AF573972

VOLUME TWO

THE LIFE AND TEACHINGS OF JESUS CHRIST

FROM THE TRANSFIGURATION THROUGH THE TRIUMPHAL ENTRY

EDITED BY
RICHARD NEITZEL HOLZAPFEL
& THOMAS A. WAYMENT

SALT LAKE CITY, UTAH

FOR BAILEY YORK HOLZAPFEL, MY WONDERFUL, KIND, AND THOUGHTFUL SON

—*Richard Neitzel Holzapfel*

FOR CATHRYNE IVORY WAYMENT, WHOSE SMILE IS CONTAGIOUS AND INSPIRING

—*Thomas A. Wayment*

Visit us at deseretbook.com

Library of Congress Cataloging-in-Publication Data

The life and teachings of Jesus Christ : from the Transfiguration through the Triumphal Entry / edited by Richard Neitzel Holzapfel, Thomas A. Wayment.

p. cm.

Includes bibliographical references and index.

ISBN 1-59038-543-8 (alk. paper)

1. Jesus Christ—Biography. I. Holzapfel, Richard Neitzel. II. Wayment, Thomas A.

BT301.3.L54 2005

232.9'01—dc22 2004025652

Printed in the United States of America 18961

R. R. Donnelley and Sons, Crawfordsville, IN

10 9 8 7 6 5 4 3 2 1

CONTENTS

KEY TO ABBREVIATIONS

BOOKS

ABD — David Noel Freedman, ed., *The Anchor Bible Dictionary*, 6 vols. (New York: Doubleday, 1992).

AJ — Josephus, *Antiquities of the Jews*, trans. Ralph Marcus, Loeb Classical Library (Cambridge, Massachusetts: Harvard University Press, 1943).

DNTC — Bruce R. McConkie, *Doctrinal New Testament Commentary*, 3 vols. (Salt Lake City: Deseret Book, 1965–73).

GEL — William F. Arndt and F. Wilbur Gingrich, *A Greek-English Lexicon of the New Testament and Other Early Christian Literature*, ed. Frederick W. Danker, 3d. ed. (Chicago: University of Chicago Press, 2000).

JD — *Journal of Discourses*, 26 vols. (London: Latter-day Saints' Book Depot, 1954–86).

JTC — James E. Talmage, *Jesus the Christ: A Study of the Messiah and His Mission according to Holy Scriptures Both Ancient and Modern* (Salt Lake City: Deseret Book, 1988).

JW — Josephus, *The Jewish War*, trans. H. St. Thackeray, Loeb Classical Library (Cambridge, Massachusetts: Harvard University Press, 1927–28).

MM Bruce R. McConkie, *The Mortal Messiah: From Bethlehem to Calvary*, 4 vols. (Salt Lake City: Deseret Book, 1979–1981).

TDNT Gerhard Kittel and Gerhard Friedrich, eds., *Theological Dictionary of the New Testament*, ed. and trans. Geoffrey W. Bromiley, 10 vols. (Grand Rapids, Michigan: William B. Eerdmans, 1964–99).

TPJS Joseph Smith Jr., *Teachings of the Prophet Joseph Smith*, comp. Joseph Fielding Smith (Salt Lake City: Deseret Book, 1976).

BIBLE VERSIONS AND STUDY AIDS

NIV New International Version
NRSV New Revised Standard Version
NJB New Jerusalem Bible
KJV King James Version
LXX Septuagint
MT Masoretic Hebrew
JST Joseph Smith Translation

ACKNOWLEDGMENTS

We thank Cory Maxwell, our publisher; Jack Lyon, our editor; and Richard Erickson, our designer, for their efforts in moving this volume from concept approval to publication. We also thank Sheri Dew and the Deseret Book Advisory Board for their willingness to approve a rather dense and scholarly three-volume work that included footnotes because they felt that Jesus' life and ministry again deserved attention.

We thank Ted Stoddard, a colleague and supporter without peer, who continued to provide editorial and content help during the final review process, as he has done with each previous volume.

Walter Rane willingly joined us in collaborating on a new visual image of the Triumphal Entry, creating with his distinctive style the painting that graces the cover of this volume—one more historically accurate than any previous painting of this well-known event.

We are especially grateful for the willingness of our colleagues, many of whom have been with us from the beginning, who dedicated significant amounts of their time and energy to provide their very best efforts to prepare thoughtful and insightful essays.

We appreciate and acknowledge our BYU student research assistants, Lindsay Grossnickle, Adam Hiatt, Jamie Karpowitz, Paul Lambert, Adrianne Gardner Malan, Elizabeth Pinborough, Justin Soderquist, Stan Thayne, and Phillip Webb, who gave invaluable help with source checking and editing.

We thank you and all those who have taken the time to read, sometimes two or three times, these volumes, joining with us on a remarkably fruitful journey of discovery, witnessing again that the life of Jesus Christ continues to command our attention and interest beyond measure.

Finally, we also thank our wives and families for their continued patience. They have remained immovable in their unsurpassed support of our efforts.

INTRODUCTION

THE PUBLIC MINISTRY

RICHARD NEITZEL HOLZAPFEL
AND THOMAS A. WAYMENT

As the final installment of a three-part series (published third in sequence), *The Life and Teachings of Jesus Christ: From the Transfiguration through the Triumphal Entry* offers fresh insights and new discoveries into the period of Jesus' public ministry.[1] Unlike the period of Jesus' birth, which tells us who Jesus was, and the period of His arrest, trial, crucifixion, and Resurrection, which tells us what He did—the Atonement—the mortal ministry is where we learn what type of teacher Jesus was, how He interacted with His own family, how the disciples came to understand Him, and other important insights into how Jesus lived.

The story of Jesus' life has not changed over the centuries, but what we know and understand about it has continued to grow; therefore, we chose to include here those subjects where there was a potential to shed new light on previous discussions. Each generation, both within and outside the Church, has seen its share of gifted biographers of Jesus' life. Within the Church, great luminaries such as James E. Talmage and Bruce R. McConkie are the most

[1] The first volume published in the series (although volume 3) is *From the Last Supper through the Resurrection: The Savior's Final Hours* (Salt Lake City: Deseret Book, 2003). The first volume in the series (although published second) is *The Life and Teachings of Jesus Christ: From Bethlehem through the Sermon on the Mount* (Salt Lake City: Deseret Book, 2005). This final volume in the series covers the period commonly referred to as the mortal ministry.

eloquent biographers of Jesus. It was upon their shoulders that we began this work, hoping to incorporate the most recent archaeological and textual discoveries, as well as access the vast amount of first-century material (such as rabbinic writings, Roman historical texts, and apocryphal writings) available to us today. Each generation will discover new avenues of discussion, and therefore they will again rewrite the past. These volumes represent what we know about Jesus today; tomorrow will cast a new light on these same subjects, but the greatness of the life of Jesus is its ability to speak anew to every generation.

One of the most powerful lessons of the mortal ministry can be appreciated by our understanding how those who knew Jesus came to understand who He really was. His early disciples had glimpses of His greatness as well as moments of misunderstanding. Some of those early disciples differentiated themselves through their own faithfulness, eventually being organized into the Quorum of Twelve Apostles. Richard D. Draper looks closely at the first attempt of the disciples to preach the gospel of Jesus Christ on their own and how their first mission became a defining moment in their spiritual progression. S. Kent Brown then looks at how the disciples became Apostles. The Twelve, as they would later be called, saw some of the greatness of Jesus, felt some of the opposition that Jesus experienced, misunderstood what He intended on occasion, but did not fully know Him until after the Resurrection.

Richard Neitzel Holzapfel looks at the experiences of Peter, James, and John on the Mount of Transfiguration, where tradition has taught us that priesthood keys were passed on. More than any other event in the mortal ministry of Jesus, the Mount of Transfiguration functions as a pivotal moment in the lives of the disciples who had recently come to testify, "Thou art the Christ, the Son of the living God" (Matthew 16:16). Building on this testimony, Jesus took three of the senior Apostles up to a high mountain and was there transfigured before them, showing them who He really was. The Father's voice was heard, testifying of Jesus' role in the plan of salvation.

Cecilia M. Peek provides a historical discussion of the arrest, imprisonment, and death of John the Baptist and their ramifications for the ministry of Jesus. John's death had important implications, as the three synoptic authors recognize it as a turning point in the public ministry. The theological importance of John's death is also the subject of discussion, providing insights into how his demise had a ripple effect on Jesus' own ministry.

Frank F. Judd Jr. and Brian Hauglid discuss the parables of Jesus and how they fit into the context of the mortal ministry. Toward the end of the public ministry, Jesus began presenting his public discourses in parable form, whereas He had previously taught the multitudes in simple prose. In His own words, Jesus explained that the reason he taught in parables was so that "whosoever hath, to him shall be given, and he shall have more abundance: but whosoever hath not, from him shall be taken away even that he hath" (Matthew 13:12). Frank F. Judd Jr. looks at what teachings were being preserved for the righteous, whereas Brian Hauglid looks at how the parables of Luke are to be interpreted in the overall context of the mortal ministry.

Eric D. Huntsman looks at the symbolically rich Bread of Life Discourse in the context of the mortal ministry. As John recorded this famous sermon in association with one of the feeding miracles of Jesus, he took the opportunity to point out how it divided Jesus' followers. Even among those who were called disciples, "when they had heard this, said, This is an hard saying; who can hear it?" (John 6:60). John sensed that when Jesus taught who He really was, some became confused that someone who appeared to be a man could make divine claims for Himself.

Charting the reactions of the multitudes, Jennifer C. Lane looks at how opinions about Jesus changed over time, particularly among the ruling class. Trying to isolate the nucleus of the opposition toward the Savior, she identifies purity concerns as the leading factor in the opposition to Jesus' teachings. Many felt that He did not keep the Sabbath day holy because of His healings or that He was not careful to observe many of the Pharisaic additions to the law of Moses. Jeffery R. Chadwick follows with a sociological analysis of how Jesus' teachings fit within their first-century Judean context and what others were teaching on the same subjects.

Two groups that have traditionally received little attention—the Gentiles and Jesus' own family—are treated in two articles by Richard Neitzel Holzapfel and Gaye Strathearn. The social dynamics of growing up with Jesus as well as the later influence of Jesus' family on the developing Christian church are the focus of Holzapfel's article. Unfortunately, but not surprisingly, Jesus' siblings did not believe in His teachings during the mortal ministry, but James, and probably the others as well, were privileged to see the Resurrected Savior. By the time Luke wrote Acts, the brothers had converted and were numbered among the believing disciples. Gentiles, who are rewarded for their faith on several occasions in the Gospels, were excluded from Israel prior to Christ's ministry. During the ministry, however, He traveled to the gentile cities of Tyre and Sidon, where He healed a Canaanite woman, exclaiming, "O woman, great is thy faith: be it unto thee even as thou wilt" (Matthew 15:28). The final statement in the Gospel of Matthew is a directive to "teach all nations, baptizing them in the name of the Father, and of the Son, and of the Holy Ghost" (Matthew 28:19).

Gaye Strathearn also looks at Jesus' relationship with His close friends Mary, Martha, and Lazarus. Of all of Jesus' followers and disciples, this small family from Bethany seems to have developed the most intimate relationship with the Master: "Now Jesus loved Martha, and her sister, and Lazarus" (John 11:5). A new dimension of Jesus' character emerges as He interacts with these loyal followers, who epitomize the faithful members who remain behind the scenes, completely devoted to Jesus.

Thomas A. Wayment looks at the story of the woman caught in adultery as a window into the process of how the canon of the New Testament developed. This story was not originally included in the majority of early manuscripts of the Bible, although its authenticity seems quite sure. The time when this story was inserted into the Gospel of John and when it began to be viewed as canonical can be accurately traced. The reasons for its initial exclusion and later reinclusions are also discussed.

Two articles discuss events from the last week of the Savior's ministry. The Triumphal Entry, which set the stage for Jesus' arrest and condemnation, is examined by Thomas A. Wayment from the perspective of history and doctrine. The event sent a powerful message to Jesus' followers as well as His opponents. Kent P. Jackson then discusses the Olivet Discourse, which Luke places before the Triumphal Entry whereas Matthew and Mark place it after. The discourse, recorded in its fullness in Matthew 24, has forever been associated with the location where Jesus delivered it—the Mount of Olives. In it, Jesus taught the disciples about the Second Coming and how their lives would be affected by it. Kent P. Jackson gives the discourse a thoughtful analysis, drawing upon insights found in the Joseph Smith Translation (Joseph Smith—Matthew).

Gospel Mosaics

To any reader who approaches Matthew, Mark, Luke, and John with more than a cursory glance, two realizations quickly come to mind: First, we see some striking similarities among the four accounts, most especially so with Matthew, Mark, and Luke, known as the synoptic Gospels because they share similar material (the Greek word *synoptikos* means "to see the whole together, to take a comprehensive view"). Second, we also see some differences among the various accounts.

People can react to the differences in at least two ways: They can realize that differences and even variances are to be expected, or they can be bothered by what they consider to be discrepancies and inconsistencies. After all, the Gospels were written by four different people, at different times, in different locales, and for different audiences. Additionally, the authors' sources, including the

Old Testament, may have contained differences already. For example, the Gospel authors had three different versions of the Old Testament available to them, the Hebrew text, the third-century B.C. Greek translation (the Septuagint or LXX), and the targums (Aramaic translations of the Hebrew texts). Some differences can be traced to their usage of these varying sources. In the story of the Triumphal Entry, for example, Matthew used the Septuagint text of Zechariah 9:9, a passage that can be mistakenly interpreted to mean that the Triumphal Entry would include a donkey and its foal. For this simple reason, Matthew, unlike the other Gospel authors, wrote, "And brought *the ass, and the colt,* and put on *them* their clothes" (Matthew 21:7; emphasis added).

Early Efforts to Make One Gospel

Scribal sensibilities would not often tolerate discrepancies between the Gospel narratives, and therefore later scribes' efforts to "correct" the texts included the practices of elimination and harmonization. That is, they retained only their favorite or preferred Gospel passages and eliminated the others. Perhaps the best-known eliminator was Marcion (mid-second century A.D.), who accepted only the Gospel of Luke, ostensibly because Luke was thought to be Paul's traveling companion (Marcion revered Paul) and also because it contained fewer references to the Old Testament, a text that Marcion found reprehensible. Tatian, a later contemporary of Marcion (latter half of the second century A.D.), composed a Gospel harmony called the *Diatessaron,* in which all four Gospel accounts were woven into a single narrative or harmony, thus eliminating the possibility of discrepancies.

A Gospel harmony, sometimes called a synopsis, endeavors to weave all the details of the Gospel tradition into a single chronological strand, composite order, or sequence. The motives for doing so are many. A synopsis can be useful, allowing students to see similarities and compare them side by side. This type of synopsis also helps avoid the cumbersome approach where every event is treated separately, thus creating a protracted discussion of a similar event. A synopsis may also be employed to show that similar events are, in reality, the same one. For example, the LDS Bible Dictionary connects the healing of the two blind men on the road to Jericho with the healing of Bartimaeus (Matthew 20:29–34; Mark 10:46–52; compare Luke 18:35–43).

There are basically two kinds of harmonies. Traceable to at least Tatian is the effort to combine the various Gospel narratives into one account. Arguing that such an attempt shares a "common goal" with other efforts to harmonize the Gospel narratives to achieve "a better understanding of the life, ministry, and teachings of the Savior and his apostles" shows a lack of understanding of the historical setting. Tatian's effort to produce one Gospel was partly an attempt to eliminate any passages Jewish or pagan critics might use to hinder Christianity in the presentation of its claims concerning Jesus. In its modern counterpart, ostensibly an attempt to make things easier for the reader, the harmony author selects unique characteristics or aspects of various Gospel events and arranges them in what seems to be a rational, cohesive order.

One of the disadvantages to such an arrangement or compilation is the elimination of the individuality of the Gospel writers. For example, it is difficult under such an arrangement to understand how the individual New Testament authors, aware of what earlier authors had written, made subtle changes to those same accounts.

Tatian's solution to the differences found in the four Gospels, the creation of a harmony, was surprisingly successful for a long time among certain groups of Christians because of its missionary appeal and its ability to circumvent controversy. Another purpose was to eliminate or harmonize passages that Christians themselves found problematic.

The Acceptance of Four Gospels

Among the most monumental decisions that were made within early Christianity was the acceptance of a four-Gospel canon. For most people, the proposal to accept a wider variety of books as canonical is appealing, yet the strong pull to accept and use only one Gospel cannot be underestimated, as it was a definite option for several centuries. In fact, strong tides moving in the various Christian communities pushed toward the acceptance of a single Gospel account as canonical. We probably need to thank Irenaeus (the second-century A.D. bishop of Lyons in Gaul) for mounting one of the most successful challenges to those who wished to accept only a single Gospel.

Some suggest that Irenaeus' defense was intended to eliminate from consideration the use of apocryphal texts, but the historical setting suggests that the main objective was to reject all the various attempts to select either one single Gospel or a harmony of known Gospels; it was thus an attempt to expand the canon rather than limit it from including competing Gospels.

While most Christians finally accepted four Gospels, it was not an easy struggle. If lost, it would have had tremendous consequences on the amount of material we have to study Jesus' life and teachings. The fact that Christians were able to accept, canonize, and utilize sources that contained contradictions speaks volumes about their willingness and desire to preserve everything possible about the life of Jesus, even if it meant they were susceptible to attack from the outside.

Harmonies

As noted above, there are two types of harmonies. The first is the creation of a single Gospel using material from the four Gospels. The second and more common type presents Gospel events in parallel columns on the same page so the reader can, with some study, isolate or extricate both the similarities and differences of the various accounts. As Latter-day Saints, we have additional voices giving us expanded and profound views of Jesus' life and public ministry. Many have undertaken to discuss these events using this broader range of sources. It is important also to examine in context what Matthew, Mark, Luke, and John had to say about these transcendent events and how their audience read or heard their Gospel narratives in the first place. A harmony cannot achieve these results; instead, it focuses attention on the linear progression of events without pausing to examine the details along the way.

Today, when using a harmony, we are attempting to use the Gospel narratives in a way other than that in which they were originally written and intended. Matthew did not write with the view that he would be creating the first book of the New Testament, or with the intent that it would be placed side by side with other Gospels. He wrote to a specific audience, with specific intentions. Therefore, in combining the accounts, we distort the historical setting of each story; as a result, we may miss the themes and insights originally intended by the author.

Undoubtedly, each writer preserved a separate and distinct account of Jesus' ministry for a good reason. This does not deny the usefulness of a harmony in some situations and for specific purposes. A study of the individual Gospels provides a nuanced portrayal of the events of Jesus' life. For example, when the accounts are harmonized, we fail to recognize that Matthew and Luke contain a significantly altered ordering of the same events found in Mark's Gospel.

The approach advocated here is not without its own deficiencies, however. Some may be concerned that they will learn *too much* about Matthew, Mark, Luke, and John and *not enough* about Jesus when focusing on individual Gospels. This problem, however, is also inherent in our usual study approach—the harmony method—because it puts forward a single Gospel account, therefore presenting only a single viewpoint. The only real difference between the two is that we may be more acutely aware of the author's presence when we study each individually, asking questions about his themes, audience, and purposes.

We would certainly like to know what Jesus Himself did, said, and thought. However, for some unknown reason, Jesus did not leave us an account of His life. In fact, we do not have any record of Jesus' writing anything. We are, therefore, left with what *others* said, recalled, and recorded about His life. Not one of the Gospels always provides the kind of details we might be interested in today because *their* audience is separated from us by time and, for the most part, by place. Yet, among those who wrote about Him are those who knew Him best, His disciples. They tell us not only who He was and how they gradually discovered who He really is but also how coming to know Him changed their lives.

The Proclamation of the Gospel

Jesus proclaimed the gospel—the good news. The English word *gospel* derives from the Anglo-Saxon *godspell,* which means "a story about God." When it is used to translate the Greek word *euangelion,* the word *gospel* acquires the popular meaning of "good news" or "glad tidings." Jesus declared the gospel: "The time is fulfilled, and the kingdom of God is at hand: repent ye, and believe the gospel" (Mark 1:15). In substance, the good news was that the kingdom of God was present in Jesus. Later, after His suffering, death, and resurrection, the New Testament writers presented the good news about Jesus. Their Gospel accounts are as much the gospel *of* Jesus as they are *about* Jesus. Among the large number of illiterate people living in the ancient world, remarkably, Jesus chose a literate group of disciples who began recording His words and deeds so early. Although ancient people certainly could tell the stories of Jesus, it took this literate group to record them and pass them along to others.

The title given to the four Gospels from the second century onward is also significant: the Gospel *according to* Matthew, the Gospel *according to* Mark, and so on. In the Joseph Smith Translation, two of the titles are changed to read, "The Testimony of St. Matthew" and "The Testimony of St. John."

So, although Jesus proclaimed a single gospel, the evangelists presented the teachings of Jesus in accordance with what they understood and experienced. Each writer thus gave his particular testimony; as a result, we now have four Gospels. Even later (in the thirteenth century), the word *gospel* took on the figurative meaning of "an authoritative account."

Separate and Distinct Views

In those Gospels, we have four separate and distinct viewpoints of Jesus' life and teachings. As noted at the beginning, each was written at a different time for a different audience by a different author. To maintain the integrity of these stories as a whole, we must examine each narrative independently of the others rather than forcing them into a single account. Each of the early Apostles and missionaries deserves a chance to be heard in his own right. Keeping the accounts separated, as the individual authors intended, may offer us a much richer way to understand the demands of discipleship in our own lives. Doing the reverse may lead us away from the messages and insights that each Gospel writer intended to preserve through his witness of Jesus.

Additionally, by combining the four individual stories into one artificially created one, we sometimes create false images not necessarily found or ever intended in the original Gospel stories. This is analogous to many university students who are exposed to Hollywood movies on Bible subjects or who grew up watching cartoon versions of the scriptures, either at home or in various church settings. They tend to visualize scenes and reproduce dialogue in their minds that does not exist in the text itself. The reality is, for the most part, that we tend to remember the Hollywood remake that includes color and background music better than we do the silent, black-and-white original.

Although we have a tendency to want just one picture of Jesus' life—a single Gospel, as it were—the Gospel narratives do not give us a single picture of Jesus but rather four beautiful mosaics. They are the words and actions of Jesus as interpreted by authentic witnesses, authors who faithfully recorded what they personally knew or who recorded the words of Jesus received through eyewitnesses.

One of the greatest evidences for the truthfulness of their work is the frank portrayal of the fundamental misunderstanding of Jesus' words and deeds during His mortal ministry by His disciples, including those closest to Him (see Matthew 16:21–23). Of note, in the cases of Mark and John at least, their Gospels portray the disciples at times in less than a positive light. Their candid admissions of struggles reminds us of Joseph Smith's testimony published in the Pearl of Great Price (Joseph Smith—History) and the revelations he received that challenged him to live up to his calling (see, for example, Doctrine and Covenants 3; 93:47). This is one of the indications that we can trust these records as being a faithful account of what they experienced and witnessed.

And although the Gospels sometimes reveal the lack of understanding of Jesus' mission by the disciples, these "testimonies" come from individuals who found forgiveness, grace, and mercy from God through Jesus Christ. We should not be blind to Jesus' own positive prophecies about their future labors. Additionally, the positive characterizations of the disciples are numerous (see Mark 1:18, 20; 2:14; 3:14; 4:11, 33; 6:1, 7). We do not need to always cut and paste them together to form a single picture.

Four Mosaics

If we had four ancient mosaics giving different representations of the same scene, it would not occur to us to say, "These mosaics are so beautiful that I do not want to lose any of them; I will demolish them and use the enormous pile of stones to make a single mosaic that combines all four."[2] Trying to combine the pieces of the mosaics to produce a single one would be an affront, not only destroying the mosaics themselves but also negating the individuality of the artists who created them in the first place. Because the

[2] See Etienne Charpentier, *How to Read the New Testament* (New York: Crossroad Publishing Company, 1984), 18.

four Gospels are different from each other, we should from time to time study each one for itself, without demolishing it and using the debris to reconstruct a life of Jesus by making the four Gospels into one.

Proper Use of a Harmony

Following a careful reading of each Gospel narrative on its own terms, we also need to study each episode in all four Gospels simultaneously. This is where the second type of harmony discussed above serves us well. Built upon the earlier foundation of individual attention to each Gospel, this approach will bring to light another set of important insights by comparing and contrasting each Gospel.

A harmony is vitally important for reconstructing a "life" of the Savior rather than a study of His teachings, which can best be achieved by looking at the sources individually. A harmony can provide a framework for discussion of the chronological order of the Lord's ministry. Jesus certainly lived a mortal life, and scattered throughout the Gospels are clues to those events of His life.

Unfortunately, the Gospel authors were not interested in such questions as whether Jesus owned a home, whether He was married, or whether He was employed. Those historical details are told only in the context of His teachings. A harmony can help identify and emphasize those details and thus help us see how His life developed.

A harmony is also useful for pragmatic purposes in presenting studies on the life and teachings of Jesus. If every study had to approach the teachings by saying "Matthew presents it this way, Mark that way," then the study of the New Testament would become too cumbersome to be useful. Scholars generally present their findings as a unified picture after they have looked at the nuances of each account; that presentation may, in turn, lead to the conclusion that a harmony approach is desirable. The results of this approach are demonstrated in the studies presented in this volume.

Studying the Life of Jesus

This contribution will certainly not be the final book written about Jesus or His teachings, but we hope that each generation of students and scholars will successively build upon the foundation laid by those who went before. As early as the time when the Gospel of John was written, its author exclaimed, "There are also many other things which Jesus did, the which, if they should be written every one, I suppose that even the world itself could not contain the books that should be written" (John 21:25).

Each author in the New Testament wrote for a specific purpose, informed through a personal witness. These writers tried to capture in print the greatness and majesty of Jesus Christ. Some of them knew Him personally, and others knew Him through the Spirit and testimony of others. Their writings merit further study and pondering. We hope this study will contribute to our understanding of His life and, at the same time, lead others to new insights in their own quests to know Him.

I.

COUNTING THE COST: THE APOSTOLIC MISSION OF THE TWELVE AND SEVENTY

RICHARD D. DRAPER

Go ye therefore, and teach all nations, baptizing them in the name of the Father, and of the Son, and of the Holy Ghost: Teaching them to observe all things whatsoever I have commanded you: and, lo, I am with you alway, even unto the end of the world.

MATTHEW 28:19–20

Blunt words, like the bitter chill of a winter breeze, brought little hope or comfort. Their bite must have surprised the twelve men who stood before the Lord that day. The successes they had experienced up to that moment seemed to argue for optimism and foretell a future full of promise, even triumph. Instead, His words discounted all the pleasant portents and boded surprisingly ill. "Beware of men," He warned, "for they will deliver you up to the councils, and they will scourge you in their synagogues; and ye shall be brought before governors and kings for my sake, for a testimony against them and the Gentiles." His dire prediction went on: "Ye shall be hated of all men for my name's sake: but he that endureth to the end shall be saved" (Matthew 18:22).

Those words served as both a warning and a guide for these men whom the Lord was now calling on their first of many missions. He warned them that their new assignment was not for the weak or fainthearted; they must be ready for the worst. However, all was not hopeless. In fact, in the end, great joy would eclipse the sorrow that lay immediately ahead. No amount of opposition, either politically motivated or satanically inspired, could stop their work.

The Meaning of *Disciple*

Though the newly minted Apostles may not have realized it at the time, their Master's guarantee of their eventual—even eternal—success lay in the fact that they were His disciples.[1] Understanding the meaning of the term opens the door to more fully understanding the significance of these men and their mission.

The word comes from the Latin *discipulus,* used to translate the Greek *mathetes,* literally, a learner. The Latin *discipulus,* associated with *disciplina,* from which our word *discipline* derives, provides an important insight into the title. A disciple was one under discipline, the discipline of a certain master. Only by staying disciplined could a follower achieve mastery of the teacher's skills. The Greek word used in the New Testament described one engaged in "the appropriation and adoption of specific knowledge or conduct" that proceeded according to a deliberate and set plan.[2] There could be no student without a teacher, for the former was incontestably dependent on the latter. Thus, education involved a corresponding personal and contractual relationship. The term *disciple,* therefore, denoted a connection between teacher and student that could not be dissolved easily. As long as the student paid the required fee and continued to work (that is, maintained discipline), the teacher could not abandon him even if he proved slow in learning.[3]

---

[1] The word is used more than 260 times in the New Testament, and only some two dozen times does it apply strictly to the Twelve. In the vast majority of instances, it denotes any follower of the Lord. See George A. Buttrick, *The Interpreter's Dictionary of the Bible*, 5 vols. (Nashville: Abingdon Press, 1962), 1: 845.

[2] Kittell and Friedrich, *TDNT*, 4:416–17.

[3] Freedman, *ABD*, 5:1158; Kittell and Friedrich, *TDNT*, 4:416–17.

Though the word *mathetes* is often translated appropriately as "apprentice," it carries the broader meaning of fellowship between the master and student that encompassed their whole relationship. Both teacher and student strove to achieve a specific and well-understood goal. Mastery is what the relationship was all about, and nothing short of mastery would do. It was critical for the master that the student learn the material, for only as the student acquired, used, and disseminated the skill was the teacher bona fide.[4] A master who could not teach was no master at all.

The Old Testament, however, unlike the Hellenistic world, had no tradition of the master-disciple relationship. It is true that the prophets had associates, such as Joshua with Moses and Elisha with Elijah, but they are never referred to as disciples (Hebrew *talmidim*). Rather, they are referred to as servants and assistants (*mesharet*). Joshua did not lead Israel as a disciple of Moses but as an independent leader whom God fully commissioned. Likewise, Elisha did not grow into the office once occupied by Elijah but rather exercised the same authority in the name of God.

The reason for the absence of the master-disciple relationship stems from the central fact that the religion of the Old Testament was based on revelation, in which God makes known His will to His servants directly. The prophet does not generate or even translate that will and, therefore, never overshadows the master's words; but a prophet may expand, interpret, extend, or explain them to others.[5] The messenger is a reporter of divine pronouncements and nothing more. No prophet presumed to interpose himself between the people and their God. This condition negated both the need for and the possibility of the Hellenistic master-disciple relationship. That condition also left no possibility of the veneration of the prophet that corresponds to that of the Greek disciples for their

---

[4] Kittell and Friedrich, *TDNT*, 4:417.

[5] See Exodus 7:2, where Moses is to speak what God commands. Note the pattern throughout Exodus and Leviticus where God commands Moses to speak His word to His people.

masters.[6] In the Old Testament, it is God and His continuous and dynamic relationship with His people that counts. Thus, where revelation prevails, there is no place for the master-disciple relationship because God is always master; Israel is always disciple.[7]

The demise of the prophets, however, opened the way for the Jews to develop the master-disciple fellowship. Between 300 B.C. and 100 B.C., Hellenism's fully developed master-disciple model influenced the Jews to an ever-greater extent. As the office of Rabbi grew in ever-greater importance, with rabbis acting as social and religious leaders and interpreters of the law, the necessity for masters and disciples developed. In the absence of direct revelation, someone needed to teach the law—and that need required both teacher and learner. Evidence suggests that at first such fellowships began in earnest about 170 B.C. The impetus, paradoxically, was to protect Palestinian Judaism from the influences of Hellenism. Therefore, though the Jews adopted much of the Hellenist master-disciple model, they did make modifications that followed their own proclivities and met their specific objectives.[8] In the first century before Christ, Jewish leaders formed actual schools and began instructing students.[9]

In the developing Jewish system, the master was the expert who understood the law and passed on that understanding to the disciple, initially the scribe, who was then prepared to stand in the

---

[6] For example, God said to Joshua, "Moses my servant is dead; now therefore arise" (Joshua 1:2). Clearly, Joshua had taken the place of Moses, and the Lord now spoke through him.

[7] For example, God told Jeremiah to speak to Israel—but only what God commanded (Jeremiah 1:7–10). In Ezekiel 2:4, the prophet is called to speak in God's name, and the people are to obey.

[8] Following the Mishnah, Jose ben Joezer and Jose ben Johanna seem to have formed the earliest master-disciple relationship, about 170 B.C. We can estimate the date by working back from the third "paired" sages, Judah ben Tabbai and Simeon Ben Shetah, who were known to have lived at the beginning of the first century B.C. See Aboth, 1.4–1.8. It is only after this era that the special class of scribes (*soferim/grammateis*) is found. See Sirach 38.25–39.11 and Kittell and Friedrich, *TDNT*, 4:438.

[9] Freedman, *ABD*, 5:1158.

master's place. The disciple's role was primarily that of listener, continually appropriating what he heard. His task, however, was not merely passive acceptance. It did not preclude critical reflection and the testing of the Rabbi's understanding of what the scriptures said. Disagreements, therefore, arose and led to rupture and reinterpretation of the law.

The need for a teacher, coupled with differing interpretations of the scripture, caused the development of schools. Those who gathered to a certain Rabbi became fellows together and promoted his views. Prominent schools, like those of Shammai and Hillel, well established in the Lord's day, gained extensive influence in the views of the people.[10]

Each disciple absorbed the tradition of his school and promoted the teachings of his master. By this means, certain traditions and interpretations were passed from generation to generation. For the Jews, the real center of concern was not, however, the teacher, but rather his particular view of the Torah. That is not to say that the teacher had only an incidental significance in the transmission process. The early Rabbis were honored as great teachers and masters of the law. Even so, their disciples did not reverence them as the disciples of the Greek philosophers, such as Pythagoras and Zeno, reverenced their masters.[11]

The Lord Gathers Disciples

As the Lord developed His own group of disciples, He adopted but also modified the Greek and Jewish models. The New Testament consistently shows a personal and deep attachment between the Lord and His disciples, an attachment that shaped the whole of their lives. Peter's words, "Thou art the Christ, the Son of the living God" (Matthew 16:16), expressed the reverence and awe in which the disciples held the Lord. He was more than Master—He was Messiah. The Messiah, however, was also God and, therefore, the

[10] Kittell and Friedrich, *TDNT*, 4:435.
[11] Kittell and Friedrich, *TDNT*, 434–35.

Master who was now calling His disciples as the foundation of the kingdom He was building and as the firstfruits of the new Israel He was creating.[12]

The Lord's relationship with His followers, therefore, had marked differences between both the Hellenistic and Jewish models. Both placed the responsibility of finding a teacher on the would-be learner. In contrast, the Lord *chose* His disciples, and He stressed that aspect: "Ye have not chosen me, but I have chosen you, and ordained you, that ye should go and bring forth fruit, and that your fruit should remain" (John 15:16). The selection, teaching, empowering, and commissioning all derived from Him.

Further, He emphasized their continued dependence on Him: "I am the true vine. . . . As the branch cannot bear fruit of itself, except it abide in the vine; no more can ye, except ye abide in me" (John 15:1, 4). These verses show that the Lord drew a distinction between Himself and His disciples. The principle that Jesus emphasized was that the disciples, in and of themselves, could not produce fruit meet for His Father, but through Him, they could do whatsoever thing was right. The point was that they were and would always be dependent on Him.

Further, His teachings did not involve the development or explication of traditional materials, proving His ideas through the application of scriptural exegesis. Jesus preached on His own authority. As a result, His disciples did not have a body of material that, once they mastered it, would allow them to earn the title of Rabbi and replace their master. He was ever teacher and Lord.[13] Because of the Savior's station, the Gospels leave no doubt that the disciples drew power and inspiration solely from Him. His words "I

[12] Old Israel dwelt under the Old Covenant and was marked by blood descent and circumcision. Unfortunately, she failed to achieve her promised blessing, even rejecting her Messiah. Therefore, as Paul notes, a new law was established. See Romans 11:7–27. Those who respond to this law make up the new Israel, whose membership is based not on descent or circumcision but on the law of faith. See Romans 3:24–31; F. F. Bruce, *New Testament History* (Garden City, N.Y.: Doubleday, 1971), 177.

[13] Kittell and Friedrich, *TDNT*, 6:964–65.

am the way, the truth, and the life" (John 14:6) meant "I am the *only* way," and He meant the disciples to take them seriously. The result was an eminently personal union between the Lord and those disciples who stayed faithful to Him.

Though the disciples could never replace the Savior, there was nothing standing in their way of becoming like Him in certain respects. The Lord's words "The disciple is not above his master: but every one that is perfect shall be as his master" (Luke 6:40) were not intended to highlight the imperfection of the student compared to the Master but rather stressed the responsibility of the student to become like the Master, with the promise that this was possible.

It is true that aspects of His mission were also unique from theirs, for He had to make atonement for the world. Hinting at this distinction, He taught them to "be not ye called Rabbi: for one is your Master, even Christ; and all ye are brethren. And call no man your father upon the earth: for one is your Father, which is in heaven. Neither be ye called masters: for one is your Master, even Christ. But he that is greatest among you shall be your servant. And whosoever shall exalt himself shall be abased; and he that shall humble himself shall be exalted" (Matthew 23:8–12). The Lord, true to His word, humbled Himself even to death, and in so doing gained exaltation.

Even so, there was much that the mission of the Lord and His disciples had in common. Both were to do the same work: preach the gospel, heal the sick, raise the dead, and, most important, lead the people into God's kingdom. Further, Jesus would be hated of men, delivered to councils, and suffer persecution and even death—and the disciples faced similar fates. All this implied that, though the disciple would not be above his master, he could become like Him. Indeed, the Lord showed there was a very close connection between Him and them: "He that heareth you heareth me; and he that despiseth you despiseth me; and he that despiseth me despiseth him that sent me" (Luke 10:16). These words make

Master and disciple as one. Indeed, He promised, "He that believeth on me, the works that I do shall he do also; and greater works than these shall he do; because I go unto my Father" (John 14:12).

Those words became a litmus test for the authenticity of the Lord and His message. If He were truly the Master, His disciples, once taught and empowered, should be able to do as He did. The Lord put Himself to the test when He called the Twelve on their first mission. Their success would demonstrate the genuineness of His claim to be Israel's Master and the source of power and life.

The Lord Calls His Apostles on Their First Mission

According to Luke, shortly after completing a healing ministry, the Lord "called his twelve disciples together, and gave them power and authority over all devils, and to cure diseases" (Luke 9:1). These men had been, up to this point, in training. Now, it was time for them to take up the ministry on their own, at least for a time.[14] Mark explained that the Lord intended "that they should be with him, and that he might send them forth to preach" (Mark 3:14).

During the course of training, covering nearly half of the Lord's ministry, they had learned much through public and private instruction and from watching the Savior.[15] Now, it was time for them to take an active role and personally push the cause of the kingdom forward—and more particularly, exercise priesthood authority by showing that the kingdom of God was truly present.[16]

According to Matthew, the disciples' call was a direct result of the Lord's work with the people of Galilee. For some time, He had been going through the towns and villages teaching and healing. Doing so, He saw that the people "fainted, and were scattered abroad" (Matthew 9:36). The nuance of the Greek text suggests

---

[14] Joseph Fitzmyer, *The Gospel According to Luke* (I–IX) in the *Anchor Bible Series*, 2nd ed. (New York: Doubleday, 1981), 752–53.

[15] Talmage, *JTC*, 328.

[16] Craig A. Evans, *New International Biblical Commentary, Luke* (Peabody, Mass.: Hendrickson Publishers, 1990), 140.

that they were less faint than spiritually harassed.[17] Apparently, certain Jews, likely the scribes and Pharisees, continually hassled and worried them. As a result, they found little solace and comfort in their religion. They were abandoned by priest and rabbi and were thus left with neither protector nor guide.

The Savior, moved with compassion for their plight and their responsiveness to His message, decided it was time to bring them into His fold. He told His disciples, "The harvest truly is plenteous, but the labourers are few; pray ye therefore the Lord of the harvest, that he will send forth labourers into his harvest" (Matthew 9:37–38). It is of interest that His call made them the initial answer to their own prayers for laborers.

The desperate need for laborers demanded not only a call to service but also a gift of power to those so called. Jesus, therefore, gave these ministers both power (*dynamis*) and authority (*exousia*)—that is, both the power to act and the right to do so.[18] Through the healing stories he had already recorded, Matthew showed that the Lord had the power. Now, He passed it on, generally as the ability to cure all maladies but specifically as power over unclean spirits.[19] This ability reveals why He called the twelve "Apostles." The word denotes, among other nuances, one who shares in the authority of the commissioning agent.[20]

---

[17] The word in Matthew 9:36 is *skullo*, meaning to worry, trouble, or bother repeatedly, thus, to harass.

[18] *Dynamis* carries the idea of power, strength, might, force. Because the word denoted the peculiar power inherent in something, it was often connected directly to the divine, such that at times it served as a title for God (see, for example, Matthew 26:64; Mark 14:62). *Exousia* denoted the right to act and to use what one had. It suggested a power derived from God but now inherent in the office of the missionary. In other words, once ordained, the power resided within each Apostle.

[19] The Jewish exorcists, having neither power nor authority, failed miserably in their attempt to cast out devils (see Acts 19:13–16). See Alfred Plummer, *A Critical and Exegetical Commentary on the Gospel According to St. Luke* in *The International Critical Commentary*, ed. Charles A. Briggs, Samuel R. Driver, and Alfred Plummer, 5th ed. (Edinburgh: T&T Clark [1900]), 239.

[20] Donald A. Hagner, *Matthew 1–13*, World Bible Commentary 33A, ed. David A. Hubbard, Glenn W. Barker (Dallas: World Books, Publisher, 1993), 265.

The disciples were moving from apprenticeship to journeymen. They had studied and kept to the discipline, and they could now be entrusted with the power. With the bequeathing of that power, the Lord proved that He was indeed the Master. As the disciples exercised that power, they testified that He was who and what He said He was.

The Purpose of the Apostolic Mission

The Savior's instructions show that the Apostles' ministry would reflect His own. Matthew described it as threefold: to proclaim that God's kingdom had come, to teach the gospel, and to heal all in need as a sign of the truth of the word (see Matthew 9:35). Though the Lord's words had eschatological overtones, they did not point to the last days. Instead, they stressed the "unquestionable urgency" and press of time necessitating the disciples' mission.[21] The central message of the Apostles revealed the urgency—God was establishing His kingdom once more on the earth, but the window of opportunity would not last long.[22] Therefore, the people must respond or miss their chance. For the disciples, it meant they must hasten the work because the time to act was short.

In Matthew 7 and 8, the Lord spelled out the purpose of their mission—to proclaim the dawning of the kingdom of God on earth. The powers to heal, exorcize, and cleanse were not ends in themselves, but they underscored the promise, power, and reality of the emerging kingdom.[23] The Lord empowered His missionaries to prepare the people to enter His kingdom, healing them of both physical and spiritual maladies, particularly satanic ailments.[24]

The Apostles' mission, the Lord explained, was to be selective. There would be no proselyting among Gentiles or Samaritans at that time; He sent them only to the spiritually lost sheep of Israel.[25]

---

[21] Hagner, *Matthew*, 260.
[22] Hagner, *Matthew*, 261.
[23] Hagner, *Matthew*, 271.
[24] Plummer, *The Gospel*, 239.
[25] For more on Jew and gentile relations, see Hagner, *Matthew*, 202–6.

The Lord's restriction would not have surprised the Apostles. In general, the Jews had little love for Gentiles, being at best tolerant and at worst hostile toward them. They had even less love for the Samaritans. A vast majority of Jews believed that both groups were religiously inferior and ceremonially unclean. The question was whether they should be converted. Some saw the Torah as hostile to foreigners and directing Israel to have no association with them. Others believed that the law protected the sojourner and even allowed strangers limited inclusion into the ranks of Israel as long as they were willing to abide by the civil requirements of the law.[26]

Many diaspora Jews, working from the positive aspects of the law, were zealous missionaries and somewhat successful in bringing Gentiles, either as God-fearers or proselytes, into the fold.[27] Many in Judea, however, especially the Essenes and Zealots, found such practices abhorrent and went to extremes to shun all contact with the Gentiles. On the other hand, Sadducees were rather open in their association, mostly because of their more literal and liberal interpretation of the law; and, being aristocrats for the most part, they had to deal with gentile authorities regularly. That is not to say they felt that Gentiles were of equal rank, but they did not disdain them, as did others. The Pharisees were much more aloof

---

[26] Passages such as Nehemiah 9:2, Isaiah 1:7, 62:8; Jeremiah 5:19, Lamentations 5:2, and Hosea 7:9; 8:7 suggested that the Jews should have nothing to do with Gentiles. On the other hand, the sojourner was to enjoy protection and even inclusion in the ranks of Israel if willing to abide by the civil requirements of the law, as in Leviticus 19:33–34; Numbers 9:14; Deuteronomy 10:19; 1 Kings 8:41, 43; Isaiah 56:3, 6; 66:18–21. There is a debate among some scholars as to the degree of tolerance manifested by the Jews of the first half of the century toward the Gentiles. See E. P. Sanders, *Judaism: Practice and Belief, 63* B.C.E.–*66* C.E. (Philadelphia: Trinity Press International, 1992), 40–42. Stephen M. Wylen, *The Jews in the Time of Jesus* (New York: Paulist Press, 1996), 141–44, feels that the Jews chafed under foreign rule and that their dislike spilled over to Gentiles in general.

[27] The King James text speaks of those who "feareth God" (see Acts 10:2, 22; 13:26). From this has come the modern term "God-fearers"—that is, Gentiles drawn to Judaism but who were not circumcised. A proselyte, on the other hand, was a Gentile who submitted even to circumcision. The writings of Philo and Sibylline Oracles 3 suggest that many diaspora Jews were zealous to convert Gentiles to the worship of Jehovah and had a sizable following.

and tended to deal with Gentiles as little as possible. Those in Judea were not active missionaries, feeling that few Gentiles could really meet the demands of the law.[28] Many of the Lord's disciples, holding Pharisaic sympathies, would have held similar views and, therefore, resonated with a restricted mission.

Matthew, however, makes it clear that this prohibition was temporary, for eventually all were to hear the Lord's gospel.[29] Even so, it was necessary that the Lord restrict His activities and those of His Apostles, at least for the present. His first priority was to rescue the lost sheep of the house of Israel within Judea and Galilee. The restriction showed God's consciousness of and faithfulness to His covenant promises. Only after Israel had a chance to respond would the gospel be taken beyond her shores.

This is an important point. Often, we see the Lord's word as going from the Jews to the Gentiles only after the Jews rejected it. That view is only partially correct. As we will see, the Lord's mission to the Jews was highly, if not completely, successful. Those faithful Jews who became Christians fulfilled the Abrahamic covenant by

---

[28] Even among the Pharisees, there were some who were freer than others, but on the whole, they had as little dealings with Gentiles as possible. When Jesus castigated the Pharisees for compassing land and sea to make one convert, he was pointing up their work to attract Jews to Pharisaism—not Gentiles to Judaism. It was former members of this sect, failing to see beyond their interpretation of the law, who gave the Church in Antioch Syria fits by insisting that gentile converts had to be circumcised and take upon them the full weight of the law. For discussion, see Willoughby C. Allen, *The International Critical Commentary on the Bible: The Gospel According to Matthew*, 3rd ed. (Edinburgh, England: T. & T. Clark, 1977), 246.

[29] See Matthew 10:18, where it is hinted at, and 21:43; 24:14, where it is clearly stated. Luke 22:35–38 suggests that the Lord's instructions for this mission were meant to be temporary and indicated the nature of this mission alone, stressing urgency, economy, and singlemindedness. See Hagner, *Matthew*, 270. There were and are some who have used these verses as if they marked the permanent requirements for missionary service. They note that Paul felt that at least the Apostles had a right to be supported, though he himself did not take advantage of it (1 Corinthians 9:4–18; 2 Corinthians 11:7). He made the same point to the Thessalonian Saints (2 Thessalonians 3:8–9), quoting the logion of Matthew 10:10 ("for the workman is worthy of his meat," but replaces *trophes*, "food," with *misthou*, "*wages*"), and to Timothy (1 Timothy 5:18). However, the Lord made it very clear at the end of His ministry that the rules had changed.

taking the gospel to the rest of the world (see Abraham 2:9–10). Thus, they opened the way by which all could become members of God's kingdom. The need for the restriction and a major reason for the disciples' mission becomes clearer in this light. They were to gather all Jews into the new Israel.[30] Those who refused to respond to the Lord's call divorced themselves from the covenant family and cut themselves off from the kingdom. Those who responded became the foundation of new Israel and took the word to the world.

The Lord's Instructions to the Twelve

The first members of God's restored kingdom, His Jewish disciples, resolutely shouldered their task and moved the work forward. The urgency of their mission is clear in the Lord's instructions that they were to "take nothing for [their] journey, neither staves, nor scrip, neither bread, neither money; neither have two coats apiece" (Luke 9:3). In other words, they were to take no provisions, no bag (that is, a scrip) that could contain provisions, and not even money to purchase provisions. The Lord explained that none of these things would be necessary because the "workman is worthy of his meat" (Matthew 10:10).[31]

There is some discrepancy among the Gospel writers about precisely which items the missionaries were not to take,[32] but the point is clear: they were to "make no special preparations; [but to] go as [they were]."[33] The nature of this mission allowed for the restrictions, requirements that would not be possible when the ministry

---

[30] These are those under the new covenant, the old one having passed away. New Israel is no longer identified with circumcision but with those who have God's law written in their minds and upon their hearts. See Hebrews 8:10–13.

[31] The word translated "meat" comes from the Greek *trophe* and means "food," not specifically flesh.

[32] Mark states they could take a staff and sandals (Mark 6:8–9), whereas Matthew says they were forbidden from taking staves or shoes (Matthew 10:9–10). It is likely that the Lord forbade them from taking extra items like two staves or an extra set of shoes or sandals.

[33] Plummer, *The Gospel*, 239.

spread to gentile lands.[34] Here it worked, because Jewish villages and towns were closely located and because local hospitality customs made it possible for the Twelve to easily find shelter and sustenance.[35] But why the restrictions? The most obvious reason is the need for immediate service. Urgency left no time for acquiring even basic equipment.[36] The time was growing short, and much labor lay ahead, leaving no time for unnecessary preparations.

The Lord commanded them to give of their time, testimony, and power freely. After all, He gave them the gospel with its attendant power and grace; now, it was their turn to give freely to others, for to do otherwise would be an abomination.[37]

The disciples were to "search out" a worthy house. The idea behind the text is not so much a house of righteous souls but rather one that could afford the expense of keeping them.[38] A worthy person, therefore, was one who had the means and was willing to provide hospitality for the necessary length of the disciples' stay.[39]

They would be able to tell where to lodge through the spirit of discernment. They were to salute the chosen house—that is, they were to invoke God's peace upon it. If the household deserved their gift of peace, they would feel that peace rest upon it; otherwise, the servants would sense that their invocation was void and were to leave.[40]

The disciples were to accept whatever the family had to offer and not expect special treatment or favors. The Lord showed that "subsistence, but not profit, was the rightful expectation of those who preached the gospel" (see 1 Corinthians 9:18).[41]

---

[34] Hagner, *Matthew*, 269.

[35] See Ralph Gower, *The New Manners and Customs of Bible Times* (Chicago: Moody Press, 1987), 241–49.

[36] Hagner, *Matthew*, 269–72.

[37] McConkie, *DNTC*, 1:325.

[38] *Axios* carries the idea of being suitable or fit for a task because it has the necessary value or worth.

[39] Hagner, *Matthew*, 272.

[40] Talmage, *JTC*, 425.

[41] Hagner, *Matthew*, 274. The Lord had explained that "the labourer is worthy of

At this point, the Lord made a transition from potential acceptance to rejection, saying that if a house or village should not receive them, they were to "let [their] peace return to [them]" (Matthew 10:13). Further, they were to shake the dust from their sandals as a sign that "they had not the smallest thing in common with the place."[42] During modern times, the Lord has given further insights into the consequence of this act, saying "that in the day of judgment you shall be judges of that house, and condemn them" (Doctrine and Covenants 75:21; see also Doctrine and Covenants 24:15; 84:92–96).

The Lord illustrated the severe consequences of rejecting His invitation by citing the example of two notorious cities, Sodom and Gomorrah, whose sins brought upon them total destruction. To be judged more harshly than these is frightening indeed, but the reason the villages and cities of Galilee could receive such a warning was simple: "Of him unto whom much is given much is required; and he who sins against the greater light shall receive the greater condemnation" (Doctrine and Covenants 82:3). The Lord and His Apostles were bringing the greatest light of all, the witness, verified by signs, that the Messiah had come and was calling them into His kingdom. They had to heed the call or suffer the consequences.

Matthew gives the most expansive account of the Lord's teachings, but much of what he records has little to do with the Apostles' first missionary effort. It may be that the Lord used the moment to give them directions and admonitions that would apply more particularly to their labors after His ascension.[43]

---

his hire" (Luke 10:7), and, in Paul, we see that the missionaries had adopted this practice. The disciples were to make one house their central headquarters. These houses then became the "house churches," which acted as the earliest meetinghouses for the early Saints (see Romans 16:5; 1 Corinthians 16:19; Colossians 4:15; Philemon 1:2). See Plummer, *The Gospel*, 240.

[42] Plummer, *The Gospel*, 240.

[43] Talmage, *JTC*, 305. Though Matthew places the discourse in the setting of the initial missionary efforts of the Twelve, both Mark and Luke have the Lord give it much later in His ministry (see Mark 13:9–13 and Luke 21:12–19), where the warning

The Lord's words make it clear that, eventually, certain Jews would do more than reject the gospel message; they would turn on the messengers. He was sending the Twelve into a hostile and dangerous world, one metaphorically infested with wolves. In that setting, they must be wary of all, possessing the shrewdness of the serpent and yet the innocence of the dove.[44] In other words, the disciples were to be prudent, give no needless offense, and not recklessly put themselves under the power of anyone[45] (see Matthew 10:16). When they were brought before magistrates and judges—for such would happen—they had no need to fear; the words they needed would be given them. Indeed, the intimate and personal force of God would be in them (Matthew 10:19–20).[46]

The Lord made no attempt to soften the grim picture of future persecution that would meet their message. Families would be divided and filial relationships broken. Hatred would mount so much that even family members would betray each other unto death. Even in the face of all this, the disciples must remain true to the cause. In spite of the trouble their message would cause and the persecution that awaited them, the disciples were not to turn from the path, for it was only "he that endureth to the end [who] shall be saved" (Matthew 10:22).

The Lord's words provide a key insight into the process of salvation. "Belief alone . . . is not enough. Nor does belief coupled with baptism and church membership suffice; these are the beginning, not the end, of the path leading to eternal life."[47] The call of the

---

actually fits conditions better. However, because Matthew organized his Gospel topically rather than chronologically, he has likely placed the discourse in this missionary setting. By the time Matthew wrote, the events described in the warning were being realized and, therefore, served to instruct and bolster the gentile as well as the Jewish Saints. See Hagner, *Matthew*, 275.

[44] The JST states that the disciples were to be "wise *servants* and harmless as doves." Because of Western society's dark view of serpents and their evil craftiness, it is little wonder a change was needed. However, the word Matthew used, *phronimos*, connoted sensible, prudent, even shrewd thinking.

[45] Talmage, *JTC*, 329.

[46] Hagner, *Matthew*, 278.

[47] McConkie, *DNTC*, 1:331.

Lord is the call to a lifetime of service. "There is, on the one hand, no flashy heroism here, no martyr complexes—they are to be crafty and to flee. Yet, on the other hand, there is a call to endurance."[48]

The Lord then made the statement that perplexes many modern readers. The disciples were to flee from the persecution from city to city, but, he said, "Ye shall not have gone over the cities of Israel, till the Son of man be come" (Matthew 10:23). On the surface, the statement appears eschatological. The Lord seems to be saying that the Second Coming would disrupt the Apostles' ministry and that the Second Coming would take place during a period in which Jewish persecution of the Christians was high. This idea, however, hardly seems the case, as Matthew is careful to record that the gospel must go to the Gentiles before the Lord will come again (see Matthew 21:43; 24:14). Further, the context suggests the Lord is talking about the specific mission to which He was then calling the disciples—namely, to bring the gospel to the Jews, not the greater mission to take the message to all the world.[49]

One interpretation seems to fit history best. It is that the Palestine Jews' harassment of the Christians would stop only when the Lord came out in judgment against them. He may have had in mind the terrible time, only one generation away, when the Romans would destroy the nation of the Jews. Because they were harassed and driven, the disciples were unable to preach to every city and town in Palestine. After the war, preaching the gospel primarily to Israel ceased as the ministry shifted almost completely to the Gentiles.[50] Thus, they hardly had time to extend the invitation to the safety of God's kingdom before war destroyed that of the Jews.

The Lord's words in Matthew 10:28–31 underscore the importance of the mission on which His servants were about to embark. He promised them that, in spite of how conditions appeared, God

---

[48] Hagner, *Matthew*, 280.

[49] Hagner, *Matthew*, 279–80.

[50] For a number of views on what the Lord's words meant, see Hagner, *Matthew*, 278–80.

was well aware of them; and, when necessary, He would protect them from any ultimate harm. That did not mean, however, that He would necessarily preserve their lives. The Savior's point was that even death itself was not to dissuade the disciples from their mission, whose importance was greater than any mortal life, especially in light of the fact that the righteous disciple's soul would be saved, whatever happened to him physically.[51] Therefore, they were not to fear those who could destroy only the body but rather "fear him which is able to destroy both soul and body in hell" (Matthew 10:28). The Lord was not here referring to Satan but rather to God, for only He has power to cast men into hell such "that in the eternal sense their souls are destroyed."[52] The Savior's point was that trials will occur, but those who deny the faith to escape them will not be saved.

The disciples' message, He warned them, might not have the effect they desired, bringing not peace to the world but war to the home. "I came not to send peace, but a sword," He lamented. Indeed, "a man's foes shall be they of his own household" (Matthew 10:34, 36).

The Lord's words point up the paradox the disciples faced. He warned them that in spite of their inclination to the contrary, they must not imagine His words would bring solace and tranquillity.[53] True, when the kingdom was fully restored and the Lord reigned, there would be peace. Until then, as hard as it was to fathom, the opposition would prevail.[54]

The Lord, to more forcefully put His point across, turned now to an ugly, even terrifying, image. His hearers had probably witnessed crucifixions and seen criminals, bearing the cross beam, on their

---

[51] Hagner, *Matthew*, 285–87.

[52] McConkie, *DNTC*, 1:334.

[53] His words, *me nomisete*, "do not imagine," suggest that it would have been the natural inclination of the disciples to expect peace to follow the message. Hagner, *Matthew*, 291.

[54] Hagner, *Matthew*, 291.

way to that horrible death.[55] Picking up on that precept, the Savior avowed, "He that taketh not his cross, and followeth after me, is not worthy of me" (Matthew 10:38). The words forced His hearers to evaluate the worth they placed on their own lives in relation to the cause of the kingdom. The imagery did not signal death as much as it did the kind of life the faithful disciple must be willing to live. On another occasion, the Lord clarified His meaning. Speaking of keeping oneself free from the lusts of the world, He revealed that "it is better that ye should deny yourselves of these things, wherein ye will take up your cross, than that ye should be cast into hell" (3 Nephi 12:30). Elder Bruce R. McConkie pointed out that "in a figurative sense men take up their cross and follow Christ when they shoulder any grievous burdens placed on their shoulders because of the cause of righteousness."[56]

The Lord demanded that His disciples exercise absolute obedience—that is, stay disciplined—and therefore practice self-denial. They must walk in His footsteps and complete their missions even as He would complete His. The Lord used the image of the cross not to portray the normal problems and difficulties that life throws at everyone but to signify the temptations, persecutions, and rejections that come when one devotes oneself fully to the cause of Christ—persecution from which the true disciple cannot turn away, even in the face of death. Only those who yield themselves fully to the service of the Lord and His kingdom, who willingly follow in His footsteps, will, paradoxically, find life—that is, fulfillment and deep, abiding joy.[57]

The Lord concluded His teaching on a positive note: "He that receiveth you receiveth me, and he that receiveth me receiveth him that sent me" (Matthew 10:40). His point was that "[He] and his servants can no more be separated than can the Father and the Son. To accept one is to accept the other. No one can believe in

---

[55] Crucifixion was familiar enough in Roman Palestine. See Fitzmyer, *The Gospel According to Luke I-IX*, 784–85.

[56] McConkie, *DNTC*, 1:336.

[57] Hagner, *Matthew*, 292–93.

Christ as the Son of God without also believing that Peter, James, and John were the apostles who bore record of him."[58] The association was so close that any who responded kindly to them would receive the same reward as if they responded personally to the Lord Himself. Using an "endearing" image, He said that "whosoever shall give to drink unto one of these little ones [the Twelve], . . . shall in no wise lose his reward" (Matthew 10:42).[59]

The Mission of the Twelve and Its Effect

With these instructions, and thus armed, the Twelve left on their important mission. Luke viewed the Twelve as embarking on a healing and preaching ministry, noting that they "went through the towns, preaching the gospel" (Luke 9:6). Mark was more specific, stating that "they went out, and preached that men should repent" (Mark 6:12). The Greek word (*metanoia*) carried the idea of a change of heart or mind.[60] It shows that repentance was not a superficial turning from sin but rather a whole-soul partaking of the gospel light. Preaching "repentance is to preach the gospel in its fulness, for it is through repentance that men accept the gospel, have their sins washed away, and get on the path leading to eternal life."[61] In this light, we see that Mark and Luke agree.

The length of the Apostles' first mission is unknown, as is the field they traversed, but it was most likely weeks rather than months. It would appear that their return occurred about the time of Herod Antipas' infamous execution of John the Baptist.[62]

When they returned, they told the Lord "all that they had done" (Luke 9:10; see also Mark 6:30). Their labor greatly augmented the spread of the new doctrine of the kingdom and the name and works of Jesus, to the point that their success reached even the ears of the civil leaders. That the work drew the attention of Herod is important

---

[58] McConkie, *DNTC*, 1:337.
[59] McConkie, *DNTC*, 1:337.
[60] Kittell and Friedrich, *TDNT*, 4:626.
[61] McConkie, *DNTC*, 1:328.
[62] Talmage, *JTC*, 331.

because it shows the dramatic effect and breadth of the power the disciples wielded. Theirs was certainly an authoritative ministration.[63] Their success can be further measured by the fact that when they did return to Jesus, they found Him surrounded by the press of a multitude to the extent they could not converse with Him, "for there were many coming and going, and they had no leisure so much as to eat" (Mark 6:31). It would appear that to find time to get a more detailed report, the Lord tried to escape to the less-settled region above Bethsaida. This strategy, however, proved fruitless, for many followed, and soon a multitude of perhaps as many as ten thousand people gathered there.[64] Certainly, the harvest was great as these first fruits bear witness, but it had only begun; therefore, as the Lord turned toward Jerusalem for the last time, He called additional laborers.

The Call of the Seventy

Selecting seventy of his choice disciples, Jesus called them to the work. Only Luke preserves the call, which he places about the time of the Feast of the Tabernacles—that is, in the late fall of the last months of the Savior's life.[65] As with the Twelve, we sense the mission's urgency in His instructions to the Seventy to pray "the Lord of the harvest, that he would send forth labourers into his harvest" (Luke 10:2).[66] The supreme importance of getting the word out and the shortness of the time remaining demanded the

---

[63] Talmage, *JTC*, 332.

[64] The estimate of the size of the multitude comes from the statement that there were "about five thousand men, beside women and children" (Matthew 14:21).

[65] The number seventy tied the Lord to the Old Testament traditions. Moses numbered seventy gentile nations (see Genesis 10:2–31), and the same number made up the elements of Jacob's family (Genesis 46:27). Thus, the number ties the mission of Israel to the people of the world, an idea Luke may have wanted to push. Eusebius, *Ecclesiastical History* 1.12.1, notes that there is no known catalog of the members of the Seventy but suggests such New Testament personalities as Barnabas, Sosthenes, Matthias, and Justus. However, because only Matthias and perhaps Barnabas were converted before the Lord's death, it is unlikely the others were part of the group.

[66] The force of the phrase, translated "send forth laborers," *hopos ergatas ekbale*, suggests the idea of haste or urgency.

large number of laborers. The Twelve, however, were not to join the mission this time. They were to remain with the Lord to the end; the Master had to use every hour of possible instruction and training for their further preparation for the great responsibilities that would rest upon them after His departure. This need meant that the Lord must call assistants because, as He had already told the Twelve, the "harvest truly is plenteous, but the labourers are few" (Matthew 9:37; compare Luke 10:2).

The number of this second wave of missionaries is significant. It reached back to Moses and the seventy elders of Israel who were endowed with the prophetic power. This ancient council of elders may have influenced the number of the members of the Sanhedrin as well, but there is another aspect that may have been at play. According to Genesis 10, the number of nations was seventy. Therefore, the number could foreshadow the eventual worldwide mission of the Church.[67]

The calling of the Seventy differed from that of the Twelve in a number of ways. First, it was not permanent. It came because of the present urgency, but the time would come when their services would no longer be necessary. Second, Christ did not give them specific power over devils, as He had their counterparts. Third, they were not restrained, as the Twelve had been, to preach only to the lost sheep of Israel. Their labors, though still somewhat confined, extended into Perea and Samaria, thus bringing the message into the realm of Samaritans and Gentiles, though it is likely they specifically targeted Jews. Even so, Perea, the seat of their mission, had a large gentile population, among whom their message must have flowed—something in which Luke, the gentile convert, would have been very interested.[68] "The narrow Jewish prejudice against Gentiles in general and Samaritans in particular was to be

---

[67] Plummer, *The Gospel*, 269. The number of bullocks slain during the Feast of Tabernacles was seventy and deliberately echoed the number of gentile nations. See Alfred Edersheim, *The Temple: Its Ministry and Services at the Time of Christ*, rev. ed. (Grand Rapids, Mich.: Eerdmans, 1994), 218–19.

[68] Plummer, *The Gospel*, 269–71.

discountenanced; and proof of this intent could not be better given than by sending authorized ministers among those people."[69]

That is not to say that they were free to preach just anywhere. The Lord specifically told them to go "before his face" (Luke 10:1)—that is, they were to precede Him and prepare His way. Their task was to give notice of the last call, which the Lord would then personally extend. Thus, their mission was critical in the Lord's last attempt to save the Jews both temporally and spiritually.

Because of the mission's importance, it is not surprising to find that His instructions to them closely paralleled those He had given the Twelve earlier. Their ministry, too, was limited to healing and preaching. Their message was that God's kingdom, with its attendant laws and ordinances, had now come, and their hearers must repent and come into the kingdom or suffer severe judgments.[70]

Like the Twelve, they were to "carry neither purse, nor scrip, nor [extra] shoes" (Luke 10:4). They were to take nothing with them, not even items that most travelers considered indispensable. In their case, all their needs were to be met on the way. The Lord stressed that they were to go directly to their destinations, not stopping to chat (that is, to greet people) along the way. His words seem designed to impress upon them the urgency and need for total devotion to the task at hand.[71] The prohibitions on what to take parallel those items the Talmud forbids a worshiper to carry into the temple, thus suggesting that they were to carry the same aura of dedication on their missions as they would in going to the temple.[72]

Like the Twelve, they were to proclaim peace to each house and town. As noted above, the idea of peace meant "more than the absence of conflict" but was actually a priesthood blessing and

---

[69] Talmage, *JTC*, 426.

[70] Though Luke does not say specifically that they preached repentance, which seems strange because the idea is dear to Luke in other places, he does use the word *euangelizesthai*—that is, "to evangelize," which would include the doctrine of repentance. See Fitzmyer, *The Gospel According to Luke I–IX*, 754.

[71] Plummer, *The Gospel*, 272–73.

[72] Edersheim, *The Temple*, 40.

carried "the idea of well-being of completeness."[73] A person of peace would be one who was attuned to the Spirit and would, therefore, receive the message gladly, whereas one who was not would reject that message and thereby forfeit the blessing. Should an entire town reject the offering of peace, the dusting off of the sandals would testify against it. As a result, that town would be in worse shape than Sodom. That city received no leniency, and there would be none for any city that rejected the kingdom.[74] Still, the disciples were not to pronounce it anathema or otherwise curse it; the Lord Himself would remember it and bring about the severe judgment.[75] If they were accepted into a house but the town rejected them, they were to leave the house (probably with a blessing) and warn the town as they left (see Luke 10:10–11).[76] He knew the sorrow that would come upon those villages that rejected the multiple testimonies. In sadness, He pronounced the end of Chorazin, Bethsaida, and Capernaum.[77] The Seventy, like the Twelve, were to accept the accommodations offered, whatever they were, but these came not as alms but as salary for the work they were doing.[78] They were bringing with them peace, a peace that came from God. As such, they were His messengers and worthy of support, but they were to be neither greedy nor fastidious.

The Effect of the Mission of the Seventy

The Seventy began their missions immediately. We do not know if they traveled and preached for weeks or months, nor do we know where they rejoined the Master. They may not have returned all at once or even to the same place. From what we can gather from the text, however, Jesus was not in the same place from which he had sent them, suggesting that some time had passed.

---

[73] Evans, *New International Biblical Commentary*, 173.
[74] Evans, *New International Biblical Commentary*, 170.
[75] Talmage, *JTC*, 396.
[76] Plummer, *The Gospel*, 275.
[77] Talmage, *JTC*, 396–97.
[78] Plummer, *The Gospel*, 274.

From the tenor of their report, they saw their ministry as most successful and rejoiced in their call (see Luke 10:17). They were delighted to exercise the Lord's power and authority. One interesting note is that, at the outset of their mission, they did not seem to have expected devils to be subject unto them (as did the Twelve; see Luke 9:1), for they had been told only to preach and heal the sick (see Luke 10:9). They soon learned, however, that they had power over demonic sickness as well as physical, and it thrilled them. Thus, the Lord's statement "I give unto you power to tread on serpents and scorpions, and over all the power of the enemy" (Luke 10:19) suggests that He was using epithets for demons and evil spirits, the great enemy being Satan himself.[79]

Luke's point seems to be that the Seventy experienced personally the power and authority of the Lord, and in that they rejoiced. The Lord, too, responded with joy. In no other place does Jesus rejoice over God's preference for His disciples as He does here (see Luke 10:21–22). Moved by the Spirit, He lifted His voice in a psalm of thanksgiving: "I thank thee, O Father, Lord of heaven and earth, that thou hast hid these things from the wise and prudent, and hast revealed them unto babes" (Luke 10:21). His words declare that God had revealed to "little children"—that is, to the Seventy—an understanding hidden from the self-appointed learned and wise.[80] The hidden things seem to have been the nature of the Lord and His power that had been kept from the intellectual aristocracy.

The Savior's words suggest that the exercise of the Lord's power had allowed the Seventy to grasp more fully the truth about His

---

[79] Evans, *New International Biblical Commentary*, 174. Satan is called the serpent in 2 Corinthians 11:3 and Revelation 12:9, 14–15; 20:2. Some scholars understand that the snake, whose head God said the "seed of the woman" would crush, to be Satan (see Genesis 3:14–15 with Romans 16:20). The *Testament of Levi* 18.12 notes, concerning the coming Priest and Savior, that "Beliar [Satan] shall be bound by him, and he shall give power to his children to tread upon evil spirits."

[80] The Savior, as is His wont, uses hyperbole here to make a point. He refers to the Seventy not simply as children but as infants (*nepios* as opposed to *pais*), His use suggesting an innocent and childlike nature not possessed by the "wise."

nature and His relationship with His Father.[81] They seem to have understood that the Father revealed or bore witness to the Son; and, at the same time, the Son revealed the nature of God (see John 3:35 and 10:15). When someone received that witness, he looked to Jesus as the source of understanding the character and will of the Father. A full understanding of what God was, however, depended on faithfulness to the Son, who would not cast pearls before swine. The Seventy caught the vision.[82]

However, they had not yet realized all they should have. The Lord pointed out that as exhilarating as exorcizing devils may have been, they were shooting too low. In other words, He had given them authority, but they had not yet glimpsed its full potential. There was something greater to rejoice about. Casting out devils did not secure eternal life. Judas himself may have done the same on his mission, but it did not guarantee him salvation. It was having their names sealed in the book of life that brought the necessary assurance. They had, indeed, been able to cast out devils in the Lord's name, but what really counted was that, in the process of properly using His power, they had their names written in His book.[83] With those insights on the personal importance of their mission, the Lord left them and turned back to His own mission.

Conclusion

These missions proved very valuable to the nascent church. First, in the short term, they served to get the word out to the Jews, the Lord's primary audience. The record shows that they were very successful. Though it is true that some rejected the Lord, even among His initial followers, the success of His missionaries brought thousands into His kingdom even before His death. Unfortunately, the missionaries' success had a downside: it threatened many elements within Jewish political and religious society. The result

---

[81] Talmage, *JTC*, 397.
[82] Evans, *New International Biblical Commentary*, 171.
[83] Plummer, *The Gospel*, 280.

was, as the Lord predicted, organized persecution. Its efforts, though successful in driving many Christians from Judea, did not stop the rapid growth of the kingdom. Those who fled continued to preach with success to the Jewish people wherever they went (see Acts 11:19)

Second, the missions acted as a training ground for the larger effort the Lord assigned the Twelve just before His ascension. To them, He commanded, "Go ye . . . and teach all nations, baptizing them in the name of the Father, and of the Son, and of the Holy Ghost: teaching them to observe all things whatsoever I have commanded you: and, lo, I am with you alway, even unto the end of the world" (Matthew 28:19–20). Because of the disciples' training as emissaries of the Lord, missionary work would continue effectively, and the gospel kingdom would eventually fill the Roman Empire and countries beyond.

Third, the missions placed Judah in a position to be judged. As noted at the beginning of this chapter, mastery of skill was what discipleship was all about. The student's acquisition and use of skill was important to the teacher, for this is what qualified him. The missions allowed the disciples to show that Jesus had imparted skills and powers to them, and, thus, the display of power proved He was who He said He was—namely, the Messiah, who was establishing His kingdom and its gospel on the earth. Further, these men had maintained discipline and, thus, acquired and mastered the power and authority of the Lord to the degree that rejecting them was tantamount to rejecting Him. Their healings and exorcisms underscored the genuineness of their message. Because of this witness, those who rejected the Lord and His disciples stood in a position worse than those in Sodom and Gomorrah. On the other hand, those who accepted the gospel message became disciples in their own right, partook of His power and exercised it, and thus had their names also sealed in His book of life.

In sum, the two missions proved critical to the work of the Lord at the time by spreading the message of the nascent church and fulfilling, at least partially, God's covenant with Abraham. The call to service also proved helpful indirectly to the next generation of Saints. The words preserved by the Gospel writers, especially Matthew, helped the Church members understand what they were about and the importance of meeting the challenge. Thus, they proved a direct boon to two generations of Saints and important counsel to all that followed.

One last sobering thought seems in order. The Lord told the Twelve, "He that loveth father or mother more than me is not worthy of me: and he that loveth son or daughter more than me is not worthy of me" (Matthew 10:37). He meant these words to be taken seriously. Long before, He had spoken from Mt. Sinai, "Thou shalt have no other gods before me" (Exodus 20:3). This commandment still stood. He demanded and still demands uncompromising loyalty. He is the only God and will not be replaced by anything—not by the things of the world or even by family loyalty. Those who would be His must be willing to shoulder His cross—that is, practice absolute obedience and self-denial. Discipline marks the disciple, and the Lord's words clearly emphasize the cost of discipleship. Before they embark on His journey, He asks all to count the cost. The question is, is it worth it? He assures us it is, for only by paying the price do we really come to know Him, and only as we know Him do we discover our own divine potential. Thus, like the Seventy, through His service, we find our names written in the Lamb's book of life.

II.

THE TRANSFIGURATION

RICHARD NEITZEL HOLZAPFEL

[Jesus] took Peter and John and James, and went up into a mountain to pray. And as he prayed, the fashion of his countenance was altered, and his raiment was white and glistering.

LUKE 9:28–29

That Jesus had an immediate and, in many cases, long-term impact on those He met is widely accepted. That Jesus' words and deeds were repeated again and again, even during His mortal ministry, and finally recorded following His death and Resurrection, reveals the astonishing influence He had on others. When examining the stories preserved in the New Testament, accounts that describe His deeds and preserve His words, we learn about those events in Jesus' life and ministry that had the most profound impression on people—the stories recalled and repeated in different settings.

Although each New Testament author wrote at a different time, to a different audience, and from a different point of view, all of them often called attention to certain events also found in other Gospel narratives. As they wove their distinctive themes into their particular telling of a common story of Jesus, themes that highlighted their unique witness and purpose, they preserved the core traditions of the stories they shared in common with each other.

Even in preserving the same stories, each author provided interesting nuances to those shared stories—fine distinctions that may help determine the reason for recording a particular event or saying of Jesus in the first place.

The Transfiguration Story

Matthew, Mark, and Luke record in some detail an incident upon a mountain when Jesus and three disciples went to pray sometime in October, just six months before Jesus' death (see Matthew 17:1–3; Mark 9:2–8; Luke 9:28–36).[1] Two participants, Peter and John, most likely mentioned this awe-inspiring episode in their personal writings. Peter recalls the events in his "farewell" letter written about A.D. 64 (see 2 Peter 1:16–19). John may have alluded to this experience in his Gospel account (see John 1:14; cf. 17:5).[2]

The Transfiguration, the name commonly associated with an experience chronicled by Matthew, Mark, and Luke, is one of the most important events in Jesus' mortal ministry.[3] It is a story about Jesus from God's perspective, and it is given for the benefit of the disciples. When examined together, the synoptic accounts of the Transfiguration provide an astonishing tapestry of traditions, variations of the same story crafted for specific use during the decades following Jesus' death and Resurrection.

---

[1] Dating the event has ranged from six months to weeks before Jesus' final week. Interpretations of this story are varied; some even suggest that originally it was an account of the Resurrection that had been transferred to the mortal ministry of Jesus. However, this radical view should be rejected because the story parallels those common within the biblical tradition and was alive during the first century. See, for example, the stories of Moses and Elijah when they ascended a mountain and stood in the presence of the Lord as noted below. See also Morna Dorothy Hooker, *The Gospel According to Mark* (Peabody, Mass.: Hendrickson, 1991), 214.

[2] Scholars have noted that the story line is remarkably consistent, as preserved in the synoptic accounts of the Transfiguration. However, there are some differences that present little problem for interpretation given the fact that these accounts are based on an oral tradition; none of the synoptic authors were eyewitnesses of the event itself. See the discussion below regarding Peter's reminiscences as preserved in Mark's account.

[3] For a discussion of how this event impacts the Twelve, see S. Kent Brown, "The Twelve," in this volume.

Additionally, insights emanating from the Restoration on this significant episode provide another opportunity to examine the Transfiguration from a unique perspective by providing detailed information about what transpired on the mount when Jesus "went to pray."

The Original Story

Before we examine the contributions gleaned from Restoration scriptures, the teachings of the Prophet Joseph Smith, or other Latter-day Saint commentators, it is helpful to carefully examine the New Testament accounts in their historical context to ascertain, where possible, the original intent of the authors when they first recorded the story. Reconstructing the original historical setting may allow us to enter the world of the first Christian disciples as we attempt to discern how those who first heard these sacred texts read out loud understood the stories themselves, in their time and place. Once we identify this historical setting, as best as is humanly possible, we are then in a better position to examine the remarkable insights available from the Restoration.[4]

Mark's Story of the Transfiguration

Probably written to Christian Gentiles living somewhere in the western Roman Empire, most likely in Rome itself, Mark's Gospel preserves Peter's reminiscences and, as a result, represents an

[4] Latter-day Saint commentators often suggest that the Restoration provides material about the Transfiguration either lost or purposely deleted from the Bible, assuming that if we had access to the original New Testament documents, known as autographs, we would have the complete picture, which would differ significantly from the accounts now preserved in Matthew, Mark, and Luke. Certainly the Joseph Smith Translation (JST) does provide such evidence for particular parts of the biblical text (see also 1 Nephi 13:26–29, 32, 34). However, another alternative is possible: the original authors of the synoptic Gospels may have had a completely different purpose in recording the stories as they did and therefore crafted their accounts to fit their needs and concerns at the time. This suggests that what has been preserved in the Greek manuscripts is basically what was originally recorded by Matthew, Mark, and Luke about the event.

eyewitness account of the Transfiguration filtered through Mark.[5] As Mark penned the first Gospel, he provided Matthew and Luke, who were not participants, the basic story outline for their own narratives. Although they relied on Mark, they were not bound by his narrative. They were also influenced by a fairly fluid oral tradition of the Transfiguration and possibly even other written sources that preserved the story from another perspective (see Luke 1:1).

Mark begins the story of the Transfiguration in chapter 8: "And Jesus went out, and his disciples, into the towns of Caesarea Philippi" (v. 27).[6] Following the well-known and often-repeated account of Peter's confession, "Thou art the Christ" (v. 29), Jesus' first prophecy about His forthcoming rejection in Jerusalem—His suffering, death, and Resurrection (v. 31), and Jesus' poignant teaching about discipleship (vv. 32–34), Mark continues his narrative, highlighting the Transfiguration: "And after six days Jesus taketh with him Peter, and James, and John, and leadeth them up into an high mountain apart" (Mark 9:2). Here, on an unnamed mountain, Jesus and these disciples find themselves alone:

> And [Jesus] was transfigured before them. And his raiment became shining, exceeding white as snow; so as no fuller on earth can white them. And there appeared unto them Elias with Moses: and they were talking with Jesus. And Peter answered and said to Jesus, Master, it is good for us to be here: and let us make three tabernacles; one for thee, and one for Moses, and one for Elias. For he wist not what to say; for they were sore afraid. And there was a cloud that overshadowed them: and a voice came out of the cloud, saying, This is my beloved Son: hear him. And suddenly, when they had looked

---

[5] Most scholars agree that Mark, the earliest Gospel account written, constitutes Peter's memoirs. See Richard Neitzel Holzapfel, *A Lively Hope: The Suffering, Death, Resurrection, and Exaltation of Jesus Christ* (Salt Lake City: Bookcraft, 1999), 22–23.

[6] Chapter divisions and versification, as they basically appear in current editions of the Bible, were added to the text beginning in the 1200s. And although helpful to the modern reader in accessing the stories, they can unwittingly destroy the continuity of a narrative by an intrusive interruption.

> round about, they saw no man any more, save Jesus only with themselves. And as they came down from the mountain, he charged them that they should tell no man what things they had seen, till the Son of man were risen from the dead. And they kept that saying with themselves, questioning one with another what the rising from the dead should mean. (Mark 9: 2–10)

Though the account is straightforward—Mark's prose is lively and his use of words moves it along—this story of the Transfiguration, like the entire Gospel, is not as simple as it first appears; it is a thoughtful and profound report of who Jesus is.

Mark commences his Gospel with a startling, bold announcement: "The beginning of the gospel of *Jesus Christ, the Son of God*" (Mark 1:1; emphasis added). The Transfiguration account affirms this declaration when the voice of God is heard saying, "This is my beloved Son" (Mark 9:7).[7] However, unlike the early declaration at the time of baptism—"Thou art my beloved Son, in whom I am well pleased" (Mark 1:11)—in this instance, God's voice is directed to the disciples, not to Jesus alone. Additionally, Mark tells his audience that both Moses, the giver of the Law, and Elias (Elijah), the representative of the Prophets, are witnesses to this bold affirmation and testify, therefore, that Jesus was He whom they had anticipated.

Of course, throughout the story, Mark preserves other witnesses to Jesus' special status as God's "beloved Son." The demonic forces, which Jesus had come to destroy, often acknowledge Jesus' superiority and testify of His filial relationship to the Father (see Mark 1:23–24; 3:11; 5:7). As many scholars have noted, Mark often drips with irony—as with this story line; those Jesus came to destroy know Him, and those He came to save do not.

[7] This is one of the very few places where God the Father speaks in the New Testament. The focus of the Gospels is centered on Jesus; even in this instance God is speaking about Jesus. One study demonstrates that God is the subject of less than .02 percent of Mark's Gospel; see Richard A. Burridge, *What Are the Gospels? A Comparison with Graeco-Roman Biography* (Grand Rapids, Mich.: Eerdmans, 2004), 325–26.

During the first part of the ministry, everyone seems to misunderstand. The Jewish leaders, who should have known who Jesus was, consistently get it wrong (Mark 2:7; 3:22; 14:63–64), as do His family (Mark 3:21–35), the crowds (Mark 4:10–12), His hometown (Mark 6:1–6), and even the disciples (Mark 8:14–18). Ironically, even when they get it right (Mark 8:29), they misunderstand what He was to accomplish in Jerusalem (Mark 8: 31–32).[8] And finally, Mark preserves a human witness, this time a Roman centurion who stood near the site of execution, bearing witness, "Truly this man was the Son of God" (Mark 15:39).[9]

The Transfiguration of Jesus itself is a key component to the story. Our current English word "transfiguration" derives from the fourth-century Latin Vulgate translation of the New Testament (*transfiguratus*), not the Greek (*metamorphōthē*), which would be translated "metamorphosis."[10]

The main point for preserving this story, which is sometimes lost in commentaries on this pericope,[11] is to demonstrate that Jesus, from a human point of view, was very ordinary, but was, in fact, extraordinary, even divine. Those who met Jesus knew He spoke a Galilean dialect of Aramaic, the common language of His world. He ate the common food of His day and dressed in the common fashion. He was probably not any taller or shorter than the average man of the period, nor was He handsome (see Isaiah 53:2). The length of His hair and beard (if He had one) would not have set him apart. He was susceptible to cuts and scrapes.

---

[8] See Jerry Camery-Hoggatt, *Irony in Mark's Gospel: Text and Subtext, SNTSMS 72* (Cambridge: Cambridge University Press, 1992).

[9] Although not part of the tradition preserved by Mark (see Mark 8:29; cf. Luke 9:20), Matthew indicated that Peter also testified, "Thou art the Christ, *the Son of the living God*" (Matthew 16:16; emphasis added).

[10] There are several other examples of Latinism in the KJV, including Calvary (*Calvaria*) for "skull" in the Greek text (see Luke 23:33).

[11] A pericope is an individual passage in the Gospels that has a distinct beginning and ending, thus forming an independent literary "unit," often in the form of a parable, miracle story, or summary. Similar pericopes are found in different places and different orders in the Gospels.

Chiseled into Jesus' maturing face and imprinted into His hands and feet were the effects of a village life of hard work, including extensive walking and manual labor. His features and stature were affected by a limited diet, both in terms of variety and quantity (fresh meat was a treat), and a lack of dental care and minimal medical attention. Most likely Jesus had an olive complexion, angular features, prominent brows, brown eyes, black hair, and a black beard (there were, however, some recessive blue-eye, red-hair genes among ancient Jews). In other words, Jesus probably looked like many other Mediterranean first-century Jews.

No one would have particularly noticed Jesus, without being prompted by the Spirit (see Luke 2:26–30), until His ministry of preaching, teaching, and healing gave Him notoriety, but this recognition was not based on any special physical features; it was based on His words and deeds (see Acts 10:38).

Mark categorically reveals in this story that the ordinary-looking son of a village carpenter was "transfigured." He no longer looked like any other Mediterranean Jew nor like any Roman emperor; Jesus' glory revealed Him as God's "beloved Son," setting Him apart from all other humans.[12]

In addition to these particular overreaching themes, Mark also provides further insights with such small details as Jesus' clothing. He states that Jesus' "raiment became shining, exceeding white as snow; so as no fuller on earth can white them" (Mark 9:3). The KJV word "fuller" is not regularly used today and sometimes cannot be found in modern English dictionaries. The Greek word *gnapheus* (used only here in the New Testament) means "bleacher, one who cleans woolen cloth."[13]

---

[12] There is a parallel among Moses (Exodus 33–34), Stephen (Acts 6:15), and Jesus (Mark 9:2). However, Jesus' Transfiguration was fundamentally different from that of Moses and Stephen. Each man reflected the glory of God in his countenance, but Jesus revealed His own glory, which He had laid aside in His birth (see John 17:5).

[13] See William F. Arndt and F. Wilbur Gingrich, *A Greek-English Lexicon of the New Testament and Other Early Christian Literature* (Chicago: University of Chicago Press, 1979), 162.

In antiquity, woven cloth was taken to a fuller, who cleaned it by treading on the cloth in a basin containing a cleaning solution (fuller's soap is mentioned in Malachi 3:2) mixed with water to remove impurities and to tighten and thicken the cloth. Additional processes made the cloth smooth. To make it white, the fuller burned sulfur under the cloth to bleach it. A recent simple and straightforward translation of the passage provides the sense of the passage: "His clothes became dazzling white, whiter than anyone in the world could bleach them" (NIV Mark 9:3).[14]

Another interesting detail is Mark's follow-up passage: "And when he came to his disciples, he saw a great multitude about them, and the scribes questioning with them. And straightway all the people, when they beheld [Jesus], were *greatly amazed* and, running to him saluted him" (Mark 9:14–15; emphasis added). Mark's Gospel is known for the use of a few favorite words throughout the narrative, such as "amazed," or the alternative KJV "astonished" and "marveled" (see Mark 2:12; 5:20, 42; 6:2, 51; 7:37; 10:26, 32; 11:18; 12:17; 15:5). Mark's use of the compound *ekthambēō* ("be greatly amazed") is found only in his Gospel.

The question naturally arises, "Why were the people greatly amazed?" One may see in this story a parallel to Moses on Mount Sinai—one of the constant themes weaving itself through the Transfiguration narratives as will be discussed below. If this is the case, then Mark may be indicating that the people were "greatly amazed" by the divine light still discernable in Jesus' countenance following the experience on the mount (for the parallel with Moses, see Exodus 34:29).

Mark's account may have reminded some of the vision recorded in Daniel where "one like the Son of man" approaches the "Ancient of days" and receives power, authority, and the kingdom (Daniel 7:13; see also verse 10), thus verifying Jesus' self-designation as the

[14] *Today's New International Version New Testament* (Grand Rapids, Mich.: Zondervan, 2002), the updated version of the tremendously successful *New International Version,* known as the NIV.

Son of Man (see Mark 2:10, 28; 8:31, 38; 9:9, 12, 31; 10:33, 45; 13:34; 14:21, 41, 62).

Another underlying theme in Mark's Gospel is the issue concerning authority to interpret Jewish scripture and law (see Mark 1:27; 3:1–3; 7:1–13; 10:2–12; 12:18–27, 28–34, 35–38). This was one of the main controversies that developed during the Intertestamental period—the era between the end of the Old Testament and the beginning of the New Testament.[15] It was a time when there was no prophet, and various individuals and groups tried to fill the void by claiming exclusive privilege to the right to interpret the Torah.

The Hebrew Bible was still an open canon during this time in Jewish history (the Torah was, for all intents and purposes, a closed canon consisting of five separate books). For many Jews, however, the authoritative writings were divided into three separate and distinct sections or divisions: the Law (*Torah*), the Prophets (*Nevi'im*), and the Writings (*Kehubim*).[16] The first part of Mark's Gospel provides experience after experience where Jesus is seen as claiming that role Himself. The Transfiguration answered the question definitively from the perspective of the synoptic Gospel authors when God spoke.

In the Transfiguration scene, Moses most likely represented the Law, and Elijah represented the Prophets. Peter, James, and John saw "Elias [Elijah] with Moses: and they were talking with Jesus" (Mark 9:4; an interesting and unexplained placement of the names with Elijah listed first). Clearly, they not only saw heavenly beings but also recognized them. Then, Mark records that the cloud "overshadowed them: and a voice came out of the cloud, saying, This is my beloved Son: *hear him*" (Mark 9:7; emphasis added).

Mark concluded this section, "And suddenly, when they [Peter, James, and John] had looked round about, they saw no man any

---

[15] See S. Kent Brown and Richard Neitzel Holzapfel, *Between the Testaments: From Malachi to Matthew* (Salt Lake City: Deseret Book, 2002), 231–38.

[16] See Jesus' reference to the threefold nature of Jewish scripture (Luke 24:44).

more, save Jesus only" (Mark 9:8). Emphatically, God informs the disciples that they are not just to listen to Jesus but also to "hear him." First, the episode ended any controversy about Jesus' right to interpret the Law and the Prophets; the disciples were to listen to (obey) Jesus, not representatives from the scribes, Sadducees, Pharisees, or Essenes, who each claimed the right themselves.

Additionally, and fundamentally more important, when Peter, James, and John looked up, they saw only Jesus. This symbolized that Jesus had been given superiority even over the Law (Moses) and the Prophets (Elijah)—for their days had ended, and now was the time of the "beloved Son."[17]

Another emphasis in the story may relate to Jesus' call of discipleship. Immediately preceding the ascent upon the mountain, Jesus taught, "Whosoever will come after me, let him deny himself, and take up his cross, and follow me" (Mark 8:34), continuing, "For whosoever will save his life shall lose it; but whosoever shall lose his life for my sake and the gospel's, the same shall save it" (Mark 8:35).

It was well known that Elijah had ascended to heaven. In addition, stories circulated about Moses ascending to heaven also.[18] Mark may have intended his audience to consider the possibility that Jesus could have ascended to heaven on the mount—He was transfigured just as Elijah and Moses were earlier. Instead, Jesus voluntarily remained on earth to finish His journey to the cross: "The Son of man must suffer many things, and be rejected of the elders, and of the chief priests, and scribes, and be killed" (Mark

[17] The command recalls the prophecy in Deuteronomy, "The Lord thy God will raise up unto thee a Prophet from the midst of thee, of thy brethren, like unto me; unto him ye shall hearken" (Deuteronomy 18:15; cf. Acts 3:22; 7:37; 1 Nephi 22:21; 3 Nephi 20:23; JS—H 1:40).

[18] Jews of the first century were fully aware of Elijah's unique status as a translated being (see 2 Kings 2:9–12). On the other hand, the Hebrew Bible records Moses' death and burial, "but no man knoweth of his sepulchre unto this day" (see Deuteronomy 34:5–7). However, first-century stories circulated that Moses had, in fact, "disappeared," suggesting a similar status as Elijah (see Josephus, *AJ*, 9.2.2).

8:31).[19] Therefore, Jesus became the model *par excellence* of dedication to God's will.

Mark also provides his audience with the fulfillment of the long-expected return of Elijah, but note how both Moses and Elijah are mentioned together in the last verses of Malachi: "Remember ye the law of Moses my servant, which I commanded unto him in Horeb for all Israel, with the statutes and judgments. Behold, I will send you Elijah the prophet before the coming of the great and dreadful day of the Lord" (Malachi 4:4–5). The appearance of Moses and Elijah on the mount further witnessed that this was a time anticipated by the prophets of Israel.

In the end, Mark informs us that even though Jesus had prophesied that He would be rejected in Jerusalem by the "elders, and of the chief priests, and scribes" (Mark 8:31), the Father verified by His own voice that Jesus' forthcoming rejection, suffering, and death in no way disqualified Him as God's "beloved Son" (Mark 9:7). Jesus' words (message) must still be obeyed, no matter what was to happen in Jerusalem.[20]

Matthew's Story of the Transfiguration

Matthew follows Mark's account very closely, more so than Luke does. Nevertheless, Matthew edits and arranges his material to suit his purposes. As in Mark, the story of the Transfiguration in Matthew is preceded, and therefore introduced, by Peter's confession (see Matthew 16:16) and Jesus' own prophecy about His fate in the Holy City (see Matthew 16:21).

Matthew, however, preserves Jesus' promise to give "the keys of the kingdom of heaven" (Matthew 16:19) to Peter, a story not found in the other Gospel. Demonstrating that Peter's confession

---

[19] This possibility is strengthened when we consider, according to Luke, that Moses and Elijah talked to Jesus about His mission in Jerusalem (see Luke 9:31, where "decease" is better translated "departure").

[20] The story continues when Jesus commands them not to tell anyone of the vision until after He has risen from the dead (see Mark 9:9–10). This leads to questions about the coming of Elias (Elijah) (see Mark 9:11–13).

(identifying Jesus as both "Christ [Messiah]" and the "Son of the living God") was accurate, adequate, and, more important, appropriate; it also reveals how individual Gospel accounts were tailored to fit a specific need at the time. Matthew continues the story:

> And after six days Jesus taketh Peter, James, and John his brother, and bringeth them up into an high mountain apart, and was transfigured before them: and his face did shine as the sun, and his raiment was white as the light. And, behold, there appeared unto them Moses and Elias talking with him. Then answered Peter, and said unto Jesus, Lord, it is good for us to be here: if thou wilt, let us make here three tabernacles; one for thee, and one for Moses, and one for Elias. While he yet spake, behold, a bright cloud overshadowed them: and behold a voice out of the cloud, which said, This is my beloved Son, in whom I am well pleased; hear ye him. And when the disciples heard it, they fell on their face, and were sore afraid. And Jesus came and touched them, and said, Arise, and be not afraid. And when they had lifted up their eyes, they saw no man, save Jesus only. (Matthew 17:1–8)

The Transfiguration setting in Matthew—the "mountain"—is an important element in the pericope and throughout the Gospel account. Matthew's highlighting the mountain setting is best understood in the context of other references to mountains in his Gospel. It is a place of divine instruction, manifestation, and revelation. A mountain plays a role in the Temptation narrative (Matthew 4:8–11); the Beatitudes and the sermon are given on a mount (Matthew 5:1); the mountain is the place where Jesus went to pray (Matthew 14:23); Jesus heals and also feeds four thousand on a mountain (Matthew 15:29–39); He enters Jerusalem from the Mount of Olives (Matthew 21:1); He delivers the Olivet Discourse on the mountain overlooking Jerusalem (Matthew 24:3); and the final commissioning of the disciples takes place on a mountain (Matthew 28:16–20).[21]

---

[21] Terrence L. Donaldson, *Jesus on the Mountain: A Study in Matthean Theology*

And like Mark's Gospel, Matthew's provides another theme in the story; Matthew wants to provide his audience the answer to the question of who Jesus was. Jesus was certainly considered many things by those who met Him or heard about His activity. He was teacher, healer, prophet, and even a messianic figure. Of these roles, that of prophet seems to have dominated the discussions about Jesus; this is well attested throughout the Gospel accounts.

Although messianic expectations may have dominated the religious discussions and dreams of the Jewish people during the first century, the coming of a prophet was a very close second concern. Additionally, the role of a prophet was by far more significant than the hope for a messiah (anointed servant) for the priestly clan as anticipated at Qumran by the Essenes.[22]

Among the debates regarding prophets and their roles was the Jewish expectation of Elijah's return (see Malachi 4:5–6). Such expectation is also alluded to in direct ways in the Gospels themselves (see Matthew 11:14; 17:10–11, Mark 9:11–12; Luke 1:17; John 1:21). There was also a concern regarding a prophet like Moses (see Deuteronomy 18:15, 18; cf. Acts 3:22–23; 7:37). And there was an expectation of an unnamed prophet (see Isaiah 61:1–3; cf. John 1:21).

People thought Jesus was a prophet, a view sustained throughout Matthew and the other texts. These rumors existed during most of Jesus' public ministry, and certainly the rumor mill continued following His death. The New Testament authors suggest that Jesus' life and ministry, to a great extent, paralleled the lives of earlier prophets. They often drew such parallels themselves as they told their stories.

However, Matthew's purpose, like that of Mark, was to demonstrate that Jesus was more than a prophet. Beginning at the baptism, where John declares it as such, Jesus is shown as God's chosen

---

JSNTS 8 (Sheffield: JSOT Press, University of Sheffield, 1985).

[22] Brown and Holzapfel, *Between the Testaments*, 197–98.

Son.[23] Here on the mount, God declares to the disciples, "This is my beloved Son, in whom I am well pleased; hear ye him" (Matthew 17:5)—thus confirming what Matthew's audience already knew from the beginning of the story (Matthew 1:23); the baptism (Matthew 3:13–17) and wilderness temptations (Matthew 4:1–11); the calming of the storm (Matthew 14:33); and Peter's inspired declaration at Caesarea Philippi (Matthew 16:16).

Matthew ends his Transfiguration narrative with the story of the descent from the mountain. As they came down, Matthew reports, "Jesus charged them, saying, Tell the vision to no man, until the Son of man be risen again from the dead" (Matthew 17:9). In this way, Jesus prepared the disciples for His death in Jerusalem—something He had begun to do while in the "coasts [regions] of Caesarea Philippi" just days before (Matthew 16:13).

Luke's Story of the Transfiguration

Like Mark and Matthew, Luke's story is preceded by Peter's confession at Caesarea Philippi (see Luke 9:18–21) and the prophecy concerning rejection (Luke 9:22). He continues his story:

> And it came to pass about an eight days after these sayings, he took Peter and John and James, and went up into a mountain to pray. And as he prayed, the fashion of his countenance was altered, and his raiment was white and glistering. And, behold, there talked with him two men, which were Moses and Elias: who appeared in glory, and spake of his decease which he should accomplish at Jerusalem. But Peter and they that were with him were heavy with sleep: and when they were awake, they saw his glory, and the two men that stood with him. (Luke 9:28–32)[24]

---

[23] See Richard Neitzel Holzapfel, "Jesus in the Wilderness: Baptism, Fasting, and Temptations," *The Life and Teachings of Jesus Christ: From Bethlehem through the Sermon on the Mount*, ed. Richard Neitzel Holzapfel and Thomas A. Wayment (Salt Lake City: Deseret Book, 2005), 167.

[24] Much has been made of Luke's "And it came to pass about an eight days after these sayings" (Luke 9:28) in relationship to Mark's and Matthew's "And after six

Luke preserves this important story apparently for several reasons. First, the episode, like that in Mark and Matthew, identifies Jesus as more than a prophet. Additionally, it also identifies Jesus as more than one of several messengers called "messiahs" (anointed ones) expected before the "great and dreadful day of the Lord."[25] He is the one Messiah after whom His predecessors are patterned. It is a clear expression that Jesus is the Son of God and, more important, that he is God's "*beloved* Son," (Luke 9:35; emphasis added) or the "chosen one," as the Greek text suggests.

Luke weaves through his account the motifs from Moses' own ascent to Mount Sinai (see Exodus 19–24; 32–34), something commentators have noticed in all the Transfiguration accounts, especially in Matthew's Gospel.[26] Additionally, Luke wants to demonstrate a parallel between the Mount of Transfiguration and the Mount of Olives, and he ties his theme of the temple with each.

Mount Sinai is the place where the Lord dwells or from which He comes (see Deuteronomy 33:2; Judges 5:5; Psalm 68:8, 17). Apparently, Sinai and Horeb are the same place. Moses ascended Mount Sinai, where the glory of the Lord was settled (see Exodus 24:15–18). On the sacred mountain, the Lord allowed Himself, or at least His glory, to be seen (see Exodus 24:11; 33:18–23) and revealed His "name" (Exodus 34:5–7). It is the place of making a covenant between Himself and His people.

The Transfiguration story is of a similar nature—it involves a natural temple—a high mountain. Like Moses, the disciples are called from the cloud. Moses enters the glory of the cloud, which is like a devouring fire (see Exodus 24:16–18). Earlier in chapter 24 of

---

days" (see Mark 9:2; Matthew 17:1). However, although Mark and Matthew are consistent on the six days, Luke says "about an eight days," a reasonable approximation.

[25] See Richard Neitzel Holzapfel, "The Hidden Messiah," *A Witness of Jesus Christ: The 1989 Sperry Symposium on the Old Testament,* ed. Richard D. Draper (Salt Lake City: Deseret Book, 1990), 81–82.

[26] See, for example, the discussion regarding this motif in Matthew's account in *Eerdmans Commentary on the Bible,* eds. James D. G. Dunn and John W. Rogerson (Grand Rapids, Mich.: Eerdmans, 2003), 1038.

Exodus, Moses has been commanded to select three disciples (Aaron, Nadab, and Abihu), together with seventy elders, to confirm the covenant (see Exodus 24:1–8). The result is that only these people are explicitly said to have seen "the God of Israel" in His court (Exodus 24:10). As was the case with Moses when he was visited by the Lord (see Exodus 34:29), Jesus' appearance was changed at the Transfiguration. The motifs of the master, three disciples, mountain, cloud, and vision in Exodus 24 recur in the Transfiguration story.

Luke, unlike Mark and Matthew, indicates that Jesus took the disciples to the mount to pray. Prayer is a central and pervasive theme in Luke—Jesus prayed often, many times on a mountain (Luke 3:21; 5:16; 6:12; 9:18, 28–29; 11:1; 22:32, 39–40; 23:34, 46).

Like a later experience at the Mount of Olives, the Transfiguration may have occurred in the nighttime—because "Peter and they that were with him were heavy with sleep" (Luke 9:32; cf. Luke 22:39 for the other experience at night).[27] This pattern has an earlier parallel: "And it came to pass in those days, that he went out into a mountain to pray, and continued all night in prayer to God" (Luke 6:12).

Another parallel with the Mount of Olives experience is the presence of Peter, James, and John in both cases. Jesus came to pray in both stories, and ultimately one or more divine messengers appeared following the prayer. As occurs often in this Gospel, the picture of Jesus at prayer precedes an event of importance (see, for example, Luke 1:9–11). In the Transfiguration, Jesus' prayer was answered by angelic administration—in this case, Elijah and Moses.

A temple context is also apparent in Luke's account. Of course, the temple is one of Luke's constant themes.[28] In this case, Jesus'

[27] Only here in the New Testament do we find the aorist participle of *diagrēgoreō*—the simple verb *grēgoreō* means "be awake." So the compound in this passage most likely means "be fully awake." Translators take different approaches to the meaning of this single word, which is the basis for the KJV phrase "when they were awake" (Luke 9:32).

[28] See "Luke and the Presence of God in the Temple," in Richard Neitzel Holzapfel

"raiment was white and glistering" (Luke 9:29). The description of the clothing is of interest because white was the color of the priestly garments and robes and of the clothing of the heavenly host who worship God in the heavenly temple (see Revelation 2:17; 6:2; 20:11)—not the clothing typically worn by Mediterranean people as they worked and walked along the dusty paths of Palestine.[29]

A final Old Testament temple context may be found in the appearance of the cloud. It is the physical representation of the glory and presence of God, whether at the holy mount, the tabernacle, or the temple in Jerusalem (see Exodus 16:10; 19:9; 24:15–18; 40:34; 2 Samuel 22:7–17; 1 Kings 8:10–11; Ezekiel 10:3–4; Psalm 18:6–13). The cloud points the way on the march out of Egypt (see Exodus 13:21). It accompanies the people throughout their journeying (see Numbers 14:14). At each special revelation, it rests on the tabernacle (see Exodus 33:9). Above all, at the making of the covenant, the cloud, with lightning on the top of the mountain, both conceals and reveals the Lord's presence (see, for example, Exodus 19:16; 24:15; Deuteronomy 5:22). Certainly, all three synoptic authors intended their audience to understand that the cloud at the Transfiguration was equated with the *Shekhinah*—the presence of God (see Exodus 25:8).[30]

Luke provides additional information about Moses and Elijah, again demonstrating how individual authors used the core tradition—Jesus was transfigured on a mount in the presences of Peter, James, and John shortly after they departed from the regions of

---

and David Rolph Seely, *My Father's House: Temple Worship and Symbolism in the New Testament* (Salt Lake City: Bookcraft, 1994), 81–117.

[29] Modern artists often represent Jesus wearing white clothing during His ministry; this, of course, provides the viewer an opportunity to visualize Jesus as fundamentally different from others depicted in various scenes. It does not, however, represent the historical and cultural reality of the first century. Similar artistic licenses, such as depicting Jesus with a halo, have always imbued religious art with a sense of the divine—allowing inner spiritual realities to be manifest outwardly for all to behold the truth.

[30] See "Shekhinah," *The Oxford Dictionary of the Jewish Religion*, ed. R. J. Zwi Werblowsky and Geoffrey Wigoder (New York: Oxford University Press, 1997), 629–30.

Caesarea Philippi—and then adapted the story to their own purposes by focusing or emphasizing different aspects of the story. As in this case, Luke is providing additional information not recorded by other authors.

Here Luke, unlike Mark and Matthew, informs his audience that Moses and Elijah also "appeared in glory" with Jesus (Luke 9:31).[31] Although this may be implied in Mark and Matthew, Luke explicitly indicates as much. Additionally, Luke provides additional information about the conversation among Moses, Elijah, and Jesus. The Greek text indicates they communicated with Jesus about His *exodus* (Greek *exodos*), not simply about His death, as the King James translators suggest by their choice of the word *decease.* The Greek word literally means "the way out" or "departure." Most likely, Luke intended his audience to understand that Moses and Elijah spoke to Jesus about His death but also about His mission in Jerusalem and ultimately His Resurrection and ascension as His "departure" to the Father.

Another aspect highlighted by Luke, as well as by Mark and Matthew, is Peter's statement, "Let us make three tabernacles; one for thee, and one for Moses, and one for Elias" (Luke 9:33). The tabernacles (Greek *skēnē*) may refer to the ancient tabernacle of Moses.[32] Whatever Luke intended with the use of "tabernacles," it seems clear from the present context that Peter misunderstood the significance of the event and was implicitly rebuked.

One proposal may be that Peter, by suggesting the construction

---

[31] Another parallel to Moses, Elijah, and Jesus may have surfaced in the story. Moses' work was continued and finished by Joshua. Elijah's work was finished by Elisha, a name related to the name Joshua. Jesus, whose Hebrew name is also related to the name Joshua, would bring to fulfillment the work of both Moses and Elijah, just as Joshua had done earlier in both cases.

[32] Some commentators suggest that what Luke had in mind were the small "booths," constructed from the branches of trees, used in connection with the Feast of Tabernacles (see Leviticus 23:42). It is the same Greek word used in the Septuagint translation (LXX). In this case, Peter misunderstood that this was not the dawning of the kingdom in glory (some Jews believed that the faithful would celebrate one final Feast of Tabernacles just before the kingdom arrived)—Jesus still needed to suffer and die before that glorious day.

of three tabernacles, implied that Jesus, Moses, and Elijah were equal, when the purpose of the event was to demonstrate Jesus' superiority to them. In essence, the voice says, "Listen to Jesus, not Moses and Elijah" (see Luke 9:35).

John's and Peter's Story of the Transfiguration

When John prepared his own Gospel account is unclear. Traditionally, it has been identified as originating at the end of the first century; however, there is good reason to believe that it was composed at a much earlier date.[33] Its relationship to the composition of the synoptic accounts is, therefore, uncertain. Scholars have noticed that the story line diverges from the accounts written by Matthew, Mark, and Luke in significant and fundamental ways.

The Transfiguration narrative is one instance where John does not record a story found in the synoptic accounts. However, some scholars suggest that the main themes found in the synoptic Gospels are often alluded to in John's Gospel. For example, the "Great Intercessory Prayer" (John 17) fits into John's narrative in the same place where the other Gospel authors record the events that transpired in Gethsemane. Therefore, this chapter replaces the Gethsemane event in the Gospel of John, which has no other reference to Gethsemane; this may be an allusion that John was aware of a fuller account of what transpired there. John may refer to the Transfiguration at the beginning of his story: "And the Word was made flesh, and dwelt among us, (and we beheld his glory, the glory as of the only begotten of the Father,) full of grace and truth" (John 1:14).[34]

Why John, an eyewitness to the Transfiguration, decided not to highlight this particular story in his Gospel is uncertain, but it does

---

[33] D. B. Wallace, "John 5:2 and the Date of the Fourth Gospel," *Biblica* 71 (1990): 177–205.

[34] Later, John recorded Jesus' prayer on the evening of the Last Supper: "And now, O Father, glorify thou me with thine own self with the glory which I had with thee before the world was" (John 17:5). The relationship to these verses andof this verse to John 1:14 is somewhat problematic but may, in fact, relate to the Transfiguration.

again demonstrate how individual authors use material specifically for their own purposes.

On the other hand, most scholars agree that the second epistle of Peter contains a direct reference to the Transfiguration. This is an important witness to the event, not only because Peter was an eyewitness (unlike Mark, Matthew, and Luke) but also because it demonstrates how a single story can be used for completely different purposes and emphases, giving new information or submerging information found in corresponding texts.

The letter begins with these words: "Simon Peter, a servant and an apostle of Jesus Christ, to them that have obtained like precious faith with us through the righteousness of God and our Saviour Jesus Christ" (2 Peter 1:1). In what may be a "farewell letter" to an unknown Christian group, Peter urges them to remain faithful despite the appearance of false teachers who deny the Second Coming of Christ.

Often seen as being composed of four separate sections, this part of the letter testifies of the Lord's Second Coming. In this context, Peter provides his personal witness when he declares that "we have not followed cunningly devised fables, when we made known unto you the power and coming of our Lord Jesus Christ" (2 Peter 1:16). The Second Coming is an event that Peter believes is proven by both the Transfiguration itself and the "more sure word of prophecy" Peter received on the mount: "But [we] were eyewitnesses of his majesty. For he received from God the Father honour and glory, when there came such a voice to him from the excellent glory, This is my beloved Son, in whom I am well pleased. And this voice which came from heaven we heard, when we were with him in the holy mount. We have also a more sure word of prophecy" (2 Peter 1:16–19).[35]

For Peter, at least in this instance, the Transfiguration provided witnesses to Jesus' ultimate victory over death and hell, providing

---

[35] Several parallels exist: see Isaiah 42:1; Psalm 2:6–7; Septuagint translation of Psalm 8:6.

the early Saints a foretaste of the Second Coming of Jesus Christ. The future event was confirmed by the "more sure word of prophecy," which Peter could not deny and which the Saints should heed.

The Holy Mount

Often, visitors to the Holy Land are interested in the geographical identification of the sites associated with the events described in the biblical narrative. Curiosity often drives the tourist to want to know the exact spot where something special happened. The location of the Transfiguration, like other places associated with Jesus' life and ministry, became the object of speculation very early, especially following the Christianization of the Roman Empire when large numbers of pilgrims made their way to the Holy Land.

Eusebius (d. A.D. 320) believed that either Mount Tabor or Mount Hermon were possible sites. The Pilgrim of Bordeaux (A.D. 333), on the other hand, associated the Mount of Olives with the event. Following Cyril of Jerusalem's identification of Mount Tabor as the site in A.D. 348, most pilgrims and tourists made the journey to this site to commemorate the Transfiguration.[36]

Some modern commentators suggest that Mount Tabor is the mountain "apart," as noted in Matthew 17:1.[37] Located about ten miles southwest of the Sea of Galilee, the geographical setting of Mount Tabor does seem to make perfect sense, as it is isolated from the surrounding hills in the northeastern portion of the Jezreel Valley, providing the visitor a commanding and breathtaking view of the valley. However, such visual identification is based on an incorrect reading of the text. Although the KJV does state that Jesus brought Peter, James, and John "up into an high mountain *apart*" (Matthew 17:1; emphasis added), the Greek text clearly indicates that Jesus brought them to a high mountain "privately" or

---

[36] See Jerome Murphy-O'Connor, *The Holy Land: An Oxford Archaeological Guide from Earliest Times to 1700* (New York: Oxford University Press, 1998), 366.

[37] See, for example, D. Kelly Ogden, *Where Jesus Walked: The Land and Culture of New Testament Times* (Salt Lake City: Deseret Book, 1991), 9–10.

"by themselves" (NIV Matthew 17:1). "Apart," therefore, does not refer to the mountain but to the disciples and cannot be used to help identify the unnamed mountain itself.

Another objection to this identification is Mount Tabor's height. Standing only 1,842 feet high, it would be difficult, but not impossible, to say it was a "high mountain."[38] Additionally, there is some evidence that a fortress existed at the summit during the first century, which suggests that it was not a place to go to be alone. Finally, the fact the Jesus was near Caesarea Philippi, about forty-five miles northeast of Tabor, before the event (see Mark 8:27) and Capernaum following the event (see Mark 9:33), a site between the two locations seems more probable.

Despite these concerns, Mount Tabor is the most well-known site associated with the Transfiguration and is visited by countless pilgrims and tourists each year. We cannot help but feel something special at this place, but that feeling may be more influenced by the fact that we are thinking about, and sometimes reading the account here, that special feelings arise in the heart and spirit. That is true at many other sites in the Holy Land.

Scholars and commentators have provided another alternative. Many believe that Mount Hermon, or a spur of that mountain, fits the context much better for two reasons: first, because it is closer to Caesarea Philippi—the vicinity of the last scene—and second, because it is higher (more than nine thousand feet) than Tabor.

As noted, Hermon is located just north of Caesarea Philippi. Additionally, as Mark noted, Jesus led the disciples "into an *high mountain*" (Mark 9:2; emphasis added), which certainly conforms to Hermon's 9,200-foot height. It dominates the landscape of northern Galilee and is covered with snow virtually year round, naturally drawing our attention to Mark's comment, "And his raiment became shining, exceeding white as snow" (Mark 9:3).

A third proposition, one that has not caught the attention of scholars and has not become a destination for pilgrims and tourists,

[38] See Jeremiah 46:18.

is Mount Meron. Located a few miles northwest from the Sea of Galilee, it stands 3,926 feet high, making it one of the tallest mountains in Galilee—only Hermon is higher. It is certainly geographically closer to Caesarea Philippi than Tabor, and its height matches the description of a "high mountain" (Matthew 17:1). Luke seems to suggest that the story that follows should be seen as happening immediately, "on the next day, when they were come down from the hill" (Luke 9:37; cf. Matthew 17:14 and Mark 9:14). If so, it might be difficult to explain the presence of a large crowd, including scribes, near Hermon.

Whichever mountain it was, the important aspect of the synoptic narratives is the fact that Jesus and the three disciples ascended a mountain where God informed those listening that they were to "hear" Jesus above all others.

The Restoration Story of the Transfiguration

The Restoration provides additional witnesses and insights to the event that occurred so many years ago on an unnamed mount during the ministry of Jesus when He "went to pray." A review of Restoration insights provides an opportunity to see how inspired authors use material. In the context of nineteenth-century America, the concerns of the first century are no longer an issue. The overwhelmingly dominant religious movement in the world, especially in America and Europe, was Christianity. Therefore, the concerns about who Jesus was and who had the right to interpret scripture had long since been answered. Naturally, then, Joseph Smith and others focused on other aspects of the story or significance of the event. None of the earlier themes outlined by the original New Testament authors even surface in this modern context, except in the Joseph Smith Translation of the Bible. Here, the concerns and the issues are the same, as we might suspect.

When Joseph Smith began his translation of the Bible in June 1830, he started a process that taught him much about the sacred events and teachings located between the covers of his 1828 King

James Version Bible, including the Transfiguration. The Joseph Smith Translation provides interesting details about this sacred story.[39] Nevertheless, the context remains basically the same, except one passage in Mark that gives a different twist to the story. Based on the previous work of Scott H. Faulring, Kent P. Jackson, and Robert J. Matthews, Thomas A. Wayment has identified some of the passages that provided changes made by the Prophet during the inspired transition (changes are highlighted in bold).

JST Mark

The most significant addition to the story from the JST is also the most enigmatic. JST Mark indicates that John the Baptist was present: "And there appeared unto them Elias with Moses, **or in other words, John the Baptist and Moses**; and they were talking with Jesus" (JST Mark 9; KJV Mark 9:4).[40]

Of course, most LDS commentators suggest that Moses, Elijah (Elias), and John the Baptist appeared on the mount—conflating or harmonizing the various accounts. However, the JST does not indicate this; such a reconstruction ignores what the text actually states when it reveals that it was "John the Baptist and Moses" who appeared on the mount.

How do we escape this exegetical difficulty? One possibility exists. We might be dealing with several different versions of the story as recorded in the synoptic accounts—confused versions based on its oral transmission. We should recall that none of the synoptic authors were eyewitnesses of the event themselves. These authors could have drawn on different traditions, oral and written, associated with the Transfiguration story. The significance of this JST change is, at present, unknown and remains open for further interpretation until some revealed clarification comes.

---

[39] See *Joseph Smith's New Translation of the Bible: Original Manuscripts* (Provo: BYU Religious Studies Center, 2005), and Joseph Smith Jr., in *The Complete Joseph Smith Translation of the New Testament: A Side-by-Side Comparison with the King James Version*, ed. Thomas A. Wayment (Salt Lake City: Deseret Book, 2005).

[40] Smith, in *The Complete Joseph Smith Translation*, 112.

JST Matthew

The JST of Matthew provides several minor but interesting changes to the KJV text. When discussing the cloud, the JST states, "While he yet spake, behold, a **light** cloud overshadowed them" (JST Matthew; cf. KJV Matthew 17:5).[41]

The JST slightly modifies the KJV: "And when the disciples heard **the voice**, they fell on their **faces**, and were sore afraid" (JST Matthew; cf. KJV Matthew 17:6).[42]

JST Luke

Although the current KJV inappropriately and inaccurately translates *exodos* as "decease," the JST captures the doctrinal significance of Luke's word choice: "Who appeared in glory, and spake of his **death, and also his resurrection,** which he should accomplish at Jerusalem" (JST Luke; cf. KJV Luke 9:31).[43]

The KJV Luke seems to indicate that Peter asked his question as Moses and Elijah were departing, whereas the JST is precise in the time: "And **after the two men** departed from him, Peter said unto Jesus, Master, it is good for us to be here: let us make three tabernacles; one for thee, and one for Moses, and one for Elias: not knowing what he said" (JST Luke; cf. KJV Luke 9:33).[44]

The JST seems to clarify who was overshadowed by the cloud: "While he thus spake, there came a cloud, and overshadowed them **all**: and they feared as they entered into the cloud" (JST Luke; cf. KJV Luke 9:34).[45]

Latter-day Saints may be surprised that none of the distinctive ideas we generally associate with the Transfiguration, such as Moses and Elijah (or, as a matter of fact, Jesus) laying their hands upon Peter, James, and John to give them the keys of the kingdom, are not mentioned in the JST. The omission is deafening. But the

[41] Smith, in *The Complete Joseph Smith Translation*, 47.
[42] Smith, in *The Complete Joseph Smith Translation*, 47.
[43] Smith, in *The Complete Joseph Smith Translation*, 175.
[44] Smith, in *The Complete Joseph Smith Translation*, 175.
[45] Smith, in *The Complete Joseph Smith Translation*, 175.

original context of the New Testament story was not concerned about this issue and therefore simply avoided mentioning it in the first place. We should not be surprised that the JST material did not deal with this issue either.[46]

The Doctrine and Covenants

During the process of the Restoration, the Prophet received additional revelations, now contained in the Doctrine and Covenants, that highlighted events mentioned in the Bible, including the Transfiguration. The nineteenth-century Saints learned that the earth itself will be transfigured (see Articles of Faith 1:10) and that a vision of this future destiny was shown to Peter, James, and John on the mount. In a revelation dated in late August 1831, the Lord states, "He that endureth in faith and doeth my will, the same shall overcome, and shall receive an inheritance upon the earth when the day of transfiguration shall come; when the earth shall be transfigured, even according to the pattern which was shown unto mine apostles upon the mount; of which account the fulness ye have not yet received" (Doctrine and Covenants 63:20–23).

In addition, the Lord informed the Church that not all that occurred on the mount had yet been revealed, indicating that more information might be forthcoming (see Articles of Faith 1:9).

Joseph Smith's Discourses

The Prophet Joseph Smith often spoke on scripture topics.[47] Therefore, it is not surprising that he said something about the

[46] The New Testament implicitly reveals that the promise given by Jesus to Peter about "the keys of the kingdom," the power to "bind [and loose] on earth" (Matthew 16:19), was at some point fulfilled (see Matthew 18:18). The fact that Elijah was known to have the power to "seal" the heavens (see 1 Kings 17:1) and appeared to Peter, James, and John on the mount between the time of the promise (Matthew 16:19) and Jesus' indication that the Twelve had the power to bind (Matthew 18:18) suggests the setting in Matthew 17 as the most likely time when that power was received under the hands of Elijah, who had held the power before.

[47] See Kent P. Jackson, *Joseph Smith's Commentary on the Bible* (Salt Lake City: Deseret Book, 1994), ix–xii.

Transfiguration. In Nauvoo, Joseph provided additional insights for the Church regarding this event, which were fortunately recorded at the time.

Some time before 8 August 1839, Joseph Smith told the Saints, "The Priesthood is everlasting. The Savior, Moses, & Elias—gave the Keys to Peter, James & John on the Mount when they were transfigured before him."[48] This, of course, corresponds to the information suggested in Matthew's account as noted earlier. According to Matthew, Jesus promised Peter "the keys of the kingdom of heaven" (Matthew 16:19) following his confession that Jesus was "the Christ, the Son of the living God" (Matthew 16:16). It was six days later when Jesus took Peter, James, and John by themselves onto the unknown mountain (Matthew 17:1). There, the disciples saw Moses and Elijah. We can assume that these prophets gave their respective keys to Peter, James, and John at the time based on the similar experience Joseph Smith and Oliver Cowdery shared in Kirtland on 3 April 1836 (see Doctrine and Covenants 110). Additionally, as already noted, Jesus implied that His Twelve Apostles had the keys (see Matthew 18:18) in a discourse following the Transfiguration experience noted in Matthew 17.

On 14 May 1843, the Prophet spoke in one of the outlying Mormon communities in Hancock County, noting:

> Though they had heard the audible voice from heaven bearing testimony that Jesus was the Son of God yet he says we have a more sure word of prophecy where unto ye do well that you take heed as unto a light shining in a dark place. Now wherein could they have a more sure word of prophecy than to hear the voice of God saying this is my Beloved Son & C[hrist]. Now for the secret & grand key though they might hear the voice of God & know that Jesus was the Son of God this would be no evidence that their election & calling

[48] Joseph Smith Jr., *The Words of Joseph Smith: The Contemporary Accounts of the Nauvoo Discourses of the Prophet Joseph*, ed. Andrew F. Ehat and Lyndon W. Cook (Provo: BYU Religious Studies Center, 1980), 9.

> was made sure that they had part with Christ & was a joint heir with him, they then would want that more sure word of prophecy that they were sealed in the heavens & had the promise of eternal life in the kingdom of God. . . . Then I would exhort you to go on & continue to call upon God until you make your calling & election sure for yourselves by obtaining this more sure word of prophecy & wait patiently for the promise until you obtain it.[49]

Joseph Smith continued to discuss the "more sure word of prophecy" a few days later when he addressed the Saints in Ramus, another outlying Mormon settlement in Hancock County on 17 May 1843: "The more sure word of prophecy means a man's knowing that he is sealed up unto eternal life, by revelation and the spirit of prophecy, through the power of the Holy Priesthood" (Doctrine and Covenants 131:5). Of course, the original context of Peter's statement recorded in his "farewell letter" suggests that the "more sure word" relates to the prophecy regarding the Second Coming of Christ. However, Joseph Smith moves beyond the original context and indicates that the "more sure word" also relates to a special knowledge received by those who know by revelation that they are "sealed up to eternal life," that is, their calling and election has been made sure.

On 27 August 1843, the Prophet told the gathered body of Saints in Nauvoo, "Men will set up stakes and say thus far will we go and not farther, did Abraham when called upon to offer his son, did the Saviour, no, view him fulfilling all righteousness again on the banks of jordon, also on the Mount transfigured before Peter and John there receiving the fullness of priesthood or the law of God, setting up no stake but coming right up to the mark in all things here him after he returned from the Mount, did ever language of such magnitude fall from the lips of any man, hearken him. All power is given is given unto me both in heaven and the earth."[50]

---

[49] Smith, *Words of Joseph Smith,* 201; spelling standardized.
[50] Smith, *Words of Joseph Smith,* 246.

In this dramatic commentary on the events of the Transfiguration, the Prophet told the Saints that Jesus received the "fulness of the priesthood" on the mount. As early as 19 January 1841, the Lord informed Joseph that He intended to restore "the fulness of the priesthood" in Nauvoo. Later, the Prophet taught on 27 August 1843 that those holding the "fulness of the priesthood" were ordained kings and priests.[51]

Following the death of Joseph Smith and the subsequent exodus and settlement of the Great Basin and the Mormon core area, little discussion of the Transfiguration is noted. However, a thoughtful and well-written discussion of the Transfiguration appeared in 1915 from the hand of Elder James E. Talmage. Now an LDS classic, *Jesus the Christ* provided a new generation of Latter-day Saints an opportunity to read a "Life of Christ."[52] However, Elder Talmage could not take advantage of the JST material because the Church and LDS scholars did not have access to the original manuscripts. Additionally, he did not access the rich collection of teachings from the Prophet Joseph Smith found in the diaries of those who recorded his sermons in Nauvoo.[53] The entire chapter dealing with the Transfiguration revolves around the same kind of issues that were on the minds of the original New Testament authors. Basically, Elder Talmage provided the Saints with a retelling of the story found in Matthew, Mark, and Luke, with a reference to Peter's statement about the "holy mount."

Later on, Elder Joseph Fielding Smith opined, "It appears that Peter, James, and John received their own endowments while on the mountain."[54] This is a significant expansion of early ideas presented by Joseph Smith, but not without thoughtful consideration of the sources. Although the Prophet said that Peter, James, and John had received the keys of the kingdom on the mount, just

---

[51] Smith, *Words of Joseph Smith,* 245; cf. Doctrine and Covenants 76:56.

[52] James E. Talmage, *JTC,* 343–48.

[53] This material would be culled and published only later.

[54] Joseph Fielding Smith, *Doctrines of Salvation*, comp. Bruce R. McConkie (Salt Lake City: Bookcraft, 1955), 2:165.

as he and Oliver had received the keys in the Kirtland Temple from the same messengers (see Doctrine and Covenants 110:11, 13–16), so Elder Joseph Fielding Smith went further to suggest that they also received the "endowment" on the same occasion, which would have been without parallel in the Restoration story. The endowments had first been administered in Nauvoo on 2 May 1842, by the Prophet, in the Red Brick store, many years following the appearance of Moses and Elijah in the Kirtland Temple.[55]

Based on these Restoration insights, particularly from the JST and the Prophet's teachings in Nauvoo, others have attempted to provide a fuller picture of what transpired at the Transfiguration, acknowledging that we do not yet have a full account of what transpired there.[56]

Conclusion

The synoptic accounts agree that the disciples did not talk about the Transfiguration "in those days" (Luke 9:36). Matthew and Mark suggest further that Jesus commanded them not to discuss what they saw and heard until after His Resurrection (Matthew 17:9; Mark 9:9).[57] However, at some point not only did they discuss the glorious events on the mount, but also their stories were eventually preserved in written form among the early Christian communities of the first century. The oral and written accounts had special significance to these early Saints and helped them respond to and answer questions about who Jesus was.

The scribes, Pharisees, Sadducees, and chief priests questioned Jesus' special claims. However, the declaration that Jesus was God's "beloved Son" upon the Mount of Transfiguration is precisely what

---

[55] See Joseph Smith, *TPJS*, 237.

[56] See, for example, Bruce R. McConkie, MM 3:53–68, and Robert J. Matthews, "Tradition, Testimony, Transfiguration, and Keys," in Kent P. Jackson and Robert L. Millet, eds., *Studies in Scripture Volume 5: The Gospels* (Salt Lake City: Deseret Book, 1986), 305–10.

[57] Just as Jesus forbids the "unclean spirits" to announce His identity (Mark 1:25; 3:12) so He forbids the disciples to do the same (see Mark 8:30; 9:9).

is affirmed by the synoptic Gospel writers throughout their accounts of Jesus' life and ministry, such as at His baptism (Mark 1:11).

Additionally, the Transfiguration prefigures Jesus' ultimate vindication by God through His resurrection and exaltation. That is, God reversed the death sentence by the earthly court when, in the heavenly court, Jesus was raised from the dead and placed on the right hand of God: "Him, being delivered by the determinate counsel and foreknowledge of God, ye have taken, and by wicked hands have crucified and slain. . . . This Jesus hath God raised up, whereof we all are witnesses. Therefore being by the right hand of God exalted. . . . Therefore let all the house of Israel know assuredly, that God hath made that same Jesus, whom ye have crucified, both Lord and Christ" (Acts 2:23, 32–33, 36).

For the original audience and the original authors, the Transfiguration was an important event in disclosing who Jesus was and how they should respond to His teachings. As Matthew closed his Gospel account, he said the disciples went "into a mountain where Jesus had appointed them" (Matthew 28:16). There, Jesus said, "Go ye therefore, and teach all nations, baptizing them in the name of the Father, and of the Son, and of the Holy Ghost: teaching them to observe all things whatsoever I have commanded you: and, lo, I am with you alway, even unto the end of the world. Amen" (Matthew 28:19–20).

III.

THE PARABLES OF MATTHEW 13: REVEALING AND CONCEALING THE KINGDOM OF GOD

FRANK F. JUDD JR.

And the disciples came, and said unto him, Why speakest thou unto them in parables? He answered and said unto them, Because it is given unto you to know the mysteries of the kingdom of heaven, but to them it is not given.

MATTHEW 13:10–11

Jesus Christ was a master teacher. As such, He certainly possessed the ability to amaze His audiences.[1] He chose, however, to teach the Jewish multitudes "on the level of their own experience and comprehension."[2] One of the ways Jesus accomplished this was through His use of parables. The English word *parable* comes from the Greek verb *paraballō,* which means "to set beside" or "to

---

[1] See Frank F. Judd Jr., "The Setting of the Sermon on the Mount," in Richard Neitzel Holzapfel and Thomas S. Wayment, eds., *The Life and Teachings of Jesus Christ: From Bethlehem through the Sermon on the Mount* (Salt Lake City: Deseret Book, 2005), 316–18.

[2] Joseph B. Wirthlin, "Guided by His Exemplary Life," *Ensign*, September 1995, 34. See also Jeffrey R. Holland, "Lift Up Your Eyes," *Ensign*, July 1983, 9; and Howard W. Hunter, "The Pharisee and the Publican," *Ensign*, May 1984, 64.

compare."[3] A parable is a story, drawn from common experience, which the narrator compares to some higher reality or truth.[4] The Savior employed different kinds of parables—"parables of instruction" and "parables of rebuke"—depending on the audience He was addressing. Jesus used parables of instruction to teach disciples and others about fundamental principles of the gospel, and He directed parables of rebuke toward those who sought to hinder the plan of God.[5] Most of His parables, including the parables in Matthew 13, were parables of instruction.

The Purpose of Parables

After the Savior recited the Parable of the Sower, He was approached by His disciples, who asked Him, "Why speakest thou unto them in parables?" (Matthew 13:10). The Savior answered, "Because it is given unto you to know the mysteries of the kingdom of heaven, but to them it is not given. . . . Because they seeing see not; and hearing they hear not, neither do they understand" (Matthew 13:11–13). Jesus told His disciples that this was a fulfillment of Isaiah's prophecy: "By hearing ye shall hear, and shall not understand; and seeing ye shall see, and shall not perceive: for this people's heart is waxed gross, and their ears are dull of hearing, and their eyes they have closed; lest at any time they should see with their eyes, and hear with their ears, and should understand with their heart, and should be converted, and I should heal them" (Matthew 13:14–15).[6]

In other words, when various groups of onlookers heard Jesus

[3] Danker, *GEL*, 758.

[4] Boyd K. Packer described a parable as "a verbal way to represent symbolically things that might otherwise be difficult to understand." Boyd K. Packer, "The Holy Temple," *Ensign*, February 1995, 34.

[5] See Frank F. Judd Jr., "The Priceless Parables," *Ensign*, January 2003, 56–58.

[6] Isaiah 6:9–10 in the King James Version differs slightly from Matthew's quotation. This difference results because the KJV of Isaiah 6:9–10 is translated from the Hebrew, whereas Matthew's quotation is from the version of Isaiah in the Greek Septuagint (LXX). The principle taught by Isaiah is also taught in other Old Testament references, such as Deuteronomy 29:4, Jeremiah 5:21, and Ezekiel 12:2.

teach gospel truths, they did not readily understand the significance of the doctrines they were hearing, and, as a result, they did not embrace the teachings. Concerning this, the Savior taught, "Whosoever hath, to him shall be given, and he shall have more abundance: but whosoever hath not, from him shall be taken away even that he hath" (Matthew 13:12). This is not a matter of mere intellectual capacity but rather of willingness and obedience. The Joseph Smith Translation clarifies the Savior's response: "For whosoever *receiveth,* to him shall be given, and he shall have more abundance; but whosoever *continueth not to receive,* from him shall be taken away even that he hath" (JST Matthew 13:10–11; emphasis added).[7] In other words, unless people received the truths they had already been taught, they would not receive additional truths and therefore would be hindered in their spiritual progression.

The prophet Alma taught the same principle to Zeezrom: "It is given unto many to know the mysteries of God . . . *according to the heed and diligence which they give unto him.* And therefore, he that will harden his heart, the same receiveth the *lesser* portion of the word; and he that will not harden his heart, to him is given the *greater* portion of the word, until it is given unto him to know the mysteries of God until he know them in full" (Alma 12:9–10; emphasis added).[8] This is not simply a choice between understanding everything at once or nothing at all. Those who heard the Savior's parables would understand those things they were prepared to receive. Elder Neal A. Maxwell concluded, "As the Master

[7] See also 2 Nephi 28:30. Joseph Smith stated concerning Matthew 13:10–16, "We understand from this saying, that those who had been previously looking for a Messiah to come, according to the testimony of the prophets, and were then, at that time looking for a Messiah, but had not sufficient light, on account of their unbelief, to discern Him to be their Savior; and He being the true Messiah, consequently they must be disappointed, and lose even all the knowledge, or have taken away from them all the light, understanding, and faith which they had upon this subject; therefore he that will not receive the greater light, must have taken away from him all the light which he hath." Smith, *TPJS*, 95.

[8] See also 1 Nephi 10:19 and Alma 26:22, as well as Talmage, *JTC*, 276–77, and Rudolf Schnackenburg, *The Gospel of Matthew* (Grand Rapids, Mich.: Eerdmans, 2002), 125.

Teacher, Christ tailored His tutoring, depending upon the spiritual readiness of His pupils."[9] Thus, by teaching in parables, Jesus revealed additional truths to those who were spiritually ready while also concealing those truths from people who were not yet able to receive sacred information. A closer look at Matthew 13 allows readers to understand what gospel truths the Savior revealed and concealed by means of these parables.

The Kingdom

A primary focus of the parables of Jesus was the anticipated "kingdom of God," a concept that has its origins in the Old Testament.[10] Approximately a millennium before the time of Jesus, Jehovah declared to King David, "When thy days be fulfilled, and thou shalt sleep with thy fathers, I will set up thy seed after thee, which shall proceed out of thy bowels, and I will establish his kingdom. He shall build an house for my name, and I will stablish the throne of his kingdom for ever. I will be his father, and he shall be my son" (2 Samuel 7:12–14).[11] Although David's son Solomon finished the temple, the reign of Davidic kings did not last forever.[12] Because of this, many Jews expected that God would fulfill this scripture by establishing His kingdom upon the earth through His

---

[9] Neal A. Maxwell, "Irony: The Crust on the Bread of Adversity," *Ensign*, May 1989, 63. See also Gerald N. Lund, "Understanding Scriptural Symbols," *Ensign*, October 1986, 24.

[10] Although all four Gospels use the phrase "kingdom of God," the Gospel of Matthew also uses the phrase "kingdom of heaven." These expressions, however, are equivalent and are used interchangeably. See David Wenham, *The Parables of Jesus* (Downers Grove, Ill.: InterVarsity Press, 1989), 23; Talmage, *JTC*, 788–89; and "Kingdom of Heaven or Kingdom of God," LDS Bible Dictionary, 721.

[11] Compare Ezekiel 34:23–24: "I will set up one shepherd over them, and he shall feed them, even my servant David; he shall feed them, and he shall be their shepherd. And I the Lord will be their God, and my servant David a prince among them; I the Lord have spoken it." See also Ezekiel 37:25; Jeremiah 23:5–6; 30:7; Zechariah 14:9.

[12] The line of Davidic kings ended with Zedekiah when the Babylonians destroyed Jerusalem and Solomon's temple in 587 B.C.. See 2 Kings 25:1–17; 2 Chronicles 36:11–21; Jeremiah 34:1–7; 39:1–7. There were other Davidic rulers after Zedekiah (for example, Shealtiel and Zerubbabel), but Zedekiah was the last king.

chosen messenger, the Messiah.[13] Isaiah prophesied concerning a future descendant of Jesse, the father of King David, "There shall come forth a rod out of the stem of Jesse, and a Branch shall grow out of his roots: and the spirit of the Lord shall rest upon him, the spirit of wisdom and understanding, the spirit of counsel and might, the spirit of knowledge and of fear of the Lord; and shall make him of quick understanding in the fear of the Lord: and he shall not judge after the sight of his eyes, neither reprove after the hearing of his ears" (Isaiah 11:1–3).[14]

Some anticipated that this future ruler would teach truth and perform miraculous deeds: "Behold my servant, whom I uphold; mine elect, in whom my soul delighteth; I have put my spirit upon him: he shall bring forth judgment to the Gentiles. . . . I the Lord have called thee in righteousness, and will hold thine hand, and will keep thee, and give thee for a covenant of the people, for a light of the Gentiles; to open the blind eyes, to bring out the prisoners from the prison, and them that sit in darkness out of the prison house" (Isaiah 42:1, 6–7).[15] Isaiah also prophesied, "They

---

[13] This scripture, of course, can be applied to David's son Solomon as well as to the future Messiah. Dallin H. Oaks taught, "Many of the prophecies and doctrinal passages in the scriptures have multiple meanings. . . . The book of Isaiah contains numerous prophecies that seem to have multiple fulfillments. One seems to involve the people of Isaiah's day or the circumstances of the next generation. Another meaning, often symbolic, seems to refer to events in the meridian of time, when Jerusalem was destroyed and her people scattered after the crucifixion of the Son of God. Still another meaning or fulfillment of the same prophecy seems to relate to the events attending the Second Coming of the Savior. The fact that many of these prophecies can have multiple meanings underscores the importance of our seeking revelation from the Holy Ghost to help us interpret them." Dallin H. Oaks, "Scripture Reading and Revelation," *Ensign*, January 1995, 8.

[14] The Prophet Joseph Smith identified the "Stem of Jesse" specifically as "Christ" (Doctrine and Covenants 113:1–2). The words *Christ* and *Messiah* are equivalent terms. The Greek word *christos* and the Hebrew/Aramaic word *meshiah* both mean "anointed one." For a discussion of these words, see M. Russell Ballard, "The Law of Sacrifice," *Ensign*, October 1998, 10.

[15] The Joseph Smith Translation adds, "For I will send my servant unto you who are blind; yea, a messenger to open the eyes of the blind, and unstop the ears of the deaf; and they shall be made perfect notwithstanding their blindness, if they will hearken unto the messenger, the Lord's servant" (JST Isaiah 42:20). The Prophet

shall see the glory of the Lord, and the excellency of our God. . . . Your God will come with vengeance, even with a recompence; he will come and save you; then the eyes of the blind shall be opened, and the ears of the deaf shall be unstopped. Then shall the lame man leap as an hart, and the tongue of the dumb sing" (Isaiah 35:4–6).[16] In sum, the expectation of the "kingdom of God" encompassed the coming of the Messiah as the king of Israel, the teaching and reception of His message, the performance of miracles, and the establishment of His kingdom upon the earth.

All of these elements found fulfillment in Jesus Christ. The Gospel of Luke records the announcement of the angel Gabriel to Mary that she would bear a son: "Thou shalt conceive in thy womb, and bring forth a son, and shalt call his name Jesus. He shall be great, and shall be called the Son of the Highest: and the Lord God shall give unto him the throne of his father David: And he shall reign over the house of Jacob for ever; and of his kingdom there shall be no end" (Luke 1:31–33).[17] About thirty years later, John the Baptist announced the fulfillment of this expectation: "Repent ye: for the kingdom of heaven is at hand" (Matthew 3:2).[18] Following the

---

Joseph Smith identified this "servant" as "our Savior," Jesus Christ. Smith, *TPJS*, 219. Matthew 12:14–21 also identifies the servant of Isaiah 42 as Jesus Christ. See also Victor L. Ludlow, *Isaiah: Prophet, Seer, and Poet* (Salt Lake City: Deseret Book, 1982), 360; Monte S. Nyman, *Great Are the Words of Isaiah* (Salt Lake City: Bookcraft, 1980), 154–55.

[16] See also Isaiah 61:1, "The Spirit of the Lord God is upon me; because the Lord hath anointed me to preach good tidings unto the meek; he hath sent me to bind up the brokenhearted, to proclaim liberty to the captives, and the opening of the prison to them that are bound." When the disciples of John the Baptist asked Jesus, "Art thou he that should come, or do we look for another?" (Matthew 11:3), Jesus offered as proof of His identity, "The blind receive their sight, and the lame walk, the lepers are cleansed, and the deaf hear, the dead are raised up, and the poor have the gospel preached to them" (Matthew 11:5). When the Pharisees questioned the source of the Savior's miracles, Jesus responded, "If I cast out devils by the Spirit of God, then the kingdom of God is come unto you" (Matthew 12:28).

[17] This is a clear allusion to Jehovah's prophecy to David in 2 Samuel 7:12–14. See also Isaiah 9:6–7.

[18] The translation "is at hand" is from the Greek verb *engizō*, which means to "draw near, come near, approach." Danker, *GEL*, 270. Elder Bruce R. McConkie interpreted John's reference to the kingdom of God as "the one true Church, the sole

imprisonment of John the Baptist, Jesus began preaching the same message in Galilee: "When Jesus had heard that John was cast into prison, he departed into Galilee. . . . From that time Jesus began to preach, and to say, Repent: for the kingdom of heaven is at hand" (Matthew 4:12, 17). When Jesus commissioned His Apostles, He instructed them to preach this very news: "As ye go, preach, saying, The kingdom of heaven is at hand" (Matthew 10:7).[19] Thus, the announcement of the kingdom was the central message of John the Baptist, Jesus Christ, and also the early disciples. A careful analysis of the parables in Matthew 13 will demonstrate that there were certain features of the kingdom of God that Jesus Christ revealed and others that He concealed.

The Parables

After giving the Sermon on the Mount (Matthew 5–7), performing numerous miracles (Matthew 8–9), and commissioning the Twelve Apostles (Matthew 10), the Savior continued His ministry among the inhabitants of Galilee (Matthew 11–12). One day during His Galilean ministry, Jesus went "out of the house, and sat by the sea side" (Matthew 13:1). Many people gathered, including His disciples—so many that Jesus "went into a ship, and sat; and the whole multitude stood on the shore" (Matthew 13:2). While in the boat, Jesus taught the people in parables.

The first parable in Matthew 13 is traditionally called the Parable of the Sower, although the focus of the parable is on the different types of soils rather than on the one who planted the seeds.[20] This parable was spoken to a crowd of people in general

---

organization through which salvation is administered." McConkie, *DNTC*, 1:114. Around 83 B.C., the prophet Alma announced the coming kingdom of God in a similar way (see Alma 5:50).

[19] In the JST, Jesus also taught this same thing to His disciples in the Sermon on the Mount (see JST Matthew 7:9).

[20] Robert J. Matthews observed that this parable "is known as The Sower or as The Soils. Since the emphasis and basic teaching of the parable is upon the various kinds and conditions of the soils, rather than upon the sower, the latter title is probably better." Robert J. Matthews, *The Parables of Jesus* (Provo: Brigham Young

while Jesus' own disciples were also near enough to hear.[21] According to the parable, there were four types of soil that received the seeds in four different ways. The seeds by the wayside were devoured by birds (Matthew 13:4); the seeds on stony ground temporarily sprang up but eventually withered away (Matthew 13:5–6); the seeds among thorns were choked (Matthew 13:7); and the seeds on good ground brought forth good fruit in varying degrees (Matthew 13:8).[22]

After the disciples came to the Savior and asked Him concerning His use of parables, Jesus interpreted this one: The seed is the word of the kingdom (Matthew 13:19); the soil by the wayside represents those who hear the gospel but are led astray by Satan because they do not fully understand it (Matthew 13:19); the soil on stony ground symbolizes those who hear the gospel and accept it but fall away after they are tried and persecuted (Matthew 13:20–21);[23] the soil among thorns stands for those who hear the gospel, but worldliness and the love of riches prevent them from receiving it (Matthew 13:22); finally, the good soil represents those who hear the gospel, understand it, receive it, and then bring forth good works

---

University Press, 1969), 10. Concerning the traditional names of parables, see Thomas A. Wayment, "Names of the Parables," *The Religious Educator* 4, no. 1 (2003): 97–106.

[21] See Matthew 13:2. The Greek word translated as "multitudes" in Matthew 13:2 is *ochlos*. In the Gospel of Matthew, this term consistently refers to the various groups of curious onlookers who were present when Jesus preached or performed miracles during His ministry. J. R. C. Cousland concluded that the term *ochlos* is used not for disciples of Jesus but "to refer to the Jewish people as distinguished from their leaders." J. R. C. Cousland, *The Crowds in the Gospel of Matthew*, Supplements to Novum Testamentum (Leiden: Brill, 2002), 22 and throughout.

[22] In the Book of Mormon, Lehi's vision of the tree of life contains similar elements: four different types of people who reacted toward the path of the iron rod in four different ways. Some wandered off and were lost in the mist of darkness; some pressed forward and partook of the tree of life but then were ashamed and fell away; some pressed forward, fell down at the foot of the tree of life, and partook; and some felt their way toward the great and spacious building. See 1 Nephi 8:19–33. On the similarities between these aspects of the Parable of the Sower and Lehi's vision, see Monte S. Nyman, *I, Nephi, Wrote This Record* (Orem: Granite, 2003), 101–9.

[23] The JST modifies verse 20 in the following way: "He that received the seed into stony places, the same is he that heareth the word, and *readily* with joy receiveth it" (JST Matthew 13:20; emphasis added).

(Matthew 13:23).[24] Concerning the Parable of the Sower, Joseph Smith concluded that "we believe that it has an allusion directly, to the commencement, or the setting up of the Kingdom *in that age*."[25] Thus, Jesus was primarily speaking of those things that would happen during His own time period.

The next three parables—the Parable of the Wheat and Tares (Matthew 13:24–30), the Parable of the Mustard Seed (Matthew 13:31–32), and the Parable of the Leaven (Matthew 13:33)—were also given to the crowds in general, with the disciples again close enough to hear.[26] The Parable of the Wheat and Tares likens "the kingdom of heaven" to a man who planted wheat in his field. After the man planted the wheat, his enemy then planted weeds among the wheat (Matthew 13:24–25).[27] When it was discovered that weeds were planted among the wheat, the servants of the sower asked, "Wilt thou then that we go and gather them up?" (Matthew 13:28). Rather than risk pulling up the good wheat sprouts with the weeds, the sower allowed both the wheat and the weeds to grow to maturity before they were harvested, separated, and gathered (Matthew 13:29–30).

Jesus also interpreted this parable for His disciples. The field is "the world," and the sower of the wheat is "the Son of Man"—Christ Himself, who spreads the gospel message.[28] Thus, the wheat sprouts, which Jesus called "the children of the kingdom" (Matthew 13:38), represent those who accept the gospel message and bring

---

[24] The JST adds that "good soil" represents those who "heareth the word, and understandeth *and endureth*" (JST Matthew 13:23; emphasis added).

[25] Smith, *TPJS*, 97; emphasis added.

[26] See Matthew 13:34, 36.

[27] The "tares" or weeds refer to a weed-grass called darnel, which "resembles wheat in its early stages of growth, and the roots of the two are often intertwined." D. Kelly Ogden, *Where Jesus Walked: The Land and Culture of New Testament Times* (Salt Lake City: Deseret Book, 1991), 83. See also S. Kent Brown, C. Wilfred Griggs, and Thomas W. Mackay, "Footnotes to the Gospels," *Ensign*, February 1975, 50.

[28] See Matthew 13:37–38. Jesus identified himself as "the Son of man" in Matthew 16:13. In a revelation to Joseph Smith, the Lord expanded the interpretation of the sower of the wheat to include not only Jesus Himself but also His Apostles, who also spread the gospel message. See Doctrine and Covenants 86:2.

forth good works. It is significant that the field represents the world rather than the Church. This suggests that the weeds, whom Jesus called "the children of the wicked one" (Matthew 13:38), are those in the world who persecute members of the Church under the influence of "the enemy," who is "the devil" (Matthew 13:39). This conclusion is supported by a revelation given to Joseph Smith in Doctrine and Covenants 86:3: "After they [the Apostles] have fallen asleep the great persecutor of the Church, the apostate, the whore, even Babylon, that maketh all nations to drink of her cup, in whose hearts the enemy, even Satan, sitteth to reign—behold he soweth the tares; wherefore, the tares choke the wheat and drive the Church into the wilderness."[29]

According to the Savior's interpretation, the servants of the sower are "the angels," and the harvest of the mature wheat and the weeds is "the end of the world" (Matthew 13:39).[30] The righteous are initially allowed to "grow together" with the wicked until "the end of the world," when they are separated and the wicked are destroyed.[31] Although the Savior's primary interpretation was that the weeds represent those in the world who persecute the Church, a secondary interpretation of the weeds is that they can also

[29] This reference is an allusion to the Book of Revelation. In chapter 17, the forces of evil are represented by a woman who is called "BABYLON THE GREAT, THE MOTHER OF ABOMINATIONS" (Revelation 17:5; all caps in KJV) and also "the great whore who sitteth upon many waters" and "reigneth over the kings of the earth" (Revelation 17:1, 18), and with whom "the inhabitants of the earth have been made drunk with the wine of her fornication" (Revelation 17:2). In chapter 12, the Church is represented by a woman (JST Revelation 12:7), and Satan is represented by a dragon (Revelation 12:9), who "stood before the woman which was ready to be delivered, for to devour her child as soon as it was born" (Revelation 12:4); then "the woman fled into the wilderness" (Revelation 12:6).

[30] The JST adds that the angels are "the messengers sent of heaven" and the harvest is "the destruction of the wicked" (JST Matthew 13:39–40). Joseph Smith taught that "the end of the world is the destruction of the wicked, the harvest and the end of the world have an allusion directly to the human family in the last days, instead of the earth, as many have imagined." Smith, *TPJS*, 101.

[31] Joseph Smith paraphrased by saying that "the Church is in its infancy, and if you take this rash step, you will destroy the wheat, or the Church, with the tares; therefore it is better to let them grow together until the harvest." Smith, *TPJS*, 98. See also Doctrine and Covenants 101:63–66.

represent those who initially accept the gospel message but then turn against it. When the angels separate the wicked from the righteous, "they shall gather *out of his kingdom* all things that offend, and them which do iniquity, and shall cast them into a furnace of fire" (Matthew 13:41–42).[32] The JST confirms this conclusion by adding that "they shall gather out of his kingdom all things that offend, and them which do iniquity, and shall cast them *out among the wicked*" (JST Matthew 13:43; emphasis added).[33]

The Parable of the Mustard Seed likens "the kingdom of heaven" to the seed of a mustard plant that was sowed in a field (Matthew 13:31). The Savior called the mustard seed "the least of all seeds," which, when fully grown, becomes "the greatest among herbs, and becometh a tree, so that the birds of the air come and lodge in the branches thereof" (Matthew 13:32).[34] Although the Savior did not directly interpret this parable, it teaches that the Church in its infancy may appear weak or small, yet it will grow until it becomes strong and mighty. The gathering of the true followers of Jesus Christ would not culminate in the early Christian period, and thus Joseph Smith applied the symbol of the mature mustard plant to "the Church as it shall come forth in the last days."[35]

---

[32] Neal A. Maxwell taught, "Church members will live in this wheat-and-tares situation until the Millennium. Some real tares even masquerade as wheat, including the few eager individuals who lecture the rest of us about Church doctrines in which they no longer believe." Neal A. Maxwell, "Becometh As a Child," *Ensign*, May 1996, 68.

[33] Joseph Smith taught that the weeds were a symbol for "the corruptions of the Church, which are represented by the tares, which were sown by the enemy, which His disciples would fain have plucked up, or cleansed the Church of, if their views had been favored by the Savior." Smith, *TPJS*, 98.

[34] D. Kelly Ogden has observed, "Although the mustard seed is not really the smallest of all seeds, proverbially or hyperbolically it denotes the strength and power inherent in even the smallest particle." Ogden, *Where Jesus Walked*, 91. See also D. Kelly Ogden, "A Sampler of Biblical Plants," *Ensign*, August 1990, 39; Sidney B. Sperry, "Hebrew Manners and Customs," *Ensign*, May 1972, 30.

[35] Smith, *TPJS*, 98. Shortly before Joseph Smith's martyrdom, Brigham Young taught, "The kingdom is organized; and, although as yet no bigger than a grain of mustard seed, the little plant is in a flourishing condition." B. H. Roberts, ed., *History*

The Parable of the Leaven likens "the kingdom of heaven" to a measure of yeast that was kneaded into "three measures of meal" (Matthew 13:33). Again, the Savior did not interpret this particular parable for His disciples. The main idea, however, is that although the gospel begins inconspicuously, its effects will eventually penetrate every part of the world.[36] On one occasion, the Prophet Joseph Smith taught, "You know no more concerning the destinies of this Church and kingdom than a babe upon its mother's lap. You don't comprehend it. . . . It is only a little handful of Priesthood you see here tonight, but this Church will fill North and South America—it will fill the world."[37]

After Jesus was approached by the disciples apart from the multitude, He gave three more short parables: the Parable of the Hidden Treasure (Matthew 13:44), the Parable of the Pearl of Great Price (Matthew 13:45–46), and the Parable of the Net (Matthew 13:47–50). In the Parable of the Hidden Treasure, "the kingdom of heaven" is likened to a treasure that a man inadvertently uncovers in a field. After the man finds the treasure, he sells all his possessions so he can purchase the field (Matthew 13:44).[38]

---

of the Church of Jesus Christ of Latter-day Saints, 2nd ed. (Salt Lake City: Deseret News, 1950), 6:354. Joseph Smith applied the Parable of the Mustard Seed not only to the Church in the last days but also to the Book of Mormon's "coming forth out of the ground, which is indeed accounted the least of all seeds, but behold it branching forth, yea, even towering, with lofty branches, and God-like majesty, until it, like the mustard seed, becomes the greatest of all herbs." Smith, *TPJS*, 98.

[36] Because the true gospel message would not cover the entire world during the early Christian era, Joseph Smith applied the Parable of the Leaven to the last days: "It may be understood that the Church of the Latter-day Saints has taken its rise from a little leaven that was put into three witnesses. Behold, how much this is like the parable! It is fast leavening the lump, and will soon leaven the whole." Smith, *TPJS*, 100.

[37] Joseph Smith, quoted in Wilford Woodruff, Conference Report, April 1898, 57. We could also be reminded of Daniel's interpretation of Nebuchadnezzar's dream in Daniel 2:44.

[38] Joseph Smith applied this to his own day: "The Saints work after this pattern. See the Church of the Latter-day Saints, selling all that they have, and gathering themselves together unto a place that they may purchase for an inheritance, that they may be together and bear each other's afflictions in the day of calamity." Smith, *TPJS*, 101.

The Parable of the Pearl of Great Price is very similar to the Parable of the Hidden Treasure. This parable likens "the kingdom of heaven" to a merchant who was seeking for, and found, an expensive pearl. After the merchant discovers the pearl, he sells all his possessions so he can purchase it (Matthew 13:45–46).[39] Richard Draper has pointed out that "whether the gospel is accidentally discovered or deliberately sought, the price of acquisition is everything one has."[40]

The Parable of the Net resembles in overall content the Parable of the Wheat and Tares. This parable likens "the kingdom of heaven" to a net that "was cast into the sea." When the net was filled and brought to shore, it had "gathered of every kind" of fish (Matthew 13:47).[41] The good and the bad catches were separated, and the bad were thrown away (Matthew 13:48). The Savior interpreted this final parable for His disciples: the man who cast the net represents "the angels," and the separating of the bad from the good signifies what will happen "at the end of the world" (Matthew 13:49).[42] The angels will separate the wicked from the righteous "and shall cast them into the furnace of fire" (Matthew 13:50).[43]

---

[39] Joseph Smith also applied this parable to his day: "The Saints again work after this example. See men traveling to find places for Zion and her stakes or remnants, who, when they find place for Zion, or the pearl of great price, straightway sell that they have, and buy it." Smith, *TPJS*, 102.

[40] Richard D. Draper, "The Parables of Jesus: (Matthew 13)," in Kent P. Jackson and Robert L. Millet, eds., *Studies in Scripture Volume 5: The Gospels* (Salt Lake City: Deseret Book, 1986), 272.

[41] Notice that the Greek word translated as "kind" is *genos*, which is often used for a "race" or "tribe" of people. Thus, "every kind" of fish represents "every nation" of people. See Craig L. Blomberg, *Interpreting the Parables* (Downers Grove, Ill.: InterVarsity Press, 1990), 202.

[42] Joseph Smith applied this parable to missionary work among the Latter-day Saints: "For the work of this pattern, behold the seed of Joseph, spreading forth the Gospel net upon the face of the earth, gathering of every kind, that the good may be saved in vessels prepared for that purpose, and the angels shall take care of the bad." Smith, *TPJS*, 102.

[43] The JST clarifies that "the world is the children of the wicked" (JST Matthew 13:50) and that the angels "shall cast them *out into the world to be burned*" (JST Matthew 13:50; emphasis added).

The Message Revealed

By teaching in parables, the Savior simultaneously revealed and concealed information, depending upon the readiness of His audience.[44] What primary message was the Savior revealing to those who heard the parables in Matthew 13? Concerning the Parable of the Sower, the Prophet Joseph Smith concluded, "This parable was spoken to demonstrate *the effects that are produced by the preaching of the word.*"[45] Thus, this parable demonstrated how different people would react to the teachings of the Savior.

This is true of the other parables in Matthew 13 as well; they also illustrate the various responses toward the gospel of Jesus Christ. The Parable of the Sower teaches that most people will not receive the truth of the gospel and that only a few will actually embrace it. The Parable of the Wheat and Tares and the Parable of the Net show that those outside the Church, and even some within the Church, will persecute those who accept the message of the gospel and will suffer the consequences. The Parable of the Mustard Seed and the Parable of the Leaven demonstrate that although the gospel message appears to be small and insignificant, it will eventually attract a following that will grow to fill the entire world. The Parable of the Hidden Treasure and the Parable of the Pearl of Great Price show that those who discover the truth of the gospel will pay any price to obtain it.

The Message Concealed

The concepts that the Savior intended His audience to understand from these parables seem fairly simple and straightforward.

---

[44] On this, Dallin H. Oaks taught, "[Jesus] told his disciples that the reason he taught the multitude in parables was that this permitted him to teach them 'the mysteries of the kingdom of heaven' (Matthew 13:11) while not revealing those mysteries to the multitude. His parables had multiple meanings or applications according to the spiritual maturity of the listener. They had a message for both children and gospel scholars." Oaks, "Scripture Reading and Revelation," 8. See also Bruce R. McConkie, *Mormon Doctrine*, 2nd ed. (Salt Lake City: Bookcraft, 1966), 553–54.

[45] Smith, *TPJS*, 97; emphasis added.

But what information is shielded from those who listened to His parables? One possibility is that the very information Jesus intended to reveal to His disciples, He also intended to conceal from the multitudes. Recall the Savior's response to the original inquiry of His disciples when He said, "It is given unto you to know the mysteries of the kingdom of heaven, but to them it is not given" (Matthew 13:11). Thus, the disciples—not the multitudes—were intended to understand the various reactions to the message of the gospel. The disciples claimed to have a grasp upon these issues. When the Savior finished explaining these parables, He asked the disciples, "Have ye understood all these things?" (Matthew 13:51). To this, the disciples answered, "Yea, Lord" (Matthew 13:51). Yet the fact that the disciples needed to ask Jesus to interpret the parables for them shows that it was not just the multitudes who failed to understand the full meaning of these teachings.[46] The Gospel of Mark records that after the disciples asked about the Parable of the Sower, Jesus said to them, "Know ye not this parable? and how then will ye know all parables?" (Mark 4:13).[47] The Savior had more information to reveal than just these explanations given to His disciples.

A closer look at the parables in Matthew 13 suggests that although they *reveal the reaction* to the message of the gospel, they *conceal the content* of that message. In other words, these parables explicitly describe how various people would respond to the teachings of the Savior, but they do not disclose which teachings would cause such responses. Something about the gospel of Jesus Christ caused most people to reject it. Something about the gospel

[46] See other examples in the Gospel of Matthew where the disciples do not completely understand or fully embrace the teachings of the Savior. For example, see Matthew 8:27 and 17:19–20.

[47] Concerning the omission of this verse from the Gospel of Matthew, one scholar has concluded, "Is this omission of reproach to be explained simply by the fact that in Matthew the disciples do in fact understand, as contrasted with Mark? Is it not rather that the note of reproach is missing, not because they do understand, but because they cannot be expected to understand?" Dan O. Via Jr., "Matthew on the Understandability of the Parables," *Journal of Biblical Literature* 84 (1965): 431.

of Jesus Christ caused those outside of—and some within—the Church to persecute those who accepted it. Something about the gospel of Jesus Christ was perceived as insignificant, but eventually it will grow to fill the whole earth. Something about the gospel of Jesus Christ caused those who truly discovered it to give up everything to possess it. What was it about the gospel message that caused these diverse reactions?

In the Parable of the Sower, Jesus stated that receiving "the seed" was equivalent to hearing "the word" (Matthew 13:20). The parallel account in the Gospel of Luke clearly states, "The seed is the word of God" (Luke 8:11). But what precisely is "the word"? The Book of Mormon contains an important interpretive key. In his sermon on faith, the prophet Alma the Younger declared, "We will compare the word unto a seed" (Alma 32:28). After Alma finished his sermon, he explicitly identified "the word": "Believe in the Son of God, that he will come to redeem his people, and that he shall suffer and die to atone for their sins; and that he shall rise again from the dead, which shall bring to pass the resurrection, that all men shall stand before him, to be judged at the last and judgment day, according to their works. And now, my brethren, I desire that ye shall *plant this word in your hearts*" (Alma 33:22–23; emphasis added). Thus, the seed or word is the life and mission of Jesus Christ, the central feature being His terrible suffering for the sins of the world and His humiliating death by crucifixion.

Although by the first century A.D. it was widely expected that the "kingdom of God" would be established at the coming of the promised Messiah, not many people understood that the Messiah would actually suffer and die to atone for the sins of the world.[48] Some Jews anticipated that the Messiah would be a powerful

---

[48] For a discussion of reasons why many Jews did not recognize Jesus as the Messiah, see Richard Neitzel Holzapfel, "I Have a Question," *Ensign*, April 1991, 53–54. The Book of Mormon contains numerous explicit references to the future suffering of the Messiah. For references and a discussion of why the prophecies concerning Christ are more explicit in the Book of Mormon than in the Bible, see Kent P. Jackson, "I Have a Question," *Ensign*, August 1999, 66–67.

military or political figure. Kent P. Jackson explained, "In the Old Testament, the term [Messiah] was primarily a royal title; the king was the 'anointed one.' Anciently, faithful followers and servants of Jehovah looked forward to the coming of *the* Anointed One, the King of Kings, who would deliver them from all enemies, particularly the bondage of sin. Sadly, teachings about this Deliverer became distorted to the point that most Jews in Jesus' day did not understand the Messiah's mission and failed to recognize him when he came. They anticipated instead one who would deliver them from Roman occupation."[49]

Isaiah prophesied of a day when the power of Jehovah would be manifest in a dramatic way by saying that "the day of the Lord of hosts shall be upon every one that is proud and lofty, and upon every one that is lifted up; and he shall be brought low. . . . And the loftiness of man shall be bowed down, and the haughtiness of men shall be made low: and the Lord alone shall be exalted in that day. And the idols he shall utterly abolish" (Isaiah 2:12, 17–18).[50] As a result of such prophecies, some Jews expected the promised Messiah to be the instrument of Jehovah's great emancipating power.[51] A Jewish document from the first century B.C. called the *Psalms of Solomon* preserves the following expectation concerning the coming Messiah: "See, Lord, and raise up for them their king, the son of David, to rule over your servant Israel in the time known to you O God. Undergird him with the strength to destroy the unrighteous rulers, to purge Jerusalem from gentiles who trample her to destruction; in wisdom and in righteousness to drive out the sinners from the inheritance; to smash the arrogance of sinners like a potter's jar; To shatter all their substance with an iron rod; to destroy the

---

[49] Kent P. Jackson, "The Eternal Ministry of Christ," *Ensign*, January 1991, 9. For an overview of various expectations concerning the Messiah throughout Jewish history, see Dan Cohn-Sherbok, *The Jewish Messiah* (Edinburgh: T & T Clark, 1997).

[50] See also Daniel 7:13–14.

[51] The irony, of course, is that Jesus was both Jehovah and the promised Messiah. When the resurrected Savior appeared to the Nephites, He declared that "the law is fulfilled that was given unto Moses. Behold, I am he that gave the law, and I am he who covenanted with my people Israel" (3 Nephi 15:4–5).

unlawful nations with the word of his mouth. . . . And he will be a righteous king over them, taught by God. There will be no unrighteousness among them in his days, for all shall be holy, and their king shall be the Lord Messiah" (*Psalms of Solomon* 17.21–24, 32).[52]

By the time of the Savior's mortal ministry, there were a variety of expectations concerning the future Messiah. Some of these expectations are evident in the New Testament. For example, some anticipated that the Messiah would perform miracles: "When Christ cometh, will he do more miracles than these which this man hath done?" (John 7:31). Concerning the origin of the Messiah, some expected that when He arrived, no one would know where He came from. On one occasion, some said about Jesus that "we know this man whence he is: but when Christ cometh, no man knoweth whence he is" (John 7:27).[53] There were some who expected that the Messiah would come from Bethlehem, just as King David had a thousand years earlier: "Others said, This is the Christ. But some said, Shall Christ come out of Galilee? Hath not the scripture said, That Christ cometh of the seed of David, and out of the town of Bethlehem, where David was?" (John 7:41–42).[54]

Even the disciples held certain expectations concerning the promised Messiah. When Jesus was at Caesarea Philippi, He asked

---

[52] According to R. B. Wright, the Psalms of Solomon were written as a "response of a group of devout Jews to the capture of Jerusalem by the Romans in the first century B.C." R. B. Wright, "Psalms of Solomon," in *The Old Testament Pseudepigrapha*, 2 vols., ed. James H. Charlesworth (Garden City, N.Y.: Doubleday, 1985), 2:639.

[53] Trypho, a Jewish man living in the second century A.D., said that "if the Messiah has been born and exists anywhere, he is not known, nor is he conscious of his own existence, nor has he any power until Elias [Elijah] comes to anoint him and to make him manifest to all." Justin Martyr, *Dialogue*, 8.4. Translation is from Thomas B. Falls, trans., *St. Justin Martyr: Dialogue with Trypho*, rev. by Thomas P. Halton (Washington, D.C.: CUA Press, 2003), 16. Interestingly, John the Baptist, whom Jesus referred to as Elias (see Matthew 17:10–13), declared Jesus to be the Messiah at His baptism (see Matthew 3:11–15; John 1:29–34), after which Jesus was anointed by the reception of the Holy Ghost (see Acts 10:38).

[54] This is a reference to the prophecy in Micah 5:2. When the wise men came to Herod the Great and asked where the "King of the Jews" would be born, Herod's advisors quoted Micah 5:2. See Matthew 2:2–10.

His disciples, "Whom say ye that I am?" (Matthew 16:15). Peter, the chief Apostle, answered, "Thou art the Christ, the Son of the living God" (Matthew 16:16). Jesus declared that this information was a revelation from God to Peter: "Flesh and blood hath not revealed it unto thee, but my Father which is in heaven" (Matthew 16:17). The Savior then commanded "his disciples that they should tell no man that he was Jesus the Christ" (Matthew 16:20). Why would Jesus demand that His disciples not share the wonderful news that He was the Messiah?

In the Joseph Smith Translation of the Sermon on the Mount, the Savior instructed His disciples, "Go ye into the world, saying unto all, Repent, for the kingdom of heaven has come nigh unto you" (JST Matthew 7:9). In other words, the announcement of the kingdom is for everyone. But there was some sacred information about the kingdom that disciples were not to share with others: "And the mysteries of the kingdom ye shall keep within yourselves; for it is not meet to give that which is holy unto the dogs; neither cast ye your pearls unto swine, lest they trample them under their feet. For the world cannot receive that which ye, yourselves, are not able to bear; wherefore ye shall not give your pearls unto them, lest they turn again and rend you" (JST Matthew 7:10–11).[55] In other words, the disciples believed that Jesus was the Messiah, but they did not understand precisely what kind of messiah Jesus was going to be. Further, neither the disciples nor other Jews in general were able to accept the fact that Jesus was not going to be a messiah who triumphed over the Romans but rather one who would suffer, be humiliated, and die.

The Savior taught His disciples, "Whosoever receiveth, to him shall be given, and he shall have more abundance" (JST Matthew 13:12). Peter's confession demonstrated his faith in Jesus' identity as the Messiah. The Savior eventually revealed additional information to His disciples: "From that time forth began Jesus to shew

---

[55] The reference to swine and dogs is an allusion to those who are not prepared or "worthy" to receive these mysteries of the kingdom. See Doctrine and Covenants 41:6.

unto his disciples, how that he must go unto Jerusalem, and suffer many things of the elders and chief priests and scribes, and be killed, and be raised again the third day" (Matthew 16:21). Peter's response demonstrates that he shared some of the popular expectations of a powerful Messiah: "Then Peter took him, and began to rebuke him, saying, Be it far from thee, Lord: this shall not be unto thee" (Matthew 16:22). Jesus responded by telling Peter that "thou savourest not the things that be of God, but those that be of men" (Matthew 16:23). Peter's expectations about the Messiah were based on human traditions rather than divine revelation. Following the events on the Mount of Transfiguration in Matthew 17, the Savior reminded His disciples, "The Son of man shall be betrayed into the hands of men: and they shall kill him, and the third day he shall be raised again" (Matthew 17:22–23). The disciples continued to find this information about the Messiah very troubling.[56] The Gospel of Matthew states that the disciples "were exceeding sorry" to hear this information again (Matthew 17:23).[57] Thus, the idea of a crucified messiah was quite offensive to a typical Jewish audience of Jesus' day—including the disciples, at first—who were expecting a military or political messiah.

The Apostle Paul declared, "The preaching of the cross is to them that perish foolishness. . . . We preach Christ crucified, unto the Jews a stumblingblock, and unto the Greeks foolishness" (1 Corinthians 1:18, 23). Here we find a key to understanding what

---

[56] The Gospel of Luke records, "But they understood not this saying, and it was hid from them, that they perceived it not: and they feared to ask him of that saying" (Luke 9:45). Compare also Mark 9:32, "But they understood not that saying, and were afraid to ask him."

[57] The Greek verb *lupeō* carries the idea of being extremely sad, distressed, or grieved. See Danker, *GEL*, 604. This is the same verb used to describe the feelings of the disciples after the Savior revealed that one of them would betray him: "[Jesus] said, Verily I say unto you, that one of you shall betray me. And they were exceeding sorrowful" (Matthew 26:21–22). The Savior reminded the disciples a third time that "we go up to Jerusalem; and the Son of man shall be betrayed unto the chief priests and unto the scribes, and they shall condemn him to death, and shall deliver him to the Gentiles to mock, and to scourge, and to crucify him: and the third day he shall rise again" (Matthew 20:18–19). This time, no response from the disciples is recorded.

was concealed in the parables of Matthew 13. This is the central feature of the kingdom of God: The Messiah will suffer for the sins of the world, experience a humiliating death upon a cross, and rise the third day from the dead. This is the information that most people will reject; that will cause non-Christians and even some Christians to persecute those who fully accept it; that will be perceived as insignificant but will grow to fill the earth; and that, when truly discovered, will cause a person to give up everything to possess it.[58] Further, this central act of the Savior's messianic mission was not explicitly revealed in the parables of Matthew 13; rather, it was concealed, not only from the multitudes in general but also from the disciples in their early years.

Conclusion

After explaining the parables, the Savior told His disciples that "every scribe which is instructed unto the kingdom of heaven is like unto a man that is an householder, which bringeth forth out of his treasure things new and old" (Matthew 13:52). This saying may sound enigmatic on the surface, but it actually contains an important lesson. The Greek verb translated as "instructed" really means "to become a disciple."[59] The followers of Jesus knew all about scribes, who "were instructed" or "became disciples" of old things—the scriptures and their interpretations.[60] Stephen E. Robinson

[58] Significantly, when Jesus finished giving the parables in Matthew 13, He returned home to Nazareth and demonstrated what He had just declared about the negative reactions to the preaching of the word. "When he was come into his own country, he taught them in their synagogue. . . . And they were offended in him. But Jesus said unto them, A prophet is not without honour, save in his own country, and in his own house. And he did not many mighty works there because of their unbelief" (Matthew 13:54, 57–58; see also John 6:60–61).

[59] The Greek verb *mathēteuō* means to "be or become a pupil or disciple." Danker, *GEL*, 609. See also Brown, Griggs, and Mackay, "Footnotes to the Gospels," 50. The same verb is used in Matthew 27:57: "There came a rich man of Arimathaea, named Joseph, who also himself was Jesus' disciple."

[60] Herod the Great appealed to scribes to know where the Messiah should be born (Matthew 2:1–10); scribes accused Jesus of breaking the law of Moses and the tradition of the elders (Matthew 15:1–2); the disciples were concerned about the

summarized, "The scribes were the lawyer class of Jewish life, the 'doctors of the law.' They were college-educated intellectuals, trained in the practical or civil aspects of the law of Moses, in applying and interpreting the law in everyday life to all denominations of Jews alike."[61] These Jewish teachers supplied and perpetuated teachings and opinions, even about the coming Messiah.[62]

But Jesus was creating a new kind of scribe, one who was a disciple not only of old things but also of new things—not only of old scripture and interpretation but also of new revelation. When Peter expressed his view about what should not happen to the Messiah, he was relying on old things "of men" rather than new things "of God" (Matthew 16:23). After time and experience, and especially after the reception of the gift of the Holy Ghost,[63] the Apostle Peter became a new kind of scribe—a disciple of Jesus Christ who relied upon and declared new revelation, specifically about the true mission of the Messiah. On the day of Pentecost, Peter declared, "Jesus of Nazareth, a man approved of God among you by miracles and wonders and signs, which God did by him in the midst of you, as ye yourselves also know: him, being delivered by the determinate counsel and foreknowledge of God, ye have taken, and by wicked hands have crucified and slain: whom God hath raised up, having loosed the pains of death. . . . Let all the house of Israel know assuredly, that God hath made that same Jesus, whom ye have crucified, both Lord and Christ" (Acts 2:22–24, 36).[64]

---

doctrinal teachings of the scribes (Matthew 17:10); and Jesus encouraged the disciples to follow the counsel of the scribes—but not their example (Matthew 23:1–3).

[61] Stephen E. Robinson, "The Setting of the Gospels," in Kent P. Jackson and Robert L. Millet, eds., *Studies in Scripture Volume 5: The Gospels* (Salt Lake City: Deseret Book, 1986), 29.

[62] When discussing what "the Son of man" would do, the disciples asked Jesus, "Why then say *the scribes* that Elias must first come?" (Matthew 17:10; emphasis added).

[63] Even after the crucifixion and before the day of Pentecost, the disciples did not completely understand the mission of the Messiah. When the resurrected Savior appeared to them, they asked, "Lord, wilt thou at this time restore again the kingdom to Israel?" (Acts 1:6).

[64] See also Acts 3:18.

We can learn many important lessons from the experiences of the earliest disciples. Modern followers of the Savior should be experts in things "old" as well as things "new." Elder Orson Pratt taught, "We are commanded over and over again to . . . make ourselves acquainted not only with ancient revelation, but with modern. . . . For every well-instructed scribe, we read in the New Testament, bringeth out of his heart things both new and old. It is not the ill-instructed scribe—it is not the person who does not study—it is not the person who suffers his time to run to idleness, but it is that man that instructs himself in all things within his reach, so far as his circumstances and abilities will allow. Such a one will bring forth before his hearers things that will edify in relation to old times, and also in relation to the present and future,—things both new and old."[65]

Likewise, the teachings of the parables are as timely today as they were when they were originally given. The primary message of the gospel has not changed. The Lord declared to latter-day missionaries, "The field is white already to harvest; wherefore, thrust in your sickles, and reap with all your might, mind, and strength. . . . Open your mouths and they shall be filled, saying: Repent, repent, and prepare ye the way of the Lord, and make his paths straight; for the kingdom of heaven is at hand" (Doctrine and Covenants 33:7, 10).[66] In our own day, the preaching of the central feature of the gospel—the Atonement of Jesus Christ—will also be met with opposition from others and be perceived as insignificant

[65] Orson Pratt, *JD*, 7:75. Note also the comments of Orson Hyde: "We must now appeal to the New Testament . . . though to me it is all alike, both the Old and New Testaments; for the scribe that is well instructed, brings out of his treasury things both new and old. This is my treasury, or rather, it is one of my treasuries, and what I cannot find there, I trust will come down from on high, and lodge in my heart. The gift of God is also my treasury, even the Holy Spirit." Orson Hyde, *JD*, 2:80.

[66] Bruce R. McConkie taught, "We, as the servants of the Lord, obedient to his command, carry his message to the world. . . . As it was with the prophets of old in their ministries, so it is with us in ours. We say as they did: Repent and believe the gospel, for the kingdom of heaven is at hand." Bruce R. McConkie, "Who Hath Believed Our Report?" *Ensign*, November 1981, 48.

by many people. But the kingdom of God will grow to fill the earth.[67] When disciples come to a true understanding of the gospel, they will also "give all that [they] have, holding nothing back" to obtain the priceless treasure the Savior has offered.[68]

[67] Joseph Smith declared, "The Standard of Truth has been erected. No unhallowed hand can stop the work from progressing; persecutions may rage, mobs may combine, armies may assemble, calumny may defame, but the truth of God will go forth boldly, nobly, and independent, till it has penetrated every continent, visited every clime, swept every country, and sounded in every ear, till the purposes of God shall be accomplished, and the Great Jehovah shall say the work is done." Roberts, *History of the Church*, 4:540. See also Bruce R. McConkie, Conference Report, October 1958, 115.

[68] Alexander B. Morrison, "For This Cause Came I into the World," *Ensign*, November 1999, 27. See also Alma 22:15, 18.

IV.

THE TWELVE

S. KENT BROWN

And when it was day, he called unto him his disciples: and of them he chose twelve, whom also he named apostles.

LUKE 6:13

They were the first called,[1] those two sets of brothers, Peter and Andrew, James and John. It seemed that they were always at the Savior's side, no matter where He went or what He did. When He first summoned them, they dropped everything; when He called, they "left their nets, and followed him" (Matthew 4:20). We sense something unusual in their character that made them respond in this way. Could they have imagined what lay ahead for them? Even after spending weeks and months with Jesus, could they have predicted what sort of messiah this man from Nazareth would be?

At the outset, it may seem a bit strange that, of these brothers, Andrew fades in the Gospel narratives, almost as if he loses his place, being known ever after merely as Peter's "brother" (Matthew

---

[1] Standard treatments of the office of Apostle appear in Bruce R. McConkie, *Mormon Doctrine,* 2d ed. (Salt Lake City: Bookcraft, 1966), 46; S. Kent Brown, "Apostle," in *Encyclopedia of Mormonism*, ed. Daniel H. Ludlow et al. (New York: Macmillan, 1992), 59–61; "apostello," Kittel and Friedrich, *TDNT,* 1:398–447; "apostolos," *Theological Lexicon of the New Testament*, ed. Ceslas Spicq, 3 vols. (Peabody, Mass.: Hendrickson Publishers, 1994), 1:186–94.

10:2; Luke 6:14).[2] After all, he was the second called and therefore stood in a position of seniority (see Matthew 4:18; Mark 1:16). But that was not how the divine economy was to work. To be sure, the first called, Peter, remained in his spot as the most senior. And it is apparent that the brothers James and John were soon elevated to places of trust next to Peter, though Andrew was possibly older than both of them. To grasp the significance of the spiritual ties that came to bind Peter with James and John, all partners in a fishing business, we need to sketch the backdrop to their early ministries, along with those of the rest of the Twelve.[3]

The most tantalizing question about these men and their brethren in the Twelve is, What was it like for them to spend years in the company of the Savior? At moments, as we shall see, scenes would have been combative and rancorous. On other occasions, the experiences must have been breathtaking. On others, shared events must have been deeply spiritual.

In broad terms, our sources, which include the New Testament Gospels, modern scripture, and a few fragmentary apocryphal texts, hint that the spiritual understanding of these men grew gradually and came to full maturity only after Jesus' resurrection. As with any of us, theirs would have been a learning experience until they themselves became filled spiritual reservoirs. In this light, if we look ahead to how God will honor the Twelve at the end of time, we see the completion of this process. For we read that they "shall stand at [the Savior's] right hand at the day of [His] coming in a pillar of fire, being clothed with robes of righteousness, with crowns upon their heads . . . to judge the whole house of Israel" (Doctrine and Covenants 29:12). The fact that the Lord early on committed into their hands the responsibility of "judging the twelve tribes of Israel"

[2] An exception is the notice in Acts 1:13 wherein Andrew's name appears in a list of the eleven Apostles. But by this point, his place within the Twelve was well established and his relationship to Peter well known. It may be noteworthy that he appears here as fourth in seniority, following Peter, James, and John.

[3] The best evidence for the business connection among Peter, James, and John appears in Luke 5:10: "James, and John . . . partners with Simon."

demonstrates His complete trust in them (Matthew 19:28; see also 1 Nephi 12:9; Mormon 3:18).

How soon did the Savior establish the office of Apostle and call twelve men to fill this lofty position? The answer differs widely among scholars. It has almost become a caricature wherein Protestant scholars interpret the early Christian evidence to question whether Jesus even established the office, and Catholic scholars see this same evidence as supporting the notion that the Savior Himself founded the institution.[4] For Latter-day Saints, the most illuminating pieces of evidence arise not from the pages of the New Testament but rather from the Book of Mormon. With the reasonable assumption that the Resurrected Jesus undertook the same tasks in His New World ministry that He had pursued in His Old World activities, we observe that on His first day at the temple in Bountiful, the Savior called a man named Nephi and "others" to whom He "gave . . . power to baptize" (3 Nephi 11:18, 22). Significantly, "the number of them who had been called [by Jesus], and received power and authority to baptize, was twelve" (3 Nephi 12:1). The Savior's action, therefore, created the institution of the Twelve at the beginning of His three-day ministry in the New World, establishing a model by which to measure His actions in the Old.[5] Moreover, the fact that these men in the New World received authority to teach, direct, and minister to others, though not reported explicitly in the record, becomes apparent on the second day when "the twelve did teach the multitude [at the temple]; and

[4] See the review by Wilhelm Schneemelcher, "Apostle and Apostolic," in *New Testament Apocrypha*, ed. Edgar Hennecke and Wilhelm Schneemelcher, 2 vols. (Philadelphia: Westminster Press, 1963–64), 2:25–31; on the Catholic side, consult Antonio Javierre, "Apostle," in *Sacramentum Mundi: An Encyclopedia of Theology*, ed. Karl Rahner, 6 vols. (London: Burns and Oates, 1968–70), 1:77–79; Ramon Trevijano, "Apostle—Apostolate," in *Encyclopedia of the Early Church*, ed. Angelo Di Berardino, 2 vols. (New York: Oxford University Press, 1992), 1:61.

[5] From the vision of Nephi, the later people of Nephi understood that one of the differences between the Twelve in the Old World and the Twelve in the New World was that of their roles in judging their respective peoples. In addition, the titles "twelve apostles" (Old World) and "twelve disciples" (New World) arose from this vision (see 1 Nephi 12:8–10).

. . . did cause that the multitude should kneel down . . . and should pray unto the Father in the name of Jesus. And the disciples . . . arose and ministered unto the people" (3 Nephi 19:6–7).[6] On the basis of the Savior's actions and those of the Twelve in the New World, we conclude that in the Old World, during His mortal ministry, as the New Testament Gospels affirm, Jesus instituted the office of Apostle and established the ecclesiastical body of the Twelve to minister the affairs of the nascent church.[7]

The Twelve in Prophecy

As we might surmise, prophecy points to the Apostles' years with the Messiah, although not in detail. More than six hundred years before Jesus' ministry, the prophet Lehi beheld in vision "One descending out of the midst of heaven" followed by "twelve others" (1 Nephi 1:9–10). Though Lehi did not identify the descending One as the Messiah, this person's association with the "twelve others" certainly points in that direction.[8] In a subsequent vision, perhaps within a year, Lehi's son Nephi also saw "the Lamb of God" accompanied by "twelve others" who witnessed "the Lamb of God going forth among the children of men" and healing those "who were afflicted with all manner of diseases, and with devils and unclean spirits" (1 Nephi 11:27, 29, 31). These two visionary experiences, occurring centuries before these twelve men were born, point to their prominence in premortal life, where, with others, they were chosen and groomed to fill their important mortal roles.[9]

---

[6] For other responsibilities, see 3 Nephi 15:12 ("ye [the twelve] are a light unto this people"); 3 Nephi 18:27–28 ("I [Jesus] give unto you another commandment . . . that ye shall not suffer any one knowingly to partake of my flesh and blood unworthily, when ye [the twelve] shall minister it"); and 3 Nephi 18:37 ("he [Jesus] gave them power to give the Holy Ghost").

[7] The title or term "apostle" seems to have been used broadly in the early Christian church to designate some individuals outside the Twelve; see Romans 16:7; 1 Corinthians 15:5, 7; 2 Corinthians 8:23 (Greek text); 11:13; Galatians 1:19.

[8] Consult Joseph Fielding McConkie and Robert L. Millet, *Doctrinal Commentary on the Book of Mormon*, 4 vols. (Salt Lake City: Bookcraft, 1987–91), 1:26.

[9] That religious leaders were chosen in premortal life for their earthly ministries is shown in Jeremiah 1:5; Abraham 3:22–23; Galatians 1:15; Ephesians 1:4.

This circumstance partly explains why Peter recognized Jesus as divine, whereas other people did not (see Luke 5:1–9).

Sources

The New Testament Gospels stand as the chief sources for the early ministry of the Twelve. And the synoptics—Matthew, Mark, and Luke—offer more information than John's Gospel.[10] How do we evaluate these documents in light of modern studies that question their historical reliability? In the prophetic words of the Book of Mormon, the New Testament records are characterized as originally containing "the fulness of the gospel of the Lord, of whom the twelve apostles bear record"; from them, "plain and precious things were [later] taken away" (1 Nephi 13:24, 29). Specifically, these documents are "of the twelve apostles of the Lamb" and reproduce "my [the Lord's] word" (1 Nephi 13:40; 2 Nephi 3:11). Further, in the Lord's grand scheme, the Book of Mormon will "establish the truth of the [Bible]," plainly indicating that the Old and New Testaments carry God's truths (1 Nephi 13:40). Bearing in mind these characterizations of the New Testament, we are justified in laying a large measure of trust in the Gospels as reliable sources for learning about the early experiences of the Twelve. If we put ourselves in the places of these men, the experiences must have been exhilarating, as we shall see.

A number of other documents, commonly called apocryphal texts, also sketch portraits of the Apostles and events that intersected their ministries. Almost without exception, however, these accounts focus on events and scenes that came after the resurrection of the Savior, often singling out one or another Apostle as the recipient of the Resurrected Jesus' special, sacred teaching. As a group, these treatises touch rarely on the ministry of the Twelve during the Savior's lifetime,

[10] The Gospel of John features the disciples in the early interactions of Jesus (see John 1:37–51); the wedding at Cana (2:1–11); the Samaritan woman (4:8, 31–38); feeding the 5,000 (6:1–21, 60–71); the man born blind (9:1–7); the raising of Lazarus (11:7-44); and the supper at Bethany (12:1–8).

which is one of our interests here.[11] A good rule for evaluating these texts is that spoken by the Lord when responding to a question from Joseph Smith about another set of writings, the fourteen books of the Old Testament Apocrypha: "There are many things contained therein that are true. . . . There are many things contained therein that are not true" (Doctrine and Covenants 91:1–2).

The Origins of the Twelve

Although these men did not all live in close proximity to one another, they each came from Galilee, as the angel's words to them disclose: "Ye men of Galilee" (Acts 1:11).[12] Such a concentration of individuals in this region hints at a divine design. It appears that Jesus had made acquaintance with some of them before calling them. John's Gospel reports that Jesus spent time—perhaps more than a day—with Andrew and one other.[13] Andrew then introduced his brother Peter to Jesus (see John 1:35–42). What is certain is that Jesus Himself initiated the first life-changing contact. As illustrated in the calling of the two pairs of brothers—Simon and Andrew, James and John—"they immediately . . . followed him," an indicator of their responsiveness to spiritual stimuli (Matthew 4:20, 22; Mark 1:18, 20). These four men evidently were living in Capernaum, as was Matthew, who worked at the customs house just east of the town.[14] It is possible that Matthew (or Levi)

---

[11] Among texts of this sort, we would include the fragmentary "gospel" accounts in Papyrus Oxyrhynchus 840, Papyrus Egerton 2, the so-called Gospel of the Nazareans, and the Gospel of the Ebionites. See Hennecke and Schneemelcher, *New Testament Apocrypha*, 1:92–97, 139–58; Montague Rhodes James, ed., *The Apocryphal New Testament* (Oxford: Oxford University Press, 1924), 8–10, 29–30.

[12] We compare "are not all these which speak Galilaeans?" (Acts 2:7).

[13] There is a sequence of a week that underlies John 1:19–2:1, ending with the marriage in Cana, which likely fell on a Wednesday, the preferred day for weddings (see Mishna *Ketuvoth* 1:1). If the marriage indeed fell on Wednesday, then John's two disciples met Jesus on Friday afternoon and thereafter spent the Sabbath with Him (see John 1:39). Consult Raymond E. Brown, *The Gospel According to John I–XII*, The Anchor Bible Volume 29 (Garden City, New York: Doubleday, 1966), 97–98.

[14] Peter's home was in Capernaum; Andrew lived nearby because they were business partners as fishermen (see Matthew 8:5, 14; Luke 4:31, 38), though they had

was the brother of "James the son of Alphaeus" because both are known as "the son of Alphaeus" (see Matthew 10:3; Mark 2:14; 3:18). If this is so, then James too may have lived in Capernaum before his call. The hometowns of the other six remain unknown. The pair of names "Simon the Canaanite" and "Simon called Zelotes" simply designate Simon's connection to the Cananean or Zealot political movement of the day (see Matthew 10:4; Mark 3:18; Luke 6:15).[15]

The Twelve were doubtless all numbered within the large group of followers or disciples whom the Savior initially called to assist, or who had begun to gather around Him, as He pressed His ministry forward in Galilee (see Matthew 4:17–5:1; Mark 1:14–20, 45). Those who received an early invitation to "follow" Him and become "fishers of men" (Matthew 4:19; Mark 1:17) were called a second time to a new body called "the twelve" (see Mark 6:7; Luke 9:1). These men now took up their lofty positions as Apostles, a term that all three synoptic Gospels introduce (see Matthew 10:2; Mark 6:30; Luke 6:13).[16]

Peter stands forth as the most prominent of Jesus' followers. James and John usually rate notice not by themselves but when they are involved with the senior Apostle. This observation leads us to conclude that, in the memory of the earliest Church members, these three men were seen as part of the same cloth, distinguishable from the other Apostles but not from one another. Lying nestled within this concept is the impression that their number formed an

---

evidently spent their youths in the town of Bethsaida a few miles to the east (see John 1:44). Moreover, James and John were business partners with the other two, and therefore they must have lived in the same community (see Luke 5:10). The customs office where Matthew worked stood just to the east of Capernaum where westbound merchants would declare their goods after crossing the Jordan River by ferry where the river entered the north end of the Sea of Galilee. Incidentally, both Mark and Luke record this man's name to be Levi (see Mark 2:14; Luke 5:27).

[15] For a summarizing treatment of the Zealots, see David Rhoads, "Zealots," in Freedman, *ABD*, 6:1043–53.

[16] John 13:16 preserves the Greek term for Apostle—but not apparently in the ecclesiastical sense; the KJV rightly translates the word "he that is sent."

essential quorum inside the body of the Twelve. That they worked closely together during their mortal ministries bridges into the modern era when the three of them restored the Melchizedek Priesthood to Joseph Smith and Oliver Cowdery in late May or early June 1829.[17]

The Learning Curve

It was during Jesus' first important Sabbath stop in a synagogue that a few disciples, soon to be Apostles, caught first wind of the extraordinary wisdom and authority in the Savior's teachings as well as the meliorating power of His miracles. They were in Capernaum. With these disciples, whose number included Peter, James, and John, Jesus "entered into the synagogue" and "taught [worshipers] as one that had authority," surpassing the imposing authority of "the scribes" (Mark 1:21–22). It was a defining moment, never to be forgotten. But the miracle that followed added a palpable thickness to the mystique that suddenly and forcefully gathered around the Savior. For "there was in their synagogue a man with an unclean spirit," which, through the afflicted one, "cried out . . . I know thee [Jesus] who thou art, the Holy One of God." Immediately, "Jesus rebuked him, saying, Hold thy peace, and come out of him." Shrieking again and convulsing the man, the unclean spirit "came out of him," freeing him in the presence of many witnesses, including the awestruck disciples. In a word, "they were all amazed." They had been touched by His words—"What new doctrine is this?" they asked—and were astonished by what they had witnessed—"With authority commandeth he even the unclean spirits, and they do obey" (Mark 1:23–27).

Within minutes and hours, these breathtaking disclosures would be multiplied, thereby engraving them on their minds and hearts. Stepping out of the synagogue and accompanying the disciples to

---

[17] Doctrine and Covenants 128:20; on the date, see Larry C. Porter, "The Restoration of the Priesthood," *Newsletter of the BYU Religious Studies Center* 9:3 (May 1995), 3–9.

the home of Peter and Andrew, the Savior found Peter's mother-in-law "sick of a fever," evidently unable to attend the synagogue service where He had uncovered His powers. But His powers had not subsided or quit Him. Instead, the Savior "took her by the hand, and lifted her up; and immediately the fever left her" (Mark 1:29–31). We can only imagine the feelings that ran through the souls of those in the home. More was coming.

At the end of the Sabbath, "at even, when the sun did set" and people could travel more than a Sabbath day's journey—two thousand cubits, or about three thousand feet[18]—townspeople who had seen or learned about the synagogue events a few hours earlier "brought unto Him all that were diseased, and them that were possessed with devils" (Mark 1:32). Clearly, people had sensed an opportunity to free themselves and loved ones from debilitating disease and demonic possession. In the words of Luke, "he laid his hands on every one of them, and healed them" (Luke 4:40).[19] It is important to note that in the presence of His disciples, the Savior "suffered [the devils] not to speak: for they knew that he was the Christ" (Luke 4:41). It must have seemed curious to the disciples, at least at first, that Jesus would muzzle the unclean spirits and prevent them from revealing to the crowds who He was.[20] They

---

[18] The regulation about a Sabbath day's journey grew out of Exodus 16:29 and Numbers 35:5. See the discussion on Acts 1:12 ("a sabbath day's journey") in Joseph A. Fitzmyer, *The Acts of the Apostles*, The Anchor Bible Volume 31 (New York: Doubleday, 1998), 213. That traveling and carrying burdens on the Sabbath ("they brought" in Mark 1:32) were under discussion in the first century A.D., see the Damascus Document of the Dead Sea Scrolls (cols. X and XI).

[19] Curiously, in contrast to Luke and Matthew, Mark records that Jesus healed only "*many* that were sick . . . and cast out *many* devils," almost as if he did not heal all (Mark 1:34; emphasis added; compare Matthew 8:16).

[20] On the so-called Messianic secret, consult, for instance, Dennis E. Nineham, *The Gospel of St. Mark* (Baltimore: Penguin Books, 1963), 31–32; Frederick C. Grant, *The Gospel According to Mark*, The Interpreter's Bible, 12 vols. (New York: Abingdon Press, 1951–57), 7:644–45.

Who were these "unclean spirits" and "devils"? Although we cannot take up a thorough review, it is significant that the Apostles received the Savior's power to "cast out" such beings from their human hosts (see Matthew 10:1; Mark 6:7; 16:17; Luke 9:1). In this connection, Moroni repeats the words that the Risen Savior said to "all

would learn as time wore on that the Savior, whose divine identity became known to them, did not intend to make a broad, noisy announcement about His true identity to everyone.

To this juncture, we sense that at virtually every turn, the Savior surprised His followers, filling their minds with celestial teaching and pouring into their hearts an enduring witness of His powers. This continued to be the case, making them a body of rock-solid witnesses to His majesty. A couple of examples of His teaching will suffice.

The first concerns the importance of revelation. In the Apostles' day, one of the strongest aspects of Jewish culture was the law of Moses. It was held up as the grand governor of a person's life, the fundamental revelation of God's will. But Jesus would modify this view by inserting His own law. He began this process in the Sermon on the Mount, which His disciples heard (see Matthew 5:1). Declaring that He had not "come to destroy the law . . . but to fulfil" (Matthew 5:17), Jesus then turned to specific requirements, alternately dismissing them—only to replace them with another

---

his [twelve] disciples, in the hearing of the multitude" that was gathered at the temple in Bountiful. These words mirror the so-called longer ending of Mark (see Mark 16:9–20; Mormon 9:22–25) and include the promise that "in my [Jesus'] name shall they cast out devils" (Mormon 9:24).

In prophesying about the Messiah who was to be born about 125 years later, an angel declared to King Benjamin that this Messiah "shall cast out devils, or the evil spirits which dwell in the hearts of the children of men" (Mosiah 3:6). Here, no distinction is made between "devils" and "evil spirits." Moreover, it seems plain that "the children of men," wherein such creatures dwell, are willing hosts either by disposition or by actions. Such a scenario is hinted at in Jesus' story about "the unclean spirit [that] is gone out of a man" but later returns to the man's soul with "seven other spirits more wicked than himself" (Luke 11:24–26). These spirits followed Satan out of the realms of God's light and positioned themselves to try to undo the work of the Savior. A close reading of the Gospels tells us that Jesus was facing an enemy from the unseen world and that His mortal experience meant dealing with this enemy in the form of unclean spirits and devils. It may also have been the case that such devils took over people's lives in greater numbers during Jesus' mortal ministry than at any other time, all in an attempt to sap His ministry of its vitality. Consult Talmage, *JTC*, 181–83, 310–12; McConkie, MM, 2:37; Jay E. Jensen, "Spirit," in Daniel Ludlow, ed., *Encyclopedia of Mormonism*, 5 vols. (New York: Macmillan, 1992), 3:1403–5.

requirement—or sharpening them. For instance, under the law, a person was to "perform unto the Lord thine oaths." However, Jesus required that an individual "swear not at all. . . . But let your communication be, Yea, yea; Nay, nay: for whatsoever is more than these cometh of evil" (Matthew 5:33–37). Here the Savior replaces a requirement of the law with another from Himself.

In a second instance, by contrast, He holds onto the law but sharpens its demand. He cited one of the Ten Commandments and repeated its dictum: "Thou shalt not commit adultery." But He wanted more: "Whosoever looketh on a woman to lust after her hath committed adultery . . . in his heart" (Matthew 5:27–28). Here Jesus jumped from act to thought, requiring purity in both.[21]

It appears that such a treatment of the Mosaic law—alternately dismissing, replacing, and sharpening—introduced among the disciples a relaxed attitude that, in general, diminished the law's importance. For at a later moment in His ministry, Jesus sought to bring them back to a proper view of its divine character: He strongly reminded them, "It is easier for heaven and earth to pass, than one tittle of the law to fail" (Luke 16:17). In this light, what were they to think about the law? Much earlier, they had heard their Master dismiss large chunks of the law. But now He was earnestly warning them against discarding it. Perhaps oddly, the answer comes in a later scene, years after Jesus' death and resurrection.

In that scene, in an important gathering called the Jerusalem Council, sat the brooding issue of whether Church leaders should require gentile converts to adhere to the tenets of the Mosaic law, particularly that of circumcision (see Acts 15). Though the meeting was momentarily captive to "much disputing" among participants, we learn that after Peter had taken control, the proceedings were graced with his personal testimony about his experience in the home of the Roman centurion Cornelius (see Acts 15:7–11).

Significantly for the meeting, Peter had come to the home of

---

[21] Compare Matthew 12:34–37 on purity of words, implying purity of thought.

Cornelius as a result of an extraordinary vision about clean and unclean foods that applied directly to the situation of gentile converts (see Acts 10:9–16). The experience with Cornelius was key to the discussion. Then followed the personal testimonies of Paul and Barnabas about the "miracles and wonders [that] God had wrought among the Gentiles" (Acts 15:12) and the relevant and illuminating scriptural reading by James (see Acts 15:13–18). Plainly, the Spirit of the Lord was in their midst (see Acts 15:28). That Spirit, "the Holy Ghost," led the gathered leaders to conclude with James "to lay upon you [Gentiles] no greater burden than these necessary things; that ye abstain from meats offered to idols, and from blood, and from things strangled, and from fornication" (Acts 15:28–29).

What had happened? Through revelation from the Spirit, the Apostles and other leaders had dealt with a pressing issue about the relevance of the Mosaic law. In a graphic experience, they had proven to themselves that Jesus' process of selecting which parts of the law were to be applicable in people's lives continued in their ministries. Thus, the responsibility, even right, for modifying the law remained within leaders' stewardship and authority, and it came to them through the influence of the Holy Ghost.

A second major teaching has to do with prayer. A person looks at the entire aggregate of Jesus' teachings to grasp the sweeping breadth of His instruction. Over time, the cumulative weight of such instruction must have settled into the Apostles' hearts. As background, the Apostles must have learned to pray as they grew up. But the words of most prayers were set. The language of prayer for major feasts was fixed. Prayers in the synagogue followed time-honored patterns. Most prayers uttered privately and with family members in homes ran in familiar paths of expression.[22] Thus, when the Savior addressed the question of prayer in His Sermon on the

[22] For a summary of prayers offered in various settings, consult James H. Charlesworth, "Prayer in Early Judaism," in Freedman, *ABD*, 5:449–50; compare Cornelius' apparently set prayer in his home at the ninth hour, the time of the evening oblation at the temple (see Acts 3:1; 10:3, 30).

Mount—the Lord's Prayer (see Matthew 6:9–15)—and elsewhere, His instructions, which drew on unusual wording, must have seemed fresh, even liberating.[23] For example, Jesus' words "Thy kingdom come" would have sounded different to the disciples, meaning as it does, "May thy kingdom come," pointing to the immediacy of the Savior's work and kingdom.

Persistence stood as a chief attribute in Jesus' teachings on prayer. For example, in a series of lessons on praying, Luke drew the obvious conclusion when he wrote that Jesus "spake a parable unto them . . . that men ought *always* to pray, and *not to faint*" (Luke 18:1; emphasis added). In the parable that followed, a widow persistently, relentlessly sought proper redress from a judge. She so wearied him with her endless pleadings that he finally took action on her behalf, an illustration of the virtue of persistence (see Luke 18:2–7).[24] In addition, in Jesus' eyes, humility joined persistence as an attribute that moves heaven. Immediately after reciting the Parable of the Widow and the Judge, Jesus told a story about a Pharisee and a publican who "went up into the temple to pray." There the Pharisee congratulated himself by intoning, "God, I thank thee, that I am not as other men are, . . . even as this publican." In sharp contrast, the publican "would not lift up so much as his eyes unto heaven, . . . saying, God be merciful to me a sinner." Jesus' words then rounded off the story by declaring that "this man [the publican] went down to his house justified . . . for every one that exalteth himself shall be abased; and he that humbleth himself shall be exalted" (Luke 18:9–14).[25]

---

[23] Most scholars believe that Jesus did not originate the Lord's Prayer and that the versions in Matthew 6:9–15 and Luke 11:2–4 reflect the liturgical interests of early church worshipers. Although worshipers may have repeated this prayer, there is no compelling reason to set Jesus aside as its originator. For a summary of modern views, see J. L. Houlden, "Lord's Prayer," in Freedman, *ABD*, 4:356–62.

[24] A similar lesson on persistence can be seen in Jesus' saying about striving "to enter in at the strait gate" (see Luke 13:24–30) and His story of the friend who came at midnight noisily seeking a loaf of bread from a neighbor (see Luke 11:5–8).

[25] Jesus taught humility in other contexts: in His saying about seeking the lowest seat at a celebration (see Luke 14:8–11); in His exchange with the rich young ruler

In the matter of miracles, the Savior's powers did not just reach into diseased and devil-infested bodies. They also healed souls, and several disciples were witnesses to this effect on people. Two examples will make our point.

The first concerns Jesus' healing of a paralyzed man, an early miracle that occurred in Capernaum. After being lowered through the ceiling of the home where Jesus was teaching, the helpless man heard Jesus say, "Son, thy sins be forgiven thee" (Mark 2:5). We ask, What sins? The man was physically unable to commit sin. But simple reflection tells us that his sins had to do with his thoughts, wherein he must have blamed God for his hopeless situation. When murmuring arose from the gathering about Jesus' right to forgive sins, He stated clearly "that [they would] know that the Son of man[26] hath power on earth to forgive sins" and, as proof, then commanded the powerless man, "Arise, and take up thy bed, and go thy way into thine house," which he did. Plainly, Jesus had healed the man's soul (as well as his spent body) by forgiving him his sins (see Mark 2:1–12).[27]

The second miracle involves the woman who "had an issue of blood twelve years" (Mark 5:25). Because the miracle happened after the choosing of the Twelve, we assume that all the Apostles witnessed this event. While the Savior was on His way to the home of a man named Jairus, "one of the rulers of the synagogue" in Capernaum, "a certain woman . . . came in the press [of the crowd] behind, and touched his garment." Astonishingly, "the fountain of her blood was dried up; and she felt in her body that she was healed." Instead of letting the matter go, Jesus "turned him about in the press, and said, Who touched my clothes?" Embarrassed—Mark

(see Matthew 19:16–30; Mark 10:17–31; Luke 18:18–25); in His teachings about little children (see Matthew 18:1–4; 19:13–15; Mark 10:13–16; Luke 18:15–17); and in His teaching about leadership (see Matthew 20:26–27; Mark 10:43–44; Luke 22:26).

[26] The title "Son of man" has occasioned a good deal of discussion among New Testament scholars. For a treatment, see S. Kent Brown, "Man and Son of Man: Issues of Theology and Christology," in *The Pearl of Great Price: Revelations from God*, ed. H. Donl Peterson (Provo: BYU Religious Studies Center, 1989), 57–72.

[27] The story also appears in Matthew 9:2–8 and Luke 5:17–26.

records that the woman was "fearing and trembling"—she "fell down before him, and told him all the truth," evidently reciting her medical history (Mark 5:22–33). It must have been an awkward moment for her, openly acknowledging her private illness before townspeople. They would have known, of course, almost since the day that she first confided her condition to an acquaintance. Hence, she would have been shunned by neighbors as an unclean person for those twelve years. It must have been a depressingly lonely time. But now Jesus had coaxed her story into the open where He could offer a healing beyond her physical condition. He next declared to her, "Daughter, thy faith hath made thee whole; go in peace, and be whole of thy plague" (Mark 5:34). At this moment, everyone in the crowd, and soon everyone in the town, knew that she was healed. The reason for shunning her had evaporated into the Galilean air. She could go into the home of another person without that person fearing ritual contamination. She could hand a morsel of food to another without the other person refusing because it was unclean. She could at last return to the synagogue, knowing that she would not render areas in the building impure by her mere presence.

Something else must have pressed itself into the minds of the Twelve: the Savior's power over natural forces. The proof stood out most vividly in the two instances when Jesus calmed the stormy Sea of Galilee.[28] In the first case, the disciples said, "What manner of man is this, that even the winds and the sea obey him!" (Matthew 8:27). What is more important for our purposes is the miracle that involved Peter's walking on the roiling water. For he would have learned firsthand what it was like to participate in the endless, seemingly raw power of the Savior. Only Matthew reports the miracle; Mark and John, who narrate the context for the story,

[28] The synoptics report one incident of walking on water among all of them: see Matthew 8:23–27; Mark 4:35–41; Luke 8:22–25. The account shared by Matthew 14:22–33, Mark 6:45–51, and John 6:16–21 is a different event.

omit it.[29] We read that, at the bidding of the Savior and in view of "his disciples" (Matthew 14:22)—the Twelve must be meant—adventurous Peter stepped "out of the ship, [and] he walked on the water, to go to Jesus." As everyone knows, he lost his courage and had to be rescued by Jesus, who Himself was still standing atop the water (Matthew 14:28–31). We can only guess what sort of impression this etched into the memories of the Twelve; the incident, of course, would have left a deeper engraving on Peter's mind.

Perhaps memories of this scene came to mind when, on the descent from the Mount of Olives into Jerusalem for the last time, Jesus, who was being hounded by Pharisees, stated firmly that if the pilgrims in His party—including the Twelve—did not sing out about Him, nature would: "If these [in the traveling company] should hold their peace, the stones would immediately cry out" (Luke 19:40).

Power over Death

The first refining indicator that the three chief Apostles stood in a select circle, besides the order in which they were called, occurred in Capernaum when the Savior restored to life the twelve-year-old daughter of Jairus, "a ruler of the synagogue" (Luke 8:41).[30] Memorably tied to the healing of the woman with the issue of blood, this account singles out Jesus as both a man of compassion and a person who takes charge.[31] The man Jairus—Ya'ir in Hebrew[32]—anxiously

[29] Because Mark and John omit the story of Peter walking on the water and because the account can be understood in symbolic terms, some commentators believe that it cannot be historical. For a sample of views, see Sherman E. Johnson, *The Gospel According to St. Matthew*, The Interpreter's Bible, 7:433–34; John Fenton, *The Gospel of St Matthew* (Baltimore: Penguin Books, 1963), 245–47.

[30] We know that the miracle took place in or near Capernaum because Jesus "returned" from the east side of the Sea of Galilee where He had healed the demoniac (see Matthew 8:28–34; Mark 5:1–20; Luke 8:26–39); Jesus soon thereafter called Matthew at the customs house just to the east of the town (see Matthew 9:9); and both Mark and Luke mention "the synagogue," which can mean only the one where the Savior was then operating, in Capernaum (Mark 5:22; Luke 8:41).

[31] The synoptics all preserve the story; see Matthew 9:18–19, 23–26; Mark 5:22–24, 35–43; Luke 8:40–42, 49–56.

approached the Savior, begging for the life of his dying daughter. It is certain that Jairus knew, perhaps firsthand, of the Savior's majestic powers in healing others from the town.[33] Before Jesus and the official could reach the home, news caught up with them that the girl had already passed away. In response, the Savior tenderly assured Jairus, "Be not afraid, only believe" (Mark 5:36). Then Jesus did something He had not done before; He allowed only the three Apostles to go with Him the rest of the way, excluding other followers (see Mark 5:37).[34] Hence, Jesus restricted the number of witnesses to the miracle. But why do this? Because principles of leadership—taking charge to create a spiritually sound atmosphere—would manifest themselves in the Savior's actions.

When Jesus arrived at Jairus' home, He found gathered mourners already "making a noise," creating a "tumult" (Matthew 9:23; Mark 5:38). In that society, friends, relatives, and neighbors gathered, almost immediately and in large numbers, to mourn the dead.[35] The situation would have been all the more poignant because it involved a child, in this case a girl who was about to emerge into the full flower of adulthood.[36] Though these people had gathered out of love and respect for Jairus and his family, the Savior did not let this fact deflect Him from His ministering path. In an understatement, and perhaps preparing Jairus for His command that he not spread word about what was to happen next,

---

[32] See the discussion in Joseph A. Fitzmyer, *The Gospel According to Luke I–IX: A New Translation and Commentary*, The Anchor Bible Volume 28 (New York: Doubleday, 1981), 745.

[33] See Matthew 8:16; 9:1–8; Mark 1:32–34; 2:1–12; Luke 4:40–41; 5:17–26.

[34] Luke says that the three Apostles were the only persons allowed to enter Jairus' home (see Luke 8:51), implying that all of the Twelve went there. But Luke's account presumably depends on Mark's; hence, we follow Mark's report.

[35] For mourning customs, consult Kittel and Friedrich, *TDNT*, 3:841–47; *Baker Encyclopedia of the Bible*, ed. Walter A. Elwell, 2 vols. (Grand Rapids: Baker Book House, 1988), 2:1500–1.

[36] The Mishnah says that a girl could become betrothed at age twelve and one-half; see Herbert Danby, *The Mishnah* (Oxford: Oxford University Press, 1972), notes on *Ketuboth* 3.1, 8 and *Kiddushin* 1.2 (248–49, 321); also Joachim Jeremias, *Jerusalem in the Time of Jesus* (Philadelphia: Fortress Press, 1969), 363–66.

Jesus said to the assembled crowd, "Why make ye this ado, and weep? the damsel is not dead, but sleepeth." Now came the challenge for the Savior in creating a spiritually inviting mood: "They laughed him to scorn." Jesus' response? He "put them all out."

Now showing that He was in charge, even in another's home, and was the bringer of life, "he taketh the father and the mother of the damsel, and [the three] that were with Him, and entereth in where the damsel was lying" (Mark 5:39–40). The setting for the miracle was now correct, and the disciples' memories would have replayed the scene again and again as they sought to lead others: quiet, respectful, enriched, and dignified by the presence of those who loved the girl most. The three Apostles would also have known to stand and observe in quiet reverence as the unbelievable then occurred: their new master raised the girl from the pale grasp of death. Here was a vibrant lesson about leadership for the Savior's chosen leaders, punctuated pointedly first by the noise of mourners and, after He took charge, by a quiet, respectful atmosphere wherein Jesus could call down the healing powers of heaven.

The Twelve as a group, of course, also witnessed the Savior's power over death in Bethany, just outside of Jerusalem. There, "a certain man was sick, named Lazarus" (John 11:1). We learn that Jesus purposely delayed His arrival in the town, even after receiving a desperate message from Lazarus' sisters (see John 11:6, 3). Jesus' action on Lazarus' behalf would not only restore him to life, thus demonstrating His control over life and death, but would also strengthen His Apostles' faith: "I am glad for your sakes that I was not there [in Bethany], to the intent ye may believe" (John 11:15; also 11:42). The fact of the Savior's absolute power over the grave would have been etched deeply into the minds of the Twelve because, by the time they reached Bethany, Lazarus had "been dead four days," a period that, in local belief, meant that the person's spirit had completely departed (John 11:39).[37] As men who had

[37] Consult the discussion in Raymond E. Brown, *The Gospel According to John I–XII*, 424.

grown up in a traditional society wherein family members were typically responsible for preparing the dead for burial, they would have already witnessed firsthand the irreversible and irresistible strength that death held in its dreaded hands. Hence, when they saw Jesus pull Lazarus from death's grasp, calling to him "with a loud voice," the impression on their souls would have been everlasting (John 11:43). Indeed, they all now stood as "eyewitnesses of his majesty" (2 Peter 1:16).

Jesus' First Prediction of His Suffering

One of the most curious of interactions between the Savior and one of His followers—Peter, in this instance—occurred as a result of Jesus' first prediction of His looming, inevitable suffering in Jerusalem. We might suspect that Peter's act and words mirrored the feelings of the others. It followed soon after Peter's famed confession, "Thou art the Christ, the Son of the living God" (Matthew 16:16). Evidently, Peter's memory—and that of the others—was short-lived. For when Jesus "began . . . to shew unto his disciples, how that he must go unto Jerusalem, and . . . be killed, and be raised again the third day . . . Peter took him, and began to rebuke him, saying, Be it far from thee, Lord: this shall not be unto thee" (Matthew 16:21–22). We can readily understand the shock that Jesus' prediction of His death carried into the hearts of the Twelve. But Peter's reaction involved more than shock: the description shows that he physically grabbed the Savior and shouted at Him in a censuring tone.[38] The situation was thoroughly acrimonious, launched by Peter's anger. Was Jesus to calm Peter and then explain in measured tones what He had just said? Not in this case. Jesus met fire with fire. Turning to Peter, He sharply hissed, "Get thee behind me, Satan" (Matthew 16:23). All the Apostles stood astonished.

We ask, Why did the Savior call Peter "Satan"? Does not this

[38] Luke omits Peter's response, but Mark preserves the story, which Matthew repeats (see Mark 8:32; Matthew 16:22).

name demean the man? Or are we witnessing a situation wherein Peter has become the temporary but willing host of Jesus' undying enemy, the devil? In the end, it does not matter whether Jesus was addressing Peter or, through him, Satan himself. The exchange between Peter and the Savior shows that Satan was somehow mixed into the scene, was somehow exerting influence, had somehow penetrated into Jesus' inner circle. This becomes apparent in Jesus' following words: "Thou art an offence unto me" (Matthew 16:23). The term translated "offence" means at base "a trap" or "an enticement," with a negative twist.[39] The one who lays traps, who fashions enticements toward evil, is Satan, who has succeeded here by injecting a climate of ill will among Jesus' closest companions, thus drawing down the strength of their fellowship and unity. It also seems plain that Peter bears some responsibility. His actions illustrate that he has swerved from "the things that be of God" and has installed in their place "those that be of men," fomenting unsavory contention along the way (Matthew 16:23). As we learn from the Savior in another setting, "the spirit of contention is . . . of the devil, who is the father of contention, and he stirreth up the hearts of men to contend with anger," a vivid depiction of Peter's acts (3 Nephi 11:29). Whatever else Jesus' two-fisted response to Peter achieved, it certainly caught the attention of all the Apostles and opened them to quietly receive further illumination about the means of His atonement.[40]

---

[39] The Greek word is *skandalon*, which comes into English as *scandal*. The Greek term points to the occurrence, whereas the English derivative points to the result. See Walter Bauer, *A Greek-English Lexicon of the New Testament and Other Early Christian Literature*, trans. W. F. Arndt and F. W. Gingrich (Chicago: University of Chicago Press, 1957), 760.

[40] The synoptic Gospels record three incidents wherein Jesus revealed that He would suffer death in Jerusalem as part of the atoning process. The first, as we have seen, brought forth a harsh response from Peter, though Luke omits this element (see Matthew 16:21–23; Mark 8:31–33; Luke 9:22). The Apostles, even after events on the Mount of Transfiguration, received Jesus' second and third disclosures with some confusion (see Matthew 17:22–23; 20:17–19; Mark 9:30–32; 10:32–34; Luke 9:43–45; 18:31–34).

The Mount of Transfiguration

In this connection, the experience that was orchestrated soon thereafter for the three chief Apostles formed the grandest and most important event in their ministries, framing ever after their perceptions of the Savior, and occurring on a lofty prominence known as the Mount of Transfiguration.[41] A careful reading of the accounts points to the Apostles as the intended recipients of this managed event. They were to be its witnesses; they were to be its beneficiaries; they were to be the ministers of its effects. While the mountain whereon the Savior's transfiguration took place remains under discussion,[42] the reality of the experience is firm. Not only do the Gospels record its happening but also both Peter's second epistle and modern revelation refer to it, underlining its importance.[43]

It is essential to notice that, even with all of the references to this event, both ancient and modern, we do not possess a full account of what happened. In speaking of the eventual transfiguration of the earth, whose pattern "was shown unto [the] apostles upon the mount," the Lord declared to Joseph Smith, "Of [this] account the fulness ye have not yet received" (Doctrine and Covenants 63:21). Even so, we can make out many of its primary elements that the Lord and scripture have disclosed.

First, that the experience was aimed at the three Apostles becomes abundantly evident first in the words of the Father, which

---

[41] Consult the important summary of this experience by Dale C. Mouritsen, "Mount of Transfiguration," in Ludlow, *Encyclopedia of Mormonism*, 5:968–69; see also Richard Neitzel Holzapfel's article in this volume, "The Transfiguration."

[42] For a brief summary of the competing sites, see Talmage, *JTC*, 376. On Mount Hermon as the location, consult McConkie, *DNTC*, 1:402; Richard Neitzel Holzapfel and David Rolph Seely, *My Father's House: Temple Worship and Symbolism in the New Testament* (Salt Lake City: Bookcraft, 1994), 96; on Mount Tabor as the place, see "Spencer W. Kimball as Extemporaneous Speaker," *BYU Studies* 25/4 (Fall 1985), 148–49.

[43] See Matthew 17:1–13; Mark 9:2–13; Luke 9:28–36; 2 Peter 1:16–18; Doctrine and Covenants 63:20–21; compare John 1:14 ("we beheld his glory") and 2 Peter 1:3 ("the knowledge of [the Savior] that hath called us to glory").

were addressed to them from "a bright cloud [that] overshadowed them: . . . This is my beloved Son, in whom I am well pleased; hear ye him" (see Matthew 17:5). Plainly, they were to be witnesses of both the Son's divine connection to His Father and the acceptable character of His ministry. Their testimony of these matters came directly from the Father, unmediated.

Second, the fact that the Savior "was transfigured before them: and his face did shine as the sun, and his raiment was white as the [sun's] light" transformed them into "eyewitnesses of his [celestial] majesty" (Matthew 17:2; 2 Peter 1:16). The day was soon coming wherein they would shoulder the responsibilities for the Savior's work beyond His death and resurrection. Part of their role as the chief guarantors of Jesus' divinity, both before and after the Resurrection, rested on this molding experience with Him.

An address by the Prophet Joseph Smith to the Twelve of his day frames the third point. In it, the Prophet revealed that "the Savior, Moses, and Elias, gave the keys to Peter, James and John, on the mount, when they were transfigured."[44] This action fulfilled Jesus' earlier promise to Peter: "I will give unto thee the keys of the kingdom of heaven: and whatsoever thou shalt bind on earth shall be bound in heaven: and whatsoever thou shalt loose on earth shall be loosed in heaven" (Matthew 16:19). These keys, the same as those delivered to Joseph Smith and Oliver Cowdery at the dedication of the Kirtland Temple, included those from Moses for "the gathering of Israel from the four parts of the earth" and, from Elijah, "the keys of this dispensation," which are designed to "turn the hearts of the fathers to the children, and the children to the fathers," basically sealing one generation to another (Doctrine and Covenants 110:11, 13–16).[45] One further dimension is worth

[44] Joseph Smith, *History of the Church*, 6 vols. (Salt Lake City: Deseret Book, 1948–50), 3:387; Smith, *TPJS*, 158.

[45] Such sealing power, connected to Elijah, is set out in an address recorded by Wilford Woodruff: see *The Words of Joseph Smith*, ed. Andrew F. Ehat and Lyndon W. Cook (Provo: BYU Religious Studies Center, 1980), 329; Smith, *TPJS*, 340; David H. Yarn Jr., "Sealing Power," in Ludlow, *Encyclopedia of Mormonism*, 3:1288–89.

noticing. The Prophet's words also seem to say that the three Apostles, "on the mount . . . were transfigured." If so, they became full participants in, or were introduced into, what Peter later calls "the divine nature" (2 Peter 1:4).

Fourth, the experience was orchestrated to show to the three, evidently in vision, "the pattern" by which "the earth shall be transfigured" at the end of time (Doctrine and Covenants 63:21). This apparent visionary aspect placed the three on a spiritual continuum with those prophets who have beheld similar views of the end of human history.[46] Thus oriented, the three effectively came to possess God's deeper knowledge of the purposes of this earth, both here and hereafter.

Fifth, the fact that Moses and Elijah appeared visibly to the Savior in the presence of the three stands as evidence that the Apostles were to grasp in a most concrete way that the long-past era of the Old Testament was tied to their own day. In this connection, we notice that Moses and Elijah still possessed their bodies, in a translated state, so that they did not die, thus allowing them to perform physical acts, such as the laying on of hands, to transmit their keys and authority.[47]

A sixth element has to do with the Savior's imminent atonement. Luke alone preserves a summary of Jesus' conversation with Moses and Elijah. Matthew and Mark record only that the two were "talking with" the Savior (Matthew 17:3; Mark 9:4). Luke's report thus clarifies that the three Apostles overheard—allowing them to hear, incidentally, was intentional—what the other three discussed together: they "spake of [Jesus'] decease which he should accomplish at Jerusalem" (Luke 9:31).

The Greek term translated "decease" in this passage is the word

---

[46] Among prophetic figures who saw to the end of time are Enoch (see Moses 7:65–67), the brother of Jared (see Ether 3:25), Daniel (see Daniel 7:1–14), and John (see Revelation 19–22).

[47] On the physical nature of Moses and Elijah, consult Joseph Fielding Smith, *Doctrines of Salvation*, 3 vols. (Salt Lake City: Bookcraft, 1954–56), 2:110–11; *DNTC*, 1:400.

exodos, which comes into English as *exodus.* Naturally, Luke's term makes a firm tie between this scene and Moses' exodus with the Hebrew slaves.[48] Moreover, it establishes the fact that Jesus' impending atonement, and the deliverance that it would offer—surpassing the deliverance of the Israelite slaves—were chief subjects of this lofty conversation.[49] The three Apostles thereby came to comprehend, at least in a limited way,[50] that Jesus would accomplish His mission in Jerusalem and that it would mean His death, thus not only receiving divine confirmation of Jesus' earlier prediction of His death and resurrection but also answering Peter's misguided "rebuke" of the Savior when he first learned these facts (see Matthew 16:21–23).

One dimension of the experience that has puzzled investigators is Peter's announced intent to set up "three tabernacles; one for [the Savior], and one for Moses, and one for Elias" (Matthew 17:4).[51] Although we do not learn whether Peter and the others actually constructed the three booths, the fact that all three synoptic accounts repeat Peter's statement, thus underscoring its integral part in the Apostles' experience, seems to say that they did.[52] If so,

---

[48] Consult Fitzmyer, *The Gospel According to Luke I–IX according to Luke I–IX,* 794–95, 800. On the term *exodos* or its Hebrew equivalent as the title for the book of Exodus, see Nahum M. Sarna, "Exodus, Book of," in Freedman, *ABD,* 2:690.

[49] On Jesus' deliverance surpassing that of the Israelite exodus, see S. Kent Brown, *From Jerusalem to Zarahemla: Literary and Historical Studies of the Book of Mormon* (Provo: BYU Religious Studies Center, 1998), 157–67; *Voices from the Dust: Book of Mormon Insights* (American Fork, Utah: Covenant Communications, 2004), 152–60.

[50] All the accounts of Jesus' repeated predictions of His death characterize the Apostles as lacking full understanding (see Matthew 17:23; Mark 9:32; Luke 18:34). Whether the reports referred to all the Twelve or to the nine who did not accompany the Savior onto the Mount of Transfiguration is not possible to say. We do know that, after events on the Mount, Jesus commanded the three "that they should tell no man what things they had seen, till the Son of man were risen from the dead" (Mark 9:9; also Matthew 17:9).

[51] Talmage suggests that "Peter's proposition" to set up three booths was intended to delay "the departure of the visitants" (*JTC,* 371); both McConkie (*DNTC,* 1:403) and Luke Timothy Johnson see Peter's proposal connected to the Feast of Tabernacles (*The Gospel of Luke,* Sacra Pagina Series 3 [Collegeville, Minn.: Liturgical Press, 1991], 153).

[52] All three mention the tabernacles: see Matthew 17:4; Mark 9:5; Luke 9:33.

why? An apparent connection to the Feast of Tabernacles stands to the fore, of course, thereby tying more tightly this experience on the Mount of Transfiguration to Moses and the Exodus. On this occasion, as Mount Sinai did for Moses, the Mount became a place of revelation and spiritual elevation for the three Apostles. But beyond these observations, the question still lingers: Why set up the three tabernacles and separate Moses and Elijah from one another and from the Savior? After all, the sight of the transfigured Jesus somehow included the accompanying appearance of Moses and Elijah to the three in the same vision—"they saw [the Savior's] glory, and the two men that stood with him" (Luke 9:32).[53] And both Matthew and Mark stress that Moses and Elijah appeared also "unto them," the three (Matthew 17:3; Mark 9:4). In response, one real possibility is that the three Apostles could meet individually with Moses and Elijah and the transfigured Savior for sacred instruction. Because of what they had so far seen and heard, their hearts would now be open to such instruction in a way that just hours before they had not been. In this connection, because receiving priesthood keys formed an important part of the experience for the three, meeting separately with Moses and Elijah would offer the two an opportunity to explain to the three Apostles, individually, the meaning and significance of those keys and what they would entail for their future ministries.[54]

The Sons of Zebedee

According to the accounts of Matthew and Mark, immediately after the Savior's third prediction of His death and resurrection, two of the three chief Apostles, James and John, approached Him and asked for a grand favor, a request that disturbed the others.[55]

---

[53] Consult Matthew 17:2–3; Mark 9:2–4; Luke 9:29–30.

[54] Joseph Fielding Smith has suggested that the instruction to the Apostles was ceremonial in nature; see *Doctrines of Salvation*, 2:165.

[55] According to Matthew, it was the mother of James and John who approached Jesus. But we follow Mark's version, thinking it to be earlier and to be based on Peter's reminiscences. On the issues of dating and Peter's influence on Mark, see S. Kent

Apparently, not long before Jesus passed through Jericho for the last time on His way to Jerusalem, the two, having grasped rather fully the Savior's destiny, asked "that we may sit, one on thy right hand, and the other on thy left hand, in thy glory." Jesus refused. He replied, "Ye know not what ye ask; . . . to sit on my right hand and on my left hand is not mine to give" (Mark 10:37–38, 40). They had apparently misunderstood the order of heaven. But there was another lesson to learn. For as soon as "the ten [others] heard it, they began to be much displeased with James and John" (Mark 10:41). In this climate, Jesus chose to teach a lesson that grew out of His own example. Pointing first to the Gentiles and their rulers, He observed, "Their great ones exercise authority upon them. But so shall it not be among you." Rather, "whosoever will be great among you, shall be your minister: and whosoever of you shall be the chiefest, shall be servant of all. For even the Son of man came not to be ministered unto, but to minister, and to give his life a ransom for many" (Mark 10:42–45).[56] Service is the key concept for the Twelve, even if it means suffering a death that ransoms others.

Conclusion

The educating of the Twelve brought them into the richly decorated corridors of spiritual sensitivity and power, of heavenly order and wisdom, of human needs and divine responses. Through the Savior, they were introduced to the sweet fragrances of celestial service. At the core of their experience stood faith: "His disciples believed on him" (John 2:11). Over time, "from the baptism of John, unto that same day that [the Risen Savior] was taken up" (Acts 1:22), their faith filled up with memories of Jesus' teaching sublime truths, of His healing the desperately ill, of His control over the natural elements. Such faith, now aimed at the future, was an

---

Brown, "The Testimony of Mark," in Kent P. Jackson and Robert L. Millet, eds., *Studies in Scripture Volume 5: The Gospels* (Salt Lake City, Utah: Deseret Book, 1986), 61–87.

[56] The gospel of Luke repeats this lesson of Jesus at the Last Supper; see Luke 22:24–27.

irreducible minimum. Why? Because theirs was to be the responsibility for the Church after the Savior's death and resurrection; theirs was to lift the souls of those who sought divine help; theirs was to lead the struggle against the powers of evil; theirs was to show the way to the lost; theirs was to stand as witnesses of the Savior's divine mission. Without faith, they would be empty of heavenly influence and power; they would be mere hollow shells. But in their association with Jesus, it was as if He had led them into a broad, verdant valley bathed in the full light of the sun. Here they would join with fellow believers in planting and harvesting, in toiling and rejoicing, all the while leading by example and precept as Jesus had done for them.

V.

FROM OPPOSITION TO HOSTILITY: CHANGING REACTIONS DURING JESUS' MINISTRY

JENNIFER C. LANE

Blessed is he, whosoever shall not be offended in me.
MATTHEW 11:6; LUKE 7:23

Opposition and hostility are not identical reactions. We can oppose an idea, a movement, or even an individual without feeling hostility. While not harboring any ill feelings, we can speak or act against ideas, movements, or people that we see as wrong, misguided, or dangerous. What is striking in the New Testament accounts is not that people maintained religious or political opposition to the teachings of Jesus but that they became hostile in that opposition. In contrast, although Jesus opposed others' beliefs and actions, He did not harbor ill will toward those who were erring. In this chapter, I will focus on explaining both opposition to Jesus and the process through which this opposition turned to hostility.

In seeking to understand the hostility that developed toward Jesus between the Sermon on the Mount and the Triumphal Entry, we must combine a close reading of the Gospels, seeking to draw out and understand the biblical evidence, with sufficient historical background to clarify actors and motives.[1] I will begin with the historical background, which will help us understand the beliefs that led to opposition. Then, using that background, I will turn to the passages in which opposition to Jesus is described. In a close reading of these passages, we can see how individuals' initial concerns and opposition grew out of their beliefs, but their hostility developed only as they heard Jesus' response and His critiques of their own weaknesses. Their opposition may initially have stemmed from different beliefs, but the hostility we see reflects the hardening of heart and enmity that grow from pride.

Jesus and those who became His opponents lived at a time when there were different forms of Judaism, known by scholars today as sectarian Judaism. The Pharisees, Sadducees, and Essenes were competing groups, each claiming to be following the right form of Jewish belief and practice.[2] In the Gospels, both the Pharisees and Sadducees appear in scenes of hostility to Jesus, but the most interactions by far occur with the Pharisees—so they will be the focus of my analysis here.[3] The Pharisees' opposition to Jesus

[1] As has been discussed elsewhere in these volumes, contemporary biblical scholarship has a different perspective on the reliability of biblical accounts of the life of Jesus than that held by Latter-day Saints. Although we accept the Bible as scripture, we need not uncritically read other historical texts from this period. Recent scholarship has shown how our other sources on the Jews in the New Testament, Josephus, and the rabbinic writings, are influenced by their authors' perspectives and agendas. It may help to see them more as painting pictures that we need to interpret rather than providing windows through which we can clearly see. I am grateful to Stephen Robinson for this analogy, which he used in the context of intertestamental literature. For a thoughtful discussion of how this critical approach to texts can be combined with the pursuit of objective knowledge about the past, see Joyce Abbleby, et al., *Telling the Truth about History* (New York: Norton, 1994), 241–70.

[2] On the tentative quality of the knowledge we have about the Pharisees and Sadducees, see Lester L. Grabbe, "Sadducees and Pharisees," in Jacob Neusner and Alan J. Avery-Peck, eds., *Judaism in Late Antiquity: Part Three, Where We Stand: Issues and Debates in Ancient Judaism* (Leiden: Brill, 1999), 61.

[3] The Sadducees do appear with the Pharisees in an early scene with John the Baptist (Matthew 3:7)—but not in the other references. In Matthew 16:1, both groups are "tempting" Jesus by asking for "a sign from heaven." At the temple in the last week, the Sadducees raise the question about marriage and the resurrection (Matthew 22:23–33; Mark 12:18–27; Luke 20:27–38). Less is known about the Sadducees than

centers on critiques of food practices and Sabbath-day observance that go against their understanding of true Judaism.[4] This historical background helps us understand the Pharisees' assumptions about how to live the law of Moses and clarifies concerns they would have had about the actions of Jesus and His disciples.

The Pharisees' practice and concern centered in their confidence in what the Gospels refer to as "the traditions of the elders," also known as "ancestral tradition."[5] The Pharisees' traditions particularly focused on details of tithes, Sabbath observance, and ritual purity in the preparation and eating of food.[6] Unlike the Sadducees' connection to the temple or the Essenes' removal of themselves from society, the Pharisees' program of holiness was integrated into

---

about the Pharisees. There are no documents produced by the Sadducees—only by their opponents. There are disagreements in scholarship over how closely the Sadducees should be associated with the high priests of the temple. One point that does consistently resurface is their rejection of a belief in the resurrection. The question of the degree of their Hellenization is debated. Some see their rejection of resurrection as a sign of Hellenization; other scholars who believe that it was a more recent belief in Judaism see them as maintaining older views; still others point out their commitment to the Torah and the fact that resurrection is not mentioned in the five books of Moses. See Cecilia Wassén, "Sadducees and *Halakah*," in *Law in Religious Communities in the Roman Period: The Debate over Torah and Nomos in Post-Biblical Judaism and Early Christianity*, ed. Peter Richardson and Stephen Westernholm (Published for the Canadian Corporation for Studies in Religion by Wilfrid Laurier University Press, 1991), 127–45; Gary G. Porton, "Sadducees," in Freedman, *ABD*, 5:892–95.

[4] Widely regarded as a critical turning point in understanding the Pharisees are the new approaches to the rabbinic texts found in Ellis Rivkin, *A Hidden Revolution* (Nashville: Abingdon, 1978), and Jacob Neusner, *From Politics to Piety: The Emergence of Pharisaic Judaism* (Englewood Cliffs, N.J.: Prentice-Hall, 1973). On this shift, see, for example, Albert I. Baumgarten's "Rivkin and Neusner on the Pharisees," in *Law in Religious Communities in the Roman Period: The Debate over Torah and Nomos in Post-Biblical Judaism and Early Christianity*, ed. Peter Richardson and Stephen Westernholm (Published for the Canadian Corporation for Studies in Religion by Wilfrid Laurier University Press, 1991), 109–25.

[5] "But what does seem certain—because it is the only thing upon which our otherwise irreconcilable sources agree—is that the Pharisees placed a great premium on something called 'ancestral tradition.'" All sources consistently assent to the Pharisees' focus on "ancestral tradition," which the rabbis would later call the oral law. Martin S. Jaffee, *Early Judaism* (Upper Saddle River, N.J.: Prentice Hall, 1997), 79.

[6] Grabbe, "Sadducees and Pharisees," 58–60; Saldarini, "Pharisees," 5:294–99.

society and daily life. Their vision was to bring the holiness of the temple into the homes of all Jews by instructing the Jews to apply the laws for priests in ordinary, everyday settings. Most scholars believe that the Pharisees were a lay movement that emphasized the solidarity of their group because of their focus on ritual purity. This solidarity should not, however, be mistaken for exclusivity in the sense that they believed this observance should be unique to them. Instead, their revolutionary claim was that the ritual temple holiness described in the law was God's will for all Jews, not just the priests.[7]

When we see how the Pharisees sought to live exemplary lives in ordinary circumstances, we can better understand their concerns and see where their Achilles' heel lay. In the Sermon on the Mount, Jesus Himself explained that the Pharisees' righteousness was a high bar that His followers had to surpass: "Except your righteousness shall exceed the righteousness of the scribes and Pharisees, ye shall in no case enter into the kingdom of heaven" (Matthew 5:20). As we read about the Pharisees, and presumably the scribes they are associated with by the Gospel writers, we may mistakenly believe that their aims were radically different from our own.[8] Without recognizing that their efforts and even their initial opposition grew out of their desire for righteous lives, we often do not identify with their efforts to justify or defend themselves. We fail to "liken them unto ourselves" (see 1 Nephi 19:23).

Developing Hostility

As we better understand the religious viewpoint of those opposing the Savior, we can explain why they questioned His behavior

---

[7] Neusner, *From Politics to Piety: The Emergence of Pharisaic Judaism*, 83.

[8] The scribes' identity is less clear than that of the Pharisees. The scribes are associated with scribal positions and may have had a role in teaching the law during this period of Jewish history. For an effort to develop the changing role of scribes and to connect to their broader ancient Near Eastern role, see Anthony J. Saldarini, *Pharisees, Scribes and Sadducees in Palestinian Society: A Sociological Approach* (Willington, Del.: Michael Glazier, 1988), 249–76.

and that of His disciples. The next challenge lies in explaining the source of their hostility. Some suggest that pressures to maintain social position explain the Pharisees' developing opposition to Jesus. This approach faces the difficulty of understanding the social position of the Pharisees based on the sources available. Although we can fairly confidently identify why the Pharisees would have had concerns about Jesus' actions, it is more difficult to make confident statements about how the Pharisees' religious positions were viewed by society in general or to understand fully their political influence at the time.[9]

The teachings and actions of Jesus and His disciples may have challenged the social status of the Pharisees, but although context helps to explain pressures and motivations, the response of hostility does not simply result from politics. At its core, hostility reflects personal, spiritual responses. The hostility described in the Gospels was informed by a particular context; but, more important, it was a universal spiritual phenomenon—the "universal sin" of pride.

The role of pride in the response of hostility can be seen in the Lord's encounter in Nazareth with individuals who, unlike the Pharisees, scribes, Sadducees, or chief priests, did not comprise the religious, political, or social elite. In Luke 4:16–29, as these ordinary individuals hear Jesus' words declaring Himself to be the Messiah, they first seem skeptical and have questions about how this could be when they know Him only as Joseph's son, but their response escalates to hostility when they themselves are called into question and compared to the unbelieving Israelites of old. When their own faithfulness is questioned by this comparison, the defensiveness of the audience turns to hostility. "And all they in the synagogue,

---

[9] An example of the debate over the social dominance of the Pharisees can be seen in the discussion of Steve Mason's essay "Revisiting Josephus's Pharisees" in *Judaism in Late Antiquity: Part Three, Where We Stand: Issues and Debates in Ancient Judaism*, vol. 2, ed. Jacob Neusner and Alan J. Avery-Peck (Leiden: Brill, 1999), 2:39–45, which argues that the primary sources support social and political dominance, and in Grabbe, "Sadducees and Pharisees," who points to the priests as leaders (60) and questions the reliability of Josephus' one comment that the Pharisees were able to impose their views on the Sadducees and direct how worship was enacted (46).

when they heard these things, were filled with wrath, and rose up, and thrust him out of the city, and led him unto the brow of the hill whereon their city was built, that they might cast him down headlong" (Luke 4:28–29).

This pattern of questioning turning into hostility because of the audience's defensiveness consistently characterizes the hostile interactions of the Pharisees and the Savior. The interactions typically begin as the Pharisees raise concerns about Jesus' practice rather than focus on His teaching or claims about Himself. These questions grow out of their understanding of the law. Their religious commitment to ritual purity and Sabbath observance puts them in a position of opposition to what they see Jesus and His disciples doing. In His responses to their questions, Jesus shows the Pharisees that scripture itself points to a higher form of holiness. As Jesus calls them into question, the Pharisees' defensive response moves them from opposition into hostility. In realizing they are being told that their efforts at spiritual excellence are falling short, they are in a position where—depending on their response—they can either be humbled or develop hostility.

Food Practices and Developing Hostility

The Pharisees' commitment to the "traditions of the fathers" or "ancestral tradition" was based on their understanding that this was the correct application of God's law as given in the Torah. A central focus of the law concerned sacrifices in the temple and rules governing the ritual purity of the priests while they officiated and ate at the temple. Although their contemporaries believed that these regulations in Leviticus applied only to the priests in the temple, "the Pharisees were Jews who believed one must keep the purity laws outside of the Temple"; in fact, they believed that "even outside of the Temple, in one's own home, the laws of ritual purity were to be followed in the only circumstance in which they might apply, namely, at the table. Therefore, one must eat secular food (ordinary, everyday meals) in a state of ritual purity *as if one were a*

Temple priest. The Pharisees thus arrogated to themselves—and to all Jews equally—the status of Temple priests, and performed actions restricted to priests on account of that status."[10]

This desire to maintain ritual purity had implications not only for what they ate and for the purification of vessels and the washing of hands but also for their emphasis on tithes. Just as the cleansing of vessels and hands helped make the meal ritually pure, the Pharisees also "tithed with great care, and so prepared foods for eating. Tithing was a dietary law, rendering food ritually acceptable."[11] Because proper tithing of the food related to its ritual purity, it was important that one know from whom one procured food.[12] It was also essential not to eat with those who did not observe these laws.[13] This combined effort to keep the ritual holiness of the family table is known as "table-fellowship." As we shall see, much of the Pharisees' initial opposition to Jesus arose over questions of His or His disciples' food practices, particularly as they reflect a breach of table-fellowship regulations. After we examine how hostility develops in discussions over eating with sinners, not fasting, and not washing hands, a discussion of the second main area of the Pharisees' critique—the observance of the Sabbath—will follow.

Eating with Sinners

New Testament accounts suggest that Jesus was invited to participate in the Pharisees' table-fellowship (Luke 11:37; 14:1), but

---

[10] Neusner, *From Politics to Piety*, 83; emphasis in original.

[11] Neusner, *From Politics to Piety*, 80.

[12] "The associates promised one another to tithe their food and to observe certain kinds of ritual purity. This means that the associates could confidently buy and sell to one another and also eat together without fear of breaking any of the laws they wished to keep. By contrast, they had to take great care in their dealings with the 'people of the land,' the *'am hā'ares*, because the 'people of the land' did not keep the special priestly laws of purity and did not tithe properly and fully. Their food was not properly sanctified and could not be eaten by associates" (Saldarini, "Pharisees," 5:300).

[13] "Pharisees furthermore ate only with other Pharisees, to be sure that the laws were appropriately observed" (Neusner, *From Politics to Piety*, 80).

we learn also that others whom He ate with were an affront to the Pharisees. Understanding the concept of table-fellowship helps us see that by eating with others who were ritually unclean, He would also threaten the purity of His Pharisaic hosts. Concerning these others, the "publicans and sinners," Neusner points out not only that it is "unlikely that these people [sinners and tax collectors] observe the laws of ritual purity at meals or tithe their food" but also that "Pharisaic law explicitly excludes tax collectors from the Pharisaic table-fellowship."[14]

In the first account of eating with publicans and sinners, the "scribes and Pharisees murmured against his disciples, saying, Why do ye eat and drink with publicans and sinners?" (Luke 5:30). "And when the Pharisees saw it, they said unto his disciples, Why eateth your Master with publicans and sinners?" (Matthew 9:11; see also Mark 2:16).

The initial "murmuring" (Greek egonguzon [*egóngyzon*])[15] of the "scribes and Pharisees" is met with Jesus' teaching that the "whole need not a physician, but they that are sick" and His saying that "I am not come to call the righteous, but sinners to repentance" (Matthew 9:12–13; see also Mark 2:17; Luke 5:31–32). On its face, it is difficult to see how these comments would rile the "scribes and Pharisees" because they would naturally concur that the sinners and tax collectors were sick and did need a physician. But in Matthew's account, we find an additional phrase that helps explain how Jesus' response calls the questioners into question.

In Matthew 9:13, between the statements about the sick and Jesus' mission to call them to repentance, we read, "But go ye and learn what that meaneth, I will have mercy, and not sacrifice." This quotation comes from the prophet Hosea, who chastised the unrighteous Israelites: "O Ephraim, what shall I do unto thee? O Judah, what shall I do unto thee? for your goodness is as a morning

[14] Neusner, *From Politics to Piety*, 73.

[15] The Greek verb is *gongýzō*, meaning "*grumble, murmur* as a sign of displeasure." Arndt and Gingrich, *GEL*, 164; emphasis in original.

cloud, and as the early dew it goeth away. For I desired mercy, and not sacrifice; and the knowledge of God more than burnt offerings. But they like men have transgressed the covenant: there have they dealt treacherously against me" (Hosea 6:4, 6–7).

Jesus here challenges the scribes' and Pharisees' interpretation of scripture in telling them, "Go ye and learn what that meaneth." Because of their understanding of the law, the Pharisees' table-fellowship kept them from eating with publicans and sinners. Their strict adherence to the requirements for priests' ritual purity had become for them "sacrifice" and "burnt offerings." Jesus challenged their fundamental understanding of the law by questioning their focus on their own ritual purity while ignoring the spiritually sick among the covenant people. As in the hostile reaction in the synagogue in Nazareth, Jesus likened His hearers to the wicked Israelites who "transgressed the covenant: there have they dealt treacherously against me" (Hosea 6:7). His critique of His questioners was not generic but was individually tailored for their own pride and assurance in their own righteousness and their ability to distinguish themselves from the less holy.

In using these words of Hosea, Jesus suggested that His questioners, like the wicked Israelites, were misunderstanding God's will as they placed their self-justifying obedience over compassion for the less obedient. "For I desired mercy, and not sacrifice; and the knowledge of God more than burnt offerings" (Hosea 6:6). Christ challenged the righteousness of the scribes and Pharisees as being based on "sacrifice" and "burnt offerings" rather than on "mercy" and "the knowledge of God." Embedded in the context of the quotation is a prophetic critique of the ultimate lack of depth and staying power of self-justifying righteousness: "O Judah, what shall I do unto thee? for your goodness is as a morning cloud, and as the early dew it goeth away" (Hosea 6:4). Although "by faith was the law of Moses given," Jesus is pointing here to "a more excellent way" (Ether 12:11), a kind of compassionate righteousness that exceeds "the righteousness of the scribes and Pharisees" (Matthew

5:20). He is pointing to a righteousness that is based on a response to the mercy of God rather than on the belief that we can be justified and saved by our own obedience to the law.

Another scene of opposition to Jesus' table-fellowship practice and His subsequent questioning of the questioners is found in Luke 15, where again the "the Pharisees and scribes murmured, saying, This man receiveth sinners, and eateth with them" (Luke 15:2). Their murmuring against His action reflects the Pharisees' understanding of holiness that is maintained through table-fellowship. For the Pharisees, those who kept the ritual cleanness of the priests in their homes allowed the holiness of the temple to reside in the home. They did not seek to be exclusive; instead, they wanted all Jews to have their homes be as temples if they would follow the laws in the Torah for the ritual cleanliness of the priests officiating at the temple. But to keep this level of holiness, it was required that they eat only with others who were equally obedient.

Jesus responded to their critique of His eating with sinners with the parable of the ninety-nine sheep that are safe and the one sheep that is lost in the wilderness. Here, the imagery of a lost, vulnerable sheep replaces His earlier explanation of eating with the sinners as ministering to the sick who need a physician, but the challenge to the spiritual caretakers remains the same. Although their question was based on their understanding that table-fellowship would make their tables as holy as the temple altar, Jesus was challenging them to look to an even higher vision of holiness. Just as Hosea had challenged the wicked Israelites to seek "the knowledge of God" rather than merely the temple worship of "burnt offerings" (Hosea 6:6), here Jesus drew on the imagery of God's care for His covenant people as shepherd as a challenge to those spiritual leaders who would be holy (see Ezekiel 34:11–12, 16).

Jesus taught that the Good Shepherd was the model for spiritual leaders. His use of the Parable of the Ninety and Nine suggests that in their focus on their own holiness in table-fellowship, they were, instead, following the example of the ancient "shepherds of Israel" (see Ezekiel 34:2) who, concerned for their own advantage, ignored those who were lost.[16] His rebuke carries with it an invitation to a higher way but, as with all spiritual correction, opens up the possibility of resentment and defensiveness in the hearer.[17]

Not Fasting

A related food practice that came under criticism is the question of why, unlike the disciples of the Pharisees and of John, Christ's disciples did not fast. In all the synoptics, this scene appears directly after the meal in which, accused of eating with publicans and sinners, Jesus responds that the sick need a physician (see Matthew 9:10–17; Mark 2:15–22; Luke 5:29–39). Jesus was questioned by "the disciples of John and of the Pharisees" (Mark 2:18),[18] who "said unto him, Why do the disciples of John fast often, and make prayers, and likewise the disciples of the Pharisees; but thine eat and drink?" (Luke 5:33). It is not clear that the Pharisees' fasting was different from that of other Jews, but fasting was part of the

---

[16] The prophet Ezekiel had been commanded to "prophesy against the shepherds of Israel, prophesy, and say unto them, Thus saith the Lord God unto the shepherds; Woe be to the shepherds of Israel that do feed themselves! should not the shepherds feed the flocks?" (Ezekiel 34:2). In this extended critique against the spiritual leaders of ancient times, the Lord tells them that they have ignored the lost sheep: "And they were scattered, because there is no shepherd: and they became meat to all the beasts of the field, when they were scattered. My sheep wandered through all the mountains, and upon every high hill: yea, my flock was scattered upon all the face of the earth, and none did search or seek after them" (Ezekiel 34:5–6.) This neglect of the lost is placed in direct contrast to the care given by Jehovah as the Good Shepherd: "For thus saith the Lord God; Behold, I, even I, will both search my sheep, and seek them out. As a shepherd seeketh out his flock in the day that he is among his sheep that are scattered; so will I seek out my sheep, and will deliver them out of all places where they have been scattered in the cloudy and dark day. . . . I will seek that which was lost, and bring again that which was driven away (Ezekiel 34:11–12, 16).

[17] An important examination of the role of defensiveness and resentment in hardening hearts can be found in LDS scholar Terry Warner's *Bonds That Make Us Free: Healing Our Relationships, Coming to Ourselves* (Salt Lake City: Shadow Mountain, 2001).

[18] In Mark 2:18, it is the disciples of John and of the Pharisees. In Matthew 9:14, it is the disciples of John coming to Jesus and asking. In Luke 5:35, the antecedent is unclear; it might still be the scribes and publicans.

law, and the Pharisees saw obedience to this aspect of the law, as well as to other parts of the law, as a means of exhibiting righteousness. We have the illustration from Jesus' Parable of the Pharisee and Publican in which "the Pharisee stood and prayed thus with himself, God, I thank thee, that I am not as other men are, extortioners, unjust, adulterers, or even as this publican. I fast twice in the week, I give tithes of all that I possess" (Luke 18:11–12).

In Jesus' teaching on this parable, the Pharisees' "fasting oft" and other works of righteousness are not condemned. He is not teaching us to become sinners like the publican but is showing that how we relate to God at any particular moment—in pride or in humility—is more important than what we have done. The publican "went down to his house justified rather than the other: for every one that exalteth himself shall be abased; and he that humbleth himself shall be exalted" (Luke 18:14). As Alma warned his son Shiblon, "Do not say: O God, I thank thee that we are better than our brethren; but rather say: O Lord, forgive my unworthiness, and remember my brethren in mercy—yea, acknowledge your unworthiness before God at all times" (Alma 38:14). The hidden danger for the righteous, as illustrated by the Pharisees, is pride.

The issue of fasting did not come up repeatedly, and this incident did not escalate into hostility; but it did signal a difference in practice that was noted by observers. The question of how to worship and how to be holy was brought here to Jesus, and He responded in a reference to His special status as the bridegroom at a wedding feast (see Mark 2:19–20).

Not Washing Hands

As the Gospel narratives proceed, an escalation in hostility to Jesus can be seen in the new questions that were raised. In the earlier issues of eating with sinners and not fasting, questions were raised about His and His disciples' practice, but there was no immediate reaction to Jesus' calling the questioners' own priorities into question. I believe, however, that in the inquiries about not washing hands, we may be able to see an escalation of hostility toward Jesus. The earlier comments about eating with publicans and sinners may have implied that these others' ritual uncleanness would diminish the holiness of Jesus and His disciples. In the challenge about not washing hands, they were accused of not being holy by not living up to the Pharisaic interpretation of how to bring the temple's holiness to every house in Israel. In Matthew 15:1–20 and Mark 7:1–23, we learn of the Pharisees' care in maintaining this understanding of ritual purity; the question was put to Jesus about why His disciples did not also follow "the tradition of the elders" in this regard (Matthew 15:2; Mark 7:3).

Although the order of the comments differs in the two Gospels, the points that Jesus made concur. He took on the issue of the authority of the "tradition of the elders" (Matthew 15:2; Mark 7:3) by illustrating with the practice of corban how obedience can be a justification for not keeping the commandments (Matthew 15:3–6; Mark 7:9–13).[19] He also quoted Isaiah's description of a hypocritical people and described it as a prophecy of His accusers (Matthew 15:7–9; Mark 7:6–8).

In Isaiah 29:13, the Lord describes a people who "draw near me with their mouth, and with their lips do honour me, but have removed their heart far from me, and their fear toward me is taught by the precept of men" (Isaiah 29:13). The emphasis is not simply on the lack of correlation between hearts and words but also on the fact that "their fear toward me is taught by the precept of men." This fits directly into Jesus' questioning the authority of the "tradition of the elders" and, in Mark, precedes His strong comment, "Laying aside the commandment of God, ye hold the tradition of men, as the washing of pots and cups: and many other such like things ye do. And he said unto them, Full well ye reject the commandment of God, that ye may keep your own tradition" (Mark 7: 8–9). In the

[19] For background on the practice of corban, see Max Wilcox, "Corban," in Freedman, *ABD*, 1:1134, and "Corban," in Geoffrey Bromily, ed., *The International Standard Bible Encyclopedia*, 1:772 (Grand Rapids, Mich.: Eerdmans, 1979).

version of Isaiah that Jesus quoted, the critique of false worship is particularly strong: "In vain they do worship me, teaching for doctrines the commandments of men" (Matthew 15:9; see also Mark 7:7).

In addition to this strong critique, the situation escalated as Jesus called "the multitude" (Matthew 15:10) or "all the people" (Mark 7:14) to Him and publicly taught that being defiled or impure is not a matter of what we take into ourselves. Instead, He taught, our concern should be on what we produce: "Not that which goeth into the mouth defileth a man; but that which cometh out of the mouth, this defileth a man" (Matthew 15:11). In teaching this "more excellent way" (see Ether 12:11), Jesus also directly and publicly refuted the authority and interpretation around which the Pharisees' understanding of holiness was built. It is not surprising, then, that at the end of Jesus' commentary, His disciples came "and said unto him, Knowest thou that the Pharisees were offended, after they heard this saying?" (Matthew 15:12).

Jesus reserved the fuller explanation of His teaching for the disciples—outside the public sphere. He taught them that "those things which proceed out of the mouth come forth from the heart; and they defile the man. For out of the heart proceed evil thoughts, murders, adulteries, fornications, thefts, false witness, blasphemies: These are the things which defile a man: but to eat with unwashen hands defileth not a man" (Matthew 15:18–20). Although the directness of this teaching against the Pharisees' traditions was not made in public, the teaching to the multitude had earlier ended with Jesus' famous statement, "If any man have ears to hear, let him hear" (Mark 7:16). In listening defensively to Jesus' teaching on holiness, the Pharisees had ears to hear the rebuke—but not the invitation. As they sought to preserve their authority as interpreters of the law and their own sense of personal justification through obedience to their interpretation, this exchange developed into an escalation in the Pharisees' hostility toward Jesus.

A similar incident is recorded in Luke 11:37–54 in which the questioning of Jesus' practice is turned around and He calls the Pharisees into question. In this scene, it is not the practice of the disciples but of Jesus Himself that is challenged. "A certain Pharisee besought him to dine with him: and he went in, and sat down to meat. And when the Pharisee saw it, he marvelled that he had not first washed before dinner" (Luke 11:37–38). In response to this questioning of His breach of the "tradition of the elders," Jesus began an extensive critique of the danger of disguising the inner self with outward righteousness. These comments touch on several practices associated with the Pharisees' program of holiness: "[making] clean the outside of the cup and the platter; but your inward part is full of ravening and wickedness" (Luke 11:39), and being exacting in tithes by "[tithing] mint and rue and all manner of herbs, and [passing] over judgment and the love of God" (Luke 11:42). As in Matthew 23 where similar critiques appear, these comments were not framed as an attack on the Pharisees' practices but rather focused on what they yet lacked (see Matthew 19:20). Concerning "judgment and the love of God," Jesus said, "These ought ye to have done, and not to leave the other undone" (Luke 11:42).

As with the incident of conflict over eating with unwashed hands found in Matthew and Mark, Christ's chastisement of the Pharisees led to heightened tension. We learn that "as he said these things unto them, the scribes and the Pharisees began to urge him vehemently, and to provoke him to speak of many things: Laying wait for him, and seeking to catch something out of his mouth, that they might accuse him" (Luke 11:53–54). Because ritual purity was central to the Pharisees' understanding of how to live the law of Moses, we can understand the Pharisees' opposition to other practices. But this hostility toward Jesus was neither fixed earlier as a part of their program nor was it a given result of the experiences they had with Him. Instead, we see, as in a mirror, our own universal response to chastisement when we respond with pride rather than humility.

Sabbath Holiness and Developing Hostility

To understand the important role of the Sabbath among the Jews in first-century Palestine, we need to be able to read obedience to the Sabbath both as a sign to God of commitment to the covenant and also as a sign of separation from encroaching Hellenistic culture.[20] Violation of the boundaries of the Sabbath threatened those commitments and suggested a rejection of God's authority. Although intertestamental and rabbinic literature testify to the regulations that were developed to clarify what was required in this commitment, different sects disagreed both among and within themselves over how to resolve certain questions.[21] By the time of the Mishnah, the prohibitions were divided into thirty-nine main tasks that were prohibited.[22] Although even among the Pharisees there were different schools of interpretation regarding different questions,[23] the general body of Sabbath-day-observance expectations was likely shared by all.[24]

To understand the situations in which the observance of the Sabbath was associated with the increasing hostility to Jesus, we need not sort through all the evidence on differences over Sabbath observance. It is, however, essential to understand that there were a few widely agreed-on actions that could appropriately be done on the Sabbath. Recognizing that there was a contemporary notion that some commandments superseded the Sabbath is important because it was this issue that Jesus and His accusers discussed.

---

[20] "The picture of the Sabbath gained from Jewish sources is confirmed and amplified by the NT writings" (Kittell and Friedrich, *TDNT*, 7:20). On the Sabbath, see E. P. Sanders, *Jewish Law from Jesus to the Mishnah: Five Studies* (London: SCM Press; Philadelphia: Trinity Press International, 1990), 6–23.

[21] On the Pharisees' and Sadducees' disagreement over the *erub*, a means used by the Pharisees of broadening the definition of a house on the Sabbath day to avoid violation of the law, see Sanders, *Jewish Law from Jesus to the Mishnah*, 8–9. Sanders also gives a good overview of the much stricter regulations in defining things as work among the Essenes; Sanders, *Jewish Law from Jesus to the Mishnah*, 8.

[22] Kittell and Friedrich, *TDNT*, 12.

[23] The schools of Hillel and Shammai both had Sabbath observance rulings that disagreed. See Sanders, *Jewish Law from Jesus to the Mishnah*, 9–12.

[24] See Sanders, *Jewish Law from Jesus to the Mishnah*, 16.

Work that was understood to supersede the observance of the Sabbath included the offerings of the priests at the temple,[25] the performing of circumcision if the Sabbath was the eighth day after a boy was born, and caring for the sick who were in mortal danger.

Initial opposition to Jesus and His disciples came as they crossed these boundaries. The issue that seems to have provoked the hostile reactions, however, was the Savior's question to the Pharisees' challenge: What supersedes the Sabbath or, in other words, Where is holiness—in the law or in the lawgiver? For example, was rejection of God's authority found in the breaking of the Sabbath as interpreted by contemporary religious leaders, or was it in neglecting the needs of God's covenant people?

Plucking Grain on the Sabbath

The first incident of Sabbath violation occurred when Jesus "went through the corn fields; and his disciples plucked the ears of corn, and did eat, rubbing them in their hands. And certain of the Pharisees said unto them, Why do ye that which is not lawful to do on the sabbath days?" (Luke 6:1–2; see also Matthew 12:1–2; Mark 2:23–24).[26] Jesus defended the Sabbath-day-observance question by comparing this action to David's eating of the shewbread at the temple, "which is not lawful to eat but for the priests, and gave also to them which were with him" (Mark 2:26).[27] The analogy put Him in a position of comparison with the quintessential king of Israel. In

---

[25] The Damascus document limits this to the Sabbath burnt offering. Kittel and Friedrich, *TDNT*, 7:14

[26] Mark and Matthew omit the "certain of" the Pharisees, leaving it more generic. The action of harvesting, which is understood here by the Pharisees as unlawful, is later listed as one of the main thirty-nine forbidden tasks in the Mishnah (see Kittel and Friedrich, *TDNT*, 7:12). Regarding taking another's agricultural produce to meet one's need, there is a provision in the law that "when thou comest into the standing corn of thy neighbour, then thou mayest pluck the ears with thine hand; but thou shalt not move a sickle unto thy neighbour's standing corn" (Deuteronomy 23:25).

[27] "Some rabb. [*sic*] took the view that David received the shewbread on the Sabbath when the old bread was always replaced by the new, Lv. 24:8. His breaking of the Sabbath was justified because on his flight from Saul he was in sorry straits and mortal danger supersedes the Sabbath" (Kittel and Friedrich, *TDNT*, 7:22).

Matthew 12:5, Jesus also made a comparison to how "the priests in the temple profane the sabbath, and are blameless."

So, Jesus had not only publicly done something conspicuously against the contemporary understanding of Sabbath observance, but He had also explained His action by, in effect, declaring Himself to be a king and a priest. His accusers did not question that these were legitimate examples of authority that superseded the Sabbath, but they likely were not pleased with Jesus' claim to be equivalent to them. But Jesus went even further in His assertion that holiness was not in the law itself but in the lawgiver. In both Mark and Luke, we have records of His comment that "the Son of man is Lord also of the sabbath" (Mark 2:28; Luke 6:5).

Mark also includes the famous and often-quoted passage that "the sabbath was made for man, and not man for the sabbath" (Mark 2:27). Taken out of context, this seems to imply that Jesus' primary concern was to humanize the law and make it bearable for individuals. Although today we may perceive the regulations that had developed about Sabbath observance as rigid and extreme, this concern of making the demands of Sabbath observance fit human needs was part of the contemporary interpretations.[28]

In Matthew, we learn more about Jesus' claim to be Lord of the Sabbath and the declaration that His holiness and authority superseded the law.[29] After Jesus commented that the priests were justified in working on the Sabbath, He then said, "But I say unto you, That in this place is one greater than the temple. But if ye had known what this meaneth, I will have mercy, and not sacrifice, ye would not have condemned the guiltless" (Matthew 12:6–7). Here

---

[28] Sanders notes that in doing so, the Pharisees themselves may have been seen as breaking the Sabbath by the Sadducees, who followed a more literal understanding of the Torah. Sanders, *Jewish Law from Jesus to the Mishnah*, 9.

[29] In the scholarly literature, there is a wide range of opinions about how the "Son of Man" passage is to be interpreted. For references to those who read it to say that as the "Son of Man" that "he is lord of the Sabbath, he decides on its confirmation or abrogation," see Frans Neirynck, "Jesus and the Sabbath: Some Observations on Mark II, 27," in *Jésus aux origins de la christologie*, ed. Jacques Dupont (Leuven: Leuven University/ Peeters, 1989), 244.

Jesus seems to have been alluding to the previous discussion in Matthew 9:13 where, in commenting on His eating with sinners as a physician caring for the sick, He said, "But go ye and learn what that meaneth, I will have mercy, and not sacrifice."

Here in Matthew 12, Jesus again addressed this fundamental question as to how God's law was to be understood. He challenged the Pharisees' interpretation of the law and their understanding of obedience alone as the source of holiness. He commented that it was their misinterpretation of the law that had led them to "have condemned the guiltless" (Matthew 12:7). He connected His statement "that in this place is one greater than the temple" with a true interpretation of the law. The concept of superseding the Sabbath is not new. The question is simply about what is important enough to do so.

I believe that, in conjunction with the comparison to the priests and to David, Jesus' claim to be greater than the temple would have had the sound of blasphemy. But this claim could have also been passed off as exaggeration or delusion by those who were not defensive. Although we do not have direct evidence of a hostile reaction within these texts, in the following scene in the synagogue, the actors seem to be the same ones; and by this point, they are clearly poised to find an offense with which "they might accuse him" (Mark 3:2).

Part of the explanation for the hostility that seems to be building lies not in Jesus' claim itself but in the response to it by His hearers. On the issue of where holiness is found, Jesus pointed away from the law and toward the lawgiver. We can, however, want holiness and authority to reside in the law itself because it is something we can control by proper interpretation and observance. When holiness and authority reside in the lawgiver, one cannot control but only worship and follow. Jesus again challenged the Pharisees' interpretation of the law upon which their entire program of holiness was built: "But if ye had known what this meaneth, I will have mercy, and not sacrifice, ye would not have condemned the guiltless" (Matthew 12:7). In challenging their interpretation, He also challenged their authority to gain position by interpreting for others as well as their ability to save themselves by obedience to the law alone.

Synagogue Healing of the Man with the Withered Hand

The following scene in the synagogue reads like a continuation of the conflict over the harvesting on the Sabbath. Luke 6:6 notes, however, that it was "on another sabbath, that he entered into the synagogue and taught" and there encountered "a man whose right hand was withered." Nonetheless, in Matthew, the connection between the scenes is suggested by the comment that from the confrontation, Jesus "went into *their* synagogue: and, behold, there was a man which had his hand withered. And they asked him, saying, Is it lawful to heal on the sabbath days? that they might accuse him" (Matthew 12:9–10; emphasis added).

The escalation in hostility leading up to this event is also suggested in Luke's comment that "the scribes and Pharisees watched him, whether he would heal on the sabbath day; that they might find an accusation against him" (Luke 6:7). In this climate of confrontation, Jesus' actions related not merely to the man with the withered hand but also to all present. Before performing any healing, Jesus questioned His questioners, again bringing them back to the issue of the interpretation of the law. The "scribes and Pharisees" believed that the law was on their side; and for them, the possibility of His healing was clearly anticipated as grounds for an accusation. A continued pattern of defiance of the Sabbath would show Jesus as unholy and a lawbreaker. He would be shown to violate not only the sanctity and separation created by purity laws but also the separation and holiness of the Sabbath.

In Mark and Luke, Jesus' question concerns the general purpose of the Sabbath: "I will ask you one thing; Is it lawful on the sabbath days to do good, or to do evil? to save life, or to destroy it?" (Luke 6:9; see also Mark 3:4). Mark fills in their response of silence: "But they held their peace" (Mark 3:4) and Jesus' understanding of their spiritual state: "He . . . looked round about on them with anger, being grieved for the hardness of their hearts" (Mark 3:5). Only then did "he saith unto the man, Stretch forth thine hand. And he stretched it out: and his hand was restored whole as the other" (Mark 3:5).[30]

As in the previous encounter over picking grain in the fields, the question of what supersedes the Sabbath comes to the front in these interactions. During this time, the law of the Sabbath was interpreted such that healing was limited to those in peril of death. That would not have applied in this instance, so in choosing to intervene and heal the man's withered hand, Jesus was also choosing to make a statement about the purpose and meaning of the Sabbath. By stressing that doing good and saving life are lawful on the Sabbath, He seems to have directly taken on the idea that it would be unholy to heal on the Sabbath.

Matthew records the exchange as starting with this same question being put to Jesus: "And they asked him, saying, Is it lawful to heal on the sabbath days? that they might accuse him" (Matthew 12:10). In response, Jesus asked who would not rescue a sheep from a pit, commenting, "How much then is a man better than a sheep? Wherefore it is lawful to do well on the sabbath days" (Matthew 12:12).[31] Again, there seems to be an implied critique as Jesus questions His questioners: What do you care more about, your property

---

[30] Sanders argues that because speaking was not considered work, no violation of the Sabbath occurred (*Jewish Law from Jesus to the Mishnah*, 21). He notes that in Luke 13:10–17, there is a synagogue healing scene that does involve the laying on of hands, but it is the ruler of the synagogue rather than the Pharisees who confronts Jesus. Sanders suggests that had Pharisees been there, they would not have backed down as easily (Sanders, *Jewish Law from Jesus to the Mishnah*, 22).

[31] The Damascus Document (CD) records a different view, presumably not that of most Jews of the time: "No man shall assist a beast to give birth on the Sabbath day. And if it should fall into a cistern or pit, he shall not lift it out on the Sabbath." G. Vermes, *The Dead Sea Scrolls in English* (Harmondsworth, England: Penguin Books, 1968), 113. There was also discussion on this question among the different schools, Kittell and Friedrich, *TDNT*, 7:25. See also Sanders, *Jewish Law from Jesus to the Mishnah*, 8.

or your fellowman? The conversation in Matthew reinterprets the condition of the man with the withered hand. Rather than seeing him abstractly as a man who is not in mortal peril and whose needs can be met on another day, instead, through the parallel with sheep, he becomes a genuine person. Note that Jesus set up the situation by asking, "What man shall there be among you, that shall have one sheep, and if it fall into a pit . . ." (Matthew 12:11). This sheep then becomes our sheep, our only sheep, and its well-being is vital for us. The man, by analogy, becomes our own and is precious to us. We can see him as God sees him. But if we know that we should see him this way and still do not act to help him, our hearts become increasingly hardened.

In all the Gospels, it is only after this conversation with those seeking to accuse Him that Jesus heals the man's withered hand. We have several indications in the text about how this particular group of Pharisees was growing in its hostility to Jesus through these interactions. We can read in Mark that Jesus looked out on them, "being grieved for the hardness of their hearts" (Mark 3:5). And every Gospel account reports that their response to Jesus' defiance of their challenge and defense of His actions enraged His hearers and further escalated their hostility toward Him: "Then the Pharisees went out, and held a council against him, how they might destroy him" (Matthew 12:14). "And the Pharisees went forth, and straightway took counsel with the Herodians against him, how they might destroy him" (Mark 3:6). "And they were filled with madness; and communed one with another what they might do to Jesus" (Luke 6:11).

Healing of the Man with Dropsy at the Pharisees' Sabbath Meal

In Luke 14, we find a scene similar to the healing of the man with the withered hand at the synagogue. In this passage, we learn that "as [Jesus] went into the house of one of the chief Pharisees to eat bread on the sabbath day, . . . they watched him" (Luke 14:1).

In this setting, a situation to do good arose because "there was a certain man before him which had the dropsy" (Luke 14:2). Jesus again proceeded first to ask the lawyers and Pharisees the question, just as the synagogue situation is described in Matthew and Mark: "Is it lawful to heal on the sabbath day?" (Luke 14:3). Also, just as in the synagogue, "they held their peace" (Luke 14:4); then Jesus proceeded to heal the man.

Before He acted in a way they clearly would have understood as being contrary to the law, He allowed them to judge the situation and the individual present before them. Then, given their unwillingness to either defend their understanding of the law or speak in favor of action on behalf of the individual, Jesus presented a further teaching about the law, again a parallel to the teaching in the synagogue: "Which of you shall have an ass or an ox fallen into a pit, and will not straightway pull him out on the sabbath day?" (Luke 14:5). In response to this question, we are told, "They could not answer him again to these things" (Luke 14:6). Unlike the passages describing the synagogue healing, this passage presents no direct evidence of hostility. The comment that "they watched him" (Luke 14:1) conveys a slight feeling of wariness, but no individuals are introduced that seek to do Jesus any harm; instead, they are present as His hosts. It may be that "the lawyers and Pharisees" (Luke 14:3) in this scene did not feel threatened by Jesus' teaching and action but were considering its merit. It may be that they did not feel as though they were being called into question and so did not feel threatened. It may be that this passage reflects differences in response among different Pharisees.

Healing of the Man Born Blind

The account of the man born blind found in John 9 depicts one of the classic scenes of Sabbath healing. The Pharisees come into the story when the neighbors take to them the man who is healed. Although making clay would have clearly been against the Sabbath regulations of the time, this scene depicts a difference of opinion among the Pharisees in how to judge the lawfulness of the act or the holiness of Jesus: "Therefore said some of the Pharisees, This man is not of God, because he keepeth not the sabbath day. Others said, How can a man that is a sinner do such miracles? And there was a division among them" (John 9:16).

In addition to illustrating that in these passages of Sabbath observance, we are not dealing with a monolithic Pharisaical bloc, we can also see a classic example of how Jesus' teachings against the Pharisees underscored His fundamental challenge to their model of holiness. As mentioned before, one of our greatest challenges as righteous, law-abiding people is to recognize that we have sins. If observing the law becomes our sense of justification before God, admitting that we are flawed will not be an option. Then, at all costs, we will exactly keep the law and judge others who do not. In this scene, Jesus commented on this common mortal outlook by returning to sickness and physical disability as an image for sin.

The Pharisees who accused Jesus of being "a sinner" (John 9:24) took pride that they were the disciples of Moses (John 9:28). After the man's defense of Jesus, he was cast out by Pharisees who judged him to be "born in sins" (John 9:34). When Jesus found the man and he believed on Him, Jesus declared His mission to him: "For judgment I am come into this world, that they which see not might see; and that they which see might be made blind" (John 9:39). This paradoxical saying seems to have caught the attention of "some of the Pharisees which were with him" because they "heard these words, and said unto him, Are we blind also?" (John 9:40). Here lies the overarching teaching of Jesus in relation to the Pharisees' vision of holiness and their confidence in their own righteousness: "Jesus said unto them, If ye were blind, ye should have no sin: but now ye say, We see; therefore your sin remaineth" (John 9:41). The great danger of pride is that, in so believing in ourselves, we fail to really believe in Christ. Being confident that we can be justified by law is to refuse to admit that we need a Savior (see 2 Nephi 2:5–6).

Developed Hostility and the Last Months of Jesus' Life

The hostility evident at the end of the Savior's life had escalated over an extended period of time. As we have seen, the Pharisees initially opposed practices involving violations of ritual purity and standards of Sabbath-day observance. This opposition would have naturally grown out of their understanding of how to follow the law of Moses. As their questions to Jesus were met with His questions of their own holiness of heart, the initial opposition sometimes changed into hostility. Although the opposition can be understood with reference to the historical context and background of those involved, the feelings of hostility have a more universal root. As with all of us, chastisement provides an opportunity for feelings of offense to develop. Those who responded with defensiveness also began to develop hostility.

In the closing months of Jesus' life, the growing hostility was translated into action, most evident when He appeared in Jerusalem. It is difficult to know the connections among all the people in the different scenes. It may be that the Pharisees in Galilee did not have strong connections in Jerusalem. It may be that even within the scenes set in Galilee or Jerusalem, there were different actors with diverse views on Jesus. It does seem, though, that by this later period, the sense of being wronged (either directly or by extension) and its related hostility were associated with Pharisees, Sadducees, and the chief priests. In the later scenes, Jesus was either provoked with the hope that His statements would discredit Him or there were direct threats on His life.

At the Feast of Tabernacles (or Sukkot) in John 7, we see that "the Pharisees heard that the people murmured such things concerning him; and the Pharisees and the chief priests sent officers to take him" (John 7:32). It is also at this point that the chief priests appeared as adversaries. The length of this chapter is too short to develop their agenda and concerns in any depth.[32] Jesus' challenge

---

[32] See Jeffrey Chadwick's "The Jerusalem Temple, the Sadducees, and the Opposition to Jesus," in *The Life and Teachings of Jesus Christ: From Bethlehem through the*

to the chief priests' authority and reputation can be seen in His earlier cleansing of the temple.[33] It is not likely that they were normally allied with the Pharisees because the Pharisees' sectarian program of holiness was centered outside the temple. But their willingness to work together against Jesus suggests that, for both, their hostility to Him exceeded their likely wariness of each other. The chief priests would have had the political and social status, as well as the temple guards, to take these actively hostile measures.

We can see that the feeling of being threatened came to be formulated in political terms by the last months of Jesus' ministry. It is not clear from the historical evidence that the Romans did see Jesus as a threat, but it is important to understand the pressures that the elite of the Jews were under. They were an occupied people, ruled by the Romans in Judea and a Roman-supported ruler in Galilee. Although the different sectarian groups had found varying strategies to negotiate the political and social pressures of Roman rule and Hellenization, it was in nobody's interest to lose what political and religious autonomy they had.

So it is not a great surprise when we read that, after the reports of the raising of Lazarus had reached the Pharisees, "then gathered the chief priests and the Pharisees a council, and said, What do we? for this man doeth many miracles. If we let him thus alone, all men will believe on him: and the Romans shall come and take away both our place and nation" (John 11:47–48). It may or may not have been an accurate fear, but it was an understandable one in light of the fragile political situation they all faced. The sense of

---

Sermon on the Mount, ed. Richard Neitzel Holzapfel and Thomas A. Wayment (Salt Lake City: Deseret Book, 2005), 1:48–88 for an argument for their central role in opposition to Jesus.

[33] John 2:13–17. The "Jews'" reaction to Jesus' actions in healing the lame man in John 5:1–16 at Bethesda may also be seen as a reaction in Jerusalem to His earlier cleansing of the temple, just as the healing of the paralytic man lowered from the roof (Mark 2:3–12) may also have been a prelude to hostility in Galilee. See S. Kent Brown, "The Arrest," in *From the Last Supper through the Resurrection: The Savior's Final Hours*, ed. Richard Neitzel Holzapfel and Thomas A. Wayment (Salt Lake City: Deseret Book, 2003), 166–67.

shared threat again may help explain why the chief priests and Pharisees were working together.

The prophetic statement of Caiaphas, who unknowingly testified of the Atonement, was also a clear statement of Jesus' opponents' feeling of justification in moving toward His death. Caiaphas said, "It is expedient for us, that one man should die for the people, and that the whole nation perish not" (John 11:49–50). The subtle escalation of hostility from offense at being challenged and rebuked had grown to the point at which they associated not just their own well-being but also the survival of their nation on eliminating this threat. By the last months of Jesus' life, the political and religious elite felt justified in working toward His demise: "From that day forth they took counsel together for to put him to death." (John 11:53)

By the final Passover of Jesus' life, the plans had been laid. Although He had evaded being captured or discredited on previous trips to Jerusalem, efforts were now focused to bring closure to what the leaders by this time had convinced themselves was a dangerous threat to the people for whom they had responsibility. The elite's hostility was not limited to isolated gatherings but had coalesced into a plan for action that was well known among the pilgrims coming to Jerusalem for the festival: "The Jews' passover was nigh at hand: and many went out of the country up to Jerusalem before the passover, to purify themselves. Then sought they for Jesus, and spake among themselves, as they stood in the temple, What think ye, that he will not come to the feast? Now both the chief priests and the Pharisees had given a commandment, that, if any man knew where he were, he should shew it, that they might take him" (John 11:55–57). From here, the hostility of the elite would drive events in the last week of Jesus' mortal ministry.

VI.

MARY, MARTHA, AND LAZARUS

GAYE STRATHEARN

Now Jesus loved Martha,
and her sister [Mary], and Lazarus.
JOHN 11:5

Only the Gospels of Luke and John recount Jesus' interaction with the remarkable family of Mary, Martha, and Lazarus. John tells us that they lived in Bethany (John 11:1), a small village 1.75 miles away from Jerusalem and on the eastern side of the Mount of Olives.[1] All the Gospels, except Luke, indicate that Jesus lodged in Bethany during His final week (Matthew 21:17; Mark 11:1; John 11:1, 18), perhaps staying at the home of these dear friends for part of that pivotal time. According to the JST (John 11:17) and some late New Testament manuscripts, the house in Bethany belonged to Martha,[2] which suggests that she may have been the oldest in the family and may also have been a woman of some means, perhaps a widow.

---

[1] John 11:18 notes that Bethany was "about fifteen furlongs (*stadia*)" from Jerusalem. One *stadion* was equivalent to approximately 606.75 feet (176 meters) or 0.11 mile. Luke does not name the village in which they lived (Luke 10:38).

[2] The following manuscripts include the phrase "into her house" at the end of Luke 10:38: Alexandrinus (A), Bezae (D), Freer (W), Koridethi (Θ), Athous Laurae (Ψ), etc. The phrase is omitted in some early manuscripts: Chester Beatty Papyrus (P^{45}), Bodmer Papyrus XV (P^{75}), and codex Vaticanus (B).

Luke 10:38–42

"Now it came to pass, as they went, that he entered into a certain village: and a certain woman named Martha received him into her house. And she had a sister called Mary, which also sat at Jesus' feet, and heard his word. But Martha was cumbered about much serving, and came to him, and said, Lord, dost thou not care that my sister hath left me to serve alone? bid her therefore that she help me. And Jesus answered and said unto her, Martha, Martha, thou art careful and troubled about many things: But one thing is needful: and Mary hath chosen that good part, which shall not be taken away from her."

For many women, in particular, this passage can elicit strong emotional responses.[3] What is the role of women as followers of Jesus Christ? When I was a young adult, I heard a woman in my Relief Society say that she was a Mary—not a Martha. She was clearly referring to our passage where Mary was the one sitting at the Savior's feet listening to Him, while Martha was presumably working in the kitchen. When I heard that saying, I immediately felt myself nodding and thinking to myself that I too was a Mary rather than a Martha. Such conclusions are modern versions of Augustine's interpretation that valued women's discipleship in terms of a contemplative rather than active life.[4] In the intervening years, as I have studied this text and those found in John's Gospel, I have come to a very different conclusion. I am both Mary and Martha. In addition, I have learned that although Mary and

[3] Frances Taylor Gench, *Back to the Well: Women's Encounters with Jesus in the Gospels* (Louisville, Ky.: Westminster/John Knox Press, 2004), 56; Veronica Koperski, "Women and Discipleship in Luke-Acts," in J. Verheyden, ed., *The Unity of Luke-Acts*, Bibliotheca ephemeridum theologicarum lovaniensium, 142 (Leuven: Leuven University Press, 1999), 517–19; Margaret Guenther, "Honoring Martha," *The Christian Century* 112, no. 21 (1995): 675; Loveday Alexander, "Sisters in Adversity: Retelling Martha's Story," in George J. Brooke, ed., *Women in the Biblical Tradition*, Studies in Women and Religion, 31 (Lewiston: The Edwin Mellen Press, 1992), 167–68; Evelyn T. Marshall, "Mary and Martha—Faithful Sisters, Devoted Disciples," *Ensign*, January 1987, 28–31.

[4] Augustine, *The Trinity* 1.10.20 and *Sermon on the Mount* 53.1–54.4.

Martha are women, the lessons of this story transcend gender and are equally incumbent upon both men and women.[5]

To appreciate the beauty and complexity of Luke 10:38–42, readers must be prepared to see it as more than an isolated snapshot—but also as one segment of a larger, detailed tapestry. It must be placed in the larger context of Luke's Gospel, both the Gospel as a whole, particularly the Travel Narrative (Luke 9:53–19:27),[6] and the Parable of the Good Samaritan that immediately precedes our story.

Jesus as an Itinerant Preacher

Luke 8:1–3 sets up two important issues that are critical for our understanding of Luke 10:38–42. It reads: "And it came to pass afterward, that [Jesus] went throughout every city and village, preaching and shewing the glad tidings of the kingdom of God: and the twelve were with him, And certain women, which had been healed of evil spirits and infirmities, Mary called Magdalene, out of whom went seven devils, and Joanna the wife of Chuza Herod's steward, and Susanna, and many others, which ministered unto him of their substance." First, we learn that as Jesus traveled throughout Galilee, He was accompanied by a number of women who "ministered (*diakoneo*) unto him of their substance" (Luke 8:2–3). It is important that we see Jesus' visit to Martha's home within the context of His reliance on the hospitality of others.

Throughout the Savior's public ministry, He was an itinerant preacher. As far as we know, He owned no house and was not

---

[5] Adele Reinhartz notes that "the evangelist's narrative purpose is not to describe the ideal female disciple in particular, but to illustrate his views on discipleship in general." ("From Narrative to History: The Resurrection of Mary and Martha," in Amy-Jill Levine, ed., *"Women Like This": New Perspectives on Jewish Women in the Greco-Roman World*, Society of Biblical Literature: Early Judaism and Its Literature (Atlanta: Scholars Press, 1991), 171; see also Dallin H. Oaks, "Spirituality," *Ensign*, November 1985, 61).

[6] Warren Carter, "Getting Martha out of the Kitchen: Luke 10:38-42 Again," *The Catholic Biblical Quarterly* 58 (1996): 266–67.

employed in a trade.[7] Although those who heard Him preach in Nazareth asked, "Is not this the carpenter (*tekton*)?"[8] (Mark 6:3), there is no evidence in the Gospel accounts that He plied His trade during His public ministry, unlike some of His disciples who periodically returned to fishing. Instead, He warned prospective disciples, "Foxes have holes, and birds of the air have nests; but the Son of man hath not where to lay his head" (Luke 9:58; see also Matthew 8:20). We also learn from His time in the wilderness that although He would later use His priesthood power to feed others, He refused to use it to satisfy His own physical needs (Luke 4:3–4; see also Matthew 4:3–4). Therefore, He relied heavily upon the generosity and hospitality of others (see Luke 7:36–50; 19:1–10).

At the beginning of chapter 10, we find Luke's account of the calling of the Seventy. Jesus directs them to "carry neither purse, nor scrip" (Luke 10:4), a notion highlighting the fact that not only Jesus but also His followers would rely on the generosity and hospitality of others. In fact, it was essential for Jesus' ongoing ministry that He and His servants had friends who opened their homes to them and fed them regularly. We must understand Jesus' visit to Martha's home within this context. He entered that home with the expectation of receiving hospitality while He was there.

Second, Luke 8:1–3 also highlights that both the Twelve and the women accompanied Jesus on His travels. This is consistent

---

[7] A number of places in Mark and Matthew link Jesus with "the house" when He is in Capernaum (Matthew 9:10, 28; 13:1, 36; 17:25; Mark 1:29; 2:1; 7:17; 9:33; 10:10). This house almost certainly refers to Peter's house and may be the place where Jesus lived. Mark 2:15 does say that Jesus "sat at meat in his house." It is unclear, however, whether the "his" refers to Jesus or to Levi. R. T. France argues that because "Mark nowhere else refers to the house in Capernaum . . . as Jesus' house, it is more likely that we should understand that Jesus went to a meal in Levi's house (as indeed Luke explicitly states [in Luke 5:29])." (*The Gospel of Mark*, The New International Greek Testament Commentary [Grand Rapids, Mich.: Eerdmans, 2002], 133).

[8] The Greek word *tekton* primarily refers to someone who works in wood, but it can also apply to craftsmen of other materials, such as stone or iron. See Chester Charlton McCown in Shirley Jackson Case, ed., *Studies in Early Christianity* (New York: The Century Co., 1928), 173–89; and Paul Hanly Furfey, "Christ as Tekton," *The Catholic Biblical Quarterly* 17 (1955): 204–15.

with Luke's broader goal to show the universality of the gospel message. In this instance, it emphasizes that Jesus extended the gospel and discipleship to both men and women.[9] The discipleship of the women is highlighted here because they actively ministered using their own resources.[10] It is significant that the Greek word for "ministering" here is *diakoneo.* This word often refers to the service of waiting on tables (Luke 4:39; 10:40; 12:37; 17:8; 22:26–27; Acts 6:2; Mark 10:45; John 12:2), but it also includes the broader sense of religious ministrations (Matthew 20:28; John 12:26; 2 Corinthians 3:3; 1 Peter 4:10–11). Luke 8:3 reminds us, therefore, that there is a cost involved in ministering. Whether that cost involves time, financial contributions, or hospitality, a disciple must consecrate himself or herself to the Lord. This interplay between ministering and consecration is at the heart of Luke's account of Jesus' interaction with Mary and Martha.

The Parable of the Good Samaritan

Luke clearly intended us to read and understand the story of Mary and Martha in concert with the Parable of the Good Samaritan. The repetition of the Greek indefinite pronoun *tis* in chapter 10 verses 25 (a certain lawyer), 30 (a certain man), and 38 (a certain woman) links the two stories. Thus, the author "pairs male and female figures in his interpretation of the two great commandments."[11] Although it is not my intent to discuss this parable in

---

[9] Other examples include Luke's description of the nativity from Mary's perspective (Luke 1:5–2:7, which is in contrast to Matthew's description from Joseph's point of view [Matthew 1:18–25]), his inclusion of male and female pairings such as Simeon and Anna at the temple (Luke 2:25–38), Simon and the woman who anointed Jesus' feet (Luke 7:36–50), and the seeming omnipresence of the women at the cross and the tomb (Luke 23:49–24:24).

[10] Joel B. Green suggests that these women were single, "not because married women had no resources but because single women would have been in an easier position to dispose of their resources as they saw fit" (*The Gospel of Luke*, The New International Commentary on the New Testament [Grand Rapids, Mich.: Eerdmans, 1997], 319).

[11] Gench, *Back to the Well*, 57–58. Contrast Joseph Fitzmyer, who argues, "It [the story of Mary and Martha] is an episode unrelated to the preceding passages" (*The*

detail, I do want to highlight the fact that Luke's intent in bringing these two stories together was to teach his readers that the discipleship needed to inherit eternal life centers on the two great commandments to love God and to love our neighbors. Jesus recites the parable in response to the lawyer's question, "Who is my neighbor?" (Luke 10:29), and a number of scholars have shown that the story of Mary and Martha, which immediately follows the parable, is a discussion on the first commandment to love God.[12] It seems to me, however, that the issue is more complicated.

The story of Mary and Martha speaks to both of the great commandments. Martha's service in ministering to the itinerant Jesus is just as important an example of loving her neighbor as was the Good Samaritan's actions in taking care of the wounded man. Instead of taking Him to an inn and leaving money for His care, Martha invited Jesus into her home and personally tended to His needs. The message that Luke portrays here is not Jesus' criticism of Martha's living the second commandment but rather His effort to reach out and raise her discipleship to the next level. Although the second commandment is necessary in the quest for eternal life, it is not sufficient. Disciples must also evidence their commitment to the command to "love the Lord thy God with all thy heart, and with all thy soul, and with all thy strength, and with all thy mind" (Luke 10:27).

Jesus Enters Martha's Home (Luke 10:38–42)

In discussing the events that took place in Martha's home, I will examine some textual issues before turning to interpretive issues. Textually, the important areas come from both the Joseph Smith

Gospel According to Luke X–XXIV, The Anchor Bible, 28A [Garden City, N.Y.: Doubleday, 1985], 891).

[12] Gench, *Back to the Well*, 57; Charles H. Talbert, *Reading Luke: A Literary and Theological Commentary on the Third Gospel* (New York: Crossroad, 1982), 120–26; Ben Witherington, *Women in the Ministry of Jesus: A Study of Jesus' Attitudes to Women and their Roles as Reflected in His Earthly Life*, Society for New Testament Studies Monograph Series, 51 (Cambridge: Cambridge University Press, 1984), 100.

Translation and ancient textual witnesses. All these changes have an impact on how we can understand the meaning of our passage.

The Joseph Smith Translation makes a change in verse 38. It reads: "Now it came to pass, as they went, they [instead of 'he'] entered into a certain village." This emendation seems to be an effort by the Prophet Joseph to harmonize with the plural form of the previous clause and shows that it was the group traveling with Jesus who entered Martha's home, not just Jesus. Although a small change, it would make a significant difference to Martha whether she was inviting an individual or a group into her home.

The remaining textual variants come from ancient sources. With verse 39, there are two textual readings. One reads, "And she had a sister called Mary, and she was sitting at the Lord's feet." Many modern English versions follow this reading.[13] Yet other ancient texts read, "And she had a sister called Mary who *also* sat at the Lord's feet" (emphasis added).[14] This is the reading followed by the King James Bible. The difference between the readings is the inclusion or absence of the relative pronoun *he,* Greek "also."[15] The change in meaning is significant. The absence of the relative pronoun emphasizes only Mary's interest in the Lord's teachings. The inclusion, however, indicates that Martha had a history of sitting at the Lord's feet and being instructed by Him.[16] Textually, it is difficult to make a firm decision about which of these two readings is original, although the Chester Beatty and Bodmer papyri slightly favor its omission. However, it is possible that the scribes of these early texts removed the relative pronoun because of the

---

[13] For example, see the Revised Standard Version, NIV, Revised English Bible, New American Bible, NJB, NRSV, and Contemporary English Version.

[14] Codices Sinaiticus (ℵ), A, B*, Ephraemi (C), D, W, Q, Y.

[15] It is omitted in texts such as the Chester Beatty (P^{45}) and Bodmer (P^{75}) papyri, the codices Sinaiticus (ℵ*), B^2, Regius (L), Zacynthius (X), the miniscule manuscript 579, and a few others (UBS). The codex Sinaiticus is mentioned in both lists because the relative pronoun was originally in the text but then was corrected by the scribe. In the case of codex Vaticanus, a second scribe has removed it from the text.

[16] John Nolland, *Luke 9:21–18:34*, Word Biblical Commentary, 35B (Dallas: Word Books, 1993), 599–600.

incongruity they envisioned between Martha sitting at Jesus' feet and the conversation that she has with Him.[17] This incongruity, however, would be valid only if the snapshot recorded by Luke were a complete description of all that happened in Martha's home that day. The interpretive significance of including the relative pronoun is that it shows that Martha, not just Mary, was a disciple who cared deeply about what Jesus had to say. This interpretation, I believe, is consistent with the Greek reading in verse 40 and also with Martha's portrayal of events in John 11. I will return to both of these issues later in the chapter.

The third textual issue comes from verse 42, where there is a variety of different readings, indicating that the ancient scribes struggled with the meaning of this verse.[18] The earliest and best manuscripts read that "one thing is needful,"[19] but one manuscript reads, "but a few things are necessary."[20] Even though the latter reading has limited textual support, it should not "be dismissed out of hand."[21] A number of good manuscripts have a conflated reading, "a few things are necessary, or one,"[22] which strengthens the possibility that the latter reading has a claim to originality.

---

[17] Mary Rose D'Angelo, "Women Partners in the New Testament," *Journal of Feminist Studies in Religion* 16, no. 1 (Spring 1990): 78–79.

[18] For a discussion with all the variants, see I. Howard Marshall, *The Gospel of Luke: A Commentary of the Greek Text*, The New International Greek Testament Commentary (Grand Rapids, Mich.: Eerdmans, 1978), 452–54.

[19] P^{45}, P^{75}, and Codices Ephraemi Rescriptus* (C*), W, Q, etc.

[20] Manuscript 38.

[21] Marshall, *The Gospel of Luke*, 453.

[22] P^{3}, B, C^{2}, Codex Regius (L), and 33, etc. This reading does not make good sense, so it should be understood as a conflation of the two readings. Against this view, see Gordon D. Fee, "'One Thing Is Needful'?, Luke 10:42," in Eldon Jay Epp and Gordon D. Fee, eds., *New Testament Textual Criticism: Its Significance for Exegesis* (Oxford: Clarendon Press, 1981), 61–75. He claims that the lack of strong textual support for the "a few things" and *lectio difficilior* suggest that the combined reading should be preferred. His arguments highlight the textual difficulty of this passage. I am more persuaded, however, by Bruce M. Metzger's position that the "variations seem to have arisen from understanding eJno/ß [*henos*] to refer merely to the provisions that Martha was then preparing for the meal; the absoluteness of eJno/ß was softened by replacing it with ojli/gwn [*oligon*]" (*A Textual Commentary on the Greek New Testament* [London: United Bible Societies, 1971], 153–54).

The difference in meaning between the two readings is substantial. If the issue is about discipleship, then the "one thing" of being attentive to Jesus and His teachings is appropriate. If, however, the issue is hospitality, then Jesus is indicating to Martha that she does not need to prepare many dishes; just a few will suffice. The two different readings indicate that early scribes were themselves probably caught up in an "either/or" mode of interpretation, unsure if this was a story about discipleship or hospitality. What happens, however, if we recognize that both strands were intentionally woven into the story's fabric? The question no longer revolves around whether Jesus favors Mary or Martha.

With these contextual and text-critical issues in mind, we are now prepared to examine the meaning of the text. Luke wants his readers to recognize that Martha's act of receiving (*hypodechomai*) Jesus into her home (Luke 10:38) "involves much more than being supplied with food and drink; it primarily denotes the embracing of the disciples' mission and its eschatological reality."[23] Thus, Martha's action was in stark contrast to the Samaritans' reaction to him in Luke 9:53: "And they did not receive (*dechomai*) him, because his face was as though he would go to Jerusalem."

Jesus' ministry in Galilee was marked by the rejection of Chorazin, Bethsaida, and Capernaum (Luke 10:13–15). He was now traveling to Jerusalem, knowing that He would be rejected again and killed (Luke 9:22). In the midst of this rejection, Martha's decision to receive Jesus provided a safe haven, not only to be fed

[23] Carter, "Getting Martha out of the Kitchen," 267. Elisabeth Schüssler Fiorenza has argued that Martha's *diakonia* involved ecclesial leadership in her household church. (*But She Said: Feminist Practices of Biblical Interpretation* [Boston: Beacon Press, 1992], 62–68). But Turid Karlsen Seim has rightly cautioned against Fiorenza's assumptions. She has shown that in early Christian communities, there seems to have been a separation between those who were patrons for the community and those who were entrusted with leadership. "Even if Martha is a householder exercising hospitality, she is not to be understood automatically, in a presupposed 'subtext,' to have been the leader of a community" (*The Double Message: Patterns of Gender in Luke-Acts* [Nashville: Abingdon Press, 1994], 100). See also the critique of Fiorenza's position by John N. Collins ("Did Luke Intend a Disservice to Women in the Martha and Mary Story?" *Biblical Theology Bulletin* 28 [Fall 1998]: 104–11).

but also to be honored, and Martha goes to great lengths to honor her guest.

Verse 40 tells us, "Martha was cumbered about much serving." Often, this verse is interpreted to mean that Martha's serving refers to being busy in the kitchen. Certainly, this interpretation fits with the concept of hospitality that I have discussed, but it should be noted that nowhere does the text explicitly mention the kitchen or the preparing of food.

As I have noted, the word *diakonia* can refer to the preparation and serving of food, but it can also refer to the work of the ministry.[24] The Greek word translated here as "cumbered about" is *perispao.* In the passive form, as it is here, it means "to be pulled, dragged away." The implication that comes from the passive form "is that Martha wished to hear Jesus but was prevented from doing so by the pressure" of *diakonia.*[25] We are here reminded of the textual variant that indicates that Mary was not the only one who sat at Jesus' feet and heard His word.

Next, we must address Jesus' rebuke of Martha, and we must be careful to clearly identify exactly what Jesus rebuked. Otherwise, we will misunderstand the intent of the story. Catherine Corman Parry, in an influential Latter-day Saint paper, has argued that His rebuke was directed at Martha's judgment of her sister. She writes, "Martha's self-importance, expressed through her judgment of her sister, occasioned the Lord's rebuke, not her busyness with the meal." Further, Parry notes, "In the same way that the father in the

---

[24] There are significant linguistic connections between Luke 10:38–42 and Acts 6:1–8 where the Grecians complained that their widows were neglected in their daily *diakonia.* The seven who are called to look after the *diakonia* are described as being "of honest report, full of the Holy Ghost and wisdom" (Acts 6:3). There is no doubt that this event refers to looking after the temporal affairs of the Grecian widows, but it is interesting that when we see two of the seven, Stephen and Philip, at work, they are involved in preaching the gospel.

[25] Marshall, *The Gospel of Luke*, 452. Barbara E. Reid, however, reads this passage as Martha's "being pulled away" from her *diakonia* (Barbara E. Reid, *Choosing the Better Part? Women in the Gospel of Luke* [Collegeville, Minnesota: Liturgical Press, 1996], 157). It seems to me that the difference in interpretation rests largely on whether we accept that Martha *also* sat at Jesus' feet.

parable of the prodigal son acknowledges his elder son's faithfulness, the Lord acknowledges Martha's care: 'Martha, Martha, thou art careful and troubled about many things' (v. 41). Then he delivers the gentle but clear rebuke."[26] Parry's assessment is valuable in that it emphasizes that Jesus' rebuke is not directed at Martha's *diakonia,* but it misses the mark when it does not recognize that verse 41 is at the heart of His chastisement. To appreciate this fact, we must look carefully at verse 41 in its context with verse 40.

In verse 40, we learn that "Martha was cumbered about [with] much serving" (*peri pollen diakonian*), but in verse 41, Jesus chastises her because she is "careful (*merimnao*) and troubled (*thorubadze*) about many things (*peri polla*)." The *peri polla* is clearly a thematic link back to the "much serving" (*peri pollen diakonian*) in the previous verse, but in this verse, Jesus makes no mention of the *diakonia.* Instead, He emphasizes the verbs *merimnao* and *thorubadze* and their object, *polla.* In contrast to Parry's assessment, this verse is not an endorsement for Martha but is a central part of the chastisement. *Merimnao* and its cognates in other New Testament passages often describe worldly attitudes and practices that hinder discipleship. Certainly, as Luke 12:22–31 shows, these cares can be associated with issues of food, but it has a much wider semantic range. In the Parable of the Four Soils, the thorns that choked the young plant are the "cares" (*merimnon*) and riches and pleasures of this life—things that "bring no fruit to perfection" (Luke 8:14); and in 1 Corinthians 7:32–34, Paul warns the Corinthians against the cares of the world that prevent people from participating in the work of the kingdom. The verb *thorybazo* is found only in this passage of the New Testament, but we find the noun form *thorybos* in numerous passages. In these passages, it carries the sense of an uproar or tumult that comes from a crowd.[27] This may reinforce the

---

[26] Catherine Corman Parry, "'Simon, I Have Somewhat to Say unto Thee': Judgment and Condemnation in the Parables of Jesus," in *Brigham Young University 1990–91 Devotional and Fireside Speeches* (Provo: Brigham Young University Publications, 1991), 116.

[27] See Matthew 26:5; 27:24; Mark 5:38; 14:2; Acts 20:1; 21:34; 24:18. See also

JST reading of verse 38 that Martha received not just Jesus but also His disciples into her home, and the reader is reminded that Martha has others to provide *diakonia* for besides Jesus.

So where is that pressure coming from that pulled Martha away from listening to Jesus and that occasioned His chastisement? Was it her own sense of duty or obligation to be the perfect hostess and put on a banquet for her honored guest, or was it some of the disciples pressuring her to get dinner ready because they were hungry? What were the *polla* that Jesus chastises? I think the passage is intentionally ambiguous. Luke wants modern readers, male and female, to become participants in the story because every reader is a Martha in some respect. Perhaps the more important question is, What are the pressures that prevent *us* from sitting quietly at the Lord's feet and being taught by him? What are the things that pull us from attending our church meetings, pondering the sacrament, listening intently to general conference, or finding a quiet time and place to pray and study the scriptures? Is it the pressure to provide well for a family? Is it the pressure to have a spotless house or yard? Or is it the pressure to overextend ourselves or our children in *many* good activities? The list of possibilities is endless, but the message is clear: The commandment to love God with all our heart and soul and strength and mind is the first great commandment because we should never allow ourselves to be distracted from it. It is the "good part." It is the "one thing [that] is needful" (Luke 10:42; cf. Luke 18:22).

It is the first commandment that enables disciples to know how to focus their obedience to the second commandment without being distracted by the cares of the world. Elder Dallin H. Oaks notes that this story "reminds every Martha, male and female, that we should not be so occupied with what is routine and temporal that we fail to cherish those opportunities that are unique and

---

Kathleen E. Corley, *Private Women, Public Meals: Social Conflict in the Synoptic Tradition* (Peabody, Mass.: Hendrickson Publishers, 1993), 140.

spiritual."[28] Likewise, Elder Neal A. Maxwell taught, "The conversation that night was eternal; the calories were not. When we get filled with Martha-like anxiety, it usually stems from failure to establish proper priorities. . . . Basically, if we are properly motivated and are proper managers of our time, there is a time and season for various good causes in our lives. The contributing emphasis, of course, must be upon keeping the commandments and being effective in our family life."[29]

Yes, Jesus chastises Martha, but He does not reject her.[30] Instead, Doctrine and Covenants 95:1 reminds us that the Lord chastises those whom He loves, and it is clear from John 11:5 that Jesus loves this woman.[31] It is His desire to help Martha reach an even higher level of spirituality that prompts the response. And the wonderful thing about Martha is that in John 11, she seems to have responded positively to His chastisement.

John 11

John 11–12 also focuses on the sisters, Martha and Mary, but these chapters also introduce their brother, Lazarus. These are pivotal chapters in John's Gospel and in the development of his message. Scholars have frequently identified chapter 11 as a transitional chapter between the two main portions of the Gospel: the Book of Signs (John 1:19–12:50) and the Book of Glory (John

---

[28] Oaks, "Spirituality," 61.

[29] Neal A. Maxwell, *Deposition of a Disciple* (Salt Lake City: Deseret Book, 1976), 69.

[30] Alexander points to other scenes where siblings are in dispute (Luke 6:41–42; 12:13; 15:25–32) and concludes that in Luke's Gospel, Jesus "shows himself remarkably unconcerned about who is in the right and who is in the wrong." Alexander argues that the father's response to the elder brother in the Parable of the Prodigal Son ("Son, thou art ever with me, and all that I have is thine" [Luke 15:31]) can "encourage us to look for gentle reproof rather than outright rejection in Jesus' reply to Martha" ("Sisters in Adversity," 181–83).

[31] Recall the statement by Elder Neal A. Maxwell about the brother of Jared, which could also apply to Martha: "The Lord is truly there to chastise those whom He loves, including the spiritually preeminent" ("Yet Thou Art There," *Ensign*, November 1987, 31).

13:1–20:31). The Book of Signs highlights seven miraculous signs that reveal Jesus' divine identity to the world.[32] Readers quickly learn, however, that although these signs generate faith in some (such as the woman at the well [John 4:1–42] and the man born blind [John 9:1–38]), they also generate hostility and rejection (the Pharisees [John 9:13–34]). In one sense, chapter 11 is the culmination of these signs. Jesus' power to restore Lazarus to life is the greatest and most convincing evidence that He comes from God. But chapter 11 is much more than the culminating event in the Book of Signs; it also prepares the reader to anticipate the crowning event in the Book of Glory—the death and resurrection of the Son of God. Perhaps the most poignant effect of the transitioning nature of this chapter is "the supreme irony that it was above all Jesus' gift of life that immediately led people to put him to death."[33]

As chapter 10 closes, we read that Jesus withdrew from Jerusalem and sought refuge in the region east of the Jordan River (v. 40). This was necessary because during the Feast of Dedication, the Jews sought to arrest Him for teaching, "I and my Father are one" (v. 30) and "The Father is in me, and I in him" (v. 38). Mention of the feast (v. 22) alerts readers to the fact that there are only about four months until the Passover and Judas' betrayal. Chapter 11 then opens with Mary and Martha sending word to Jesus that their brother Lazarus is sick. Although this is the first time we hear of this family in John's Gospel, the account presupposes that Jesus already had a close relationship with them.[34] Mary and Martha

---

[32] The seven signs are the following: (1) turning water into wine (2:1–11); (2) healing the nobleman's son from a distance (4:46–54); (3) healing the invalid by the pool of Bethesda (5:1–9); (4) the feeding of the five thousand (6:1–14); (5) Jesus walking on the water (6:16–21); (6) the healing of the blind man (9:1–38); and (7) the raising of Lazarus (11). In these passages, where we find the word *miracle*, it is actually the Greek word *semeia*, which literally means "sign" (see 2:11; 4:54; 6:2, 14, 26; 9:16; 11:47).

[33] Raymond E. Brown, *The Gospel and Epistles of John: A Concise Commentary* (Collegeville, Minn.: Liturgical Press, 1988), 62.

[34] Readers may assume that the account in Luke 10:38–42 stands in the background of this chapter, although John never mentions it.

identify their brother as "he whom thou lovest" (John 11:3),[35] and John informs his readers, "Jesus loved[36] Martha, and her sister, and Lazarus" (v. 5).[37] These expressions of love prefigure Jesus' later declaration in John 15:13, "Greater love hath no man than this, that a man lay down his life for his friends."[38]

Jesus clearly understood the ramifications of choosing to return to Judea, and the disciples' declarations in chapter 11, verses 8 and 16, show that they too were keenly aware of the dangers. Jesus, however, was committed to doing "the works of him that sent me, while it is day." He was fully aware that "the night cometh, when no man can work" (John 9:4). It is in this context that He reiterates to His disciples His commitment to "continue doing God's work in the short time remaining before the onset of the 'night' of the Passion."[39] Thus, He declares, "Are there not twelve hours in the day? If any man walk in the day, he stumbleth not, because he seeth the light of this world. But if a man walk in the night, he stumbleth, because there is no light in him" (John 11:9–10).

Jesus' love for this family meant that He was willing to lay down His life for them. Although these events can be understood in the broader terms of His crucifixion, they should also sharpen the reader's attention to the more immediate danger of His choice to journey to Bethany. The fact that He tarried for two days meant that Lazarus died before He came, but Jesus makes clear that His

---

[35] Some scholars suggest that this identification indicates that Lazarus was the unnamed disciple whom Jesus loved as mentioned throughout this Gospel. For a discussion of the issues, see Raymond E. Brown, *The Gospel According to John I–XII*, The Anchor Bible, 29 (Garden City, N.Y.: Doubleday, 1966), xciii–xcviii.

[36] In the canonical Gospels, Mary, Martha, and Lazarus are the only named people described as being loved by Jesus. John, of course, also mentions the unnamed disciple "whom Jesus loved" (John 13:23; 20:2; 21:7, 20).

[37] The purpose of this verse seems to be to assure readers that Jesus did not delay His journey to Bethany because He was indifferent to Lazarus' condition (Brown, *The Gospel According to John I–XII*, 423).

[38] Wendy E. Sproston North, *The Lazarus Story within the Johannine Tradition*, Journal for the Study of the New Testament Supplement Series, 212 (Sheffield: Sheffield Academic Press, 2001), 41–57.

[39] North, *The Lazarus Story*, 55.

delay was intentional, that "the glory of God" could be made manifest (v. 4).

Even before Jesus arrived in Bethany, Martha heard of His coming. In this chapter, we see a different Martha from that of Luke 10:38–42. We know that Martha's home was filled with guests: Jews who came "to comfort [Martha and Mary] concerning their brother" (John 11:19). As owner of the home, Martha would have been just as obligated to offer *diakonia* to her visitors as she was in Luke 10; but this time Jesus is the focus of her attention, and she leaves her guests behind to rush out to meet Him as He approaches the outskirts of Bethany (vv. 20, 30). In the tender scene that follows, we catch a glimpse of the powerful, albeit still growing, testimony Martha has of her Lord. Martha's first words to Jesus, which will later be echoed by her sister, were, "Lord, if thou hadst been here, my brother had not died" (v. 21, cf. v. 32). Unlike Mary, however, Martha goes further and declares, "But I know, that even now, whatsoever thou wilt ask of God, God will give it thee" (v. 22). Jesus responds to her faith by reassuring her, "Thy brother shall rise again" (v. 23). His response is calculated to convey two levels of meaning: an immediate return to life and the future resurrection of the dead. Martha interprets it in terms of the latter (v. 24),[40] and Jesus uses her reply to make the powerful declaration, "I am the

[40] North, *The Lazarus Story*, 143. Jewish understanding of the resurrection during the time of Jesus was not uniform. The Sadducees, in contrast to the Pharisees, did not believe in a resurrection (Mark 12:18; Acts 4:1–2; 23:8). Daniel 12:2 teaches, "And many of them that sleep in the dust of the earth shall awake, some to everlasting life, and some to shame and everlasting contempt." In contrast, 2 Maccabees 7:14 taught that "there will be no resurrection to life" for the wicked. Others believed that immortality was independent of the body. Josephus says the following about the Essenes: "Their doctrine is this:—That bodies are corruptible, and that the matter they are made of [is] not permanent; but that the souls [that is, spirits] are immortal, and continue forever" (*JW* 28.154–55). A fragment from the Dead Sea Scrolls (4Q521) talks about resurrection during the messianic age, where it seems that the Messiah is God's agent in performing the resurrection (John J. Collins, "A Herald of Good Tidings: Isaiah 61:1–3 and Its Actualization in the Dead Sea Scrolls," in Craig A. Evans and Shemaryahu Talmon, eds., *The Quest for Context and Meaning: Studies in Biblical Intertextuality in Honor of James A. Sanders*, Biblical Interpretation Series, 28 [Leiden: Brill, 1997], 234–35).

resurrection, and the life: he that believeth in me, though he were dead, yet shall he live: and whosoever liveth and believeth in me shall never die" (vv. 25–26). Jesus here uses the divine expression, I AM (*ego eimi*), to emphasize the power and authority by which He provides resurrection and life to those who believe in Him. With this power and authority, death is nothing more permanent than sleeping (see vv. 11–14).

Then, Jesus poses a question meant to probe the depths of Martha's faith, as the death of a loved one can lead to a crisis of faith for many people. "Believeth thou this?" (v. 26). Did Martha *really* believe that Jesus was the resurrection and the life? Did she *really* believe that He was the Son of God? Martha's affirmation of faith and testimony is powerful. "Yea, Lord: I believe that thou art the Christ, the Son of God, which should come into the world" (v. 27). This testimony is second to none among the New Testament believers of Jesus. It ranks alongside those of Peter given at Caesarea Philippi (Matthew 16:16) and at the conclusion of the Bread of Life Discourse (John 6:69). In John's Gospel, Martha is *the* exemplar of what it means to be a disciple. Her testimony "echoes the central christological claim of the Gospel" found in John 20:30–31:[41] "And many other signs truly did Jesus in the presence of his disciples, which are not written in this book: but these are written, that ye might believe that Jesus is the Christ, the Son of God; and that believing ye might have life through his name."

Martha's testimony has two other significant aspects. First, we need to appreciate that Martha "makes her confession as a response to Jesus' words, without having seen the miracle."[42] Martha's testimony is grounded firmly in Jesus' teachings, not in His miracles.

---

[41] Martinus C. de Boer, "John 4:27—Women (and Men) in the Gospel and Community of John," in George J. Brooke, ed., *Women in the Biblical Tradition*, Studies in Women and Religion, 31 (Lewiston, N.Y.: The Edwin Mellen Press, 1992), 209.

[42] Craig R. Koester, *Symbolism in the Fourth Gospel: Meaning, Mystery, Community*, 2nd ed. (Minneapolis: Fortress Press, 2003), 66. See also Turid Karlsen Seim, "Roles of Women in the Gospel of John," in Lars Hartman and Birger Olsson, eds., *Aspects on the Johannine Literature*, Coniectanea biblica. New Testament Series, 18 (Uppsala: Almqvist & Wiksell International, 1987), 72.

Many people in John's Gospel believed in Jesus because of His miracles (see John 2:23; 6:2), but unfortunately they also turned away when they did not get the miracle they were looking for (John 6:22–66). Her declaration is in stark contrast to a later statement by Thomas, "Except I shall see . . . I will not believe" (John 20:25); it is a poignant reminder that "blessed are they that have not seen, and yet have believed" (John 20:29). Second, the perfect tense of the verb translated as "I believe" (*pepsiteuka*) can indicate that her faith was established prior to this event, not as a result of it.[43]

It is Martha's declaration of faith in Christ and the resurrection that enables the second level of Jesus' assurance, "Thy brother shall rise again," to be realized (John 11:23). As Moroni teaches, "Ye receive no witness until after the trial of your faith" (Ether 12:6; see also Doctrine and Covenants 35:8). Jesus had come to Bethany not just to teach about the resurrection but also to provide yet another sign that He was "the coming one" sent by God who would give sight to the blind, heal lepers, and make the lame to walk and the deaf to hear. He had also come to raise up the dead (see Matthew 11:4–5).

We know from the synoptic Gospels that Jesus had performed this miracle before; He had already raised Jairus' daughter (Mark 5:35–43) and the widow of Nain's son (Luke 7:11–15). But, at this point, it does not appear that Martha anticipated that her family would be blessed with *that* miracle.

We do not know why Martha then went secretly to call Mary. Perhaps, given the danger mentioned in verse 8, it was an unsuccessful attempt to keep the fact of Jesus' arrival away from the Jews gathered at the house.[44] Nevertheless, they followed Mary and witnessed the miracle of Lazarus' return from the dead. When Mary met Jesus, she fell at His feet and repeated Martha's earlier declaration: "Lord, if thou hadst been here, my brother had not died"

[43] Francis Moloney, "The Faith of Martha and Mary," *Biblica* 75, no. 4 (1994): 477.

[44] Brown, *The Gospel According to John I–XII*, 425.

(John 11:32).[45] Unlike Martha, Mary makes no further statement. This may be because "grief clouds her vision, and the arrival of the 'consolers' prevents any further conversation."[46] It is clear from John's editorial comment in verse 2 that he sees Mary's actions in a positive light. This is the same Mary who, in chapter 12, will anoint "the Lord with ointment, and [wipe] his feet with her hair" (John 11:2).

At the site of the tomb, Jesus is moved to tears when He sees Mary's pain.[47] Even though he was about to bring Lazarus back to life, Jesus was sensitive to the very real emotions that death evokes. It is also possible that Lazarus' death, like that of John the Baptist's (Matthew 14:3–12), was a reminder of the nearness of Jesus' own death and that the magnitude of that event surely weighed heavily upon His soul.[48] Just as Jesus could have prevented Lazarus' death, but chose not to, Jesus knew that neither would His Father prevent that which was foreordained in the premortal councils. Both the deaths of Lazarus and of the Son of God were "for the glory of God" (John 11:4), which, in Jesus' case, was "to bring to pass the immortality and eternal life of man" (Moses 1:39).

John's specific mention that Lazarus was entombed in a cave with a stone sealing the entrance (John 11:38) is meant to reinforce

---

[45] Many scholars have noted the similarity between the two sisters' response. Many believe that the description of one of the sisters is a later literary addition to the original story, although there is no consensus about which is the addition. For a discussion, see Brown, *The Gospel According to John I-XII*, 432–33. It is a natural reaction, however, for people who have faith in Jesus, and so it is not at all necessary to conclude that one is a later literary addition.

[46] George R. Beasley-Murray, *John*, Word Biblical Commentary, 36 (Waco, Texas: Word Books, 1987), 192.

[47] We do not know the cause of Lazarus' death, but Barnabas Lindars has argued that the Greek word *embrimasthai* in verses 33 and 38 suggests that the miracle was linked with other exorcisms that Jesus performed ("Rebuking the Spirit: A New Analysis of the Lazarus Story of John 11," in Adelbert Denaux, ed., *John and the synoptics*, Bibliotheca ephemeridum theologicarum lovaniensium 101 [Leuven: Leuven University Press, Uitgeverif Peeters, 1992], 542–47).

[48] The Greek word translated as "troubled" in John 11:33 is *tarassein*. John often uses this word in association with Jesus' death (John 12:27; 13:21; 13:38–14:1). See Koester, *Symbolism*, 67.

the link between this event and the one that would occur on Easter Sunday (John 20:1). Verse 39 reminds the reader that Lazarus had been dead for four days.[49] Martha's protest here when Jesus ordered the removal of the stone, "Lord, by this time he stinketh" (John 11:39), reminds us that, despite her early testimony of the resurrection, she was not prepared for the events that followed.

From a literary perspective, I have noted that the raising of Lazarus was a type of Jesus' own resurrection. There are, however, important differences between the two events of which readers should be aware. First, when the stone was rolled away from the tomb and Jesus had prayed to His Father, we learn from verse 43 that "he cried with a loud voice, Lazarus, come forth." The Greek verb for "cried" is *kraugazein.* It occurs six times in John's Gospel, once in this verse, once in 12:13 where the crowds cried Hosanna during Jesus' triumphal entry into Jerusalem, and four times in chapters 18–19 (18:40; 19:6, 12, 15). In all four of the last cases, it is used to describe the crowd's shouts to Pilate calling for Jesus' death.[50] Again, the reader is reminded of the irony that in spite of Jesus' cry to Lazarus that results in life, the crowd ultimately will cry out for His death.

Second, verse 44 reads, "And he that was dead came forth, bound hand and foot with graveclothes: and his face was bound about with a napkin. Jesus saith unto them, Loose him, and let him go." In contrast to Lazarus, who exited his tomb still wearing his graveclothes and facial napkin, Jesus left them behind in His tomb (John 20:6–7). John wants all his readers to remember that although Lazarus would eventually die again and need his burial clothes, Jesus would never need them again.[51] As important as this miracle was, it paled in significance to what Jesus would do in just a

---

[49] It has been suggested that the Rabbis believed that the spirit "hovered near the body for three days but after that there was no hope of resuscitation" (Brown, *The Gospel According to John I–XII*, 424). We must be careful, however, about assuming that the beliefs of later rabbis always reflect the reality and beliefs of the first century.

[50] Brown, *The Gospel According to John I–XII*, 427.

[51] Brown, *The Gospel and Epistles of John*, 65.

matter of months, but it is an important reminder of what Jesus had earlier promised He would do for all. "Jesus called one man, Lazarus, out of the tomb in order to show that in the future 'all who are in their graves' will hear the voice of the Son of Man 'and will come out' (5:28–29)."[52] Likewise, Paul taught the Corinthians, "For since by man came death, by man came also the resurrection of the dead. For as in Adam all die, even so in Christ shall all be made alive" (1 Corinthians 15:21–22).

The raising of Lazarus "gives the most incontrovertible proof for Jesus' claim stated earlier in the course of the narrative: Jesus really does the works of his Father, which shows that the Father is in him and he is in the Father (10:37–38)."[53] Yet, as we can expect in the narrative of John's Gospel, the response to this miracle is varied: "Many of the Jews which came to Mary, and had seen the things which Jesus did, believed on him. But some of them went their ways to the Pharisees, and told them what things Jesus had done" (John 11:45–46). The Sanhedrin was convened under Caiaphas' leadership. Their greatest fear was that the Romans would see the rising public support for Jesus as a threat to their hegemony and respond with force. Caiaphas' assessment that "it is expedient for us, that one man should die for the people, and that the whole nation perish not" resulted in their "counsel together for to put him to death" (vv. 50, 53). As a result, "Jesus therefore walked no more openly among the Jews" (v. 54).

John 12:1–9

In the discussion of the previous two texts, I have purposely omitted any detailed discussion of Mary's involvement. For the most part, Luke 10 and John 11 have been the story of Martha, not Mary. Luke notes Mary's presence in the house, but she is not an

[52] Koester, *Symbolism*, 122.

[53] Raimo Hakola, "A Character Resurrected: Lazarus in the Fourth Gospel and Afterwards," in David Rhoads and Kari Syreeni, eds., *Characterization in the Gospels: Reconceiving Narrative Criticism*, Journal for the Study of the New Testament Supplement Series, 184 (Sheffield: Sheffield Academic Press, 1999), 229.

active participant in the proceedings. In John 11, Mary's role also takes a back seat to that of Martha, although John's editorial comment in 11:2 that Mary is the same person "which anointed the Lord with ointment" is an important linking together of chapters 11 and 12. As chapter 12 opens, Jesus has returned to Bethany. It is just six days before the Passover and Jesus' atoning sacrifice. At this time of foreboding, He returned to the home of those whom He loved. Again, He partakes of Martha's *diakonia,* but unlike Luke 10, she is not cumbered about with it. Also, in this chapter, we find Mary for the third time sitting at Jesus' feet. In this instance, however, her actions are the central focus of the story.

The story in John 12 has remarkable affinities with two other anointing stories in the synoptic Gospels—one in the house of Simon the leper (Mark 14:3–9; Matthew 26:6–13) and one in the home of Simon the Pharisee (Luke 7:36–50). The account in Luke appears to be a different episode than that in John 12. There is no evidence that Mary had an immoral past, and the event in Luke takes place in Galilee, not Bethany. The account in Mark seems to describe the same event as the one in John 12, although with some differences. Both events take place in a house in Bethany; both emphasize the expense of the perfume; in both there is a complaint about using such costly perfume at the expense of administering to the poor; and chronologically both situate the anointing during the passion week.[54] In the Markan account, however, the woman who anoints Jesus remains anonymous. There is no mention of Mary, Martha, or Lazarus—only Simon the leper. This has led some scholars to speculate that Simon was their father.[55] In addition, in the Markan account, it is Jesus' head, not his feet, that is anointed. The latter difference is difficult to reconcile but may reflect emphases on different events that took place that day. Mark emphasizes

[54] Although John's account specifies six days before the Passover (12:1), the context of Mark's story is that it was only two days. Mark 14:1 has reference to the chief priests and scribes wanting to put Jesus to death, not explicitly to the anointing.

[55] Bruce R. McConkie, "Our Sisters from the Beginning," *Ensign*, January 1979, 62–63.

the anointing of Jesus' head in remembrance of His triumphal entry as David's royal heir. John, however, emphasizes the anointing of Jesus' feet in anticipation of the ordinance of washing of feet that He will perform for the Twelve in chapter 13.

Mary anointed Jesus' feet with a pound of oil (*myron*) extracted from true (*pistikos*) nard (*nardos*) grown in the mountains of India.[56] This was expensive oil that she had been saving "that she might anoint [Jesus] in token of [His] burial" (JST John 12:7). Mary's actions have profound theological significance in John's Gospel. As I have already noted, the raising of Lazarus intensified efforts to put Jesus to death. Unlike the synoptic Gospels, throughout John's Gospel, Jesus has made pointed statements about His death (John 7:33–34; 8:21). His disciples who heard these statements misunderstood their meaning (John 7:35; 8:22). Of all the disciples, "only Mary anticipates and grasps the human significance of Jesus' words, and she displays her love accordingly. . . . Her reckless act of pouring out a pint of expensive perfume on Jesus' feet and wiping them with her hair dramatizes for Jesus—and for us—the truth that love is stronger than death."[57] Elder McConkie captures the tenderness of Mary's actions in the following statement: "To understand this solemn scene one must both know and feel the religious significance of Mary's act. Here sat the Lord of Heaven, in the house of his friends, as the hour of his greatest trials approached, with those who loved him knowing he was soon to face betrayal and crucifixion. What act of love, of devotion, of adoration, of worship, could a mere mortal perform for him who is eternal?"[58] For Mary, it was to sit at His feet in humility and pour out the feelings of her heart by pouring out the oil and then lovingly wiping His feet with her hair. Six days later, in another meal setting, in a similar act of love and service, Jesus humbled Himself and washed the feet of the Twelve and then said, "I have given you an example, that ye

[56] Brown, *The Gospel According to John I–XII*, 448.

[57] J. Ramsey Michaels, "John 12:1–11," *Interpretation: A Journal of Bible and Theology* 43, no. 3 (July 1989): 288.

[58] McConkie, *DNTC*, 1:700.

should do as I have done to you" (John 13:15). Even before Jesus issued this directive to the Twelve, Mary had understood and practiced this eternal principle.

Conclusion

Jesus loved Mary, Martha, and Lazarus. In John's Gospel, many people who interact with Jesus remain anonymous (for example, the Samaritan woman and the man born blind). But with this family, it is different. "Each member of this family from Bethany receives a proper name as soon as they appear in the story. As such, they stand out in [John's] Gospel as a special group."[59] They were not perfect individuals. At times, He chastised them. They were not part of the inner circle of the Twelve. The glimpses we get of them show that they still had things to learn about Jesus and His divine mission, but still He loved them. This family in Bethany stands out as exemplars to all those who have a testimony of Jesus and who constitute the rank and file of His Church. They are His sheep whom "he calleth . . . by name" (John 10:3) and for whom He has laid down His life (John 10:15).

[59] Hakola, "A Character Resurrected," 234.

VII.

WHAT JESUS TAUGHT THE JEWS ABOUT THE LAW OF MOSES

JEFFREY R. CHADWICK

What is written in the law? how readest thou?

LUKE 10:26

The early spring sun shone high in the western sky on a mild afternoon in the month of Adar.[1] Thousands of Jews from all over the land of Israel were gathered on a gently sloping plain near the north shore of Lake Kinneret—the Sea of Galilee.

Atop a high hill covered with long green grass, strewn with dark grey basalt boulders, and spotted with thousands of colorful wild flowers, Jesus of Nazareth stood silhouetted against the clear blue sky. A gentle Mediterranean breeze carried His words eastward to the multitude, which included not only those who considered themselves His disciples but also many who were investigating His miracles and doctrines. Centuries later, this event would become known as the Sermon on the Mount.

Many of the Jews present believed that Jesus was the promised

---

[1] The Jewish month of Adar occurs in the late winter/early spring period equivalent to late February through the middle of March in our calendar. The rainy winter season is still in progress, but sunny dry days are not uncommon. Temperatures in Israel during Adar are usually mild but not hot, similar to those in the southern United States.

Messiah. Others were not yet sure, but they had come hoping it could be so. The fame of Jesus, His miraculous healings, and His opposition to the corrupt Jerusalem Sadducees had spread throughout the land. But what, they wondered, would He teach them about the law of Moses on this day? The answer: "Think not that I am come to destroy the law, or the prophets: I am not come to destroy, but to fulfill. For verily I say unto you, Till heaven and earth pass, one jot or one tittle shall in no wise pass from the law, till all be fulfilled" (Matthew 5:17–18).[2]

By the time Jesus finished expounding the commandments from Mount Sinai that day, "the people were astonished at his doctrine: for he taught them as one having authority, and not as the scribes" (Matthew 7:28–29). So impressed were they by His teachings on Mosaic law that "when he was come down from the mountain, great multitudes followed him" (Matthew 8:1).

Jesus' statement about the enduring nature of the Mosaic law—"till heaven and earth pass, one jot or one tittle shall in no wise pass from the law"—can be a confusing concept for Christians in general and for Latter-day Saints in particular. Just what did Jesus mean when He said those words? And just what did Jesus teach the Jews about the law of Moses?

Stumbling Block or Stepping Stone?

The law of Moses has always been a difficult subject to discuss with Latter-day Saints. On one hand, when we teach the Old Testament, we point out that the Mosaic law was the sacred law of the eternal God, given by the great Jehovah Himself to Moses in the wilderness. We teach that Jehovah is the Savior Jesus Christ, and we quote Him saying, "I am he that gave the law" (3 Nephi 15:5). In the Old Testament, the law of Moses is the law of Jehovah. Obedience to it was the way of life and salvation for the house of Israel.

[2] The Joseph Smith Translation words this passage differently. But for the purposes of this chapter, I will rely on the KJV itself to understand what Jesus taught about the law of Moses in the New Testament period.

But when Latter-day Saints teach the New Testament, and even the Book of Mormon, the divinity, sacred character, and eternal nature of the law of Moses are often discounted. It is called everything from a lower or lesser law to a stone of stumbling. It is alleged that Jesus came to do away with the law and to replace it with a higher and truly spiritual gospel code. But is such a characterization accurate? Is this what Christ actually said of the law He gave to Israel? What does the New Testament itself say?

The approach taken in this chapter will demonstrate that the Lord did not revoke the law of Moses for His Jewish disciples, who constituted the large majority of His Church during the New Testament period. But He did exempt all Gentiles (meaning anyone who was not Jewish) from having to abide by its customs and ordinances. Because the law of Moses was so culturally and religiously foreign to Gentiles, it would have represented a stumbling block to them in terms of proceeding toward their salvation—a stumbling block that the Lord directed the Church to remove. But for Jews who believed in Jesus as the Messiah and who lived it, revered it, and made the effort to understand it, the law of Moses was no stumbling block. Rather, it was a divinely designed stepping stone that the Lord left firmly in place to assist His "ancient covenant people" (2 Nephi 29:5) in their upward progress toward the fulness of His gospel.

The approach here requires that we start over from the beginning in our attempt to analyze, or rather reanalyze, what Jesus taught His Jewish disciples about the law of Moses. The path will be line upon line and precept upon precept, along a necessarily circuitous path through not only the four New Testament Gospels but also the book of Acts and even some of the apostolic letters. All of these are germane to understanding what Jesus taught about the law. To set the stage for our analysis, we turn first to the Apostles and disciples themselves.

By Their Fruits Ye Shall Know Them (Matthew 7:20)

The most obvious way to discern with validity what Jesus taught His New Testament Church about the law of Moses is to observe what the Church actually did with regard to that code. After Jesus' death, resurrection, and ascension, the Church was led by the Apostles whom Jesus designated and to whom He revealed His will. From Peter, James, and John all the way down to Paul, the Apostles, as well as the members of the Church who faithfully followed them, were the righteous fruit of the good tree Jesus planted. Their actions with regard to the law of Moses are significant indicators of what Jesus must have said (or not said!) about the law.

It has long been recognized that the New Testament Church continued to actively practice and revere the law of Moses for decades after Jesus' departure. The Apostles themselves led the way in adhering to the performances of the ancient law, including observance of the Saturday Sabbath, the Mosaic festivals (Passover, Pentecost, the Day of Atonement, and the Feast of Tabernacles), the Aaronic rituals of the Jerusalem temple, and the sacrifice of animals that attended those holidays and rituals. This may come as a shocking surprise to those who have not carefully read the book of Acts and the apostolic letters. But to those familiar with the New Testament writings, the continuing practice of the law has always been clear.

In Acts 3, for example, "Peter and John went up together into the temple at the hour of prayer, being the ninth hour" (Acts 3:1). This would have been the afternoon service at the temple of Herod—a prayer service that involved the Aaronic priests offering both animal sacrifice at the great outdoor temple altar and the burning of incense inside the holy place of the temple itself. Once inside the temple complex, Peter and John met "a certain man lame from his mother's womb" at the gate called Beautiful, which led from the outer court into the temple's inner court, where the prayer service was conducted (Acts 3:2).[3] After Peter and John blessed the man (Acts 3:6–7), he stood up "and entered with them into the temple" (Acts 3:8). Because the miracle happened at the "Beautiful gate," this means the three men actually entered the inner court and attended the prayer service. Only afterward did they exit and proceed to "the porch that is called Solomon's" (Acts 3:11) at the eastern limit of the outer court of Gentiles, where Peter gave his inspired address to the gathered crowd. The context of this report is clearly that Peter and John took part in the Mosaic prayer ritual at the temple of Herod.[4]

In Acts 10, another example, Peter was shown a vision of "a great sheet knit at the four corners, and let down to the earth: wherein were all manner of fourfooted beasts of the earth, and wild beasts, and creeping things, and fowls of the air" (Acts 10:11–12). This was essentially a tablecloth spread with animals and birds that were not permitted for consumption by the law of Moses—in other words, food that was not kosher. "And there came a voice to him, Rise, Peter; kill, and eat" (Acts 10:13). This would have violated the commandments of kashrut, which was why Peter responded, "Not so, Lord; for I have never eaten any thing that is common or unclean" (Acts 10:14). Peter had obviously continued the Mosaic law practice of keeping kosher in the years following Jesus' Resurrection. The voice responded, "What God hath cleansed, that call not thou common" (Acts 10:15). It is important to remember that this vision was a symbol—not about food but about people. Peter indicated this clearly when he explained, "God hath shewed me that I should not call any man common or unclean" (Acts 10:28),

---

[3] The LDS Bible Dictionary identifies the "Beautiful Gate" as the entry between the court of the Gentiles and the court of women. More probably it was the Nicanor gate, which led from the court of women into the court of men, where the prayer service was conducted. But either scenario supports the notion that Peter, John, and the man they healed actually entered the temple's inner court.

[4] A contrasting viewpoint was maintained by Bruce R. McConkie, who held that Peter and John's prayer-time entry into the temple was "not to engage in ritualistic Jewish prayers." See McConkie, *DNTC*, 2:46. But this position is difficult to reconcile with the context of the passage.

using no food imagery at all. Every indication in the book of Acts is that Peter and the other Jewish Church members continued to regard themselves as bound by the Mosaic dietary commandments, and they observed those regulations faithfully.

The Apostles Barnabas and Paul, on their mission together, "went into the synagogue on the sabbath day, and sat down" (Acts 13:14). The New Testament context for the word "sabbath" is always the Saturday Sabbath of the Old Testament and the law of Moses. To enter the synagogue to "sit down" indicates active participation in the Sabbath service, which included the Jewish prayers. Only this, "after the reading of the law and the prophets," would qualify Paul for an invitation to speak a "word of exhortation" to the congregation of the synagogue (Acts 13:15–16), which he did. Throughout his ministry, Paul resorted to the synagogue many times on the Sabbath, actively participating in the Mosaic worship there. As we shall now see, Paul strove throughout his life to abide by the law of Moses with exactness in all his personal affairs.

The Jerusalem Conference and the Gentile Exemption

Although commentaries generally refer to Paul as the Apostle to the Gentiles and Peter as an Apostle to the Jews, the fact is that it was Peter who received the initial revelation to invite Gentiles into the Church, and it was Peter—the senior Apostle, who held and could exercise all the keys of the kingdom—who was above all others the Apostle to the Gentiles. The best historical evidence is that Peter arrived in Rome long before Paul and actively built up the Church there among the Gentiles of ancient Italy.[5] And though Paul was certainly a catalyst, it was Peter who directed the apostolic conference in Jerusalem (Acts 15) that ruled on the status of Gentiles converted to the gospel.

Many commentaries have suggested that the Jerusalem conference (sometimes also called the Jerusalem council) moved officially

[5] See F. F. Bruce, *New Testament History* (New York: Doubleday, 1980) 395–96.

to discontinue the law of Moses and obligated all Church members to cease its practice. But this view is incorrect and contradicts the very text of Acts 15. It is out of harmony with what the rest of the book of Acts clearly describes the Apostles as doing. What happened, in reality, was that the Apostles, after careful consideration of all the issues and after consultation and prayer, prepared an official declaration that exempted Gentiles (and only Gentiles) from the obligations of the law of Moses. Jewish members, who constituted the great majority of the Church, were to continue gospel observance of Mosaic law.

It is evident that Peter and James,[6] the two leading Apostles in the account, solicited and listened to contrasting opinions and positions of various brethren within the Church, including Paul and his companions, before deciding whether "it was needful to circumcise them [the gentile converts], and to command them to keep the law of Moses" (Acts 15:5). Then, after a good deal of discussion (the word "disputing" in Acts 15:7 is too harsh a translation), "Peter rose up" and explained that the precedent for this question had been set at the time he had baptized the Roman officer Cornelius and his household (Acts 10), all uncircumcised Gentiles who, though they kept not the law of Moses, had received the Holy Ghost. If God could so accept Gentiles who did not observe Mosaic law, Peter maintained, so then could the Church. With that guiding principle, James then pronounced what the new policy of the Church would be.

The declaration formulated by James (Acts 15:19–20, 23–29) was addressed only to converts who were "Gentiles in Antioch and Syria and Cilicia," areas outside the land of Israel (Acts 15:24). In

---

[6] In Acts 15, it is not James the brother of John who is acting—he had been killed by order of King Herod Agrippa I around A.D. 41, as reported in Acts 12:1–2. The James of Acts 15 was evidently the same person known as "James the Lord's brother" (Galatians 1:19), who also wrote the epistle of James. He may have been the Apostle known as "James the son of Alphaeus" (Matthew 10:3, Mark 3:18, Luke 6:15), although there is debate on this issue. See Talmage, *JTC*, 209–10, note *rr*. He may also have been a cousin to Jesus, rather than a literal half-brother.

terms of circumcision for Gentiles, it noted that there was "no such commandment." In terms of biblically mandated Mosaic practices, it required only that Gentiles refrain from eating three types of unclean things: (1) food offered to idols, (2) blood, and (3) "things strangled"—a reference to animal flesh not specifically butchered for consumption (see Exodus 20:3 and Genesis 9:3–4). The fourth requirement of the declaration was that Gentiles, like Jews, abstain from "fornication," an inclusive reference to all sexual impurity or misbehavior.

Gentile converts were thus exempted from all Old Testament laws and practices that Jewish members were under covenant obligation to observe. Both peoples were still governed by the spiritual and ethical principles that were the heart of Christ's gospel and the true essence of Mosaic law. James noted that even Jews living outside the land of Israel would have no trouble observing the law of Moses in their gospel living: "For Moses of old time hath in every city them that preach him, being read in the synagogues every sabbath day" (Acts 15:21).

The rest of the New Testament era saw the Church of Jesus Christ operate on two tracks in terms of its widely diverse membership: the one track, which regulated the great majority of members, who were Jewish, required adherence to the biblical law of Moses as part of gospel living, and the other parallel track, the "gentile exemption," which governed the small but increasing number of non-Jewish converts to the Church, operated without Mosaic ritual and restriction while inculcating the spirit and ethic of the same gospel. It may seem strange to modern members that such a two-track situation could exist in the Church. But that it did, and that gospel unity was able to grow and prevail under the dual system, is New Testament history.

The Jewish Members Kept the Law of Moses

After the Jerusalem conference, the rest of the book of Acts records that the Apostles and Jewish members faithfully lived the gospel and observed the law of Moses, seeing no contradiction in the combination but regarding the two as one harmonious whole. In this they were abiding the Lord's admonition in the book of Malachi: "Remember ye the law of Moses my servant, which I commanded him in Horeb for all Israel, with the statutes and judgments" (Malachi 4:4). This was the same chapter of Malachi that predicted "the coming of the great and dreadful day of the Lord" and Elijah who should come before Messiah (Malachi 4:5–6).

The Jewish members' gospel observance of the law of Moses seems to have been similar to that recorded of the early Nephites in the Book of Mormon: "They observed to keep the law of Moses and the sabbath day holy unto the Lord" (Jarom 1:5), and "the prophets, and the priests, and the teachers, did labor diligently, exhorting with all long-suffering the people to diligence; teaching the law of Moses, and the intent for which it was given; persuading them to look forward unto the Messiah, and believe in him to come as though he already was" (Jarom 1:11). There was nothing inherently contradictory or difficult in living the gospel within a law of Moses operational construct, either for the early Nephites or for the New Testament Jewish members.

There are numerous evidences in the last half of the book of Acts demonstrating that the Jewish members faithfully adhered to Mosaic law in all its aspects. A convenient list of ten such evidences will be considered here:

1. *Circumcision.* In Acts 16:1–3, Paul had Timothy become circumcised. Timothy was a son of a Jewish woman who was a member of the Church, "but his father was a Greek." Jewish interpretation of the law of Moses regarded the child of a Jewish woman to be Jewish also, even if the father was a Gentile. Therefore, according to Jewish law, and also Church policy that regarded Jews as subject to Mosaic law, Timothy was Jewish. His belated circumcision was not only proper but also necessary if he was to be a missionary companion of Paul and a credible representative of the Church.[7]

[7] In saying that Paul "circumcised him because of the Jews which were in those

2. *The Sabbath.* In Acts 16:12–13, Paul and his party continued to regard the Sabbath on Saturday as the day of prayer and rest, even though there was no synagogue or Jewish community in Philippi. They went to the riverside "where prayer was wont to be made" and worshiped and preached there as best they could among the Gentiles. The Saturday Sabbath was an intrinsic part of the law of Moses from which the Gentiles were exempted but which was obligatory for observant Jews, including Jewish members of the Church. The instance of Saturday-Sabbath observance in a non-Jewish setting shows Paul's faithfulness in observing the law of Moses.[8]

3. *The Nazarite vow.* In Acts 18:18, Paul "had a vow" that involved the shaving of his head. It is almost universally assumed in New Testament commentaries that this vow was the Nazarite vow of the Mosaic law, described in Numbers 6:1–21.[9]

---

quarters" (see Acts 16:3), Luke was not indicating that Paul was caving in to some sort of Jewish pressure, as has sometimes been alleged (see McConkie, *DNTC*, 2:147). Any local Jewish pressure for Timothy to be circumcised would certainly have occurred much earlier in his life. Rather, Luke seems to be telling us that Paul knew that the Jews of the region (members of the Church or otherwise) would expect a young person presented as a minister of the word of God to have conformed to the ordinance required by scripture. Paul and Timothy were scrupulously abiding by the policy set down by the Apostles in Acts 15, which exempted only gentile converts (not Jewish members) from the law of Moses. In this, they were obeying with exactness.

[8] Sunday, the first day of the week, became an important day of prayer and assembly for the Saints in the New Testament. This was probably because it was the day of Jesus' resurrection. Sunday was probably the day referred to in Revelation 1:10 as "the Lord's day." But Sunday was not otherwise regarded as a Sabbath (or as *the* Sabbath day) in the New Testament. It was long after the close of the New Testament era that gentile Christians, exempt from the Saturday Sabbath, eventually adopted Sunday as a Sabbath day. Sunday has been approved as a Sabbath for the Church by revelation in the latter days (see Doctrine and Covenants 59). But Paul and the Jews of the New Testament Church observed the Saturday Sabbath of the law of Moses.

[9] See McConkie, *DNTC*, 2:165, where the assumption of the Nazarite vow is followed by McConkie's assessment that Paul "was performing an unnecessary and improper rite, for the apparent purpose of humoring either the Jewish segment of the Church or prospective Jewish converts or both." But this view seems inconsistent with the report of Paul's subsequent travel to Jerusalem to fulfill the vow, which could not have been witnessed by the Ephesians. Generally speaking, the Nazarite vow was a temporary obligation, accepted freely by the person taking it, regarding some issue or

4. *The Feast of Tabernacles.* In Acts 18:20–21, Paul's intent to attend "this feast that cometh in Jerusalem" demonstrates his commitment to participate in Mosaic law festivals. In this case, the festival was most likely the fall month of holidays, including the climactic Feast of Tabernacles (called *Sukkot* in Hebrew). Paul's quick and safe sailing through the Mediterranean from Ephesus in western Turkey to the land of Israel is best placed in the calm weather and seas of late summer.[10]

5. *The Feast of Passover.* In Acts 20:6, Paul departed from Philippi (a locale without a Jewish community or synagogue) only "after the days of unleavened bread." This was the seven-day period directly connected with Passover, the main spring festival of the Mosaic law. That Paul would not depart for travel during the seven days of Passover and unleavened bread, even from a non-Jewish community, indicates that he and Luke and their other companions must have been personally observing the Sabbaths of Passover and the days of unleavened bread (Leviticus 23:5–8).[11]

6. *Pentecost: The Feast of Weeks.* In Acts 20:16, Paul skipped a visit to Ephesus because he was anxious to get to Jerusalem for the day of Pentecost. "Pentecost" is the New Testament Greek name for the one-day Mosaic law festival that the Old Testament calls the Feast of Weeks (*Shavuot* in Hebrew). This holiday was celebrated in

---

action in which that person wished to commit himself to God. After the temporary period of the vow came to an end, the head was again to be shaved (Numbers 6:18), and a series of Mosaic offerings were to be made at the Jerusalem temple, including the sacrifice of one lamb, one ewe, and one ram (Numbers 6:12). In Acts 18, the purpose of Paul's Nazarite vow appears to have been his promise to God to attend the coming Mosaic festival at Jerusalem (Acts 18:21).

[10] During the fall holiday period, Paul would probably have participated in the Jewish New Year (*Rosh HaShannah*) and the Day of Atonement (*Yom Kippur*) as well as the Feast of Tabernacles (*Sukkot*). Mosaic animal sacrifices and prayer services at the Jerusalem temple were part of all these holidays. After *Sukkot*, Paul's trip back to Syria and then Turkey in Acts 18:22–23 seems to have been by land ("he departed, and went over all the country of Galatia and Phrygia"), as late fall and winter conditions would have made sailing difficult.

[11] The Passover festival itself was held only in Jerusalem at that time, but observing the Sabbaths associated with the beginning and ending of the week-long period was obligatory for all Jews everywhere who observed the law of Moses.

the early summer, on the fiftieth day after Passover—the day after a "week of weeks" (forty-nine days) since the Passover feast was eaten (Exodus 34:22; Leviticus 23:15–16). The Feast of Weeks involved animal sacrifice at a temple convocation and was the Jewish remembrance of the giving of the law of Moses on Mount Sinai following the weeks of travel in the wilderness after the exodus from Egypt. Paul's desire to participate in the Mosaic law's festivals and Sabbaths is clear here.

7. *Jewish members zealous of the law.* In Acts 21:17–21, when Paul returned to Jerusalem from his third missionary journey, he reported his success among the Gentiles to James and the other leaders of the Church. James then related to Paul "how many thousands of Jews there are which believe; and they are all zealous of the law"—meaning that the Jewish members of the Church in the land of Israel faithfully observed the law of Moses in their adherence to the gospel of Jesus Christ. Unfortunately, those Jewish members had heard false reports that Paul had tried to teach Jews in other countries to abandon the Mosaic law, something he had never done or advocated. James then gave Paul instructions to demonstrate to the Jerusalem Church members that he, too, was a faithful gospel observer of the law of Moses.

8. *Mosaic ritual immersion in a mikveh.* Acts 21:23–24 records James' instructions to Paul to take four local Jewish members who had taken a vow upon them (undoubtedly the Nazarite vow) and "purify" himself with them and "be at charges with them." This was so that everyone would see and know that "thou thyself (Paul) also walkest orderly, and keepest the law." To purify oneself meant to immerse oneself in water, according to the requirements of the Mosaic law—an ordinance related to, but separate from, the gospel ordinance of baptism by immersion for remission of sins. In Jerusalem, such purification immersion usually took place in an artificially constructed basin or font called a *mikveh.* Such fonts (called *mikvaot* in the plural) were located at the southern entry to the temple mount.

9. *Personal animal sacrifice at the temple.* Acts 21:25–26 relates Paul's conformance with James' instructions. After noting that Gentiles were not required to observe these things, Luke records that "Paul took the men, and the next day purifying himself with them entered into the temple . . . that an offering should be offered for every one of them." As explained earlier, the offering at the end of the Nazarite vow included the sacrifice of a lamb, a ewe, and a ram, in addition to certain food and drink offerings (see Numbers 6:13–17).

This passage is one of the clearest indicators of the full participation in the law of Moses—including the sacrificial rites—in which the vast majority of New Testament Church members (tens of thousands of Jews) freely engaged. This was done not against the counsel of the Apostles and elders of the Church, and not merely with their reluctant permission, but with their active and enthusiastic encouragement. For Jewish members to observe the law of Moses, including even its animal sacrifices, was to live the gospel of Jesus Christ in its divinely and apostolically approved fullness.

10. *The fast of the Day of Atonement.* Acts 27:9 mentions the dangerous sailing weather of late fall and early winter, sometime after the "fast" was past. The "fast" is mentioned in reference to annual timing, and in this case can have been only the Day of Atonement (*Yom Kippur*), the most solemn day of the Mosaic law calendar (Leviticus 23:27–28), a day of fasting that occurs each fall ten days after the New Year (*Rosh HaShannah*). It is unlikely that this "fast" would be mentioned in this passage of Acts unless Paul and his Jewish traveling companions had observed this Mosaic ritual themselves.

Why Did the Jewish Disciples Observe the Law of Moses?

That the Jewish Church members—all of them, including the Apostles—observed and kept the law of Moses as part and parcel of their adherence to the gospel of Jesus Christ is clear from the New Testament. The question for us in the latter-day Church, who do not do so and would not dream of doing so, is why? Why did the early Jewish disciples do this?

There are different ways to answer this question. One is what might be termed the "apostasy approach." It is sometimes suggested that the Jewish members of the New Testament Church, including the Apostles themselves, were willfully engaging in apostate or otherwise unauthorized practices in the years after Jesus departed—practices of the law of Moses that they "knew" had been abolished. This approach was taken by, among others, Bruce R. McConkie, who asked, "Why? What justification can there possibly be for these early saints to reject the spirit and practice of true religion and pretend to conform to the dead letter of a dead law, to a law which can lead nowhere except to spiritual death? The explanation lies in the semi-converted status of the Jewish saints of Jerusalem. As with all men, the Lord was giving gospel truths to them line upon line, precept upon precept. It was better to have them in the Church, seeking the Spirit, striving to keep the commandments, and trying to work out their salvation, than to leave them without the fold until they gained a full knowledge of all things. Even Peter was not converted to the full gospel until long after he was ordained an apostle."[12]

---

[12] See McConkie, *DNTC*, 2:183–84. In his commentary on Acts 21, where James instructs Paul to demonstrate his observance of the law, Elder McConkie said the following: "This is an extremely difficult passage to explain in such a way as to do credit to Paul, or to James the Lord's brother, or the leading brethren in the Church, or to the Jewish segment of the Church established in Jerusalem.

"A quarter of a century has passed since the death of the Lord; the law of Moses is fulfilled; circumcision is no longer an approved part of true worship; the peculiar customs and practices of the Jews are false and damning; the Nazarite system of vows and sacrifices is destructive of that faith which, centered in Christ, leads to life and salvation.

"And yet to humor Jewish-Christians—particularly converted church members who still practice false rites and cling to false ordinances; who are giving lip service to Christ while following Mosaic performances which Christ abolished; who are Christian in name, but largely Jewish in act; who have had the laying on of hands for the gift of the Holy Ghost, but have never attained the spiritual maturity to gain the full companionship of that member of the Godhead—to humor these weak members of the Church, Paul is asked, officially, as a matter of church discipline to pretend that he is a Jew who keeps the Law of Moses."

A more moderate approach might be referred to as the "tolerance approach," which is the suggestion that although God did not approve of the Apostles and the Church practicing the law of Moses, He tolerated their actions. It is reasoned that they were doing so for cultural reasons, in order not to offend their Jewish fellows, and that they deliberately chose to be ambiguous about the abolition of the law of Moses. An example of this approach is the following statement by Robert J. Matthews, "There is no question that Peter and the other brethren knew that the law of Moses was fulfilled. The doctrinal question was settled. The law was no longer a requirement for salvation now that Jesus had made the Atonement. Missionary work among the gentile nations could go forth directly and without impediment. But there was a conflict between culture and doctrine. The brethren were clear on the matter, but long-standing culture and tradition persisted among many Jewish members of the Church even after the doctrinal question had been settled. Latter-day revelation leaves no doubt that the law of Moses was fulfilled in Christ (3 Nephi 15:4–5; Moroni 8:8; Doctrine and Covenants 74)."[13]

The main difficulty with both the "apostasy" and "tolerance"

---

[13] See Robert J. Matthews, "The Jerusalem Council," in *The Apostle Paul: His Life and His Testimony: The 23rd Annual Sidney B. Sperry Symposium* (Salt Lake City: Deseret Book, 1994), 106–9. In his discussion on the Jerusalem conference of Acts 15 (which he calls by the alternative title "Jerusalem council"), Matthews made the following remarks in assessing the decisions taken by the Apostles: "As forward reaching and beneficial as the decision by the Jerusalem Council was, it was only a half step forward in the progress of the Church. For one thing, the council did not decisively declare an end to the law of Moses. The announcement part of the epistle sent from the council does not use the words "law of Moses" nor declare its fulfillment or its final and absolute end as a practice in the Church. Furthermore, the epistle was addressed not to all members of the Church but only to the Gentile members in Antioch, Syria, and Cicilia [*sic*]. The council settled the matter of observing the law of Moses with respect to the Gentiles; it did not address the subject with respect to Jewish Church members. So far as the epistle is concerned, the Jewish members of the Church could continue to observe the ordinances of the law of Moses as a supposed requirement for salvation. Why would the Brethren have been so ambiguous and non-declarative? They seem to have said as little as they could about the matter. Perhaps they hoped to avoid dividing the Church and alienating the strict Jewish members."

approaches, however, is that they view the Jewish membership of the Church, both the Apostles and the general rank and file, as the problem, the weak link, and the unworthy element. Both of the approaches take the view that the term "fulfill" meant "abolish" and that when Jesus described Himself as fulfilling the law of Moses, He meant thereby that the law was to be discontinued.

Are we unalterably forced into the conclusion that the early Apostles were weak, vacillating, and ambiguous practitioners of apostasy, willing to compromise on true doctrine and ordinance to accommodate an unspiritual Jewish Church membership? Were Peter, James, and John—apostolic giants who not only led and fed the ancient Church but also wrote parts of the New Testament and even figure in the latter-day restoration—really such fatally flawed vessels? Was the Apostle Paul, author of so many New Testament letters, a hypocrite of similar weakness and disingenuity?

Another Approach to Understanding the Law

There is another legitimate way to approach the law of Moses question—one that takes a positive view of the early Apostles as well as of the Jewish Church members. It is completely in harmony with the context of the New Testament while not contradicting a single facet of the Book of Mormon or Doctrine and Covenants. It is simply that the Jewish Apostles and members of the New Testament Church observed and practiced the law of Moses because that is exactly what Jesus told them to do.

Latter-day Saints have often thought that Jesus, in saying He had come to "fulfill" the law of Moses, was indicating that with His death and resurrection, He would bring that law to a close. It was to be discontinued, abolished, done away with. But this interpretation of the word "fulfill" is not consistent with its true definition. The English word "fulfill" as it appears in Matthew 5:17 is an accurate translation of the Greek term *plērosai.* "Fulfill" is correctly defined in Webster's Dictionary as "to carry out (a promise) / to obey (a law, command) / to satisfy (a prayer, desire) / to complete, accomplish (a task) / to answer (a purpose) / to comply with (conditions) / to prove true (a prophecy) / to realize (a destiny)."[14]

There is not a hint of "discontinue" or "abolish" or "do away with" in the definition of the word "fulfill." Nor was there any hint of "ceasing" in the way Jesus used the verb on any occasion or in any tense throughout the four Gospels.[15] The discontinuance of certain practices such as animal sacrifice in the early Church is not an indication that all aspects of the law were similarly ended. For example, when, at His baptism, Jesus said that "it becometh us to fulfill [again, Greek *plērosai*] all righteousness" (Matthew 3:15), Jesus was certainly not advocating the discontinuation of either righteousness or baptism.

Likewise, when He stood on the mount and said, "Think not that I am come to destroy the law," He was definitively asserting that He had *not* come to do away with or abolish Mosaic law or to discontinue it in any way. In saying "I am not come to destroy, but to fulfill" (Matthew 5:17), Jesus positively indicated His intention to faithfully carry out, obey, satisfy, accomplish, comply with, prove true, and even perpetuate every aspect of the law of Moses.

He went on to warn His audience gathered in the plain that if they violated even the least commandment in the law of Moses, or taught others to do so, their status in the kingdom of heaven would be correspondingly reduced. But whoever would observe and teach the precepts of that law would "be called great in the kingdom of heaven" (see Matthew 5:19).

He also encouraged them to abide by the law of Moses more faithfully than even the scribes and Pharisees, who were among the law's strongest advocates. In fact, said He, unless the Jewish

---

[14] *The New Lexicon Webster's Encyclopedic Dictionary of the English Language* (New York: Lexicon Publications, 1990), s.v. "fulfill, fulfil," 383.

[15] Although the present/future term "to fulfill" (Greek *plērosai*) occurs only twice in Matthew, the past tense word "fulfilled" (same Greek verb) occurs thirty-nine times in the four Gospels. In addition to Matthew 5:18, Jesus Himself used the past tense in fifteen other passages: Matthew 13:14; 24:34; 26:54; 26:56; Mark 14:49; Luke 4:21; 21:22; 21:24; 21:32; 22:16; 24:44; John 13:18; 15:25; 17:12; 17:13.

Church members were truer to the law than the scribes and Pharisees, they would "in no case enter into the kingdom of heaven" (see Matthew 5:20).

Of course, it is true that when Jesus, as resurrected Savior, repeated the "sermon on the mount" to a Nephite audience halfway around the world, He changed the wording of these last two passages (see 3 Nephi 12:19–20). But that fact does not alter the reality of what He told His Jewish audience. There were valid reasons for the changes in the sermon when it was delivered to the Nephites. The wording to the Jewish members was as it still stands in our Bible canon. Jesus told them they must be the most faithful observers of Mosaic law it was possible to be.

As strange as it may sound to Latter-day Saints, this is the correct and contextual reality of the Sermon on the Mount. This is what the Jewish Church members and investigators heard Jesus say. Those faithful Jewish followers, including all the New Testament Apostles, earnestly observed the law of Moses for decades after Jesus' resurrection because that is precisely what He had told them to do. Thus, He instructed by precept in the Sermon on the Mount and by example in all His other dealings and teachings.

A further word on the notion of "fulfilling" the law of Moses: Not only is it clear in Matthew 5 that Jesus' use of the term "fulfill" did not mean cessation; we can also see this in the Book of Mormon account of the sermon. Speaking to the Nephites, Jesus said that "one jot nor one tittle hath not passed away from the law, but in me it hath all been fulfilled" (3 Nephi 12:18). This remarkable statement, uttered after Jesus' atoning work, death, and resurrection were accomplished facts, was voiced in the past tense. In suffering, dying, and rising again, Jesus had "fulfilled" the law of Moses. But even here the term did not mean discontinuation, and that the Nephites did not understand "fulfilled" to mean "discontinued" is evident in their reaction to the sermon. After it was over, Mormon reported that "there were some among them who marveled, and wondered what he would concerning the law of Moses"—they did not immediately equate "fulfill" with cessation, and "they understood not the saying that old things had passed away, and that all things had become new" (3 Nephi 15:2).

The risen Christ then indicated that He wished the Nephites to cease practicing the Mosaic law and ordinances (something He never told His Jewish disciples). But understanding the English translation of this directive presents some challenges. When Jesus said, for example, "I have come to fulfil the law; therefore it hath an end" (3 Nephi 15:5) and "the law which was given unto Moses hath an end in me" (3 Nephi 15:8), did this mean He had altogether ended the law? Or should we understand the term "end" here in the same context as it was used in the New Testament? New Testament examples would suggest that "the end" referred rather to the fulfillment of the law's purpose or intent. An example of that context is Paul's observation that "Christ is the end of the law" (Romans 10:4), where the word translated as "end" (Greek *telos*) actually means "goal" or "purpose." This meant that the whole goal or purpose of the law of Moses (the "end of the law") was to bring Israel to Christ. Our English New Testament never uses the word "end" to indicate a cessation of Mosaic law. Because Jesus directed the Nephites to cease practicing the law, it may be that He used the term to refer its literal end, or He may have intended to refer to fulfillment of the law's goal or purpose. The term "fulfill" clearly did not mean cessation in the New Testament.

So how did Jesus "fulfill" the law of Moses? In one sense, He fulfilled it the way any other Jewish person of His day could fulfill it—by living it. In His daily life, He kept the commandments of the law, and, perhaps more importantly, He acted as an example of the true spirit of the law.

But in a more significant and even eternal sense, He fulfilled the law by fulfilling its prophecies concerning His atoning sacrifice and resurrection. Those events did not bring the law to cessation (at least not among the Jewish disciples)—for such was not the meaning of the word "fulfill." But Jesus' crucifixion and resurrection did fulfill the inspired passages in the law of Moses that either directly predicted or symbolically foreshadowed His messianic works, including His death and His rising again. Jesus made this clear in His own words to the disciples on the very day of His resurrection: "These are the words which I spake unto you, while I was yet with you, that all things must be fulfilled, which were written in the law of Moses, and in the prophets, and in the psalms, concerning me. Then opened he their understanding, that they might understand the scriptures, and said unto them, Thus it is written, and thus it behoved Christ to suffer, and to rise from the dead the third day: and that repentance and remission of sins should be preached in his name among all nations, beginning at Jerusalem" (Luke 24:44–47).

Jesus fulfilled the law of Moses in that He fulfilled what the law predicted of Him.

The Nephites and the Latter-day Saints

That the Jewish disciples lived the law of Moses for decades after Jesus' resurrection is clear. That the Nephites were instructed to discontinue living the law of Moses is also clear. And that the Latter-day Saints do not operate by Mosaic precept is modern reality. Why the difference in the way these groups have been governed?

My approach suggests that the answer to this question is the principle behind the "gentile exemption" enacted in Acts 15. This principle is that only Jews, who revered the law of Moses and were trained in understanding its procedures and symbols, were benefited by continuing to live the law once the Messiah came to fulfill it. Non-Jews, whether Romans and Greeks of the Old World, Nephites and Lamanites of the New World, or Latter-day Saints of the modern world, have neither the history nor the heart for living the Mosaic law. That is not to say that Jews are superior and Gentiles inferior in any gospel sense, nor is it to say the opposite. It is simply a reality—and one for which the Lord prepared long prior to the point in antiquity when Jew and Gentile were differentiated.

The "gentile exemption" does not explain *why* Jews were instructed by the Lord to live the law of Moses "till heaven and earth pass," whereas the Nephites were to cease its works. Acts 15 itself does not elaborate at any length on the Lord's reasons for exempting Gentiles from Mosaic performance. We just know that it was so. For now, at least, that is all we can conclude.

But it must be clear to Latter-day Saints that we, today, are under no obligation to live Mosaic law. In fact, the Lord has specifically told us that we "cannot enter in at the strait gate by the law of Moses" (Doctrine and Covenants 22:2). Let no discerning soul be in doubt about this fact—the Latter-day Saints are *not* to perform their religion or pursue their salvation by the law of Moses.

In this regard, it is perhaps helpful to remember that the Lord has, throughout history, regulated different gospel dispensations in different ways. The specific laws and performances of the dispensation of Adam were different from those of Moses, and both were different from those of Joseph Smith. Perhaps contrasting gospel dispensations need not be viewed as separated only by time. Perhaps they can also be separated by space—by continents or oceans—at least in ancient settings where worldwide communication was not possible and where a worldwide Church leadership had not been introduced. The Book of Mormon, in whole or in part, may represent one or more different dispensations from those of the Bible. Different modes of operation, even with regard to the law of Moses, need not be deemed implausible.

Jesus Expounded and Expanded the Law of Moses

In the New Testament and the Sermon on the Mount, Jesus proceeded to teach His expectation that His Jewish followers faithfully observe the law of Moses in perpetuity, or "till heaven and earth pass" (Matthew 5:18)—a very long time. Commentaries have generally suggested that Jesus was replacing an "old law" with a much better "new law"—that is to say, replacing the supposedly inferior law of Moses with a better and more perfect gospel code.

But Jesus did not do away with any "old law." The Mosaic commandment "Thou shalt not kill" (Matthew 5:21; compare Exodus 20:13) was not done away with, nor was "Thou shalt not commit adultery" (Matthew 5:27; compare Exodus 20:14) or "Thou shalt not forswear [perjure] thyself," which is to say "Thou shalt not bear false witness" (Matthew 5:33; compare Exodus 20:16). What Jesus did was to expand His disciples' understanding of these basic but important precepts of the law of Moses and to inform them of His expectation that they live those commandments more perfectly.

Jesus' expansion on the Mosaic commandment "Thou shalt not kill" was to not even get angry (Matthew 5:21–22). This is remarkably wise counsel, as almost all murder is preceded by anger. Anger is nigh unto insanity—people do things when they are angry that they would never do under normal circumstances. Continuing the expansion, Jesus told His hearers to avoid insulting others—the term "Raca," which He condemned, was an Aramaic slur meaning "worthless."[16] He also directed that His Jewish followers be reconciled to anyone they might have offended, prior to taking any sacrificial gift to the altar of the Jerusalem temple (Matthew 5:23–24). Additionally, He advised that they avoid getting entangled in the legal system—"Agree with thine adversary quickly, whiles thou art in the way with him" (Matthew 5:25–26) meant, in today's terms, "settle out of court." Becoming entangled in the legal system, with "the judge" and "the officer" down to "the uttermost farthing," often resulted in financial disaster. This is as true today as it was two thousand years ago.

The Savior's expansion on the law of Moses commandment "Thou shalt not commit adultery" was to not even think about such things (Matthew 5:27–28). If we do not look on other persons to lust after them, sexual misconduct cannot occur. Employing the time-honored device of hyperbole (deliberate exaggeration), Jesus

[16] Literally, the Aramaic term "Raca" (*reyka*) meant "empty one"—it was a way of saying that a person was devoid of value. There is no basis, however, for the notion that this term was also Greek (see Matthew 5:22, footnote d).

taught that it was better to pluck out a diseased eye or cut off a diseased hand rather than let the disease claim the whole body (Matthew 5:29–30). In other words, as He reworded the idea for the Nephites (who may not have understood Jewish hyperbole), it is better to deny one's sexual temptations than to commit the impure acts and risk "that ye should be cast into hell" (3 Nephi 12:29–30). Carrying the warning against adultery one step further, Jesus set out what the Mosaic law allows as reasons for seeking a divorce (see Matthew 5:21–22).

The point being made here is that the Sermon on the Mount was all about the law of Moses. The law of Moses was not being laid aside or somehow discontinued in the sermon. Jesus was explaining the law to His Jewish disciples so they could abide by it more fully. He was expanding the law so that its central meaning and individual regulations could be applied in a variety of situations that His Jewish followers might not have otherwise considered. In this, Jesus was teaching in ways that continued existing Jewish religious traditions, including some Pharisee traditions. One such tradition, well known in the first century A.D., was recorded in the Talmud: "Moses received the law at Sinai and passed it to Joshua, and Joshua to the elders, and the elders to the prophets, and the prophets passed it to the men of the great Knesset: They said three things—Be careful in judgement, raise up many disciples, and put a fence around the law."[17]

Jesus set a perfect example for the Jewish nation in His performance of these traditional "three things." His warning that "with what judgment ye judge, ye shall be judged" succinctly expressed the need to "be careful in judgment" (see Matthew 7:1–2).[18] His work to "raise up many disciples" is well known. And in teaching and expanding the law of Moses, whether in the Sermon on the Mount or on other occasions, Jesus, through His inspired interpre-

[17] Babylonian Talmud, *Avot* 1 (author's translation).

[18] Jesus' advice on judgment in Matthew 7:1–2 is a case where the Joseph Smith Translation aptly illuminates the meaning of Jesus' original words: "Judge not *unrighteously . . . but judge righteous judgment*" (JST Matthew 7:1–2; emphasis added).

tations and expansions, "put a fence around the law" that assisted His disciples to avoid transgressing it.

The Jewish idea of "a fence around the law" was that God approved of developing principles and practices to help Israel stay well away from the sins outlined in the Mosaic code. Jewish tradition, as recorded in the Talmud, is replete with such principles and practices. Although some of these precepts may be "the commandments of men" (as Jesus noted in Matthew 15:9), many others are imbued with divine wisdom and intent. Jesus' way of teaching consistently set up inspired fences around the law of Moses. Around the law "Thou shalt not kill," He set a wide fence—do not even get angry, and seek to reconcile with adversaries. Around the law "Thou shalt not commit adultery," the fence was to not even think lustfully and to rid oneself of temptation.

Sometimes the expansion or "fence" taught by Jesus places a Mosaic principle in an entirely new light for modern readers. An example of this is the "eye for an eye, and a tooth for a tooth" passage (Matthew 5:38; compare Leviticus 24:20). The modern world generally judges this passage to be a call for retribution, a justification for revenge, or even an excuse for mayhem. As a result, modern commentaries deem the passage barbaric and criticize its graphic harshness. Detractors of the Bible in general, and the Mosaic law in particular, wonder out loud why a just God would devise such a principle. But the world, as usual, fails to understand the reality that the God of Israel set in place.

In biblical days, the "eye for an eye" passage was never understood as a license to take physical revenge on one's adversary, even for an injury. The understanding that was developed in Old Testament times, and that was perpetuated by Jewish tradition down to the time of Jesus and beyond, was that "an eye for an eye, and a tooth for a tooth" was a statement of theoretical liability, a standard to be used in court proceedings when monetary damages could be awarded where physical loss or injury had been incurred.[19] There is

[19] The term "theoretical liability" is used by Jewish author Herman Wouk, who

no report, either in the Bible or any other Jewish literature, of an injured person having the eye or tooth of the offender taken in retribution. It never happened, because the original meaning of "an eye for an eye" in the law of Moses was never literal. The hyperbolic statement was understood by the Jews as a clause of plausible liability, setting the standard that one who injured another, depriving him of the use of an eye or hand or some other body part, was to be held financially liable for compensation by the judges in Israel. Today, we call it tort law.

In the event an offender was found guilty of injuring or depriving another, the court was to determine monetary compensation, or some other form of compensatory service, to be awarded the aggrieved party. The standard was that the award for a lost eye should be equal to the value of that eye to the owner; the award for a lost tooth should be equal to the value of that tooth to the owner; and the same applied for a hand, a foot, an ox, an ass, a tool, a house, or any other item. Modern tort law is not much different. The true meaning and intent of the "eye for an eye" passage was never barbaric.

This is clear in the way Jesus expounded upon the "eye for an eye" passage. When He uttered the passage, His listeners would have known that He was addressing the possibility of their being found guilty or liable for damages by a court. If we understand this, His instructions afterward then make sense. When He said "resist not evil," He was not advising capitulation to wickedness; "evil" in this context refers to the judgment of the court. "Do not resist the court's negative sentence" was the essential message. "Whosoever shall smite thee on thy right cheek, turn to him the other also" (Matthew 5:39) was advice to accept any corporal punishment the court might order without resistance. (Physical punishment was often meted out rather than a prison sentence.) Better to get it over with and move on. In saying "if any man will sue thee at the law,

gives a useful exposition on the legal context of "an eye for an eye." See Herman Wouk, *This Is My God* (New York: Little, Brown, and Company, 1959), 189–91.

and take away thy coat, let him have thy cloke also" (Matthew 5:40), Jesus advised His hearers that if found liable for a tort, they were to pay the judgment without resistance and even offer additional compensation for the damage they had caused. Should the person found liable lack the resources to pay, he was not to resist a court decree to render compensation through servitude: "whosoever shall compel thee to go a mile, go with him twain" (Matthew 5:41). In teaching and expanding the "eye for an eye" passage, Jesus emphasized the principles of personal responsibility, just compensation for misdeeds we might commit, and even the principle of "going the extra mile" to make sure that we put right whatever we might do wrong. This was one true intent of the law of Moses.

Other Ways Jesus Taught the Law of Moses

Let us observe that there is not a single passage in the four New Testament Gospels that depicts Pharisees or other Jews as complaining that Jesus opposed or undermined the law of Moses or somehow sought or predicted its discontinuation.[20] Even at Jesus' trial before the Sadducee-controlled Sanhedrin, no charge was made that He had advocated or worked toward the abolition of Mosaic law. Jesus simply never taught any of the Jews, whether they were His disciples or otherwise, that the law of Moses was to cease. On the other hand, there are several passages where Jesus either advocates the living of the law, teaches the divine meaning of the law, or both.

Matthew records that after Jesus had delivered His Sermon on the Mount, He encountered a man suffering from leprosy, who said, "Lord, if thou wilt, thou canst make me clean." Jesus touched him and said, "I will, be thou clean. And immediately he was cleansed" (Matthew 8:1–3). The instructions that Jesus gave to the newly

[20] The passage in Acts 6:13–14 also cannot be used to indicate that Jesus taught the discontinuation or alteration of the law of Moses, because although the witnesses against Stephen claimed, "We have heard him say that this Jesus of Nazareth shall destroy this place and shall change the customs which Moses delivered us," the passage clearly indicates that these were "false witnesses" whose testimony was untrue.

cleansed leper have often baffled modern readers: "Jesus saith unto him, See thou tell no man; but go thy way, shew thyself to the priest, and offer the gift that Moses commanded, for a testimony unto them" (Matthew 8:4). Commentaries often suggest that Jesus was insisting that the man keep his miraculous healing a secret, but they also strain to provide plausible reasons why Jesus would do this. The reality was much different.

Jesus' instruction to "tell no man" had nothing to do with secrecy. In fact, the Savior meant for the man to make his miracle widely known—but only in due time. First, the man was to follow the law of Moses regulations governing a recovery from leprosy. The warning "tell no man" was a reminder not to engage in any kind of discourse with anyone until pronounced clean by the appropriate Aaronic authority. Otherwise, those with whom the man might interact would become unclean themselves. He was first to present himself to the priest of Aaron and arrange for the appropriate Mosaic rituals, which included the sacrifice of birds and at least one lamb (see Leviticus 14:1–32). These rituals, performed openly at the Jerusalem temple, would be part of "a testimony unto them" (Matthew 8:4)—the man's public declaration of his miraculous healing. He would then be free to share his experience with anyone he pleased. In all this, Jesus was urging the man to obey the law of Moses with exactness.

On the subject of the Sabbath (contextually Saturday), Jesus continually demonstrated the true intent and meaning of the law of Moses. One example of this will suffice for our current study. On one occasion, Jesus was asked "Is it lawful to heal on the sabbath days?" (Matthew 12:10). Whether it was permissible on the Sabbath to exercise medical arts (which could include the mixing or cooking of medicines, the application of balms or salves, the binding or tying of bandages, and so forth) was a vexed issue among Jewish teachers at the time of Christ. Some of the labors involved were specifically forbidden on the Sabbath by Mosaic law. And the fact that medical arts could be practiced as a vocation, for money, was an additional complication. Jewish authorities were divided on the subject. The Sadducees and certain Pharisees of the academy of Shammai were adamant that medical arts were inappropriate on the Sabbath. On the other hand, Pharisees of the academy of Hillel held that threats to life or health suspended Sabbath prohibitions. Jesus was actually being asked to rule on this divisive point of Mosaic law.

Without entering the debate over individual issues, He definitively stated that "it is lawful to do well on the sabbath days" (Matthew 12:12). In saying "lawful," Jesus clearly meant that His ruling was the correct interpretation of the law of Moses. Efforts that might normally be considered improper on the Sabbath could be deemed not only permissible but also "good" when the intent was to bless life and spirit. In this, Jesus validated the earlier position of the respected teacher Hillel, whose pragmatic view in time became the basis of later Jewish practice. (For example, in Israel today, hospitals and ambulances operate on the Sabbath, as do police and emergency services.) This ruling was the practical expression of Jesus' teaching on another occasion: "The sabbath was made for man, and not man for the sabbath" (Mark 2:27). This, too, was an observation on the priorities of Mosaic writ—in the earliest chapters of the law, the account of the creation of the world, God's creation of man was accomplished prior to the designation of the Sabbath (see Genesis 1:26–2:4). The Sabbath really was made for man and not vice versa.

Jesus' Teachings on Marriage and Divorce

Jesus applied the same teaching techniques—the principles of priority—when dealing with issues of marriage and divorce in the law of Moses. On this issue, too, Jewish opinion was divided. Among the Pharisees, according to the Mishnah, the strict academy of Shammai felt that marriage was so important that a man could utilize the law's divorce passage (see Deuteronomy 24:1) only if his wife was guilty of "a matter of sexual impurity"—meaning adultery or other unfaithful acts of physical sexuality.[21] But the more pragmatic academy of Hillel took the unusually loose view that a man might divorce his wife for any cause at all, even if she ruined food in cooking it. Matthew 19 records that Pharisees came to Him to assess His position on the vexing issue.[22] They asked Him, "Is it lawful for a man to put away [divorce] his wife for every cause?" (Matthew 19:3).

Jesus' response was a classic example of priority examination. Instead of responding immediately on the issue of divorce, He directed His questioners to the initial chapters of the law of Moses, pointing out that in the beginning, God made male and female and caused them to come together as one flesh (Matthew 19:4–5; compare Genesis 1:27–28, 2:21–24), a reference to the divine origin of marriage. Jesus then confirmed the divine priority of the marriage covenant, exclaiming, "What therefore God hath joined together, let not man put asunder" (Matthew 19:6). In other words, the question that should really be addressed is not the issue of divorce but the importance of marriage. With that made clear, the discussion could proceed.

To the Pharisee query "Why did Moses then command to give a writing of divorcement?" (Matthew 19:7), Jesus' answer was simply

---

[21] Babylonian Talmud, *Gittin* 90:a—"[They of] Beyt Shammai say: A man shall not divorce his wife unless he has indeed found in her a matter of sexual impurity, as is it written: (Deuteronomy 24:1) because he discovered in her a sexually impure matter; but [they of] Beyt Hillel say: even if she spoiled the food in cooking it" (author's translation). The Hebrew text of the Mishnah reads literally *davar ervah* ("a matter of genitalia"), and the phrase was interpreted by the academy of Shammai as a reference to forbidden types of physical sexual contact. In the Latter-day Saint edition of the Bible (English), the similar Hebrew term in Deuteronomy 24:1 is simply translated "uncleanness," and footnote b suggests that this should be understood as "unchastity" or "indecency."

[22] The King James Version use of the word "tempting" in Matthew 19:3 fails to accurately represent the event. The Greek verb in this passage (*pierazo*) is more properly rendered as "test, try, or prove." See note 35a for Matthew 22:35 in the LDS edition of the Bible, where the same Greek term is employed. The Pharisees in Matthew 19 had not come to tempt or entrap Jesus. They had come with a legitimate question and wished to assess His position. His immediate, respectful, and detailed response indicates that He took their inquiry seriously.

pragmatic: human nature does not always measure up to divine standards, and the law must be able to respond to man's weakness. The law of "Moses because of the hardness of your hearts suffered you to put away your wives: but from the beginning it was not so" (Matthew 19:8). In other words, God's priority is marriage; man's occasional failure to make marriage work would be provided for—but only in a subsequent addendum. Then, and only after the discussion of priority was complete, did Jesus respond to the initial question posed to him, "Is it lawful for a man to put away his wife for every cause?"

On this occasion, to the astonishment of His own disciples (since His positions more often paralleled those of Hillel), Jesus' ruling was nearly identical to the earlier position of Shammai: "Whosoever shall put away his wife, except it be for fornication, and shall marry another, committeth adultery" (Matthew 19:9). In His interpretation of the law of Moses on this matter, the Master deliberately emphasized the primary importance of marriage over any pragmatic benefits of a divorce obtained too easily.

When considering this ruling, however, whether in Matthew 19 or in the Sermon on the Mount (Matthew 5:31–32), Latter-day Saints should keep in mind that it is a law of Moses ruling. Although the principle of respect for marriage should be as important to us today as it was to the Jews of Jesus' time, Latter-day Saints are not governed by the law of Moses, and the regulations of that law regarding divorce are not those that are germane in the Church today. Latter-day Saints are subject to the civil divorce laws in the states or countries where they reside, and Church law applies only in matters of worthiness for membership or temple activity. In any case, members of the modern church need not worry that they are automatically judged guilty of adultery if they have remarried after experiencing a legal divorce for a legally valid cause. Though we have many commandments and precepts in common, the law of Moses is not the law of the Latter-day Saints.

The Most Important Commandment in the Law

Matthew 22 and Mark 12 record an exchange about the law of Moses that Jesus had with a Pharisee at Jesus' last public appearance at the temple in Jerusalem. Matthew called the Pharisee a lawyer, Mark called him a scribe, but the sincerity of his question[23] was evident: "Master, which is the great commandment in the law?" (Matthew 22:35–36; compare Mark 12:28). Jesus replied by quoting Deuteronomy 6:4–5, the introductory lines of the passage the Jews called *Shema:* "Hear, O Israel; the Lord our God is one Lord: and thou shalt love the Lord thy God with all thy heart, and with all thy soul, and with all thy mind, and with all thy strength: this is the first commandment" (see Mark 12:29–30, quoting a longer version than Matthew 22:37). "And the second is like unto it," Jesus continued, recalling Leviticus 19:18, "Thou shalt love thy neighbor as thyself. On these two commandments hang all the law and the prophets" (Matthew 22:39–40).

Though this was essentially Jesus' last public appearance, there was no hint here that the law of Moses was to go out of effect within days—because that was not the case. Quite the contrary, Jesus had once again extolled the law, noting that its chief function was promoting the love of God and fellow man. What higher or more celestial law could there be than this?

The account was extended, however, by Mark, who recorded the Pharisee's reply: "Well, Master, thou hast said the truth: for there is one God; and there is none other but he: and to love him with all the heart, and with all the understanding, and with all the soul, and with all the strength, and to love his neighbor as himself, is more than all whole burnt offerings and sacrifices" (Mark 12:32–33). The true essence of the law of Moses is neither the mere repetition of ritual nor the bringing of animals to a horned altar. Correctly

---

[23] Again, in Matthew 22:35, the King James assertion that the Pharisee was "tempting" Jesus is a misrepresentation. The Greek term (*pierazon*) is more correctly translated as "test, try, or prove," as per note 35a for that verse in the LDS edition of the Bible.

understood, it was endued by God with the spirit necessary to guide those for whom it was intended to a celestial reward. This is clear from the Savior's response to the noble scribe: "When Jesus saw that he answered discreetly, he said unto him, Thou art not far from the kingdom of God" (Mark 12:34).

Conclusion

From the ten commandments to the "golden rule" that was the point of the law (Matthew 7:12), from the nature of the Sabbath to the performance of the sacrifices, and from the sanctity of marriage to the pure love of God, what Jesus taught the Jews about the law of Moses was the same message He has taught us in Doctrine and Covenants 14:7: "If you keep my commandments and endure to the end you shall have eternal life, which gift is the greatest of all the gifts of God."

VIII.

THE DEATH OF JOHN THE BAPTIST

CECILIA M. PEEK

But what went ye out for to see? A prophet? yea, I say unto you, and more than a prophet. For this is he, of whom it is written, Behold, I send my messenger before thy face, which shall prepare thy way before thee. Verily I say unto you, Among them that are born of women, there hath not risen a greater than John the Baptist.

MATTHEW 11:9–11

In every one of the Gospel narratives, a summary of the career of John the Baptist precedes and acts as prologue to the career of Jesus.[1] The comparatively brief scriptural account of John's activities becomes the rhetorical forerunner to the account of Jesus' public ministry—a reflection of the prophesied function of the Baptist's life, in which John becomes that absolutely essential figure

[1] Mark 1:2–8; Matthew 3:1–12; Luke 3:1–20; John 1:6–8, 19–36; 3:23–30. See Catherine M. Murphy, *John the Baptist: Prophet of Purity for a New Age* (Collegeville, Minn.: Liturgical Press, 2003), 7–8; F. F. Bruce, *New Testament History* (New York: Doubleday, 1971), 152; Raymond E. Brown, *An Introduction to the New Testament* (New York: Doubleday, 1997), 128. On the connection between the end of John the Baptist's career and the beginning of Jesus' public ministry, see Cecilia M. Peek, "Early Galilean Ministry and Miracles," in *The Life and Teachings of Jesus Christ: From Bethlehem through the Sermon on the Mount*, ed. Richard Neitzel Holzapfel and Thomas A. Wayment (Salt Lake City: Deseret Book, 2005), 271–77, with notes.

foretold to "prepare . . . the way of the Lord," a man whose own course marks the path Jesus would both parallel and surpass in birth, in life, and in death.[2]

This chapter will concern itself primarily with the death of John the Baptist, considering it as a historical and theological event. First, a number of historical questions must be answered. What scriptural and extrascriptural evidence is available on John's death? What is known of the individuals and events surrounding that death? Based on surviving evidence, who and what were responsible for John's arrest and execution? Finally, the death of John the Baptist will be considered in the context that surrounds his story as represented, however briefly, in the Gospels. This chapter will investigate the unique significance of his death in view of the specific setting and rhetorical purpose of those individual Gospels that discuss the end of his life, as well as the symbolic import of his death in the larger religious framework of the life and ministry of the man called to "go before the face of the Lord to prepare his ways" (Luke 1:76).[3]

Sources of Information

There are six sources of evidence for John the Baptist that are judged to be most original and, therefore, most important. These earliest available texts on John are almost exclusively canonical. Five of the six are among the books of the New Testament: the Gospels of Matthew, Mark, Luke, and John all feature John the Baptist; the book of the Acts of the Apostles also refers to him in several settings. Indeed, New Testament references to John the Baptist are numerous,[4] although for information on his arrest and

[2] See Matthew 3:3. Compare Isaiah 40:3; Mark 1:3; Luke 3:4; John 1:23. Also, see Malachi 4:5–6.

[3] John's father, Zacharias, whose voice had just been restored to him after many months of muteness, proclaimed this to those present at the infant boy's naming and circumcision. See Luke 1:62–79.

[4] Including, to name just a few examples, Luke 1:5–25, 39–56, 57–79 for the announcement of John's birth, the visit of Mary to Elizabeth, and John's naming and circumcision; Mark 1:2–6; Matthew 3:1–6; Luke 3:1–6; and John 1:6–8 for the start of

death we are dependent specifically upon the Gospels. All four report John's arrest (Mark 1:14; 6:17; Matthew 4:12; 14:3; Luke 3:19–20; John 3:24), but only the synoptics comment on his execution. Luke only mentions it (7:9), whereas Mark and Matthew give lengthier and more detailed descriptions thereof (Mark 6:14–29; Matthew 14:1–12).[5] The sixth of the main sources is Antiquities of the Jews, by the Jewish historian Josephus. His sketch of John the Baptist occurs within the larger chronicle of Herod Antipas, the son of Herod the Great.[6]

These texts provide the key surviving evidence about John's life, his violent end, and the individuals and causes associated with it. The details differ somewhat from text to text; blame is variously attached, and motives are variously imputed. However, as we shall see, certain elements remain constant among those sources that mention and discuss the fate of John the Baptist.[7]

The Story in Josephus

Josephus introduces the account of John's death as part of his consideration of a key defeat of the forces of Antipas by the Nabatean King Aretas IV. In A.D. 36, the Nabatean King Aretas IV

John's public ministry and for his performance of baptism; Mark 1:7–8; Matthew 3:7–12; Luke 3:7–18; and John 1:15–27 for the content of John's preaching; and Mark 1:9–11; Matthew 3:13–17; and Luke 3:21–23 for the baptism of Jesus.

[5] As for the Gospel of John, it provides no account of John the Baptist's death and will not formally make up part of this discussion.

[6] Josephus, *AJ* 18.5.1–2.

[7] All these sources are discussed in detail by J. Ernst, *Johannes der Täufer. Interpretation—Geschichte—Wirkungsgeschichte* (Berlin and London: Walter de Gruyter, 1989), 4–216 (for the five New Testament texts), 253–60 (for Josephus) and by Murphy, *John the Baptist*, 3–13. See also C. R. Kazmierski, *John the Baptist: Prophet and Evangelist* (Collegeville, Minn.: Liturgical Press, 1996), 7, and H. Hoehner, *Herod Antipas* (Cambridge: Cambridge University Press, 1972), 110–24. On additional texts featuring references to John the Baptist, see Ernst, *Johannes*, 217–51. For more particular consideration of the noncanonical sources and their comparative value, see Walter Wink, *John the Baptist in the Gospel Tradition*, SNTSMS 7 (Cambridge: Cambridge University Press, 1968); Ernst Bammel, "The Baptist in Early Christian Tradition," *New Testament Studies* 8 (1971–1972): 95–128; and Robert L. Webb, *John the Baptizer and Prophet: A Socio-Historical Study*, JSNTSup 62 (Sheffield: JSOT Press, 1991).

crossed the border of his kingdom into Antipas' territory and invaded Perea, pointing to Antipas' rejection of his Nabatean wife, the daughter of Aretas, as justification for the hostility. Aretas soundly defeated the forces of Antipas, destroying, according to Josephus, the whole of his army. When Herod informed the emperor Tiberius of the attack, he ordered Lucius Vitellius, the legate of Syria, "to make war upon [Aretas] and either to take him alive, and bring him to [Tiberius] in bonds, or to kill him, and send him his head."[8] As it happened, news of the emperor's death reached Vitellius in Jerusalem before he had fully undertaken the expedition, and the legate called off the campaign.[9] Josephus says that certain Jews believed the destruction of Antipas' army at the hands of the Nabatean king to be a manifestation of divine punishment for what he had done to John the Baptist: "Now, some of the Jews thought that the destruction of Herod's army came from God, and that very justly, as a punishment of what he did against John, that was called the Baptist; for Herod slew him."[10] The Jewish historian and apologist lays the blame for the Baptist's death squarely on the shoulders of Herod and explains it thus: "Now, when, others came in crowds about [John], for they were greatly moved by hearing his words, Herod, who feared lest the great influence John had over the people might put it into his power and inclination to raise a rebellion (for they seemed ready to do anything he should advise), thought it best, by putting him to death, to prevent any mischief he might cause."[11] The author specifies that John was consequently sent as a prisoner to the Herodian fortress of Machaerus in Jordan and there put to death.[12]

---

[8] Josephus, *AJ* 18.5.1.

[9] Josephus, *AJ* 18.5.3.

[10] Josephus, *AJ* 18.5.2 (emphasis in original).

[11] Josephus, *AJ* 18.5.2.

[12] Josephus, *AJ* 18.119. Pliny the Elder calls Machaerus "the most important Jewish stone fortress just after Jerusalem" (*Natural History* 5.15.72). The fortress where John the Baptist was imprisoned and executed would have been the second of two successive fortresses built on the site: the first erected by Alexander Janneus in c. 90 B.C., the second by Herod the Great in 30 B.C. (Josephus, *JW* 7.171–72). See

Before we examine the text, let us consider the identity and history of this Herod. The Herod referred to here by Josephus is one of the many offspring of Herod the Great. This son, known as Herod Antipas, or simply Antipas, was the issue of Herod the Great and his wife Malthace.[13] At the death of Herod the Great in 4 B.C., Antipas inherited a portion of his father's kingdom. Over the course of his reign, Herod had changed his mind many times about the disposition of his territories and the order of succession at his death, but in the end, his will settled upon three sons: Archelaus, Antipas' elder brother by the same mother, was to receive Judea, Samaria, and Idumea, as well as the royal title; Herod Antipas was to rule Galilee and Perea as tetrarch;[14] and Herod Philip, a son of Cleopatra of Jerusalem, was to be tetrarch of Gaulonitis, Trachonitis, and Paneas, territory that Herod the Great had received from Augustus to the east and northeast of the Sea of Galilee.[15]

Before any of the designated sons could inherit, the last will of Herod had to be ratified by the emperor.[16] After their father's

---

"Machaerus," in Freedman, *ABD* 4:457. For the location of John's imprisonment and death, we are dependent upon Josephus; the Gospels provide no information on the subject.

[13] This Malthace, the mother of Antipas (and of a brother Archelaus), was only one of several wives of Herod. Others included Doris; two wives named Mariamme—one a Hasmonean princess, the other a daughter of the high priest Simon Boëthus; and Cleopatra of Jerusalem, mother of the Philip who would, along with Archelaus and Antipater, become one of Herod the Great's political heirs. On the marriages of Herod the Great, see Josephus, *JW* 1.562–63.

[14] The term *tetrarch* technically means "ruler of a fourth part," and it strictly referred to one of four governors of a province. The term, however, also came to be used more generally of a subordinate or dependent prince or a petty sovereign. With Herod Antipas, the term suggests that he was ruler of only a portion of the larger Jewish territory (although not of precisely a fourth part), and he was also a petty sovereign. See H. D. Westlake, "Tetrarchy," in *The Oxford Classical Dictionary*, ed. Simon Hornblower, 3rd edition (Oxford and New York: Oxford University Press, 2003), 1489.

[15] Josephus, *AJ* 17.8.1–2; *JW* 1.33.8. On the various wills of Herod the Great, see Hoehner, *Herod Antipas*, 269–76. Compare Bruce, *New Testament History*, 22–24.

[16] Until the will could be ratified, Archelaus was careful not to accept the title of king or to allow himself to be crowned, although he did become the *de facto* leader. See Josephus, *AJ* 17.9.3; *JW* 2.2.1.

demise, Archelaus and Antipas made their way to Rome to advance their interests, and Philip remained in Palestine.[17] Antipas campaigned for the royal title in rivalry to his brother, Archelaus. While the brothers, with the help of their respective supporters, were pressing their claims before Augustus, a deputation of fifty Jewish aristocrats also traveled to the city and requested the establishment of a Roman governor in Palestine in place of Herodian rule.[18] After hearing the petition of the delegation and the arguments for and against both Antipas and Archelaus, Augustus ratified the originally proposed settlement of Herod's will, except that he demoted Archelaus from king to ethnarch.[19]

Meanwhile, Palestine was subjected to a series of disruptions. Indeed, just after the death of Herod the Great, even before his heirs departed for Rome, some Jews demanded of Archelaus revenge on behalf of those who had been killed by his father for removing the Roman eagle from the temple gate. Archelaus expressed himself willing to fulfill at least one of their requests—namely, to choose a new high priest—but urged them through his general to withhold other petitions until he could be established in his government. This request was not well received, and at the feast of the Passover, revolutionaries in attendance at the feast in Jerusalem openly lamented their old losses. Archelaus responded by sending out his troops to prevent a full-scale uprising and ended by

---

[17] Josephus, *AJ* 17.11.1; *JW* 2.6.1–2. Although Philip remained in Palestine initially, he later traveled to Rome, with the approval of Quintilius Varus, the Roman legate of Syria. See *AJ* 17.11.1; *JW* 2.6.1.

[18] Josephus claims that the delegation, which was joined by eight thousand Roman Jews, demanded direct Roman rule, a request that was not granted at the time but that would affect part of the region in the relatively near future. See *AJ* 17.11.1; *JW* 2.6.1. According to Nicolaus of Damascus (*Life of Augustus* IIa, 424), the delegation petitioned for Roman rule but was prepared to accept Antipas if necessary.

[19] Josephus, *AJ* 17.9.3, 11.1–4; *JW* 2.2.3–6.3. See Hoehner, *Herod Antipas*, 21–33; Bruce, *New Testament History*, 24. *Ethnarch* literally means "ruler of a people (*ethnos*)." It is a lesser title than king but greater than tetrarch. Augustus determined to withhold from Archelaus the honored title of king but still allowed that Archelaus was the ruler of a people and not just of a territory. See F. F. Bruce, "Palestine (Administration of Roman)," in Freedman, *ABD* 5:97.

killing three thousand people.[20] This outcome did not, however, put an end to disturbances.

While the terms of Herod's will were being debated in Rome, word arrived of more trouble at Jerusalem during the feast of Pentecost.[21] The problems seem to have spread from there throughout Palestine, including the appearance of pretenders to the throne and the outbreak of several armed revolts. In Judea, the revolt was led by old soldiers of Herod the Great.[22] Elsewhere, a certain Simon, once a slave of Herod, assumed the diadem and was declared by some to be a king. "He burnt down the royal palace at Jericho, and plundered" its remains. He also destroyed others of the king's residences throughout the country.[23] An otherwise unknown shepherd by the name of Athronges likewise set himself up as king and, along with his rebel brothers, "retained his power for a great while." According to Josephus, they "did their own nation also a great deal of mischief" before they were finally subdued.[24] In addition, Beth-Ramptha in Perea—part of the territory inherited by Antipas as tetrarch—was burned by insurgents. But perhaps the most serious threat occurred in Galilee, another of the areas assigned to Herod Antipas. A rebel named Judas attacked the Herodian palace at Sepphoris and seized control of the armory there.[25] This site may well have become the "headquarters of the rebellion."[26]

The threat posed by Judas, along with the several simultaneous risings elsewhere in Palestine, was considered sufficiently grave to justify Roman intervention. Quintilius Varus, the legate of Syria, was ordered to quell the insurrections. With the assistance of his armed forces, he subdued the troubled region, including the

[20] Josephus, *AJ* 17.9.1–3; *JW* 2.1.2–3.

[21] Josephus, *AJ* 17.10.1–10; *JW* 2.9.

[22] Josephus, *AJ* 17.10.4; *JW* 2.4.1.

[23] Josephus, *AJ* 17.10.6; *JW* 2.4.4; Tacitus, *Histories* 5.9.

[24] Josephus, *AJ* 17.10.7–8; *JW* 2.4.3.

[25] Josephus, *AJ* 17.10.5; *JW* 2.4.1.

[26] Hoehner, *Herod Antipas*, 83, believes this to have been the case and believes this explains the particularly brutal punishment eventually inflicted on that city.

recapture and burning of Sepphoris, whose surviving inhabitants were made slaves.[27]

Because of the uprisings at home and the political perils in Rome, the territories and positions to be held by Herod's sons were not easily secured. Archelaus, Antipas, and Philip all faced serious threats to the security of their offices and to the stability of Palestine itself at the start of their rule. When once these early threats were overcome, the brothers could, for a time, settle into their places.

When Herod Antipas returned to Palestine, he found a region devastated by war. During his tenure as tetrarch, he repaired much of the damage that had been done by various insurgent forces at his father's death, rebuilding two cities, Sepphoris and Beth-Ramptha, and founding one new, Tiberias, established on the western shore of the Sea of Galilee and named in honor of the emperor Tiberius. The work of rebuilding probably occurred soon after his return from Rome.[28] When Antipas repaired Beth-Ramptha in Perea, he fortified it as an outpost against the bordering Nabatean kingdom and renamed it Julias, or Livias, for the wife of the emperor.[29] He also magnificently rebuilt Sepphoris, which, in its restored condition, Josephus calls "the ornament of all Galilee."[30] This fortified site

[27] Josephus, *AJ* 17.10.9; *JW* 2.5.1. On the wide variety of disturbances and the eventual Roman response to them, see Josephus, *JW* 2.4.1–3; *AJ* 17.10.4–10.

[28] Hoehner, *Herod Antipas*, 84. Compare S. J. Case, "Jesus and Sepphoris," *Journal of Biblical Literature* 45 (1926): 17–18n4.

[29] Josephus, *AJ* 18.2.1; 20.8.4; *JW* 2.9.1, 13.2; 4.7.6, always refers to the city as "Julias," specifying that it is named for the emperor's wife. Other ancient sources, however, regularly refer to the site as "Livias." Compare Pliny, *Natural History* 13.9.44, and Ptolemy, *Geographia*, 5.16.9. Some scholars assume that the city was originally named "Livias," in honor of Augustus' famous wife, but that the name was changed to "Julias" when that same Livia was adopted into the Julian *gens* in accordance with the terms of Augustus' will. For the terms of Augustus' will, cf. Tacitus, *Annals,* 1.8, 1–2; Suetonius, *The Twelve Caesars* 2.101. On the assumption that the name of the rebuilt city may have been changed after Livia's adoption, see, for example, E. Schürer, *The History of the Jewish People in the Age of Jesus Christ (175 B.C.–A.D. 135)*, ed. Geza Vermes et al., rev. ed., 3 vols. in 4 (Edinburgh: T&T Clark, 1973–87), 2:214–15.

[30] Translated in Hoehner, *Herod Antipas*, 84–87. Josephus, *AJ* 18.2.1: "*proschêma tou Galilaiou.*" This phrase might also be translated "the security of all Galilee." See

became and remained Antipas' capital city until he founded Tiberias.[31] Even after he transferred his attention to his new capital, Sepphoris continued to be the largest city in Galilee.[32] Nevertheless, the city of Tiberias, founded about A.D. 18, proved to be Antipas' most famous and most important building project.[33]

Antipas' building activity is significant—because at least for the years this activity lasted, the tetrarch would have been reminded of the original insecurity of his territory. Specifically, his efforts to rebuild Beth-Ramptha and Sepphoris, two sites devastated by rebellion and revolt, would have driven home the memory of his early troubles. The fact that he named and renamed sites in honor of the most influential members of the imperial family suggests that Antipas acknowledged the ongoing insecurity of the tetrarchy, the value of Roman support, and the continuing need for that support in his office.

The potential weakness of Antipas' position would have been particularly poignant in Galilee. The revolt under Judas in 4 B.C. was by no means the first instance of unrest there. Judas' own father was Hezekiah, whom Josephus calls a "bandit chief" (*archilêstês*). Forty-three years earlier, he had been caught and executed by Herod the Great.[34] As Bruce reads it, Hezekiah was not merely a "bandit-chief" but rather a "patriotic resistance leader" and forerunner to the future Zealot movement.[35] The genealogy of Judas

---

Bruce, *New Testament History*, 27–28. Some scholars believe that Antipas also renamed Sepphoris, calling it "Diocaesarea." See G. Dalman, *Sacred Sites and Ways: Studies in the Topography of the Gospels*, trans. P. P. Levertoff (New York: Macmillan, 1935), 75; Bruce, *New Testament History*, 27–28. There is, however, no surviving material evidence for Sepphoris' being called "Diocaesarea" until the reign of Antoninus Pius (A.D. 138–61). See Hoehner, *Herod Antipas*, 86.

[31] Hoehner, *Herod Antipas*, 85. Compare Dalman, *Sacred Sites*, 75.

[32] Josephus, *Life* 37.

[33] Josephus, *AJ* 18.2.3; *JW* 2.9.1. According to Josephus, the city had the status of a *polis*, with its own archon, a Council of Ten, and a Senate of Six Hundred. See *JW* 2.21.9; *Life* 13, 54, 57. Compare Hoehner, *Herod Antipas* 91–100.

[34] Josephus, *JW* 1.10.5; *AJ* 14.9.2.

[35] Bruce, *New Testament History*, 97–99, points to uses of the term *archilêstês* (and variants) in Josephus and elsewhere. He also indicates that Hezekiah's likely political

suggests that the Galilean uprising he led may itself have been a politically charged "zealot rising."[36] His family background at least demonstrates that there was a history of anti-Herodian and anti-Roman feeling in Galilee, a key location of Herod Antipas' territory, of which hostility the tetrarch was clearly reminded in 4 B.C. and to which he would be sensitive ever after.[37] These considerations must be borne in mind when we read Josephus' account of John the Baptist's death.

Later events must also be taken into account. Antipas' brother, Archelaus, lost his office only ten years after assuming it. He was deposed and sent into exile at Augustus' orders in A.D. 6.[38] According to Josephus, two embassies—one from Judea and one from Samaria—went to Rome to complain of Archelaus' tyrannical rule and to ask that he be removed.[39] The rare cooperation of the Jewish and Samaritan communities suggests that their objections to Archelaus were both serious and justified.[40] Augustus certainly believed so. Persuaded that Archelaus' continued tenure might cause a large-scale revolt, the emperor deposed the ethnarch,

---

identity is suggested by the angry response of the Sanhedrin to the news of John's death.

[36] Bruce, *New Testament History*, 98. Compare William R. Farmer, "Judas, Simon, and Anthronges," *New Testament Studies* 4 (1957–8): 147–55.

[37] Indeed, the Galilean revolt of 4 B.C. may still have been recalled with concern well into Jesus' ministry. Ritt believes that Jesus' Galilean origins aroused suspicion specifically because of Judas' revolutionary activity in that area twenty years earlier. See H. Ritt, "Wer war am Schuld am Tod Jesu?" *Beihefte zur Zeitschrift für die neutestamentliche Wissenschaft* 31 (1987): 170–72.

[38] On the duration of Archelaus' ethnarchy, see Hoehner, *Herod Antipas*, 301–2.

[39] Josephus, *AJ* 17.13.2; *JW* 2.8.3. Other ancient sources differ slightly in the accounts they give of Archelaus' deposition. Strabo, *Geographica* 16.2.46, suggests that all three sons of Herod the Great encountered opposition from their subject populations, although he provides no specific information about the accusations leveled against them, saying instead that the sons of Herod "were not successful, but became involved in accusations." Archelaus was banished as a result of these unnamed "accusations." Dio Cassius, *Annals* 55.27.6, claims that Archelaus was accused by his *brothers* of some misdeed and that he was banished because of *this* accusation, although the specific charge is again absent from the account.

[40] A. H. M. Jones, *The Herods of Judaea* (Oxford: Clarendon Press, 1938), 167. Compare Hoehner, *Herod Antipas*, 104.

banished him to Vienna, and reorganized Judea as a part of the Roman province of Syria.[41] Just before recounting the visit of the complaining embassy to Rome and the deposition of Archelaus in response thereto, Josephus gave a short summary of the ethnarch's misdeeds. Prominent among them was the fact that he had "transgressed the law of our fathers, and married Glaphyra," his dead half-brother Alexander's wife.[42] The structure of the history implies that the opposition to Archelaus was a direct response to the cited offenses and that those offenses, including the unlawful marriage to his deceased brother's spouse, precipitated his removal.

During Antipas' reign, he made a similarly unsanctioned marriage when, after approximately twenty years of marriage to a daughter of the Nabatean King Aretas IV, he transferred his affection to his sister-in-law. On a journey to Rome, Antipas lodged with his half-brother Herod (Philip).[43] During this visit, he saw and

---

[41] Josephus, *AJ* 17.13.2; *JW* 2.1.3. Compare Strabo, *Geographica* 16.2.46; Dio Cassius, *Annals* 55.27.6.

[42] *AJ* 17.13.1, 4–5; *JW* 2.7.4. The marriage to Glaphyra was deemed a transgression because Jewish law did not allow marriage to a dead brother's wife, except in cases where the earlier marriage had been childless. In that case, provision had been made for a surviving brother to marry the widow in order to produce a legal heir for the dead brother. For the injunction against marriage to a brother's wife, see Leviticus 18:16, 20:21. On the exception to this rule, see Deuteronomy 25:5–6; Ruth 3:9–13; Mark 12:19. According to Josephus, *AJ* 17.13.1, Alexander had, in fact, fathered three children by Glaphyra, and the Deuteronomic exception could not be invoked to justify her marriage to Archelaus. See Hoehner, *Herod Antipas*, 104n1; Bruce, *New Testament History*, 25.

[43] There is some uncertainty about the identity of Herodias' first husband. The Gospels of Mark and Matthew call him Philip, whereas Josephus gives his name only as Herod. Adding to the confusion, Josephus tells us that Herodias' daughter Salome married a Philip, also the half-brother of Antipas and the tetrarch of Trachontis. The Herod referred to by Josephus as Herodias' first husband may have been known, as some assume, by the full name Herod Philip. This would explain the use of the name Philip for Herodias' husband in the Gospels. If the evangelists rightly give the name Philip to the husband Herodias abandoned for Antipas, then it is another son of Herod the Great with the name Philip and not the tetrarch of Trachontis. See Josephus *AJ* 18.5.3. Compare Hoehner, *Herod Antipas*, 131–36, where he discusses the identity of Herodias' first husband and concludes that he was, in fact, Herod Philip, the son of Mariamme II, and "that both Josephus and the Gospels are correct." Bruce, *New Testament History*, 28, likewise identifies Herodias' husband as Herod Philip.

became enamored of Herodias, his brother's wife and Antipas' own niece. He proposed marriage, which she accepted, provided he divorce his Arabian wife.[44] Antipas agreed. Although Josephus does not explicitly assert that the marriage made the tetrarch unpopular with his Jewish subjects, he strongly hints his disapproval, and it seems likely to have generated some Jewish opposition in view of Archelaus' earlier trouble. Indeed, Antipas' proposed marriage was an even more egregious violation of the law, for Herodias' husband, unlike Glaphyra's, was still living, and there was no possible justification for the union under Jewish law.[45] And Josephus certainly does assert that Antipas' broader political position was threatened by the affair. For, as mentioned earlier, king Aretas took offense at the slight to his daughter and "made this the first occasion of his enmity between him and Herod," an enmity that would eventually result in armed conflict.[46] Antipas must have been aware that the marriage to Herodias or, more to the point, the dissolution of his marriage to Aretas' daughter rendered him politically less secure.

In general, Antipas seems to have ruled as tetrarch long and successfully.[47] Nevertheless, the memory of events following his father's death, the removal of his brother Archelaus from his office, the transformation of that brother's territory into a Roman province, and the stresses apparently caused by his own marriage to Herodias must all have made Antipas a very watchful politician. The possibility of future rebellion by his own people, of future

---

Contrast Murphy, 62, who believes the Gospels are in error in calling that husband Philip.

[44] Josephus, *AJ* 18.5.1.

[45] See references in note 42 above.

[46] Josephus, *AJ* 18.5.1. When King Aretas' daughter learned of Antipas' plan to divorce her, she made her way to Machaerus, the stronghold built by Herod the Great on the borders of her father's territory. From there she made her way to Aretas and informed him of her husband's intentions. Josephus notes that the mistreatment of his daughter was only one reason for Aretas' hostility to Antipas. There was also a dispute over boundaries. Compare Hoehner, *Herod Antipas*, 140–44.

[47] See Bruce, *New Testament History*, 27–31.

complaints to Rome, and of future reprisals from the Nabatean kingdom ever loomed.

With this background in mind, let us return to Josephus' account of John the Baptist's death. A number of important points emerge about the historical John, largely confirming what is known of him from the New Testament. Josephus establishes that he was known as the Baptist, that he exhorted the Jews to be virtuous and pious, and that he called his listeners to be baptized.[48] As for John's death, Josephus speaks of it only in general terms. He mentions no specific misdeed or offense against Herod Antipas. The tetrarch had John killed neither because he had done anything illegal nor, indeed, because he actively threatened rebellion but because he was influential, popular, and, to Herod's mind, potentially dangerous. Herod noted that people "seemed ready to do anything [John] should advise," and he worried that "the great influence John had over people might put it into his power and inclination to raise a rebellion."[49] So Antipas sent him in chains to Machaerus, lest he eventually cause some sort of revolt. In view of Antipas' personal history, his worry over a figure like John is perhaps understandable. During his public ministry, John seems to have been active on the Perean bank of the Jordan Valley,[50] an area within Herod's tetrarchy that had manifest anti-Herodian feelings and active revolt in the past. With an appropriately charismatic leader, rebellion might happen again. As Josephus describes it, Antipas feared that John might turn out to be just such a leader. In the Jewish historian's account, Herod's interest in John is primarily political; his treatment of John is preventative.[51]

The motives ascribed to Herod by Josephus may, of course, be explicable without being justified, and they tell us more about the tetrarch than they do about the Baptist. Antipas apparently could not imagine a man enjoying the sort of influence John did without

[48] Josephus *AJ* 18.5.2. See Murphy, *John the Baptist*, 5–6.

[49] Josephus *AJ* 18.5.2.

[50] John 1:28. See Bruce, *New Testament History*, 160.

[51] Hoehner, *Herod Antipas*, 137, 140.

putting it to work in the interest of personal advancement. But Herod badly misjudged him, for never was a man less intent on personal advancement than John the Baptist. He generously proclaimed to the Jews who questioned him about Jesus' activity, "Ye yourselves bear me witness, that I said, I am not the Christ, but that I am sent before him. He that hath the bride is the bridegroom: but the friend of the bridegroom, which standeth and heareth him, rejoiceth greatly because of the bridegroom's voice: this my joy therefore is fulfilled. He must increase, but I must decrease" (John 3:28–30). Jesus is the bridegroom, but John himself is content to be the friend who rejoices at the groom's good fortune and to have his own public life wane while Jesus' increases.

If Herod Antipas misjudged John the Baptist, Josephus did not necessarily misjudge Herod, for the Gospel accounts that treat the death of John likewise hold the tetrarch responsible, although the reasons advanced are more specific and more personal than those given by Josephus.

Mark's Representation of the Arrest and Execution

Mark's first mention of the arrest of John the Baptist says nothing of its causes. It is simply introduced as the immediate chronological precursor to the start of Jesus' public ministry: "Now after that John was put in prison, Jesus came into Galilee, preaching the gospel of the kingdom of God" (Mark 1:14). Having informed the reader that John has been arrested, Mark abandons the account of the Baptist's situation. However, the Gospel writer returns to the subject as part of a later and larger reminiscence on the arrest and execution,[52] in which he establishes an explicit link between Antipas' marriage to Herodias and the arrest and death of John the Baptist:

> For Herod himself had sent forth and laid hold upon John, and bound him in prison for Herodias' sake, his brother Philip's wife: for

[52] Murphy, *John the Baptist*, 60.

he had married her. For John had said unto Herod, It is not lawful for thee to have thy brother's wife. Therefore Herodias had a quarrel against him, and would have killed him; but she could not: For Herod feared John, knowing that he was a just man and an holy, and observed him; and when he heard him, he did many things, and heard him gladly. And when a convenient day was come, that Herod on his birthday made a supper to his lords, high captains, and chief estates of Galilee; and when the daughter of the said Herodias came in, and danced, and pleased Herod and them that sat with him, the king said unto the damsel, Ask of me whatsoever thou wilt, and I will give it thee. And he sware unto her, Whatsoever thou shalt ask of me, I will give it thee, unto the half of my kingdom. And when she went forth, and said unto her mother, What shall I ask? And she said, The head of John the Baptist. And she came in straightway with haste unto the king, and asked, saying, I will that thou give me by and by in a charger the head of John the Baptist. And the king was exceeding sorry; yet for the oath's sake, and for their sakes which sat with him, he would not reject her. And immediately the king sent an executioner, and commanded his head to be brought: and he went and beheaded him in prison, and brought his head in a charger, and gave it to the damsel: and the damsel gave it to her mother. And when his disciples heard of it, they came and took up his corpse, and laid it in a tomb. (Mark 6:17–29)[53]

In Mark's account, Herod Antipas, whom he inaccurately refers to as king,[54] arrested John the Baptist "for Herodias' sake." John

[53] There are a number of difficulties with the King James translation of this passage, particularly of verse 20, for the modern English reader. Some assistance can be found in the Joseph Smith Translation of that verse: "For Herod feared John, knowing that he was a just man and *a holy man, and one who feared God and observed to worship him;* and when he heard him he did many things *for him*, and heard him gladly." Some of the implications of the Joseph Smith Translation are borne out by the Greek. The term translated in the King James Version as "observed"—*sunetêrei*—would be better translated "protected." Arndt and Gingrich. *GEL*, 792. The idea that Herod "protected" John may be inferred from Joseph Smith's phrase, "and when he heard him he did many things for him."

[54] Herod Antipas' technical title was undoubtedly tetrarch, but the term "king" (*basileus*) may represent popular usage. Similar misapplication of nomenclature is, for example, found in Josephus' references to the ethnarch Archelaus. The problem is

had challenged Herod's marriage to Herodias on the grounds that it was unlawful for Herod to have his brother's wife.[55] Although Josephus confirms that Herod Antipas had, in fact, unlawfully married his brother's wife, he does not mention that John the Baptist condemned the marriage and asserts no clear connection between the marriage and John's arrest.

Mark's interests are, of course, predominantly theological; Josephus' interests are political. Nevertheless, the two accounts need not be read as mutually exclusive. For a devout Jewish audience, religion and politics could be, and frequently were, closely intertwined. Herodias was presumably enraged at John's condemnation of the union—not because she was ashamed of her religious infraction nor solely because she was embarrassed by public criticism but because that criticism threatened her husband's powerful position and therefore her own.

If Archelaus' experience is any guide, a Jewish ruler who violates Jewish law may find his status seriously compromised or, indeed, completely undermined. Should the objections of Antipas' subject population and of their priestly leaders become sufficiently strong, they might complain to Rome of his leadership. John had denounced the marriage and thereby threatened Herod and earned Herodias' enmity. And the marriage did have political consequences, weakening, as Josephus says, Anitpas' relationship to his erstwhile father-in-law, Aretas IV, and, as Mark implies, to his own people as well.[56]

Herod, however, is not the particular enemy of John in the Gospel of Mark, which holds Herodias, with the assistance of her unnamed daughter, mainly responsible for the Baptist's death. Indeed, the daughter, whom Josephus identifies as Salome,[57] may remain unnamed to underscore the centrality of Herodias in the

---

discussed by Bruce, *New Testament History*, 27, and Hoehner, *Herod Antipas*, 149–50, with references.

[55] See note 42 above, with references.

[56] Hoehner, *Herod Antipas*, 137–46.

[57] Josephus, *AJ* 18.5.4.

course of events—her daughter is submissive to her mother's wishes and acting on her mother's orders.[58] Antipas, Mark tells us, kept John safe (sunetêrei), when his wife "would have killed him" (6:19). Here the woman plays the central role as the plotter and the enemy. The similar story of Elijah, Ahab, and Jezebel comes to mind as a comparison. When Elijah condemned the actions of the royal household, Jezebel was out for the prophet's blood.[59] In Mark's account, John the Baptist becomes the Elijah figure to Herodias' Jezebel, although John, unlike the prophet of old, failed to escape the cruel fate wished upon him by the king's wife.[60]

Herod Antipas is, in apparent contrast to his wife, a weak character, ambivalent about John the Baptist and swayed by the opinions of others: by Herodias, by her dancing daughter, and by the guests at his birthday celebration. He regrets what he does, but he beheads John for the sake of those "which sat with him" and "for the oath's sake." Although Herod's guests are men of rank and importance (Mark 6:21), his apparent fear of risking his reputation with them establishes a critical contrast to John the Baptist, who famously declares and does what is right, even if it involves the condemnation of the most powerful family in the land at the risk of his own life.

Herod's other justification for beheading John—"for the oath's sake"—at first glance seems to strengthen the reading of Herod as a weak-minded man. He has made a promise, and even though the consequences of that promise are evil, he is determined to see it through rather than be made to look foolish. But the term employed to describe Herod's decision may have more troubling implications. The phrase puts us in mind of the story of Lamech

---

[58] Compare Ben Witherington III, "Salome," in Freedman, *ABD*, 5:907, who adds, however, that Salome herself seems to have contrived the perverse request for John's head "on a platter."

[59] 1 Kings 18:17–18; 19:1–2, 9–10, 13–14.

[60] Henry B. Swete, *The Gospel According to St. Mark* (London: Macmillan, 1909), 194. Compare Hoehner, *Herod Antipas*, 162. As John is elsewhere in the Gospels likened to Elijah, this account strengthens that comparison.

and presents Herod in a disturbing light. Lamech, a descendant of Cain, had "entered into a covenant with Satan, after the manner of Cain." When a young man by the name of Irad began to reveal to others the "great secret" of Lamech's pact with Satan, Lamech "slew him, not like unto Cain, his brother Abel, for the sake of getting gain, but he slew him for the oath's sake" (Moses 5:49–50). There is something uniquely sinister about murdering primarily for the sake of an oath—without some deeper emotional interest in the act. The use of the phrase in conjunction with Herod Antipas recalls Cain and his descendants who bound themselves by oath to Satan. The execution of John the Baptist becomes thereby a death of epic status, like one of the earliest known murders among the fallen race of men.

Mark's Context

Mark's complete discussion of John's arrest and death occurs, we should recall, much later than its initial introduction, and we naturally might wonder why the evangelist delays it. The context must be taken into consideration. Shortly before providing the full report of John's death, Mark describes the types of miracles performed by Jesus and by His Twelve Apostles on their first mission (see Mark 6:7–13).

The reports of these miracles had given rise to troubling rumors about the identity of Jesus. According to Mark, Herod himself thought Jesus might, in fact, be John the Baptist "risen from the dead": "And king Herod heard of him; (for his name was spread abroad:) and he said, That John the Baptist was risen from the dead, and therefore mighty works do shew forth themselves in him. Others said, That it is Elias. And others said, That it is a prophet, or as one of the prophets. But when Herod heard thereof, he said, It is John, whom I beheaded: he is risen from the dead" (Mark 6:14–16).

The anxiety the tetrarch underwent at the news of Jesus' miracles, as well as the guilt and fear he seems to have experienced from his involvement in John the Baptist's death, is underscored by the repetition of Herod's assertion that the miracle-working Jesus must be John returned from the grave. Yet if this Jesus is John reincarnated, then John must have died, but Mark has not yet offered any account of that event. Up to this point in the narrative, the reader has heard only that John was arrested. Hence, there is an immediate logical necessity for the extended aside on John's death at this juncture in the Gospel.

This does not, however, wholly explain the matter, for the location of the story remains the writer's choice. Mark could have provided more extended details when he first told of John's arrest, and then the reader would already have known of John's execution as well. The more specific and immediate context for Mark's finished account is the moment when Jesus sends the Twelve on what seems to be their first mission, the instructions Jesus gives them before the start of that mission, and a summary statement about their preaching and their performance of many miracles (Mark 6:7–13).

Directly following the explanation of John's death, Mark returns to the tale of the Apostles, who have returned from their labors and report to Jesus, "And the apostles gathered themselves together unto Jesus, and told him all things, both what they had done, and what they had taught" (Mark 6:30). Why does Mark make the first mission of the Twelve the framework for the arrest and execution of John the Baptist?

The relationship between the work of the Twelve and the death of John the Baptist recalls the relationship between the start of Jesus' public ministry and the imprisonment of John mentioned elsewhere in Mark (1:14). In that earlier setting, the removal of John by arrest acts as a kind of "cue" for Jesus to begin His ministry and further looks ahead to the perils of that ministry. Similarly, Mark ties the beginning of the public work of the Twelve to the fate of the Baptist. The fact that the Apostles' departure for and their return from their mission surrounds the tale of John's arrest and execution may well hint at the dangers (even perhaps violent death) Jesus and His disciples will face in their own careers.[61]

The context also, and perhaps more importantly, highlights a critical transition. John is a pivotal prophetic figure: "The law and the prophets were until John: since that time the kingdom of God is preached" (Luke 16:16).[62] His ministry, being of the order of the Aaronic Priesthood, belongs partly to the world of the law and the prophets, but it also moves Israel beyond those boundaries by foretelling and foreshadowing the gospel covenant to come with Jesus Christ.

John is the last prophet of the pre-Christian era and the first prophet of the Christian era. His arrest and death generally mark the end of the old prophetic order, and the specific location of that death in Mark's Gospel announces the introduction of the new order that succeeds the old—that of Jesus (begun after John's arrest) and also that of His Apostles. The proof of the real import and power of that new ministry is to be found in its new work. For Mark records no miracles done by John the Baptist but surrounds the account of John's death with references to the miracles being performed by Jesus and by His Apostles.[63]

This is a new priestly order under Jesus' leadership. These are the successors to John and to the priesthood of Aaron, and the content and accomplishments of their ministries necessarily surpass his. The Apostles are directed and overseen by Jesus and by His

[61] See, Brown, *Introduction*, 135–36: "The fate of [John the Baptist] is a warning of what the fate of Jesus is likely to be—and the fate of those sent to carry on his work." What is only suggested in Mark's Gospel is explicit in Matthew's, where Jesus, in warning His disciples of the hazards inherent in their adherence and service to Him, uses the same verb as that used to characterize the arrest of John (*paradidōmi*). See Matthew 10:17–21: "But beware of men: for they will deliver you up (*paradidōmi*) to the councils" (10:17) and "But when they deliver you up (*paradidōmi*), take no thought how or what ye shall speak" (10:19). On the verb *paradidōmi*, see W. Popkes, *Christus Traditus: Eine Untersuchung zum Begriff der Dahingabe im Neuen Testamentum*, ATANT 49 (Zurich: Zwingli, 1967), 53–55, 152–69, 180–81.

[62] Compare Brown, *Introduction*, 250.

[63] The Gospel of John is clearer in this regard and says explicitly that John the Baptist "did no miracle" (John 10:41).

priesthood and are fully come into their own just as John is removed from the account.[64]

Matthew's Representation

Matthew's account of the arrest and execution of John the Baptist is closely akin to Mark's. As with Mark, Matthew's first reference to John's arrest is to introduce Jesus' move to Galilee, where He began His public ministry: "Now when Jesus had heard that John was cast into prison, he departed into Galilee" (Matthew 4:12). Matthew likewise postpones further discussion of John's fate until significantly later in his narrative, and the backdrop for that discussion is again the miracles performed by Jesus and Herod's fear that the miracle worker might, in fact, be John the Baptist risen from the dead (Matthew 14:1–12). Matthew also declares that Herod had John bound and put into prison "for Herodias' sake," again because John had challenged the legality of their union (Matthew 14:3–4; compare Mark 6:17–18). Matthew differs, however, in his explanation of why Herod was hesitant to put John to death.

According to Mark, Herodias was anxious to have John removed but could not because "Herod feared John" and was interested in what he taught (6:19–20). On the other hand, Matthew reports that "when [Herod] would have put [John] to death, he feared the multitude, because they counted him as a prophet" (14:5). Matthew attributes the desire to have John put to death to both Herodias and Herod; the tetrarch fears the opinion of the multitude rather than the prophet himself; and he has no personal investment in John or his message. In Matthew's version, the blame, both for motive and action, is more soundly Herod's.

As for the more elaborated portrayal of John's demise, the details remain largely unchanged in Matthew's Gospel. The reader

[64] Contrast this reading to Murphy, *John the Baptist,* 71, who claims that "the entire Baptist interlude . . . interrupts the sending and return of the Twelve, thus 'buying time' at the level of the story for the disciples to be out and about."

still finds Herod's birthday celebration, although Matthew says nothing of whom the tetrarch invited to the event. The daughter of Herodias dances, and Herod promises to give her whatever she asks. At her mother's instruction, and apparently by prearrangement, she requests the head of John the Baptist on a platter.[65] Herod is sorry but complies "for the oath's sake" and for the sake of his reputation among those at the feast. John's head is presented to the daughter, who gives it to her mother. The disciples of the Baptist arrive, take the body, and bury it (Matthew 14:6–12). Unique to Matthew is the claim that John's followers went and reported his death to Jesus (14:12). This claim is the most significant difference in Matthew's depiction of John's actual execution. It has the effect of making Jesus' immediately ensuing actions a reaction to the news of John's death: "When Jesus heard of it, he departed thence by ship into a desert place apart: and when the people had heard thereof, they followed him on foot out of the cities. And Jesus went forth, and saw a great multitude, and was moved with compassion toward them, and he healed their sick" (Matthew 14:13–14).

In Matthew, Jesus seems to go away alone and in direct response to word of John's execution. Jesus had gone alone into the desert once before (Matthew 4:1–11). That had been a time of temptation and preparation before the beginning of His activity in Galilee, which activity originated just after Jesus heard of John's arrest (Matthew 4:12) and was characterized from the start by the performance of miracles (4:12–25). After John's death, Matthew provides effectively a reintroduction of Jesus' ministry. In both the earlier transition and the later, John the Baptist, having prepared the way, moves aside for the One foretold. That John's ultimate removal in Matthew is violent foreshadows, as in Mark, the perils that await Jesus and His disciples. That Jesus' work includes miracles once again confirms the superiority of Jesus and His

[65] This differs from Mark's version (6:24), where Herodias' daughter seems to leave Herod's presence to ask her mother what she should request.

priesthood labors as well as the new relationship between God and man that He Himself mediates.

Luke's Content and Structure

Like the Gospels of Mark and Matthew, the Gospel of Luke's account touches on the arrest of John the Baptist fairly early in the Gospel narrative: "But Herod the tetrarch, being reproved by him for Herodias his brother Philip's wife, and for all the evils which Herod had done, added yet this above all, that he shut up John in prison" (Luke 3:19–20).

Rather than merely mentioning the arrest in this first instance, Luke also explains its causes, eliminating the necessity of offering a fuller explanation later. Both Mark and Matthew precede the reference to the arrest with a description of Jesus' baptism and His temptation in the wilderness; they follow it with the introduction to Jesus' public ministry. Luke organizes his Gospel differently. Before telling of John's arrest, the evangelist makes no reference to the adult life of Jesus. He provides instead an elaborated summary of the ministry of John the Baptist. Therein the reader learns that John's career constitutes a fulfillment of prophecy as expressed in the book of the prophet Isaiah (Luke 3:3–6), just as Jesus, at the very outset of his public ministry, declares His own activity to be the fulfillment of prophecy from Isaiah (Luke 4:16–21).[66] The reader also discovers that the content of John's preaching is explicitly reminiscent of the ideals later expressed and encouraged by Jesus.[67] John is so significant a figure that people wonder whether he could be the Christ. But John himself proclaims the coming of one mightier than he (Luke 3:15–17). Thus, Luke presents John's career as a prophetic parallel to the coming career of Jesus and prepares his reader, through John's own words, for the arrival and preeminence of the Savior.

---

[66] Matthew 3:1–3 and Mark 1:2–4 certainly also treat John's ministry as a fulfillment of Isaiah's prophecy.

[67] Compare, for example, John's advice in Luke 3:10–14 to Jesus' sayings in Luke 6:30–35.

Luke concludes his review of John's career with the report of John's arrest as cited above (3:19–20). In contrast to the other synoptic Gospels, he removes John from the scene not only before the start of Jesus' public ministry but even before His baptism and the announcement of His divine Sonship. John's arrest, in fact, makes way for the whole of Jesus' adult ministry. The Baptist's removal "has the effect," as Murphy points out, "of giving Jesus the entire stage," leaving him with no peer and allowing for the unrivaled demonstration of the very superiority John the Baptist ascribed to Him.[68]

Just after the arrest of John, Luke recounts Jesus' baptism, the descent of the Holy Ghost, and the associated pronouncement of Jesus' divine Sonship: "Thou art my beloved Son; in thee I am well pleased" (Luke 3:22).[69] This scene is quickly followed by an extended aside on Jesus' genealogy through His adoptive father, Joseph. Having confirmed His heavenly ancestry, Luke establishes Jesus' sovereignty through His mortal family, tracing the connection through Joseph back to King David, to Abraham, and to Adam (Luke 3:23–38). The baptismal scene with its heavenly declaration and the presentation of Jesus' lineage thereafter confirm that Jesus

---

[68] Murphy, *John the Baptist*, 62. A comparison Luke already made in the corresponding infancy narratives of John and Jesus, wherein Jesus emerges as the greater of the miraculous sons. See R. E. Brown, *The Birth of the Messiah: A Commentary of the Infancy Narratives in Matthew and Luke* (Garden City, N.Y.: Doubleday, 1977), 248–53. Compare Murphy, *John the Baptist*, 42–43. Hans Conzelmann, *The Theology of St. Luke*, trans. G. Buswell (New York: Harper and Row, 1961), 21, similarly believes that Luke is drawing a distinction between "the epochs of salvation," with the moment between the ministry of John the Baptist and that of Jesus marking the critical point of demarcation. In contrast to this view, see Wink, *John the Baptist in the Gospel Tradition*, 46–58.

[69] Murphy, *John the Baptist*, 24–27, assumes that Luke locates John in prison when Jesus was baptized in order to suggest that John cannot have baptized Him. This is, according to Murphy, one part of Luke's effort to deal with the problem of Jesus' baptism, which, as a religious gesture typically undertaken by sinners to demonstrate their repentance, becomes "an embarrassing" detail when applied to Jesus. We may consider, however, that Luke's structure may be designed more to clarify the relative positions of Jesus and John—the one the forerunner; the other the mightier one foretold—than to establish a precise chronology of events.

is that mighty one foretold by John. Together, they verify that He has the right to the throne of Israel as the legitimate heir of kings, of patriarchs, and of God.

Once John the Baptist is removed by his arrest, Luke never details, here or elsewhere, John's fate. He does, however, later make explicit reference to the fact that John's imprisonment ended in death and to the fact that Herod Antipas was responsible for that end: "Now Herod the tetrarch heard of all that was done by him: and he was perplexed, because that it was said of some, that John was risen from the dead; and of some that Elias had appeared; and of others, that one of the old prophets was risen again. And Herod said, John have I beheaded: but who is this, of whom I hear such things? And he desired to see him" (Luke 9:7–9).

Like Mark and Matthew, Luke mentions John's execution in connection with Herod's reaction to the reports of Jesus' miracles. In Luke's version, the possibility that the miracle-working Jesus might be John the Baptist risen from the dead does not apparently occur to Herod but is put forward by unnamed people referred to simply as "some."[70] The tetrarch seems more confused than distressed and wishes to see Jesus. As in Mark, Luke has Herod admit responsibility for John's death but provides no further explanation. The reader learns that Herod had John put in prison because of the Baptist's condemnation of his marriage to Herodias. It later becomes clear that Herod had followed that arrest with an execution; nothing more is said.[71]

Although much information is passed over by Luke, the location of what he does say of John's death is significantly reminiscent of

[70] In both Mark (6:14) and Matthew (14:1–2), Herod *himself* suggests that Jesus might be John risen from the dead.

[71] Various explanations have been offered for Luke's failure to include the particulars of John's fate. Hoehner, *Herod Antipas*, 112–13, with notes, provides a summary of explanations and critiques them, although several of his reasons overlap and seem redundant. Compare R. Bultmann, *The History of the Synoptic Tradition*, trans. John Marsh (Oxford: Oxford University Press, 1963), 301; Raymond E. Brown, *The Death of the Messiah: From Gethsemane to the Grave: A Commentary on the Passion Narratives in the Four Gospels* (New York: Doubleday, 1994), 764.

Mark. Luke's brief aside on the beheading of John the Baptist is immediately preceded by Jesus' sending out the Apostles on their first mission and a summary of the work they did—"preaching the gospel, and healing every where" (Luke 9:6). Just after the parenthesis on Herod's perplexity and John's death, the evangelist records that the Twelve returned and reported to Jesus "all that they had done" (Luke 9:10). Mark similarly framed his rather thorough account of John's execution with this first mission of the Twelve. Presumably, the intent of the imitative structure of Luke is similar to that of Mark. Luke's version of the arrest of John the Baptist introduced Jesus in His public ministry and confirmed His personal legitimacy as the Son and heir of God and of His ancient covenant with man. John's death marks the realization of that inheritance, as Jesus Christ and His Apostles actively succeed the old prophetic order. The proof of that succession and of the superior power of the Christian covenant is here, as elsewhere in the synoptics, to be found in the miracles wrought both by Jesus and by His Apostles. As noted above, Luke's primary interest seems to be in the transition to Christ's epoch of salvation, and he accomplishes it with the most abbreviated reference to John's execution.

The Symbolic Import of John's Death in the Framework of the Gospels

John was, according to Jesus, "more than a prophet" (Matthew 11:9).[72] The Hebrew term for prophet—*nabiy'*—denotes one who is a mouthpiece of the true God, or God's spokesman, calling individuals and nations to repentance.[73] In Greek, the word "prophet"

---

[72] Multiple meanings may be suggested by this phrase, such as John's transitional role between the prophets of the Old Testament and the Savior of the New and his super-prophetic task, reminiscent of Joshua and Elijah, of leading Israel to the promised land (or, in John's case, the promised Messiah), and of preparing Israel "for God's action." See Brown, *Introduction*, 183. Only one of many possible interpretations will be considered in this context.

[73] See Francis Brown, S. R. Driver, and Charles A. Briggs, *The Brown-Driver-Briggs Hebrew and English Lexicon* (Peabody, Mass.: Hendrickson, 1997), 611.

(*profêtês*) is related to the word *profêmi*, literally "to say before."[74] A prophet is, in this sense, one who foretells, who announces events before they happen.

But John the Baptist is more than either of these terms allows. He does not just call men to repentance, nor does he merely foretell events of salvation history. John is a forerunner, sent to "prepare the way of the Lord," and in many particulars of his personal history, John's life actively anticipates the life of Jesus Christ. John's mission was foretold by the same ancient prophets who foretold the mission of Jesus (Isaiah 40:3; Malachi 3:1; John 1:23; compare Isaiah 7:14; 11:1). His birth and Jesus' birth were both announced by the angel Gabriel (Luke 1:5–38). Miraculous events attended John's birth, circumcision, and naming, as they did those of Jesus (Luke 1:57–79; 2:21–39). The same terms are used in Luke's Gospel to describe their respective youthful development: they both "grew and waxed strong in the spirit" (Luke 1:80; 2:40). John spent time in the desert before the start of his public ministry, as did Jesus (Luke 1:80; 4:1; compare Matthew 4:1; Mark 1:12). Some of the Baptist's own disciples later became disciples (and at least two—John and Andrew—became Apostles) of Jesus (John 1:35–42; compare Acts 1:21–22).[75] Like Jesus, John suffered, finally, a brutal and unjust death at the order of a misguided temporal authority.

What becomes clear from the details of and the sequel to John's end is that his death looks ahead to the violent manner and the vital message of the final acts of Jesus' own mortal life. John was beheaded, and his severed head was then presented upon a platter, in seeming mockery of a feast. This image explicitly evokes the Last Supper, the paschal meal to be shared by Jesus and His disciples, wherein Jesus speaks of His own body and blood as the ingredients of the feast, the atoning sacrifice foreshadowed by that meal, and the sacramental ordinance that will ever after recall that sacrifice.

---

[74] See Henry G. Liddell and Robert Scott, comp., *A Greek-English Lexicon* (Oxford: Clarendon Press, 1968), 1539.

[75] In addition to the shared details of their lives, the content of John the Baptist's preaching anticipates the messages of Jesus' ministry. See above.

Jesus becomes the bread and wine of the new covenant, a covenant that will be established and sealed by His suffering in the Garden of Gethsemane, His death on the cross, and His Resurrection.[76]

John the Baptist is the last representative of the pre-Christian relationship between God and man and of the order of the priesthood that administered it. His death symbolizes the end and the ultimately insufficient nature of that order and of that relationship. John's body and blood thus cruelly presented by Herod Antipas upon a platter are without the power to save, whereas Jesus' body and blood, signified in the feast of the Last Supper and in the repetition of that feast in the sacrament, have the necessary power. As Jesus Himself informs us, "My Father giveth you the true bread from heaven. For the bread of God is he which cometh down from heaven, and giveth life unto the world" (John 6:32–33). Christ is the true bread that "giveth life unto the world." His is the saving feast, and He, in His atoning sacrifice, proves Himself again the successor and superior to His forerunner.

This is not to undervalue the mission and greatness of John the Baptist, "the outstanding bearer of the Aaronic priesthood in all history" and the one "entrusted with its most noble mission,"[77] of whom Jesus said, "Among them that are born of women there hath not risen a greater than John the Baptist" (Matthew 11:11). John did not, after all, choose the nature of his death, nor did he himself intend it as a mock feast. His fate was imposed upon him by sinful men and women. But his death, like his birth and his life, prepared the way for the one foretold, and that death informs the reader of the Gospels to whom one must finally look for salvation—namely, to the Christ of God that "giveth life unto the world."

---

[76] In each of the synoptic accounts, the first miracle detailed after the Baptist's gruesome execution is Jesus' famous feeding of the five thousand (Mark 6:34–43; Matthew 14:14–21; Luke 9:12–17). This meal, miraculously provided by Jesus, in such close proximity to John's death, looks ahead to and confirms the representation of Jesus as the giver of the covenant "meal" that promises eternal life.

[77] LDS Bible Dictionary, s.v. "John the Baptist," 32.

IX.

LUKE'S THREE PARABLES OF THE LOST AND FOUND: A TEXTUAL STUDY

BRIAN M. HAUGLID

He spake many things unto them in parables.

MATTHEW 13:3

Luke 15, "rightly described as the heart of the Third Gospel"[1] or "the Gospel for the Outcast,"[2] presents three parables emphasizing the love of God: His interest in seeking out those who wander from the fold, those who are lost from our view, and those who have rebelled and then penitently find their way back. Subsequently, each parable focuses on the joy that is shown after the lost has been found. Frequently referred to as the parables of the lost and found, the parables of the Lost Sheep, the Lost Coin, and the Prodigal Son in Luke 15 are essentially narrative parables—that is, parables that can be applied differently depending on the reader's point of view, needs, or circumstances.

Jesus taught with parables on many occasions. During a certain part of His Galilean ministry, it is recorded that "without a parable

[1] Greg W. Forbes, *The God of Old: The Role of the Lukan Parables in the Purpose of Luke's Gospel*, *Journal for the Study of the New Testament*, Supplement Series 198 (Sheffield, England: Sheffield Academic Press, 2000), 109.

[2] I. Howard Marshall, *The Gospel of Luke: A Commentary on the Greek Text* (Grand Rapids, Mich.: Eerdmans, 1978), 597.

spake he not unto them" (Mark 4:34). In Greek, the word for parable is *parabolé,* which denotes a "setting beside," giving the sense of setting something side by side in a comparative state. It is related conceptually to the Hebrew *mashal,* which also means "to be similar, like" in the same sense of a comparison, implying that the usage of parables certainly did not begin with the New Testament period but extends much further back into the Hebrew tradition. A good example of a Hebrew parable in the Old Testament is the prophet Nathan's comparing David to a rich man who has many lambs but takes the only lamb (that is, Bathsheba) of a poor man (that is, Uriah the Hittite) to give to a hungry traveler passing through the area (2 Samuel 12:1–6).

Jesus used different types of parables:

Aphoristic parables are metaphors that may or may not be introduced with the term *parable*—for example, "No man also seweth a piece of new cloth on an old garment; . . . no man putteth new wine into old bottles" (Mark 2:21).

Extended parables have a predictable unfolding of the meaning implicit in aphoristic parables. An example is Luke 6:47–49, which compares the man who hears and obeys the Savior to a house built on a rock, whereas the one who does not hear and obey builds his house on a sandy foundation.

Narrative parables are more unpredictable than the other two types, and in which the application depends on how a reader reads the story.

The narrative parables, in particular, were carried forth in the oral tradition and generally included people, objects, and events common to normal situations in life.[3] Good examples of narrative parables include those in Luke 15 and that of the Good Samaritan (Luke 10:30–35).

Parables can be interpreted both externally and internally. If externally interpreted, the context drives the commentary, whereas an internal interpretation will yield manifold possibilities because of

[3] Freedman, *ABD*, 5:148–50.

the details embedded in the story as it is told and retold.[4] In this chapter, the parables in Luke 15 will be examined both externally and internally. Internal interpretation of Luke 15, especially the Parable of the Prodigal Son, provides numerous possibilities of application as evidenced in the many published studies on the subject.[5] Four basic principles of interpretation will be followed: (1) discovering the main theme of the parable, (2) seeking to understand the *Sitz im Leben* (setting in life) in which the parable was uttered, (3) seeking to understand how the evangelist interpreted the parable, and (4) determining what God is saying to us today through the parable.[6]

In what follows, Luke 15 will first be examined contextually—that is, possible reasons will be explored for Luke's citing of these parables from a vantage point many years after the Savior initially spoke them. Next, each parable will be discussed separately within the contextual Jewish background of the Savior's and of Luke's day. Finally, various applications, ancient and modern, will be noted so we can examine the variety of interpretations that can emerge from these parables. From a discussion of the above points, a clear understanding of the richness of the parables in Luke 15 will emerge, along with a deep appreciation of the love that God has for all His children.

Love of God: The Main Point of the Parables in Luke 15

As mentioned, the main theme of the three parables in Luke 15 is the love of God. Because of His love, He is willing to search for those who are lost and to forgive those who rebel and then repent. Particularly from a gospel perspective, Luke 15 illustrates the value of a human soul[7] and "is a distillation of the plan of salvation, a message within the Message, the gospel within the Gospel. The

---

[4] Freedman, *ABD*, 5:150–51.

[5] The most notable will be cited throughout the chapter.

[6] Robert H. Stein, *An Introduction to the Parables of Jesus* (Philadelphia: Westminster Press, 1981), 53–71.

[7] J. Kent Jolley, "The Parables of Jesus: The Lost Coin," *Ensign*, June 2003, 30.

brief sermon of Luke 15 is deep and profound: God loves his children, all of them, and he will do everything in his power to save them."[8]

General Contextual Background of Luke 15

Although Matthew's Gospel was written for the Jews, Luke's Gospel is generally directed more toward the Gentiles and to those who are oppressed, depressed, or beaten down through their own weaknesses and sins.[9] Luke presents a God who is intimately interested in all of His children and reaches out in love to them. Some scholars argue that Luke uses the earlier Gospels of Mark (also written for the Gentiles) and Matthew as a basis for writing his own Gospel. Concerning the former, the Gospel of Luke "consistently amends Mark in the direction of correctness, clarity, and consecutiveness." For example, Luke "upgrades Mark's diction, grammar, and syntax while retaining as much as possible of his source's original flavor. . . . Luke improves Mark by inserting earlier on in the story the proper preparation for a later development."[10]

By isolating Luke's changes to Mark, we can identify Luke's focus. These improvements are seen mainly in two related themes that are two major focuses of Luke 15: (1) Jesus defends His ministry as an outgrowth of carrying out the will of the Father, and (2) Jesus invites His questioners to view sinners as He and the Father view them. Luke accomplishes these outcomes through his presentation of the three narrative parables in Luke 15 that are set in the context of verses 1–2.[11] Although the context of Luke 15 fits

---

[8] Robert L. Millet, *Lost and Found* (Salt Lake City: Deseret Book, 2001), 8.

[9] The parables in Luke 15 "make a major contribution to the Lukan theme of God's love and mercy for sinful human beings and of Jesus' call for repentance and conversion" (Joseph A. Fitzmeyer, *The Gospel According to Luke [X–XXIV]*, The Anchor Bible [New York: Doubleday, 1985]), 1071.

[10] Luke Timothy Johnson, *The Gospel of Luke*, Sacra Pagina Series vol. 3, ed. Daniel J. Harrington (Collegeville, Minn.: The Liturgical Press, 1991), 11–12. See also Mark Goodacre, *The Case Against Q* (Harrisburg, Penn.: Trinity Press International), 19–45; 105–20.

[11] Joel B. Green, *The New International Commentary on the New Testament*, ed.

well into the general approach of Luke's portrayal of God reaching out to the lost, the contextual setting provides a glimpse into the purposes that may have prompted Luke to cite the three parables of the lost and found.

Scholars have debated about whether the first two verses in Luke 15 are pre-Luke or Luke's composition. One scholar solves the dilemma by focusing on the close parallels between Luke 5:29–30 and Mark 2:15–17. Both deal with Jesus' eating with publicans and sinners; but Luke, likely using Mark's account, puts the story into his own words and somewhat refashions the context according to what is taking place in his own day.[12] This change in wording and context is significant because it indicates that these verses are probably Luke's later reworking of Mark's text that he rewords to reflect his own time and circumstances. For instance, verses 1 and 2 refer to the Pharisees and scribes, but the first parable about a shepherd losing a sheep would not be used in Pharisaic circles because shepherding was a despised occupation, revealing that Luke may not have been aware of the social setup of Jesus' day. Moreover, these contextual verses are followed by three parables when only one is referred to, suggesting that the introductory verses were initially inspired by Mark but rewritten later by Luke.[13]

In Luke 7:29–30, the evangelist sets up a dichotomy between the publicans (toll collectors) and the Pharisees/lawyers: "And all the people that heard him, and the publicans, justified God, being baptized with the baptism of John. But the Pharisees and lawyers rejected the counsel of God against themselves, being not baptized of him." Luke interjects this same dichotomy in Luke 15:1–2 to preface the three parables: "Then drew near unto him all the

Ned B. Stonehouse, F. F. Bruce, and Gordon D. Fee (Grand Rapids, Mich.: Eerdmans, 1997), 569.

[12] Marshall, *The Gospel of Luke*, 598.

[13] Marshall, *The Gospel of Luke*, 598–99. One scholar "goes so far as to claim that Jesus deliberately addressed an audience of Pharisees as shepherds in order to shock their sensitivity and expose their prejudice against a despised occupation" (Marshall, *The Gospel of Luke*, 599).

publicans and sinners for to hear him. And the Pharisees and scribes murmured saying, This man receiveth sinners and eateth with them. And he spake this parable unto them." Why would Luke introduce this dichotomy before the parables of the lost and found?

That Jesus Himself was concerned about the rebelliousness of the Pharisees and scribes is well established in all four Gospels. However, because only the Parable of the Lost Sheep is attested in another synoptic Gospel (cf. Matthew 18:11–14), it is difficult to ascertain if Luke's context of the three parables is comparable to that of the other Gospel writers.[14] Matthew's recitation of the parable is placed within an entirely different context than Luke's. In fact, it is generally accepted that Matthew's context for the Parable of the Lost Sheep is a charge to Church leaders to be responsible for their flock, whereas Luke's context emphasizes that it is God's will that no one should perish.[15] Of course, it is important to view both of these as independent and inspired versions through Matthew and Luke respectively. Yet it seems clear that Matthew is more concerned that leaders not lose perspective of their role as shepherds of the flock, whereas Luke emphasizes God's love for the sinful, downtrodden, and oppressed. In other words, the same parable is to be considered equally inspired as it is applied appropriately within its unique context, whether in Matthew or Luke.

Luke is writing from a vantage point of approximately thirty to forty years after Jesus. Therefore, he has a keen knowledge of the resistance of the Pharisees in his own day; and, if his Gospel dates after A.D. 70, he has already seen that God's judgments upon the

[14] The Parable of the Lost Sheep can also be found in two Gnostic accounts, the Gospel of Thomas (107) and the Gospel of Truth (31:35–32:9). See James M. Robinson, *The Nag Hammadi Library in English* (New York: Harper & Row, 1977), 44, 129.

[15] Forbes, *The God of Old*, 109. "Tax-collectors were ritually defiled by contact with Gentiles and further despised due to their collaboration with the Romans. Sinners represent the immoral, who deliberately and consistently violated the law."

Jews, as prophesied by the Savior, have been fulfilled with the great destruction of Jerusalem and the temple at the hands of the Romans. It is, therefore, reasonable to conclude that the level of Pharisaic defiance Luke sees in his own day could, through inspiration, be easily projected back to the time of Jesus. The rebelliousness of the Pharisees in Luke's day may also suggest why Luke is juxtaposing the sheer joy of the lost being found with the murmuring of the Pharisees and scribes. They (Pharisees and scribes) do not appreciate Jesus' "receptivity to the lost among God's people: they should be joining in the celebration!"[16]

As Jesus probably did not put forth the contextual dichotomy between the publicans and the Pharisees in 15:1–2 (this was Luke's doing), it is also more than likely that Jesus did not contextualize the three parables that follow as well. This, of course, does no injury to Luke's inspired rendering of the text but instead reinforces Luke's sensibilities to his own environment and, at the same time, distinguishes Jesus' three parables as authentic and independent of each other. Furthermore, if Luke is showing, in the retrospective specific context of 7:29–30 and 15:1–2, that the lost being found is offensive to the Pharisees and scribes of Luke's day, then it is equally true that Jesus' message of joy over the lost being found, within the context of Jesus' own day, can apply to the publicans and to the Pharisees and scribes as well.

Interestingly, Joseph Smith, too, interpreted 15:1–2 as important to understanding the three parables, particularly the Prodigal Son. He said, "I have a key by which I understand the scriptures. I enquire, what was the question which drew out the answer, or caused Jesus to utter the parable?" The Prophet then cited the Pharisees' complaint, "This man receiveth sinners, and eateth with them" (15:2), pointing out that this phrase "unlocks the parable of the prodigal son. It was given to answer the murmurings and questions of the Sadducees and Pharisees, who were querying,

[16] Johnson, *The Gospel of Luke*, 240.

finding fault."[17] Whether viewed from Luke's day or the Savior's, the fact is that "Jesus openly had table fellowship with those with whom the Pharisees refused to associate. . . . The parables of this chapter strongly attack such an attitude."[18]

Interpreting the Three Parables in Luke 15

There also appears to be a structural unity between this chapter and the individual parables themselves. It is quite clear that the "chapter begins and concludes with grumbling, initially by the Pharisees and scribes (15:2), and finally by the elder son (15:28–30). Seen another way, the chapter begins with the opposition of two groups and ends with the opposition of two sons."[19] Each parable is also "meant to be read as a unit, with each parable informing, and being informed by the other two to some degree."[20] It is also noteworthy that the three parables in Luke 15 have a characteristic shape, of which the "most striking feature is that the crisis happens in the middle, and not, as is so often the case in Matthew's parables, at the end."[21]

The Lost Sheep

In the Parable of the Lost Sheep, Jesus recounts that a shepherd loses one of his one hundred sheep because it strayed from the flock. He leaves the ninety-nine and searches diligently until he finds it and brings it back upon his shoulders (implying the weakened condition of the sheep), calls his neighbors and friends, and joyously celebrates its return. At the conclusion of the parable, Jesus says that "likewise joy shall be in heaven over one sinner that repenteth" (7).

According to one scholar, Luke's context of the Parable of the

---

[17] Smith, *TPJS*, 276–77.

[18] Forbes, *The God of Old*, 110.

[19] Forbes, *The God of Old*, 112.

[20] Forbes, *The God of Old*, 113.

[21] John Drury, *The Parables in the Gospels: History and Allegory* (New York: Crossroad, 1985), 112.

Lost Sheep (as opposed to the context set forth in 15:1–2) is different (perhaps earlier) than Matthew's context. For Luke, the parable is directed against the opponents of Jesus, but in Matthew's context, it has changed and has become addressed to the disciples of Jesus. "This change of audience has resulted in a shift of emphasis." Luke's more apologetic parable has assumed the character of giving an exhortation in Matthew.[22] A side-by-side comparison of the Parable of the Lost Sheep as found in Luke 15:4–7 and Matthew 18:12–14 shows some of the specific contextual differences between the two accounts.

Luke	*Matthew*
World at large	Church discipline
Wilderness	Mountain
Calls friends, neighbors to rejoice	Rejoicing over found sheep
Joy in heaven over one sinner who repents	Not one soul should perish
Three words of rejoicing	Three uses of going astray
Focused on sheep (a sign of what's to come in the prodigal son)	Focused on shepherd
Mid-term crux (party after)	Final crux
Sheep is any sinner	Erring Christian
Shepherd = Jesus	Shepherd = church leader[23]

From the ancient New Testament social perspective, the occupation of shepherding was looked down upon, "for it was deemed

[22] Joachim Jeremias, *The Parables of Jesus* (New York: Charles Scribner's Sons, 1963), 40, 42, 43.

[23] This comparison is found in Drury, *The Parables in the* Gospels, 140. "Occasionally Matthew alone [not Luke] allegorizes parables of the logion material. Thus, in Luke, the parable of the Lost Sheep depicts an activity drawn from life [15:4–7], while in Matthew, on the other hand, it has become an ecclesiological allegory [18:12–14]; the shepherd represents the leader of the Christian community, and the lost sheep an erring member" (Jeremias, *The Parables of Jesus*, 69–70).

impossible for a shepherd to adhere to the law." Hence, "in identifying his audience with shepherds, Jesus is, at the outset, making a powerful attack on Pharisaic prejudice."[24] In ancient Middle Eastern culture, it was common to say "The sheep went astray" rather than "I lost the sheep."[25] This is a stinging rebuke against the Pharisees, who were quick to blame others for their waywardness and slow to take accountability for their own shortcomings. Joseph Smith also interpreted this parable as a chastisement against the Sadducees and Pharisees. He noted, "The hundred sheep represent one hundred Sadducees and Pharisees, as though Jesus had said, 'If you Sadducees and Pharisees are in the sheepfold, I have no mission for you; I am sent to look up sheep that are lost; and when I have found them, I will back them up and make joy in heaven.' This represents hunting after a few individuals, or one poor publican, which the Pharisees and Sadducees despised."[26]

Ancient Bedouin culture suggests that one hundred sheep would be a medium-sized flock and that the shepherd who possessed them would not likely be able to afford a watchman. Furthermore, before putting them into the fold at night, the shepherd would count his sheep; hence, the scriptural recording of the number ninety-nine implies that the shepherd has counted his sheep. "Experts on Palestinian life all agree that a shepherd cannot possibly leave his flock to itself. If he has to look for a lost animal he leaves the others in the charge of shepherds who share the fold with him (Luke 2:8; John 10:4 f.), or drives them into a cave."[27] Ironically, the Jewish leaders who claim responsibility for leading the flock, but "delight in the downfall of others," not only should look for the lost sheep but should also rejoice and celebrate when one is found.[28] Of course, this is not happening, and it results in the most

---

[24] "Furthermore, they were often suspected of driving their flocks into foreign ground and embezzling the produce of the flock" (Forbes, *The God of the Old*, 115).

[25] Forbes, *The God of Old*, 123.

[26] Smith, *TPJS*, 277.

[27] Jeremias, *The Parables of Jesus*, 133.

[28] Forbes, *The God of the Old*, 123.

poignant condemnation against the Pharisees and Sadducees. It is interesting that "in light of the Pharisees' and scribes' self-righteousness, the story's moral also becomes a caricature of smugness when the Savior says, 'I say unto you, that likewise joy shall be in heaven over one sinner that repenteth, more than ninety and nine just persons, which need no repentance'" (Luke 15:7).[29]

Other interpreters tend to leave out the Pharisees and scribes to one degree or another and then apply this parable in other ways. For instance, we could argue that this parable needs to be understood within the context of three Old Testament passages that develop a similar theme.[30] In this sense, the parable takes on the more general interpretation, applying the responsibility of caring for the flock to any leader, which would, of course, include the Pharisees and scribes. A common Latter-day Saint point of view that fits well within a Christian interpretation departs from the contextual message against the Jewish leaders and portrays the love that God has for all His children, and especially those who stray from the fold. In other words, the "Savior's mission is to try and save us all."[31]

The Lost Coin

In the Parable of the Lost Coin (8–10), there is a coin instead of a sheep and a woman instead of a shepherd, but the context and interpretation are similar to those of the Parable of the Lost Sheep. Here Jesus is perhaps stressing the important place that women hold in the kingdom of God and is communicating more directly to the female disciples.[32] In this parable, a woman loses one of her ten coins and searches frantically to find it.[33] Like the finding of the lost

---

[29] Richard Lloyd Anderson, "Parables of Mercy," *Ensign*, February 1987, 21–22. Of course, the idea that there are ninety-nine just persons is untenable, as all people, even the Pharisees and scribes, need repentance.

[30] Cf. Psalm 23:3; Jeremiah 23:1–8; Ezekiel 34:1–24.

[31] Elder David B. Haight, "Feed the Flock," *Ensign*, May 1975, 12.

[32] Forbes, *The God of Old*, 125.

[33] Fitzmyer says that the woman lit a lamp, "indicating the darkness of the ancient (likely windowless) house in Palestine" (*The Gospel According to Luke*, 1081).

sheep, there is a celebration at the recovery of the coin. It is likely that the coin in this parable was a silver Greek drachma, approximately equivalent to a Roman denarius, and was worth about a day's wages.[34] Some scholars have argued that the ten silver coins the woman has may have been a part of her dowry (the headdress decorated with coins).[35]

From both of these parables, we can see that if a human being exerts this much effort to recover lost property, how much more effort will God put forth to recover lost souls. Jesus pointedly answers the criticism of the scribes and Pharisees, and He demonstrates why He socializes and eats with those perceived as sinful.[36] With both the lost sheep and the lost coin, it is interesting that neither of the two can fully represent repentance because repentance is a human act. However, Luke leaves the indirect "symbolic treatment of the sheep and the coin for the direct treatment of a human being"[37] in the Parable of the Prodigal Son.

The Prodigal Son

If the first two parables demonstrate God's initiative to search out those who are lost and then hold subsequent celebrations, the Parable of the Prodigal Son shows that sometimes God will wait for the lost to choose to repent and return and still hold a celebration.[38] The parable can be divided into two parts: verses 11–24 focus on the father and the younger son, and verses 25–32 deal with the father and the elder son. In the first part, the father waits

[34] Forbes, *The God of Old*, 125.

[35] Fitzmyer, *The Gospel According to Luke*, 1081.

[36] Fitzmyer, *The Gospel According to Luke*, 1080.

[37] Drury, *The Parables in the Gospels*, 141.

[38] Forbes, *The God of Old*, 118. "But whilst the Lost Sheep and the Lost Coin focus on the activity of the one who finds, in the PS the father does *not* go out searching. He stays at home, where he welcomes the 'lost and found' son and has a feast prepared for him" (Heikki Räisänen, "The Prodigal Gentile and His Jewish Christian Brother," in *The Four Gospels 1992, Festschrift Frans Neirynck*, ed. F. Van Segbroeck, C. M. Tuckett, G. Van Belle, J. Verheyden, vol. II [Leuven: University Press, 1992], 1618).

for his wayward son to come to his senses and return to his home after squandering his inheritance in riotous living; the elder son is offended at the celebration his father brings about at his brother's penitent return. It has been argued that the second part is Luke's adaptation directed against the Pharisees and is made to form a link with chapter 16.[39] However, it is more likely and reasonable for this parable to be an authentic creation of Jesus,[40] for this parable illustrates best Jesus' mission to those who are despised and cast out.[41]

A number of new elements are interjected to make this parable unique not only from the other two in Luke 15 but also from all other parables, with the result that it is one of the most quoted and studied parables of Jesus. Although it has peculiarities and is not attested in the other Gospels, parallels have been found in the Joseph of Egypt story (as well as other Old Testament stories)[42] and in "Babylonian and Canaanite literature, in the Lotus Sutra, and in Greek papyri." None measure up to the Savior's, however.[43] One unique element is this parable's bipartite structure, meaning it is essentially two parables in one. The first concerns the lost son (Luke 15:11–24) and the second the elder son (Luke 15:25–32). This has led Joseph Fitzmyer to view it as the "Parable of the Father's Love," unifying both parts into one central message.[44] In addition, unlike other parables, it ends without a specific application, which leaves the reader with the option of deciding how the elder son turned out. Most important, this parable illustrates that God is willing to forgive and celebrate with those who have consciously sinned and wish to repent and return.

---

[39] Forbes, *The God of Old*, 128. Drury says that out of the 380 words (22 verses) in the Parable of the Prodigal Son, 36 words or phrases are considered to be purely from Luke (*The Parables in the Gospels*, 141–42).

[40] Luke would likely have a "harsher portrayal of the father's relationship to the elder son" (Drury, *The Parables in the Gospels*, 128–29).

[41] Jeremias, *The Parables of Jesus*, 128.

[42] Forbes, *The God of Old*, 130.

[43] Fitzmeyer, *The Gospel According to Luke*, 1084.

[44] Fitzmyer, *The Gospel According to Luke*, 1084.

Because this parable is more complex and nuanced than the other two, it is useful to examine it both within the context of its general background and purpose and then, in the details embedded in the story, to help the reader see that internal interpretations and applications of the narrative can be wide and varied. As far as contextual background is concerned, Heikki Räisänen argues that the "one" parable pointed to in Luke 15:2 is that of the Prodigal Son.[45] Räisänen argues that the story has one contextual background in which two separate interpretations emerge: (1) The lost son represents the publicans and sinners while the elder son represents the Pharisees, or (2) The lost son signifies converted Gentiles while the elder son represents the Jewish-Christian brethren of the book of Acts. He concludes that the figure of the lost son represents the publicans and sinners, and the elder son the Jewish-Christian brethren.[46] However, the primary context of this parable is that of the Pharisees' and scribes' accusation that Jesus is dining with publicans and sinners. This interpretation is in accord with the Prophet Joseph Smith's statement that the Luke 15:2 wording, "This man receiveth sinners, and eateth with them," "is the keyword which unlocks the parable of the prodigal son."[47]

With this context in mind, we can easily see two general purposes for the Savior's giving this parable. (1) Jesus is responding "to those who question his choice of table companions." These "table companions" are people who have responded positively to the message of Jesus, and God welcomes them and celebrates their willingness to return to Him. "In welcoming such persons Jesus is only giving expression to the magnitude and consistency of the grace of God." (2) Jesus is inviting the Pharisees and scribes to be as welcoming and to join the celebration.[48] These general contextual

[45] Heikki Räisänen, "The Prodigal Gentile and His Jewish Christian Brother," 1618.

[46] Heikki Räisänen, "The Prodigal Gentile and His Jewish Christian Brother," 1627, 1635–36.

[47] Smith, *TPJS*, 277.

[48] Green, *The New International Commentary on the New Testament*, 579.

observations provide some helpful guidance in understanding and applying this parable; still more can be gained from a detailed analysis.

In the opening of the parable, the younger of two sons comes to his father with the request, "Father, give me the portion of goods that falleth to me. And he divided unto them his living" (Luke 15:12).[49] According to Greg Forbes, "No Middle Eastern son ever asks for an inheritance, let alone is given it."[50] However, in the Jewish legal system, there were at least two ways for a son to be given an inheritance while the father was still living. This could be accomplished through a will or a gift. "In the latter case the rule was that the beneficiary obtained possession of the capital immediately, but the interest on it only became available upon the death of the father."[51] In this case, of course, the younger son demanded not only the possession of the property but also the right of disposing of it in any way he pleased. From this, it is obvious that the younger son desired the early inheritance because he sought a life independent of his father.[52] But in the end, his unusual request shows a clear rejection of his family.[53] It appears from the parable that the son turned his possession into cash[54] and then "took his journey into a far country, and there wasted his substance with riotous living" (Luke 15:13).[55] Interestingly, the text also states that the father

[49] The parable implies that the younger son was unmarried. Because marriage normally took place between the years of eighteen to twenty, he "may well have been about 17 years or more" (Marshall, *The Gospel of Luke*, 607).

[50] Forbes, *The God of Old*, 133. The portion allotted to the younger son would amount to a third of the property. Cf. Deuteronomy 21:17; Jeremias, *The Parables of Jesus*, 128. "If, however, a disposition was made to take effect earlier, the share would be less, possibly two-ninths" (Marshall, *The Gospel of Luke*, 607).

[51] Jeremias, *The Parables of Jesus*, 128.

[52] Jeremias, *The Parables of Jesus*, 129.

[53] Green, *The New International Commentary on the New Testament*, 580.

[54] Marshall, *The Gospel of Luke*, 607. Cf. also Jeremias, *The Parables of Jesus*, 129.

[55] "The size of the Diaspora which has been estimated at over four million, as against a Jewish Palestinian population of half a million at the most, may give us some idea of the extent of the dispersion which was stimulated by the inducement of the more favourable living conditions in the great mercantile cities of the Levant, and by the frequent occurrence of famine in Palestine" (Jeremias, *The Parables of Jesus*, 129).

"divided unto them" his living, meaning the elder son received his portion as well, a point that will rise again when the parable returns to the elder brother in verse 25.[56]

Verses 12–13 bring out a significant detail that sets this parable apart from the previous ones. Although they focused on a sheep and a coin, this parable is explicitly of human application and focuses on family relationships. We can appreciate the loss of a sheep or a coin, but the losing of a son is certainly of greater concern. Obviously, from verses 12–13, the actions of the younger son constitute a blatant disregard for familial relationships; this detail also serves to magnify the merciful actions of the father, who is willing to reinstate the prodigal son as a son into the family. However, the "shocking breach of familial ties" begins not so much with the asking for his portion but with the son turning it into cash and then shamefully disposing of his property in a wasteful manner.[57]

One bad situation leads to another as the young man receives his property, converts it into cash, and squanders it in "riotous living." As he has been living like a Gentile in a gentile country, now he must work as a Gentile when he runs out of money and a famine occurs. Had he not "spent all," he likely could have survived the famine. However, his bad choices bring the most loathsome of consequences as he cannot even feed himself "the husks that the swine did eat." No one would share food with him, so he joined "himself to a citizen of that country; and he sent him into his fields to feed swine" (Luke 15:15–16).

Of course, the occupation of feeding pigs (as with the eating of them) is absolutely forbidden in Jewish law, so this act underscores the desperate and despicable state the young man had brought upon himself. As a feeder of pigs, "he was forced to be in contact with unclean animals (Leviticus 11:7) and could not have observed the Sabbath; hence, he must have been reduced to the lowest

[56] Green, *The New International Commentary on the New Testament*, 580.
[57] Green, *The New International Commentary on the New Testament*, 580.

depths of degradation and practically forced to renounce the regular practice of his religion."[58] From the text, it appears that the young man may not have actually eaten swine, for the scripture says that "he would fain have filled his belly with the husks that the swine did eat: and no man gave unto him" (Luke 15:16). The NIV translation says, "He longed to fill his stomach with the pods that the pigs were eating, but no one gave anything to him." Because he was too disgusted to eat swine and because no one shared food with him, he had to resort to stealing food to live, according to Joachim Jeremias.[59]

Finally, in his misery, the young man "came to himself" and wanted to return home. This phrase in both Hebrew and Aramaic is an expression of repentance.[60] But it is actually more than repentance; the phrase can also signify "coming to one's senses." According to one New Testament commentary, "What he comes to recognize is his loss of status, the deteriorating social condition that has developed from a series of actions outlined in vv 12–14 by which he shamed his father as he distanced himself further and further from his household."[61] When the young man "came to himself," he said, "How many hired servants of my father's have bread enough and to spare, and I perish with hunger! I will arise and go to my father, and will say unto him, Father, I have sinned . . . and am no more worthy to be called thy son: make me as one of thy hired servants" (Luke 15:17–19). He comes to realize that it would be better for him to go back to his father, confess his sins, and serve as a hireling than to remain in his present condition. "This recognition serves as a barometer of the depths to which the younger son had sunk."[62] It is also interesting that the realization of this low point comes to the younger son in the very midst (v. 17) of

[58] Jeremias, *The Parables of Jesus*, 129.
[59] Jeremias, *The Parables of Jesus*, 129–30.
[60] Jeremias, *The Parables of Jesus*, 130.
[61] Green, *The New International Commentary on the New Testament*, 581.
[62] Green, *The New International Commentary on the New Testament*, 581.

the first section of the parable (vv. 11–24).[63] From here on, the situation of the young man improves dramatically.

When the younger son returns home, the scripture states that his father saw him "a great way off . . . and had compassion, and ran, and fell on his neck, and kissed him" (Luke 15:20). In the Middle Eastern tradition of the day, it was humiliating for a father (a nobleman) to run and meet his son. It was a private matter, and drawing a crowd would be inappropriate. In fact, in this situation, the father would normally lock his son up, finish the banquet, and have him beaten.[64] However, even though the son no longer has any claim on the father, for food or clothing, his father responds with a sign of forgiveness by kissing him and treating him as an honored guest instead of a wage earner.[65]

Although the boy tries to give his predetermined confession, the father, like the Pharaoh to Joseph of Egypt, gives three orders: to place upon him the best robe, to give him a ring and shoes, and to feed him a fatted calf.[66] In these three orders of the father can be found "the manifest tokens of forgiveness and reinstatement,

---

[63] Drury, *The Parables in the Gospels*, 112–14.

[64] Forbes, *The God of Old*, 138, 142. Jeremias notes that this is "a most unusual and undignified procedure for an aged oriental even though he is in such haste" (*The Parables of Jesus*, 130).

[65] Jeremias, *The Parables of Jesus*, 130. Forbes argues that there are two verbs that give insight into the father's character. "The former reflects his compassionate heart, a compassion which precedes his son's confession. The latter signifies his forgiveness . . . with the preposition compound indicating either repeated kissing or tender kissing" (*The God of Old*, 138). "The father's feeling precedes any confession of repentance and corresponds to the seeking and searching in the two preceding parables" (Marshall, *The Gospel of Luke*, 610).

[66] Jeremias observes that "when Joseph was appointed chief vizier he received from Pharaoh a ring, a robe of fine linen, and a golden chain [cf. Genesis 41:42.]: (1) First comes the ceremonial robe, which in the East is a mark of high distinction. . . . The returning son is treated as a guest of honour. (2) The ring and shoes. Excavations have shown that the ring is to be regarded as a signet ring; the gift of a ring signified the bestowal of authority (cf. I Maccabees 6.15). Shoes are a luxury, worn by free men; here they mean that the son must no longer go about barefoot like a slave. (3) As a rule meat is rarely eaten. For special occasions a fatted calf is prepared. Its killing means a feast for the family and the servants, and the festal reception of the returning son to the family table" (Jeremias, *The Parables of Jesus*, 130).

evident to all."[67] Even though the son himself may initially view the relationship as that of a master and his hired hand, "at odds with his father's persistence in regarding him in filial terms," in the end, the younger son accepts his status as son and "is reconciled to his father and restored as a member of the family."[68] This section of the parable, concerning the younger son, concludes with two "vivid images in synonymous parallelism; both describe the change: resurrection from the dead, and the finding of the lost sheep."[69]

In the second section of the parable, the elder son "was in the field: and as he came and drew nigh to the house, he heard musick and dancing" (Luke 15:25). Upon hearing from one of the servants the cause of the celebration, "he was angry, and would not go in" (Luke 15:28), "thus physically distancing himself from the family and his own role as elder son in a celebration of this magnitude."[70] His absence from the party denotes "his refusal to share in the meal, a symbolic act of gargantuan proportions in a culture where kinship boundaries are secured through the sharing of food."[71] However, this physical separation from the family may be evidence of a possibly deeper resentment the elder son feels toward the father, perhaps alluding to strained relations that had occurred long before the present event. This possibility is reinforced in the way in which the elder son speaks to his father. Unlike the younger son, who repeatedly addressed his father as "Father" (Luke 15:12, 18, 21), the elder son does no such thing in verse 29 but instead reproaches his father for celebrating the return of the younger son. In fact, speaking to his father, the elder son refers to his brother as "thy son" (Luke 15:30) and not as "my brother." Therefore, it may be more accurate to say that "this son is not so much angry that the other has come home as he is angry that his parents are so happy

[67] Jeremias, *The Parables of Jesus*, 130.

[68] Green, *The New International Commentary on the New Testament*, 579.

[69] Jeremias, *The Parables of Jesus*, 130.

[70] Green, *The New International Commentary on the New Testament*, 584.

[71] Green, *The New International Commentary on the New Testament*, 584–85.

about it."[72] It is ironic that, in his meeting with the father, the elder son acts more like a hireling than a son.[73]

The father's response to his elder son is telling. Instead of giving an apologetic answer such as "I had to make a feast," the father, in a loving but reproachful manner, says, "You ought to be glad and make merry, since it is *your* brother who has come home."[74] The father is not angry at his son; he is trying in a kind but corrective way to help his elder son see his true relationship in the family. From the father's touching and simple response, we see "what God is like, his goodness, his grace, his boundless mercy, his abounding love."[75]

Moreover, the father ends this second half of the parable in much the same way as the first with "this thy brother was dead, and is alive again; was lost, and is found" (Luke 15:32). Why did Jesus repeat this? "There can be only one answer because the parable was addressed to men who were like the elder brother, men who were offended at the gospel. An appeal must be addressed to their conscience."[76]

Although the younger son "had been a prisoner—a prisoner of sin, stupidity, and a pigsty . . . the older brother lives in some confinement too. He has, as yet, been unable to break out of the prison of himself. . . . He has yet to come to the compassion and mercy, the charitable breadth of vision to see that *this is not a rival returning*. It is his brother."[77] In the end, we are not given further information as to whether the elder son had a change of heart—but only that his attitude toward his brother was not appropriate. Whether the Pharisees and scribes saw themselves as the elder son and changed is not clear. However, as this is an open-ended parable, it is fair to say that the parable was an open invitation to

[72] Jeffrey R. Holland, "The Other Prodigal," *Ensign*, May 2002, 63.

[73] Green, *The New International Commentary on the New Testament*, 585.

[74] Jeremias, *The Parables of Jesus*, 131; emphasis in original.

[75] Jeremias, *The Parables of Jesus*, 131.

[76] Jeremias, *The Parables of Jesus*, 131.

[77] Holland, "The Other Prodigal," 63.

them, and now to anyone else, to rejoice in the spiritual progress of those who have consciously chosen to stray from the path, return, and be forgiven, which is a clear reminder of the goodness, grace, and mercy of God.

The Parable of the Prodigal Son generally concerns the unconditional love of the father, but it is also related to three other important issues: (1) it is related to the two previous parables, emphasizing the joy and celebration over the younger son who was lost and now is found; (2) it connects the attitude of the elder son to the grumbling of the Pharisees and scribes;[78] and (3) it clearly brings out that Jesus consorts and dines with publicans and sinners because "such persons can find acceptance with God himself."[79]

Conclusion

Like other editors of sacred texts such as Mormon and Moroni, Luke is an inspired editor who takes three original parables of Jesus and places them together in one coherent unit to teach that God is ever willing to search and find souls who have strayed, are lost from view, or have consciously chosen to disobey. That the parables of the lost and found illustrate God's love for all His children is of paramount significance. No other grouping of parables in scripture can emphasize this point as well as Luke 15.

In both its context and interpretation, Luke 15 stands out as a timeless invitation to all for self-reflection and change. With his specific emphasis on the Pharisees and scribes, Luke is able to show that even those who are adherents to the faith need to realize that God's thoughts and ways are higher than man's (Isaiah 55:8–9), demonstrating that man, in many cases, must repent and return to the Lord. With the parables of the Lost Sheep and the Lost Coin, this repentance and returning may occur after we stray from the Lord's path or get lost on a forbidden path. In both cases, the Lord rejoices at the finding of such souls.

---

[78] Fitzmyer, *The Gospel According to Luke*, 1085.

[79] Fitzmyer, *The Gospel According to Luke*, 1086.

In the Parable of the Prodigal Son, the Savior makes explicit reference to the younger and elder sons who need to change and return to the father. In both cases, the sons have chosen to stray from the flock and must have a change of heart to return. Again, however, the father, who represents our Heavenly Father, is joyous and celebrates the return of the younger son and, if it takes place, the elder son as well. Here, the father's deep love of his sons represents the unconditional love of God, who stands ready with open arms to receive all who come to their senses after choosing to stray and to receive those who overcome their pride and jealousy.

In examining these parables in their textual context and within various interpretations and applications, we can clearly see why they have stood the test of time and will continue to challenge the human conditions that keep us from completely submitting ourselves to the Lord. These three parables will ever be a reminder that no matter our circumstances and choices, the Lord is working to save as many of His children as possible.

X.

THE BREAD OF LIFE SERMON

ERIC D. HUNTSMAN

Whoso eateth my flesh, and drinketh my blood, hath eternal life; and I will raise him up at the last day. For my flesh is meat indeed, and my blood is drink indeed. He that eateth my flesh, and drinketh my blood, dwelleth in me, and I in him. As the living Father hath sent me, and I live by the Father: so he that eateth me, even he shall live by me. This is that bread which came down from heaven: not as your fathers did eat manna, and are dead: he that eateth of this bread shall live for ever.

JOHN 6:54–58

These concluding statements in Jesus' powerful and heavily symbolic Discourse on the Bread of Life caused confusion, consternation, and even anger among many of the sermon's original hearers, both among "the Jews" and some of Jesus' own disciples. The complete discourse (John 6:26–58) is the central one of seven that, in John, teach important truths about who Jesus is and what He does for mankind.[1] Thus, this sermon, along with the others in John, focuses on Christology—understanding *the person* and *the work* of Jesus as the Messiah or Anointed One.

[1] The seven are The New Birth (3), The Water of Life (4:1–42), The Divine Son (5:17–47), The Bread of Life (6:35–58), The Life-Giving Spirit (7:16–52), The Light of the World (8:12–59), and The Good Shepherd (10:1–18).

Biblical scholarship has, for the most part, interpreted the sermon along one of three lines. One approach tends to focus on its sacramental aspect, using the Lord's Supper to interpret it. A second view interprets it largely as a metaphor, seeing in the sermon a description of Jesus' role and the believer's response to Him. A third position does both, seeing the original discourse delivered by Jesus as primarily symbolic while acknowledging that John could well have intended the imagery to be applied to the sacrament.[2] These approaches echo the questions that Elder Bruce R. McConkie raised at the beginning of his own analysis of the discourse: "How do men eat the Lord's flesh and drink his blood? Is this literal or figurative? Does it have reference to the sacrament of the Lord's Supper or to something else?"[3]

The discourse's focus on Christology was necessitated by the historical circumstances at the time of its delivery, and this makes the third approach to the sermon—seeing it primarily as symbolic but recognizing that its symbolism has been extended to the ordinance of the sacrament—particularly useful for understanding it. Jesus' immediate audience consisted of several different groups: the crowd whose members had been present at or heard about the miraculous feeding of the five thousand (6:26–40), a specific group that John identifies as "the Jews" (6:41–59), and, finally, Jesus' followers, both a general group of disciples and His innermost circle of the Twelve (6:60–71). Each of these groups misunderstood in some way either *who* Jesus was or *what* His mission was, allowing

[2] See the surveys of scholarship by Vernon Ruland, "Sign and Sacrament: John's Bread of Life Discourse (Chapter 6)," *Interpretation: A Journal of Bible and Theology* 18 (1964): 450–52; Leon Morris, *The Gospel According to John*, rev. ed., The New International Greek Commentary on the New Testament (Grand Rapids, Mich.: Eerdmans, 1995), 311–15; and Raymond E. Brown, *An Introduction to the Gospel of John*, ed. Francis J. Moloney (New York: Doubleday, 2003), 229–34. G. H. C. MacGregor, "The Eucharist in the Fourth Gospel," *New Testament Studies* 9 (1962–63): 114, observes that confessional biases have tended to affect the interpretation of the discourse, Catholic writers generally interpreting it sacramentally and conservative Protestants denying any reference to the sacrament.

[3] Bruce R. McConkie, *DNTC*, 1:358.

Jesus to expand the meaning of the discourse with each group. Understanding the particular lessons needed by each of these original audiences leads readers of the sermon in every age to a better understanding of Jesus and His mission.

The Passover

Jesus' sermon on the Bread of Life forms an integral part of the sixth chapter of John, with the chapter's setting and the miracles of the Feeding of the Five Thousand and the Walking on Water providing important interpretive clues.[4] The chapter's introduction provides some geographic and chronological context (6:1–4). First, Jesus traveled to the east side of the Sea of Galilee, which included the largely gentile region of the Decapolis on the southeast and the mixed regions of Herod Philip on the north and northeast. Luke 9:10 identifies the site as being in the latter region, in the territory of Bethsaida, which was the home of Philip and the original home of Peter and Andrew. Next, "a great multitude [*ochlos polys*] followed him, because they saw his miracles which he did on them that were diseased" (John 6:2, perhaps parallel with Matthew 14:14)—although these healings are not among the signs that John selected for his narrative.[5] Jesus then climbed a mountain or hill, where He sat with His disciples (6:3), an act that, like the Sermon on the Mount in Matthew 5–7, was reminiscent of Moses' ascent of Sinai.[6]

---

[4] The sixth chapter of John constitutes a self-contained textual unit that divides into sections, or pericopes, that include a narrative introduction (6:1–4), the miracle stories of the Feeding of the Five Thousand (6:5–14) and Jesus' Walking on Water (6:15–21), a narrative transition (6:22–25), and Jesus' Discourse on the Bread of Life itself (6:26–58). See Thomas R. Valletta, "John's Testimony of the Bread of Life," in *The Lord of the Gospels*, ed. Brent L. Top and Bruce A. Van Orden; The 19th Annual Sidney B. Sperry Symposium (Salt Lake City: Deseret Book, 1991), 173–86.

[5] In the synoptic accounts (Matthew, Mark, and Luke), this gathering of the multitude that necessitated the miracle of the loaves and the fishes follows Herod Antipas' execution of John the Baptist (Matthew 14:1–12; Mark 6:14–29; Luke 9:7–9) and the return of the newly selected and ordained Twelve from their first mission (Mark 6:30; Luke 9:10).

[6] Valletta, "John's Testimony of the Bread of Life," 181.

John's account adds one important time reference that is missing in the synoptics: "And the passover, a feast of the Jews, was nigh" (6:4). This reference associates the events of John 6 with a group of episodes in John's Gospel that illustrate how Jesus replaced or fulfilled important Jewish feasts (5:1–10:42).[7] It also strengthens the association of Jesus as the New Moses and provides the imagery of deliverance and bread that made Jesus' feeding the multitude in the wilderness so reminiscent of the Lord's sustaining the children of Israel under Moses.[8] This Passover setting establishes some of the fundamental symbolism necessary for understanding the Discourse on the Bread of Life, including deliverance, the crossing of the Sea, miraculous feedings in the wilderness, and the saving role of the paschal lamb. Although this episode does not take place in Jerusalem where the Passover was properly celebrated, it does associate this scene closely with the final Passover of Jesus' ministry, at which He died to bring life to the world.

The Miracles Preceding the Sermon

The two miracle stories of John 6, both of which are connected to the Passover setting of the chapter, are fundamental to the interpretation of Jesus' sermon on the Bread of Life. The miraculous Feeding of Five Thousand in a rural area outside Bethsaida is the only miracle other than the resurrection recorded in all four Gospels (John 6:5–14; parallels Matthew 14:13–21; Mark 6:33–44; Luke 9:11–17).[9] Seeing the famished condition of the multitude

---

[7] For the arrangement of many of the early chapters of John according to the festivals of the Jewish year, see Brown, *An Introduction to the Gospel of John*, cxliv; F. F. Bruce, *The Gospel of John: Introduction, Exposition and Notes* (Grand Rapids, Mich.: Eerdmans, 1983), 121.

[8] John Painter, *The Quest for the Messiah: The History, Literature, and Theology of the Johannine Community*, 2d ed. (Edinburgh: T&T Clark, 1993), 264. For an older, but detailed, discussion, see Bertil Gärtner, *John 6 and the Jewish Passover*, Coniectanea Neotestamentica 17 (Copenhagen: Ejnar Munksgaard, 1959), 14–19.

[9] The similarities between this miracle and the Feeding the Four Thousand in Matthew 15:32–39 and Mark 8:1–9 have led some scholars to suggest that these two miracles were actually a single incident that different traditions remembered with varying details. See, however, the detailed discussion of Brown, *An Introduction to the*

and having received a mere five loaves and two fish from a local boy, Jesus offered thanks and distributed the bread and then the fish, either first to the disciples and then to the multitude seated on the grass or directly to those sitting on the grass (6:11–12a).[10] The filling meal of bread and fish for the multitude, in effect, re-created the table fellowship of the Passover meal, Jesus thereby extending the blessings of the meal to the thousands whom He fed, all the while hearkening back to Jehovah's provision of manna and flesh in the wilderness.

Jesus then directed the disciples to gather up the remaining fragments "that nothing be lost" (6:12). Significantly, the manna that was given to the Israelites during the Exodus was *not* to be gathered; indeed, it spoiled if extra was ever collected on any day other than that preceding the Sabbath (Exodus 16:16–31). The gathered remnants of bread filled twelve baskets, a fact that may have had significance on several levels. Gathering the remaining food avoided waste, perhaps even signaling the importance of valuing the Lord's gifts, and the mere fact that there was extra bread emphasized that Jesus had provided in abundance.[11] For those who

---

Gospel of John, 236–44. R. T. France, *The Gospel of Mark: A Commentary on the Greek Text*, New International Greek Testament Commentary (Grand Rapids, Mich.: Eerdmans: 2002), 306–7, argues for two separate and historical accounts.

[10] The synoptics all have Jesus look up to heaven in an attitude of prayer, break the bread, and then distribute the bread to the disciples, who then distribute it to the seated multitude (Matthew 14:19; Mark 6:41; Luke 9:16). John 6:11 omits the more obvious sacramental (eucharistic) gestures such as looking up to heaven and breaking the bread; and the critical Greek text based on older and presumably better manuscripts lacks "gave it the disciples" *(edōken/edidou tois mathētais)*, although the Textus Receptus used by the King James translators and derived from later Byzantine manuscripts has added "distributed to the disciples" (*diedōken tois mathētais*) before "distributed to those who were sitting" (*diedōken tois anakeimenois*).

Following the synoptic account, we can see here a model for Jesus' working through His Apostles, thereby "teaching the order of priesthood government" (Kent P. Jackson, "The Bread of Life," in Kent P. Jackson and Robert L. Millet, eds., *Studies in Scripture Volume 5: The Gospels* [Salt Lake City: Deseret Book, 1986], 290). The only qualification is that in all four Gospels, the term "disciples" (*mathētai*), when not accompanied explicitly with "the twelve," commonly refers to more followers than just the Twelve Apostles.

[11] Talmage, *JTC*, 334, for instance, wrote, "Our Lord's direction to gather up the

see the miracle and the subsequent discourse as being primarily sacramental, carefully gathering the remaining fragments also stresses the sacredness of the sacramental bread.[12] The twelve baskets, like the Twelve Apostles, connects this miracle with the house of Israel, and as the Twelve Apostles and the Church represented Jesus' establishment of a new Israel replacing the old, the twelve baskets full of bread may signify Jesus' ability to continue sustaining this New Israel, which the Twelve were to gather. Jesus Himself, however, gave the fact that none of the fragments was lost new meaning when He later used the imagery of the miracle in His Discourse on the Bread of Life.

Elder Bruce R. McConkie identified three reasons that Jesus miraculously fed the five thousand. First, He did it out of compassion because they were hungry and, away from towns or markets, were in real need of bread. Second, it was a sign that as the Son of God, He had all power and was, in fact, the creator of all things. Third, it provided the setting "for one of his strongest and deepest recorded discourses," as a "prelude . . . that men must eat spiritual bread to gain eternal life."[13] This "prelude," however, was not immediately or correctly understood by its audience. By feeding the multitude in the wilderness, Jesus performed a "sign of deliverance" that linked Him in the minds of the crowd not only with Moses but also with current expectations of a deliverer.[14] Thus, in what Perry calls "a eucharistic midrash on the Exodus story," Jesus' act established Him as the New Moses feeding Israel in the wilderness.[15]

---

fragments was an impressive object-lesson against waste; and it may have been to afford such a lesson that an excess was provided." McConkie, *DNTC*, 345, also sees this primarily as a "lesson in economy." See my discussion of John 6:39 below.

[12] MacGregor, "The Eucharist in the Fourth Gospel," 115.

[13] McConkie, *DNTC*, 1:343–44.

[14] Josephus, *AJ* 20.97–99, 20.168, and 20.188 and *JW* 2.259 and 6.285. The first of these references, *AJ* 20.97–99, notes in particular the case of the false prophet Theudas, who led a crowd to the Jordan River, which he claimed would divide before them as the Lord had divided the Red Sea for Moses. See Painter, *The Quest for the Messiah*, 260–62.

[15] John M. Perry, "The Sacramental Tradition in the Fourth Gospel and the synoptics," in *Jesus in the Johannine Tradition*, ed. Robert T. Fortna and Tom Thatcher

Nevertheless, in the Bread of Life sermon that soon followed, Jesus made clear that the Father, not Moses, was the one who gave the children of Israel bread in the wilderness (6:32). The miracle of the feeding, then, associated Jesus more closely with divinity, and the second miracle story recorded in John 6, Jesus' Walking on the Water (6:15–21), continued the Passover imagery of Exodus, recounting the crossing of the Red Sea. It also made an important Christological statement, identifying Jesus directly with Jehovah and providing an important corrective to the contemporary messianic expectations encouraged by the Feeding of the Five Thousand.[16]

Whereas the feeding miracle could be interpreted too narrowly as a sign that Jesus was only a messianic king, His walking on the water and miraculous completion of the sea voyage served as a sign that He was far more. The first verse of this passage records, "When Jesus . . . perceived that they would come and take him by force, to make him a king, he departed again into a mountain himself alone" (6:15). The crowd's desire to make Jesus a temporal ruler reflected many of the messianic expectations of the time, which, at least since the time of the Maccabees, had suffered an overly political interpretation that, in actuality, presented a false Christology of *who* the Messiah would be (a political ruler) and *what* He would do (deliver them from Herodian rule and Roman occupation).

Jesus' power over the water revealed, however, that He was far more than a great ruler or worldly deliverer. He was, in fact, king of heaven and earth and, implicitly, their creator. John emphasizes this fact by employing the formula "I Am" (Greek *egō eimi*) even

(Louisville: Westminster John Knox Press, 1989), 157. See also Charles H. Dodd, *The Interpretation of the Fourth Gospel* (Cambridge: Cambridge University Press, 1958), 335.

[16] Of the synoptics, only Luke, for reasons that are not immediately clear, lacks an account of Jesus' walking upon the water (see Matthew 14:22–33; Mark 6:45–52). John's version of the episode is considerably briefer than those of Matthew's and Mark's, lacking details provided by the other two and, like Mark, omitting Peter's attempt to join Jesus on the water. On the surface, this miracle indicates Jesus' power over the elements and, in Matthew, teaches a valuable lesson about faith. In the context of John 6, however, Jesus' walking on water focuses on His identity.

more explicitly than do Matthew and Mark.[17] In John's substantially briefer account, Jesus' controlling of the raging sea and bringing His disciples safely to shore manifests Him as the one exercising the power that the Old Testament attributes to Jehovah alone (Job 9:8; 38:16; Habakkuk 3:15).[18] Thus, in the Passover context of the Bread of Life sermon, Jesus' walking on the water revealed Him as the one who both created the deep and also brought the Israelites through it. As Gärtner has written, "Just as the Lord ploughed a path for Israel through the sea, leading them to freedom from bondage, so Jesus, when he walks on the water, shows that as Messiah he has power over the seas."[19]

Bread Come Down from Heaven

> Then Jesus said unto them, Verily, verily, I say unto you, Moses gave you not that bread from heaven; but my Father giveth you the true bread from heaven. For the bread of God is he which cometh down from heaven, and giveth life unto the world (John 6:32–33).

In a narrative transition, "the people," which in Greek is once again *ho ochlos* or "the multitude," follow Jesus and the disciples across the Sea of Galilee to Capernaum (6:22–25). This is the setting for the first section of the Discourse on the Bread of Life,

---

[17] Simply translated, *egō eimi* means "I am," and when used by Jesus, the formula sometimes appears as a simple self-identification (John 6:20, emphasis added: "*I* that speak unto thee *am he*"), with a predicate (for instance, John 9:5, emphasis added: "*I am* the light of the world"), or absolutely without a predicate (John 8:58. emphasis added: "Verily, verily, I say unto you, Before Abraham was, *I am*"). See the detailed discussion of Brown, *An Introduction to the Gospel of John*, 533–38, and Catrin H. Williams, "'I Am' or 'I Am He'?" in *Jesus in the Johannine Tradition*, ed. Robert T. Fortna and Tom Thatcher (Louisville: Westminster John Knox Press, 2001), 343–48.

[18] As in the earlier stilling of the storm as recorded by the synoptics (Matthew 8:18–27; Mark 4:35–41; Luke 8:22–25), the raging sea resonates with the image found in both the Old Testament and throughout Near Eastern mythology of the great deep's representing the surging force of uncreated chaos. See Williams, "'I Am' or 'I Am He'?" 346.

[19] Gärtner, *John 6 and the Jewish Passover*, 18. See also Brown, *An Introduction to the Gospel of John*, 245; Valletta, "John's Testimony of the Bread of Life," 182.

which apparently began in front of the crowd on the spot where they found Him. The first part of the discourse, delivered to the multitude, divides into two distinct sections, a more general discussion of the Bread come down from heaven, which focuses on correcting the crowd's incorrect expectation of *who* the Messiah would be (6:26–34), and a specific pronouncement that Jesus Himself is the Bread of Life, the major message of which is *why* Jesus came into the world (6:35–40).

In the first section, Jesus notes that the multitude sought Him not because they had seen the miracles, perhaps referring to other divine signs of His identity, but because they had eaten of the bread He had provided the previous day (6:26). The manna that Israel had enjoyed under Moses came six days a week for forty years until it ceased after the last Passover celebrated before Israel came into Canaan.[20] Because Deuteronomy 18:15 had promised that a prophet "like unto [Moses]" would come, the expectation arose that the Messiah would perform the same miracles that Moses had, including the provision of manna. Intertestamental writings, for instance, confirm that a tradition had arisen that a second deliverer, the Messiah, would bring a new dispensation of manna at the opening of the new age even as Moses, the first deliverer, had provided manna during the Exodus.[21]

Although Jesus had avoided the multitude's attempt to make Him king the day before, the crowd's desire for more bread betrayed that they still had a worldly conception of a Messiah whose primary purpose was not only to deliver them politically but also to provide for their temporal needs. Accordingly, Jesus immediately tried to move the multitude away from the precedent of the manna under Moses and, in fact, even beyond His own miraculous feeding of the crowds the previous day. Recalling that the Mosaic manna quickly decayed and that even His own bread had not permanently satisfied their need for food, Jesus enjoined, "Labour not for the meat which

---

[20] See Brown, *An Introduction to the Gospel of John*, 1:265.

[21] 2 Baruch 29:8.

perisheth, but for that meat which endureth unto everlasting life, which the Son of man shall give unto you" (6:27).

The Joseph Smith Translation adds an important idea to the previous verse: "Ye seek me, *not because ye desire to keep my sayings,* neither because ye saw the miracles, but because ye did eat of the loaves, and were filled" (JST John 6:26; emphasis added). This helps explain why the multitude, subtly rebuked for their false expectation of what the Messiah was to do for them, began to realize that they had a responsibility to respond in some way to Jesus in order to receive this imperishable food.[22] Without waiting for an answer, the crowd returned to the theme of bread, proclaiming, "Our fathers did eat manna in the desert; as it is written, He gave them bread from heaven to eat" (6:31; see Psalm 78:24), to which Jesus responded, "Verily, verily, I say unto you, Moses gave you not that bread from heaven; but my Father giveth you the true bread from heaven" (6:32). Besides qualifying that God, not Moses, gave Israel the manna that sustained Israel in the wilderness, Jesus' response focused His audience on *true* bread, as opposed to perishable food that sustains life only for the day. Although actual bread sustains physical life, both the bread and human life are temporal and perish. More important is what both the manna and the loaves at the feeding of the five thousand represented.

Old Testament images of eating and drinking, wherein God's people eat His word (Jeremiah 15:16; Ezekiel 2:8, 3:1), specifically established food as a metaphor for spiritual sustenance.[23] The later

[22] Accordingly, Jesus' injunction that they "labour not for the meat which perisheth" prompted their question, "What shall we do, that we might work the works [*erga*] of God?" (6:28). Jesus' response immediately shifts from the plural "works" (*erga*) to the singular (*ergon*), noting, "This is the work [*ergon*] of God, that ye believe on him whom he hath sent" (6:29), prompting the crowd to ask again for a sign that they can see and believe, inquiring, "What dost thou work [*ergazē*]?" (6:30). Their question ironically creates a verbal echo with Jesus' earlier discourse on the Divine Son (5:17–47), when Jesus, following His healing of the lame man at the Pool of Bethesda, is accused of working on the Sabbath. There Jesus' statement, "My Father worketh [*ergazetai*] hitherto, and I work [*ergazomai*]" (5:17), emphasizes that by Jesus' doing His Father's will, the signs show His relationship to the Father.

[23] Morris, *The Gospel According to John*, 301.

Jewish understanding that manna represented the *Torah* or Law[24] is supported by Jesus' own words regarding bread and the word of God. Although John lacks a temptation narrative, the use of bread in the synoptics is illuminating (Matthew 4:1–4; Luke 4:1–4). There Satan tests Jesus, encouraging Him to make bread out of stones, an act that, if performed, would have foreshadowed turning water into wine or the multiplication of bread here. Jesus' response was to quote part of Deuteronomy 8:3, which, when quoted in full, has particular bearing upon the Bread of Life Discourse: "And he humbled thee, and suffered thee to hunger, and fed thee with manna, which thou knewest not, neither did thy fathers know; that he might make thee know that man doth not live by bread only, but by every word that proceedeth out of the mouth of the Lord doth man live." Therefore, as Moses had given spiritual food in the form of the law, Jesus, here the Son of Man, was offering true bread from heaven not to support merely physical life but rather spiritual, everlasting life.

Because manna could represent the Torah in this context, the multitude no doubt expected their question regarding "working the works of God" to be answered in terms of keeping the injunctions and ceremonies of the law. As a result, they may well have misinterpreted Jesus' next saying: "For the bread of God is he which cometh down from heaven, and giveth life unto the world" (6:33). Although the Aramaic or Hebrew original is not preserved, the Greek for "which cometh down" (*ho katabainōn*) is ambiguous because *ho katabainōn* can be taken substantively either as "he who comes down" or in agreement with the preceding "bread" (*artos*).[25] In other words, the multitude may have heard "the bread of God is *that* which came down from heaven," which they took to mean the word of the Lord or the law that came from heaven, leading them to exclaim, "Lord, evermore give us this bread" (6:34).

---

[24] Dodd, *The Interpretation of the Fourth Gospel*, 336–37; Gärtner, *John 6 and the Jewish Passover*, 41; Morris, *The Gospel According to John*, 319.

[25] Brown, *An Introduction to the Gospel of John*, 262–63; Painter, *The Quest for the Messiah*, 273; Morris, *The Gospel According to John*, 322–23.

Jesus, the Bread of Life

> And Jesus said unto them, I am the bread of life: he that cometh to me shall never hunger; and he that believeth on me shall never thirst (John 6:35).

Although the people in the crowd might not have understood what Jesus meant when He taught them about bread come down from heaven, their request for that bread was rewarded with the clear pronouncement, "I am the bread of life," the first of seven significant "I Am sayings" in the Gospel of John that couple the *egō eimi* formula with a predicate describing Jesus and His role.[26] Jesus' declaration, nevertheless, also lays specific responsibility upon His hearers: "He that *cometh* to me shall never hunger; and he that *believeth* on me shall never thirst" (6:35; emphasis added). In the first part of His teaching to the multitude, Jesus had led them away from their previous expectations of *who* He was—He was not (at least in this coming) a political deliverer and an earthly king, nor was He merely a miracle worker who could provide for His people's needs and usher in the new messianic age of peace and prosperity. By identifying Himself as the Bread of Life, He corrected the idea that He was a new prophet and giver of law in the mode of Moses, and in His succeeding statements to the multitude in this section, He began to explain *why* He had come into the world and what must be the response of those who would receive Him.

Ecclesiasticus 24:19–22, otherwise known as "The Wisdom of Jesus, Son of Sirach," has Wisdom state, "Come to me, you who desire me, and eat your fill of my fruits. For the memory of me is

[26] See Morris, *The Gospel According to John*, 323, who observes, "His 'I am' is a solemnly emphatic statement, and in this context has overtones of divinity." The others of these statements are "I am the light of the world" (8:12), "I am the door" (10:7–9), "I am the good shepherd" (10:11–14), "I am the resurrection, and the life" (11:25), "I am the way, the truth, and the life" (14:6), and "I am the vine" (15:1–5). Although these may be simple predications ("Jesus is X"), Jesus' bold statement in the Light of the World Discourse, "before Abraham was, I am" (8:58) explicitly identified Him with the Old Testament *YHWH*, or Jehovah.

sweeter than honey, and the possession of me sweeter than the honeycomb. *Those who eat of me will hunger for more, and those who drink of me will thirst for more*" (emphasis added). Likewise, the Mosaic manna, the loaves of the miraculous feeding and what they represent, filled only temporary needs. Ruland has noted that "the Old Law, symbolized in the physical bread of Exodus manna and now in the miraculous loaves, will not satisfy man's basic archetypal hunger and thirst for familiarity and communion with God, for a share in his life, for a pledge of immortality and resurrection."[27]

Contrast this hunger with Jesus' promise that those who come to and believe in Him will never hunger or thirst (6:35), a statement that resonates immediately with His words to the woman of Samaria in the Discourse on the Water of Life (4:4–42). There Jesus had said, "But whosoever drinketh of the water that I shall give him shall never thirst; but the water that I shall give him shall be in him a well of water springing up into everlasting life" (4:14).[28] Thus, Jesus combines the Exodus symbolism of both manna and the water from the rock (Exodus 17:6; Deuteronomy 8:15), a fact confirmed by Paul who wrote, "Moreover, brethren, I would not that ye should be ignorant, how that all our fathers . . . did all eat the same spiritual meat; and did all drink the same spiritual drink: for they drank of that spiritual Rock that followed them: and that Rock was Christ" (1 Corinthians 10:1, 3–4).

At this point, Jesus makes no explicit reference to eating the Bread of Life, saying simply that those who come to Him will not hunger. The earlier images of eating manna or eating the word of the Lord, however, made this implicit, albeit still comfortably metaphorical. Here and throughout the discourse, the symbol of eating powerfully represents accepting Jesus fully and internalizing Him and what He represents. A precedent for this may be found in the Bread of the Presence (*lehem panim*, KJV "shewbread") used in

[27] Ruland, "Sign and Sacrament: John's Bread of Life Discourse," 457.

[28] Painter, *The Quest for the Messiah*, 269–70. After the dialogue with the Samaritan woman, Jesus told His disciples, "I have meat [*brōsin* or "food"] to eat that ye know not of" (4:32), a foreshadowing perhaps of this very discourse.

the tabernacle and in both Jerusalem temples. The "Bread of the Presence" represented the presence of the Lord in the temple and was "most holy," meaning that it conveyed holiness to those who touched it—in this instance, to the priests who each week ate it.[29]

Like the manna that seemingly fell from heaven, Jesus directly declares, "I came down from heaven, not to do mine own will, but the will of him that sent me" (John 6:38), answering both Christological questions in a single pronouncement. As a proclamation on the person of Jesus, "I came down from heaven" is an identification of His divine origins, one already used by Jesus with Nicodemus (3:13) and by John the Baptist with his disciples (3:31). Thus, Jesus was not simply a messiah in a general sense—an anointed Davidic king or high priest; rather, He was *the* Messiah, the one who came down from heaven. As for the work of the Messiah, He did not come to do His own will but the will of the one who sent Him. Jesus' doing the will of the Father is an important theme in John's Gospel (4:34; 5:30; 6:38–40), one closely associated with doing the Father's work: "Jesus saith unto them, My meat is to do the will of him that sent me, and to finish his work" (4:34; cf. 17:4).

Jesus defines the Father's will and work for Him by saying, "And this is the Father's will which hath sent me, that of all which he hath given me I should lose nothing, but should raise it up again at the last day (6:39)." The reference to losing nothing that the Father has given to Him gives added significance to Jesus' earlier direction to the disciples to "gather up the fragments that remain, that nothing be lost" (6:12). Jesus' statement "This is the will of him that sent me, that every one which seeth the Son, and believeth on him, *may have everlasting life*" (6:40; emphasis added) suggests Moses 1:39, perhaps the best definition of the work of the Christ: "This is my work and my glory—to bring to pass the *immortality* and *eternal life* of man."

John 1:11, however, noted that when Jesus "came unto his own"

---

[29] Margaret Barker, *The Great High Priest: The Temple Roots of Christian Liturgy* (London: T&T Clark, 2003), 70–71, 87–91, 93.

(*ta idia*), His own (*hoi idioi,* "His own people"), for the most part, did not receive Him. This freedom to accept or reject Jesus occasions Jesus' definition of the Father's will for all men and women: "This is the will of him that sent me, that every one which seeth the Son, and believeth on him, may have everlasting life: and I will raise him up at the last day" (6:40). Seeing—that is, recognizing who Jesus is as the One who came down from heaven—and having confidence and trust in Him (another rendering of *pisteuōn eis auton,* KJV "believing on him") indicate that Jesus taught not only "*who* He was" and *what* He would do but also "what a person's relationship with him must be in order to obtain eternal life."[30]

Murmuring of "the Jews" and Jesus' Response

Up to this point, John has described Jesus' audience as the multitude (*ho ochlos*), translated variously in the KJV as "a great multitude" (6:2), "a great company" (6:5), and "the people" (6:22, 24). Suddenly, John's description shifts to a group he calls *hoi Ioudaioi,* or "the Jews" (6:41, 52).[31] This shift may also signal a change of scene from the harbor or some other outside setting where the crowd first found Jesus to the synagogue in Capernaum, which John 6:59 identifies as the place where much of the discourse was delivered.[32] Although members of the multitude and certainly many of Jesus' disciples may have followed Him into the synagogue and heard this second part of His discourse, the sudden change of tone and markedly sharper rhetoric in 6:41–59 strongly suggest that Jesus was focusing His attention on a new, more hostile audience. Like the teachings to the multitude, this part of the discourse divides into two sections. The first, the murmuring of "the Jews"

[30] Jackson, "Bread," 293.

[31] Painter, *The Quest for the Messiah,* 267.

[32] Painter, *The Quest for the Messiah,* 253, 278; Morris, *The Gospel According to John,* 327. Talmage, *JTC,* 339, however, places the entire discourse in the synagogue, and Gärtner, *John 6 and the Jewish Passover,* 14–19, makes an interesting argument that connects explicitly the feeding, walking on water, and sermon with the Jewish texts that could have been read in the Capernaum synagogue as part of a Passover festival for those who could not travel to Jerusalem for the feast.

and Jesus' response to them, focuses largely on the issue of who Jesus is (6:41–50). The second, through the use of the jarring image of flesh and blood, concentrates on the central act of Jesus' work, His salvific death, and how believers appropriate it (6:51–59).

John's use of *hoi Ioudaioi* throughout his Gospel is problematic and has been the focus of much debate in studies of John's writings. The Greek term is first used for the Hebrew *yehûdîm* in the Septuagint version of 2 Kings 16:6, where it describes the citizens of the pre-exilic kingdom of Judah. This is the sense in which Nephi uses the term in 2 Nephi 33:8, and it occurs again at 2 Kings 25:25 and is well established in Jeremiah, Esther, Ezra, and Nehemiah. In the New Testament, Acts and the writings of Paul use it broadly as an ethnic description that particularly refers to followers of the Jewish faith. Rare in the other Gospels,[33] it is common in John. John's usage, however, is idiosyncratic, given that in many ways this is the most Jewish of the Gospels and that Jesus, the disciples, and John himself were all Jewish. Furthermore, in John, *hoi Ioudaioi* is often, although not always, negative, leading scholars to propose a number of explanations. These include seeing *hoi Ioudaioi* as simply an ethnic term, distinguishing Jews from Samaritans and other national groups; as a geographic term, referring to Judeans as opposed to Galileans and other Jews; as a political term, denoting "the rulers of the Jews" in the political and religious sphere; as "experts in Jewish law" in a more general sense, which would include Pharisees and other strict adherents in the law; and, in some compositional theories, as a term more reflective of traditional Jewish antagonists of the early Jewish-Christians that was retrojected to apply to the Pharisaic and Sadducean opponents of Jesus.[34]

---

[33] With the exception of Matthew 28:15; Mark 7:3; Luke 7:3; and 23:51, all appearances of "the Jews" in the synoptics occur in the formula "King of the Jews." See Brown, *An Introduction to the Gospel of John*, 157n18, for a detailed analysis of the term in the four Gospels.

[34] Painter, *The Quest for the Messiah*, 29–31 and especially 278; Morris, *The Gospel According to John*, 115–16; Adele Reinhartz, *Befriending the Beloved Disciple: A Jewish*

None of these explains every use of "the Jews" in John satisfactorily,[35] although one working theory that combines several of these proposals suggests that the term refers more generally to the aristocracy, particularly those descended from those of Judah's former nobility who returned from the Babylonian exile. Upon their return in the early Persian period, they regained control of most of the land as well as the political and religious institutions, often to the exclusion of the *am 'Haretz* or "people of the land" who had not been taken into captivity and whose descendants constituted the peasantry and urban masses of Jesus' time. Religious developments during the captivity had transformed the exiles into a confessional group recognizable by its beliefs and practices. Upon the return of this group to Judea and under the influence of figures such as Ezra, the *Ioudaioi* imposed many of its practices upon the Jews who had remained in the land. Subsequently, this group formed the heart of both the Sadducean aristocracy that dominated the temple and the Pharisaic movement, whose members were among the leadership in Jerusalem and who also dominated the synagogues in the towns and perhaps villages of the countryside.[36]

According to this view, "the Jews" of 6:41 and 52 were either part of this group or members of the local aristocracy and religious leadership who had accepted their religious views and been assimilated to the *Ioudaioi.* This explanation is in line with the observation of Elder James E. Talmage, who wrote, "There were present in the synagog some of the rulers—Pharisees, scribes, rabbis—and

Reading of the Gospel of John (New York: Continuum, 2001), 46–47, 72–75; and especially Brown, *An Introduction to the Gospel of John*, 157–72.

[35] The occurrence of *hoi Ioudaoi* in John 6 illustrates the difficulty in finding one comprehensive theory. The geographic explanation does not work well here because the setting is Galilee, not Judea. Furthermore, the Jews who murmur and strive with Jesus in 6:41 and 52 are not the chief priests and elders who constitute the "rulers of the Jews" in Jerusalem, excluding the political explanation.

[36] Daniel Boyarin, "The Ioudaioi in John and the Prehistory of 'Judaism,'" in Janice C. Anderson, Philip Sellew, and Claudia Setzter, eds., *Pauline Conversations in Context: Essays in Honour of Calvin J. Roetzel*, JSNT Sup 221 (New York: Sheffield, 2002), 218–39.

these, designated collectively as the Jews, criticized Jesus. . . . Chiefly to this class rather than to the promiscuous crowd who had hastened after Him, Jesus appears to have addressed the remainder of His discourse."[37] In this section, the group identified as "the Jews" have a particular, and increasingly violent, theological reaction against who Jesus testifies that He *is*. Their "murmuring" resulted directly from Jesus' claim that He was "the bread which came down from heaven" (6:41), which identified Him as the Son of the Father. To counter this claim, they responded by charging, "Is not this Jesus, the son of Joseph, whose father and mother we know? how is it then that he saith, I came down from heaven?" (6:42).

By attributing Jesus' paternity to Joseph the carpenter, the synagogue leadership was clearly trying to negate Jesus' claim to be God's son, but their murmuring echoes that of the children of Israel against both Moses and the Lord during the Exodus, which was later understood to be caused by unbelief (Psalm 106:23–25).[38] By not believing Jesus' testimony, they were repeating the mistake of their fathers in the wilderness and keeping themselves from coming to Christ: "No man can come unto me, except he doeth the will of my Father who hath sent me. And this is the will of him who hath sent me, that ye receive the Son; for the Father beareth record of him; and he who receiveth the testimony, and doeth the will of him who sent me, I will raise up in the resurrection of the just" (JST 6:44).

Their emphasis on Jesus' presumed parentage suggests that they understood fully the implications of the claim that Jesus had come down from heaven. In fact, their response presupposes the reaction of the *Ioudaioi* in Jerusalem who had reacted so vehemently to the Discourse on the Divine Son (5:17–18).[39] As a result of Jesus' pronouncement that He was doing the work of His Father, "the

[37] Talmage, *JTC*, 341.

[38] Painter, *The Quest for the Messiah*, 279; Morris, *The Gospel According to John*, 327 n. 111.

[39] Dodd, *The Interpretation of the Fourth Gospel*, 340.

Jews sought the more to kill him, because he not only had broken the sabbath, but said also that God was his Father, making himself equal with God" (5:18). After a detailed discourse on His relationship to the Father, Jesus identified the major obstacle keeping them from seeing Him for who He was: an almost blind devotion to the law that kept them from understanding what it symbolized. Although the King James Translation renders 5:39 as "Search the scriptures; for in them ye think ye have eternal life: and they are they which testify of me," the Greek text and its translation is ambiguous. The form of "search" (*eraunate*) is as easily indicative as imperative, resulting in "You *are searching* the scriptures because *you think* that you have eternal life *in them*" (translation and emphasis mine). As Bruce observed, "'Search the scriptures,' the AV rendering of the first clause of verse 39, is excellent advice. But the men whom Jesus was addressing were already diligent Bible searchers. The form of the verb may be either indicative or imperative, but the indicative is more appropriate in the present context."[40] Here "the Jews"—in this instance probably Pharisees or those of similar traditions—had Hebrew scriptures before them and were constantly reading and studying them, thinking that eternal life is in the texts themselves, all the while failing to see that scriptures all point to Jesus as the Son of God. Consequently, Jesus' pointed statement "Your fathers did eat manna in the wilderness, and are dead" (6:49) took on particular significance for this audience.

The Christological error of the multitude was mostly concerned with *what* Jesus would do, but once they began to grasp the idea that He had come to give them new bread as Moses—or, more properly, God through Moses—had given them the law, they appear to have been eager to accept "this bread." "The Jews," on the other hand, resistant to changing their idea of *who* Jesus was, clung more tenaciously to Moses and the old law. Although Moses

[40] Bruce, *The Gospel of John*, 136; see Morris, *The Gospel According to John*, 292–93.

is not explicitly named, the return to the theme of manna in the wilderness, which represented both the Lord's sustaining His people in the wilderness and also typified Moses' giving of the law, compares the law of Moses unfavorably to the grace of Christ: "For the law was given by Moses, but grace and truth came by Jesus Christ" (1:17).[41] For them, manna represented both the miracles that the Lord worked for their fathers through Moses *and* the law that He gave through Moses. Those ancestors were given the means to maintain their physical lives for a season, but now they were dead, and likewise the law that the manna could also represent failed to give life. Jesus, on the other hand, was "the bread which cometh down from heaven, that a man may eat thereof, and not die" (6:50).

Flesh and Blood

> I am the living bread which came down from heaven: if any man eat of this bread, he shall live for ever: and the bread that I will give is my flesh, which I will give for the life of thc world. . . . Verily, verily, I say unto you, Except ye eat the flesh of the Son of man, and drink his blood, ye have no life in you (John 6:51, 53).

The second section of Jesus' address "to the Jews" moved to the central act of His role as the Christ or Anointed One: His salvific death whereby He brought life to the world. Describing this gift as giving His flesh immediately led the *Ioudaioi* to complain, "How can this man give us his flesh to eat?" (6:52). This complaint seems to have been disingenuous, because even the broader crowd had been able to see bread as a symbol for the law, and those educated in religious discussions and imagery should have been able to see that Jesus was using a metaphor.[42] In response to their reaction, Jesus extended the metaphor, solemnly declaring, "Verily, verily, I say unto you, Except ye eat the flesh of the Son of man, and drink his

[41] Dodd, *The Interpretation of the Fourth Gospel*, 337.

[42] Talmage, *JTC*, 342 and 347–48n10.

blood, ye have no life in you. Whoso eateth my flesh, and drinketh my blood, hath eternal life; and I will raise him up at the last day" (6:53–54). Modern, particularly Christian, readers—accustomed to the sacramental imagery of partaking of bread and wine (or water), which represent the body and blood of Christ—may not always appreciate the impact of this imagery on its original audience. Given biblical injunctions against consuming blood,[43] the addition of "drinketh my blood" sharpened the response of "the Jews," but this addition is vital for correctly understanding Jesus' teaching.[44]

The Exodus imagery of the discourse's Passover setting provides an important, although often overlooked, image that connects this flesh and blood symbolism directly to the original discourse that Jesus delivered—namely, the paschal lamb who was sacrificed so that His blood could ward off death and whose flesh was eaten in a festive meal. Nevertheless, comparisons between the sacrament of the Lord's Supper and the flesh and blood section of the Bread of Life Discourse must be qualified, because the symbolism of the sacrament is actually much broader than what Jesus' statement focused on here. Although the sacrament is certainly commemorative, causing Christians since Jesus' mortal ministry to look *back* at His death, it is also proleptic, encouraging them to look *forward* to His glorious return and to celebrate as a type of the great end-time messianic feast (see, for instance, Isaiah 25:6–8; Ezekiel 39:17–20; Zechariah 9:15; Doctrine and Covenants 27:4–14).

---

[43] Note that the Old Testament injunctions against drinking blood (Genesis 9:4; Leviticus 19:26) were reaffirmed in the New Testament (Acts 15:29; 21:25).

[44] The change in rhetoric and indeed the shift in symbolism from bread to flesh and blood have led some scholars to propose that the verses in 6:51–58 are actually an interpolation, added by John or later editors to make explicit sacramental associations with this discourse (see Brown, *An Introduction to the Gospel of John*, 231, cites opponents of sacramentalism, especially the earlier work of Bultmann, who attributed this passage to the "ecclesiastical redactor"). Such attempts are motivated partially by John's surprising omission of the institution of the sacrament at the Last Supper. One way of explaining this is to see sacramental imagery woven throughout the body of the Gospel—seeing foreshadowings of it, for instance, in the miracle of water to wine, the Discourse on the Water of Life, and here in the final section of the Discourse on the Bread of Life (see Brown, *An Introduction to the Gospel of John*, 234).

Perhaps because of this, all Eucharistic references in the New Testament are to Jesus' body (*sōma:* Matthew 26:26; Mark 14:22; Luke 22:19; 1 Corinthians 11:24, 27, 29) rather than specifically to His flesh (*sarx/sarka:* John 6:51, 53–55).[45] Jesus' institution of the sacrament among the Nephites may illustrate the difference, for there He explains that the sacramental bread is "in remembrance of my body, *which I have shown to you*" (3 Nephi 18:7; emphasis added), a reference in that instance to His resurrected, immortal body as opposed to the mortal body of His prepassion ministry. Accordingly, as both a commemorative and a proleptic act, the celebration of the sacrament in Latter-day Saint theology not only focuses on what Jesus has done for us, looking back to His atoning death, but also points forward to the resurrection and emphasizes the possibility of current and future communion with Him, symbolized by the Last Supper with His disciples and His celebration of the sacrament with the Nephites.

Although this distinction between body (*sōma*) and flesh (*sarx*) should not be pressed too far,[46] the combination of flesh *and blood* emphasizes that Jesus was speaking of His mortal body, because the phrase "flesh and blood" consistently refers to a living, albeit mortal, body (Ether 3:8–9; see Leviticus 17:11–14; 1 Corinthians 15:50), as contrasted with "flesh and bone," which can refer to immortal, resurrected bodies (Doctrine and Covenants 129:1–2; 130:22).[47] More immediately important is the use of *sarx* in the

---

[45] See Morris, *The Gospel According to John*, 331–32, especially note 125. For the semantic ranges of the respective nouns, see Arndt and Gingrich, *GEL*, "sarx" and "*sōma*," 743–44, 799–800.

[46] 3 Nephi 18:28–29, for instance, speaks of partaking of the sacrament improperly as "[partaking] of *my flesh* and blood unworthily" (emphasis added), although this may have particular reference to improperly trying to lay hold of the fruits of the Atonement, being somewhat analogous to crucifying the Lord "afresh" (Hebrews 6:6) and even "[assenting] unto [His] death" (Doctrine and Covenants 132:27). On the other hand, see also Doctrine and Covenants 20:40, which refers to "[administering] the bread and wine—the emblems of the flesh and blood."

[47] "After the resurrection from the dead our bodies will be spiritual bodies, but they will be bodies that are tangible, bodies that have been purified, but they will nevertheless be bodies of flesh and bones, but they will not be blood bodies, they will

Johannine corpus itself, where it is antithetical to spirit (*pneuma*), emphasizes the earthly as opposed to the divine, and, when used of Jesus, emphasizes His incarnation as the Word made flesh (1:14).[48]

Therefore, whereas the sacrament serves as a memorial of a wider range of Jesus' atoning acts—His suffering, death, resurrection, and return in glory to live with His saints—the flesh and blood of the final section of the Bread of Life Discourse has particular reference to the fact that Jesus has really come in the flesh and that He, the Lamb of God, would sacrifice that flesh for His people. Hence, the imagery of the discourse, following the progression of the Gospel's prologue from the premortal Word to the Word made flesh, moves from "I am the bread of life" (6:35) to "the bread . . . is my flesh" (6:51b), and its use of flesh points unwaveringly to Jesus' death on Calvary.[49] Although "flesh" refers back to the teachings of the Gospel's opening section, "blood" then points forward to one of the Gospel's final climactic scenes as a spear point's thrust brings forth blood and water (19:34).[50]

As already discussed in regard to the bread of life and the shewbread, eating was a symbol of accepting something fully, internalizing it, and conveying its holiness. Hence, consuming the flesh and blood meant accepting Jesus' salvific death and incorporating it

---

no longer be quickened by blood but quickened by the spirit which is eternal and they shall become immortal and shall never die." (Joseph Fielding Smith, Conference Report, April 1917, 63).

[48] MacGregor, "The Eucharist in the Fourth Gospel," 116–17. See the discussion of Eduard Schweizer, "sarx," in Kittel and Friedrich, *TDNT*, 7:138–40, for its use in the Gospel of John. This emphasis on the divine Jehovah's becoming the man Jesus was central to the teaching of the Book of Mormon prophet Abinadi, notably in Mosiah 15:1–9. The "authorities" of Abinadi's day resisted it as strongly as "the Jews" of Jesus' time, so much so that Limhi reported that they put Abinadi to death largely for this reason, because he taught that "God should come down among the children of men, and take upon him *flesh and blood*, and go forth upon the face of the earth" (Mosiah 7:27; emphasis added).

[49] Ruland, "Sign and Sacrament: John's Bread of Life Discourse," 461.

[50] Brown, *An Introduction to the Gospel of John*, 234, notes how both water and blood in 19:34 show how both sacramental water and eucharistic blood have their source in the death of Jesus.

fully into one's own being.[51] This point of acceptance or initial conversion—unlike the sacrament, which is celebrated regularly as a means of remembrance—is, ideally, a one-time action: "eat" (*phagē/phagēte*) and "drink" (*piēte*) in 6:51 and 53 are aorist subjunctives, with the aspect of this tense suggesting a one-time rather than repeated action. [52] Nevertheless, although the significance is not completely clear, the word for "eat" in 6:54 and 56 changes from *phagē* to the substantive present participle *ho trōgōn*. Although this is rendered simply as "he eats" or "whoever eats" in virtually all English translations, the word actually means "to gnaw (chew)" or "eat audibly." [53] Furthermore, the tense changes from an aorist one-time action to a continuous present. The text thereby suggests the notion of eating with enjoyment, with the present tense perhaps "[pointing] to a continuing appropriation" once the decision to accept Jesus' sacrifice has been made.[54]

Thus, although the symbolism and purpose of the sacrament overlap in many ways with the imagery of the Bread of Life Sermon, interpreting the discourse backward solely from the ordinance that Jesus established at the end of His mortal ministry can limit to some extent our current understanding of both. The sacrament holds a wider range of symbolism—particularly for the body (*sōma*)—but the flesh and blood in the last portion of the Bread of Life Sermon

---

[51] Jackson, "Bread," 294, writes, "The ordinance of the sacrament, in which we consume the symbolic emblems of his redemptive act, signifies profoundly our consuming of his atoning grace and of his plan that makes it effective in our lives."

[52] Morris, *The Gospel According to John*, 335. Daniel B. Wallace, *Greek Grammar Beyond the Basics: An Exegetical Syntax of the New Testament* (Grand Rapids, Mich.: Zondervan, 1996), 554–55. Morris may overstate the significance of the aorist aspect because in both of these verses, the grammar is a bit more complicated, since in each instance the aorist subjunctive verbs appear in the protasis of a third-class condition (present general by Classical convention), but the aspect is probably maintained even in the general nature of the condition.

[53] Arndt and Gingrich, *GEL*, "*trōgō*," 829; see Ruland, "Sign and Sacrament: John's Bread of Life Discourse," 450: "Christ's words here are abrasively ultra-realistic: the graphic verb *trōgein*, recurring emphatically four times within four verses, means literally to 'crunch' his flesh. These shocking words provoke an agonized schism among his followers."

[54] Morris, *The Gospel According to John*, 335 n. 136.

illustrate a particular Christological point about the work of Jesus, specifically the salvific nature of His death. Eternal life can be found only in Jesus as the Son of God who came down from heaven specifically to die for the world, a fact that "the Jews," placing their trust in Moses and the law, could not accept.

Reactions to the Bread of Life Discourse

> From that time many of his disciples went back, and walked no more with him. Then said Jesus unto the twelve, Will ye also go away? Then Simon Peter answered him, Lord, to whom shall we go? thou hast the words of eternal life (John 6:66–68).

At the conclusion of the Sermon on the Bread of Life, Jesus moved out of the synagogue and addressed the final groups mentioned in John 6. Just as the previous audiences were identified twice as "the crowd/the people" (*ochlos,* 6:22 and 24) and "the Jews" (*hoi Ioudaioi,* 6:41 and 52), so John specifies Jesus' new listeners by identifying the first group as "his disciples" (6:60 and 66) and the second as "the twelve" (6:67 and 71).[55] Whereas the crowd had an incorrect idea of the person and work of Jesus, and "the Jews" rejected the truth when it was taught to them, the body of Jesus' followers, collectively referred to as "his disciples" (6:61), did not reject the idea of a divine Son who came down from heaven. Although the "flesh and blood" passages were disturbing if taken literally, even for those followers of Jesus who may have understood that they were a metaphor for accepting the death of Jesus, they proved to be "a hard saying" (6:60). They, too, began to "murmur" at the proposition that their Messiah would need to give His flesh and blood by dying (6:61).

The general reaction of the disciples here finds some parallel in the reaction of the Twelve in the synoptics when Jesus began to teach them more directly that He must go to Jerusalem, suffer there, and die. In the three great "Passion Predictions," Peter and

---

[55] Painter, *The Quest for the Messiah*, 267.

the other members of the Twelve, who had accepted who Jesus *was*, having gained a testimony by revelation, still found it difficult to embrace what He must *do.*[56] Elder McConkie has written, "By the simple expedient of teaching strong doctrine to the hosts who followed him, Jesus was able to separate the chaff from the wheat and choose out those who were worthy of membership in his earthly kingdom. Before entering the synagogue in Capernaum to preach his great discourse on the Bread of Life, Jesus was at the height of his popularity . . . [but] unable to believe and accept his strong and plain assertions about eating his flesh and drinking his blood, even many classified as disciples fell away."[57]

John records, "From that time many of his disciples went back, and walked no more with him," at which point Jesus, turning to His final audience, poignantly said to the Twelve, "Will ye also go away?" (6:67). Peter's response, "Lord, to whom shall we go? thou hast the words of eternal life. And we believe and are sure that thou art that Christ, the Son of the living God" (6:68–69),[58] contrasts sharply with the position of "the Jews" in the Discourse on the Divine Son (5:39): Jesus, not the Jewish scriptures of themselves, had the words of eternal life. Peter and the other members of the Twelve now understood the answer to the first part of the Christological question, who Jesus was, and their determination to follow Him after the Discourse on the Bread of Life indicated their willingness to continue to follow Him even if they did not at this time fully understand the hard saying that represented the answer to the second Christological question, which focused the "work" of Jesus on the necessity of His giving His life for life of

[56] First prediction: Matthew 16:21–28; Mark 8:31–9:1; Luke 9:19–27. Second prediction: Matthew 17:22–23; Mark 9:30–32; Luke 9:43b–45. Third prediction: Matthew 20:17–19; Mark 10:32–45; Luke 18:31–34.

[57] McConkie, *DNTC*, 1:361.

[58] Although harmonizing events in John with the synoptics is difficult, Peter's confession following the Bread of Life Discourse appears to anticipate that delivered at Caesarea Philippi shortly before the Transfiguration (Matthew 16:13–20; Mark 8:27–30; Luke 9:18–21). See Ruland, "Sign and Sacrament: John's Bread of Life Discourse," 452.

the world. The complete meaning of Jesus' "flesh and blood" was not clear to the Twelve or to any of the disciples until after the Passion and Resurrection. Indeed, John's notice that Jesus concluded His discussion of the Bread of Life by alluding to Judas' future treachery creates an echo with Judas' leaving to betray Jesus during the Last Supper.[59] Even one of the Twelve would, in the end, reject the Savior's saving mission.

Nevertheless, the fact that the Son of God, who had come down from heaven and become flesh, must lay that flesh down and shed His blood is the fundamental definition of the gospel that believers must fully accept and internalize. What Jesus taught in metaphor in the Bread of Life Discourse He taught directly to the Nephites following His resurrection:

> My Father sent me that I might be lifted up upon the cross; and after that I had been lifted up upon the cross, that I might draw all men unto me, that as I have been lifted up by men even so should men be lifted up by the Father, to stand before me, to be judged of their works, whether they be good or whether they be evil—and for this cause have I been lifted up; therefore, according to the power of the Father I will draw all men unto me, that they may be judged according to their works. And it shall come to pass, that whoso repenteth and is baptized in my name shall be filled; and if he endureth to the end, behold, him will I hold guiltless before my Father at that day when I shall stand to judge the world. (3 Nephi 27:14–16)

For the Latter-day Saints and all Christians today, "To eat the flesh and drink the blood of the Son of God is, first, to accept him in the most literal and full sense, with no reservation, whatever, as the personal offspring in the flesh of the Eternal Father," and "to work the works of God" in practical terms "[by keeping] the commandments of the Son by accepting his gospel, joining his Church, and enduring in obedience and righteousness unto the

---

[59] Ruland, "Sign and Sacrament: John's Bread of Life Discourse," 454.

end."[60] To this we can add the lesson taught by "the Jews" and the faithless disciples: part of accepting Jesus as the Son of God includes accepting—indeed, focusing on—the salvific necessity of His suffering, death, and resurrection.

[60] McConkie, *DNTC*, 358.

XI.

JESUS AND THE GENTILES

GAYE STRATHEARN

Many shall come from the east and west, and shall sit down with Abraham, and Isaac, and Jacob, in the kingdom of heaven.

MATTHEW 8:11

Shortly before the Feast of Dedication, Jesus taught, "Other sheep I have, which are not of this fold: them also I must bring, and they shall hear my voice; and there shall be one fold, and one shepherd" (John 10:16; cf. 3 Nephi 15:17). Later, after His resurrection, when He appeared to the descendants of Lehi, He explained its meaning. He taught them that "not at any time hath the Father given me commandment" that He should tell the people in Jerusalem of the "remnant of the house of Joseph" who lived in other lands (3 Nephi 15:12, 14). All He was allowed to tell them was the passage in John 10:16. "Because of stiffneckedness and unbelief they understood not my word; therefore I was commanded to say no more of the Father concerning this thing" (3 Nephi 15:18).

As a result, "they understood me not, for they supposed it had been the Gentiles; for they understood not that the Gentiles should be converted through their preaching. And they understood me not that I said they shall hear my voice; and they understood me not that the Gentiles should not at any time hear my voice—that I should not manifest myself unto them save it were by the Holy Ghost" (3 Nephi 15:22–23).[1]

As we turn to the New Testament, we find a more complicated scenario. The New Testament makes it clear that Jesus understood Hisministry to be directed to the "lost sheep of the house of Israel" (Matthew 15:24), but it is also clear that, at times, Gentiles sought Him out for special blessings, and that Jesus responded to their faith (see Matthew 8:5–13; 15:21–31). It is also clear that He anticipated a time when they would also share in the blessings of the gospel.

This chapter is divided into three sections and will briefly discuss the etymology of the word *Gentile,* examine the historical dynamic between Jews and Gentiles, and then discuss this dynamic in the context of Jesus' ministry, as recorded in Matthew's Gospel.

The Hebrew and Greek Etymology of the Word *Gentile*

The word *Gentile* is a translation of either the Hebrew word *goy* (pl. = *goyim*) or the Greek word *ethnos* (pl. = *ethnoi* or *ethna*). Both the Hebrew and Greek words have the basic sense of "nation." In the King James Version (KJV) of the Old Testament, we find numerous places where "nation" is the translation of choice (see Genesis 10:20, 31–32; 12:2; 17:4). Other times, it is translated in a more pejorative way as either "heathen" (e.g., Leviticus 25:44; Ezra 6:21; Psalm 2:1) or "gentile" (e.g., Isaiah 11:10; 42:1, 6; 49:6, 22; 54:3; 60:3, 5, 11, 16; Micah 5:8 [Heb. = Micah 5:7]; Zechariah 1:21 [Heb. = Zechariah

[1] Even a cursory look at modern discussions on John 10:16 shows that people still interpret the "other sheep" as the Gentiles. Raymond E. Brown writes, "That there are other sheep who do not belong to the fold introduces the Gentile mission" (*The Gospel According to John I–XII: A New Translation with Introduction and Commentary,* The Anchor Bible 29 [New York: Doubleday, 1966], 396). See also Andreas J. Köstenberger, *John* (Grand Rapids, Mich.: Baker Academic, 2004), 306–7; Craig S. Keener, *The Gospel of John: A Commentary,* 2 vols. (Peabody, Mass.: Hendrickson, 2003), 1:818–19; James D. G. Dunn and John W. Rogerson, *Eerdmans Commentary on the Bible* (Grand Rapids, Mich.: Eerdmans, 2003), 1187; Thomas L. Brodie, *The Gospel According to John: A Literary and Theological Commentary* (New York: Oxford University Press, 1993), 370–71.

2:4]; Malachi 1:11, etc.). In one place, in the same verse, we find *goy* used twice, and it is translated once as "nations" and once as "gentiles" (see Genesis 10:5). In the KJV New Testament, *ethnos* is translated with the same semantic range: sometimes it is translated as "nation" (see Matthew 21:43; Acts 2:5; Romans 1:5), sometimes as "gentile" (see Matthew 4:15; 6:32; 10:5, and so forth), and sometimes as "heathen" (see 2 Corinthians 11:26; Galatians 1:16; 2:9; 3:8). In both the Old and New Testaments, many other English translations are more consistent in their translations and choose a neutral translation of "nation" or "people."[2]

In the Old Testament, *goy* is sometimes seen in distinction from another Hebrew term for people, *ʿam,* but while we do find the phrase *ʿam yhvh* (people of Yahweh/Jehovah; 2 Samuel 1:12; Ezekiel 36:20), we do not find a corresponding phrase using *goy.*[3] In addition, the peoples whom the Assyrians imported into the northern kingdom, who brought their own gods and worshiped them in the houses of the Samarians, are identified as *goyim* (Gentiles).[4] Thus, *goyim* in this sense are viewed as people who worship different gods than those of the people of Israel. We also find a few references where "certain *goyim,* left historically and politically undefined, constitute a political threat to Israel and to its anointed king" (Psalm 2:1, 8; 46:6 [Heb. = Psalm 46:7]).[5] In some passages, the context helps us see a contrast between *goy* and the covenant people. Isaiah tells his people, "The Gentiles [*goyim*] shall come to thy light" (Isaiah 60:3). We find a similar distinction in the New

[2] For example, the New International Version, English Standard Version, New Living Translation, American Standard Version, etc.

[3] Ronald E. Clements, *Theological Dictionary of the Old Testament,* ed. G. Johannes Botterweck and Helmer Ringgren, trans. John T. Willis (Grand Rapids. Mich.: Eerdmans, 1975), 2:427.

[4] Although the KJV uses the word "Samaritans" here, I have chosen to use "Samarian" to indicate there is no evidence that the Samaritans of the New Testament existed as a separate religious group until the second century B.C. See Gaye Strathearn, "Jesus Teaches at Jacob's Well," in *The Life and Teachings of Jesus Christ: From Bethlehem through the Sermon on the Mount,* ed. Richard Neitzel Holzapfel and Thomas A. Wayment (Salt Lake City: Deseret Book, 2005), 1:247–68.

[5] Clements, *Theological Dictionary of the Old Testament,* 2:431–32.

Testament where Jesus instructs His disciples, "But when ye pray, use not vain repetitions, as the heathens [*ethnikoi*] do: for they think that they shall be heard for their much speaking" (Matthew 6:7). Likewise, Paul's efforts to take the gospel to the Gentiles are clearly viewed by some of his opponents as a rejection of the law of Moses (Acts 15:1–5; 21:18–24).

In discussing the historical dynamic between Jews and Gentiles, therefore, we must be aware that the term *gentile* was a fluid term that only over time took on a contrasting role to that of the covenant people.

The Abrahamic Covenant and the Gentiles

When God covenanted with Abraham in Haran, He promised him, "I will make of thee a great nation [*goy*], and I will bless thee, and make thy name great; and thou shalt be a blessing: and I will bless them that bless thee, and curse him that curseth thee: and in thee shall all families of the earth be blessed" (Genesis 12:2–3). We find a more detailed account of the covenant in Abraham 2:8–11:

> My name is Jehovah, and I know the end from the beginning; therefore my hand shall be over thee. And I will make of thee a great nation, and I will bless thee above measure, and make thy name great among all nations, and thou shalt be a blessing unto thy seed after thee, that in their hands they shall bear this ministry and Priesthood unto all nations; and I will bless them through thy name; for as many as receive this Gospel shall be called after thy name, and shall be accounted thy seed, and shall rise up and bless thee, as their father; and I will bless them that bless thee, and curse them that curse thee; and in thee (that is, in thy Priesthood) and in thy seed (that is, thy Priesthood), for I give unto thee a promise that this right shall continue in thee, and in thy seed after thee (that is to say, the literal seed, or the seed of the body) shall all the families of the earth be blessed, even with the blessings of the Gospel, which are the blessings of salvation, even of life eternal.

As Abraham left Haran and entered Canaan, the Lord reassured him that his seed would be as the stars in the heaven, promising "to give [him] this land to inherit it" (Genesis 15:5–7). In these blessings, we note two important elements that would have a profound impact on Jewish/Gentile relations throughout history. The covenant promised Abraham that his seed would become a "great nation" and that through them "all the families of the earth" would be blessed. As we examine both of these promises, we will see that now and again they stood in some tension to each other. To become a great nation, Israel, at times, had to distance itself from other nations to establish its geographical, political, and religious boundaries. Throughout its history, Israel was not always able to maintain this distinction, which led to frequent prophetic calls for repentance and attempts at religious reform by leaders such as Josiah and Ezra. At other times, however, particularly during the intertestamental period, Israel became a light that attracted Gentiles to Jehovah and His teachings. As we examine the historical underpinnings of each of these covenantal blessings, we will be better able to appreciate Jesus' interaction with Gentiles in the New Testament.

Israel Will Become a Great Nation

The first part of the Abrahamic covenant was the promise that Abraham's posterity would one day become a great nation (*goy*). In the Genesis account, this is significant because previously Genesis 10 outlined the Table of Nations—the nations that sprang from Noah's posterity after the Flood. In the Old Testament, we find implied in the notion of becoming a nation the requirements of having a people with a territorial possession and a governing structure. All three of these requirements are central features in the blessings that Jehovah promised Abraham. In addition, nations were distinguished from other nations by a common language and the worship of a national God.[6] But Abraham was not just promised

[6] Clements, *Theological Dictionary of the Old Testament,* 2:427–30. For a discussion of Abraham and his God vis-à-vis other national gods, see Gaye Strathearn, "The

that he would be one among many nations; Jehovah promised that he would become a "great nation." This greatness would not come from superior numbers or victories on the battlefield; it would come because of the priesthood of God. Jehovah instructed Abraham's descendants, "If ye will obey my voice indeed, and keep my covenant, then ye shall be a peculiar treasure unto me above all people: for all the earth is mine: and ye shall be unto me a kingdom of priests, and an holy nation" (Exodus 19:5–6; cf. 1 Peter 2:9).

Historically, this aspect of the covenantal promise has evolved into some uneasy tensions between Abraham's covenant descendants and the other nations of the world. In an effort to maintain the purity of the covenant community, Abraham did not want his posterity to marry outside the covenant. He gave specific instructions to his servant "that thou shalt not take a wife unto my son of the daughters of the Canaanites, among whom I dwell" (Genesis 24:3). Isaac placed the same injunction upon his son Jacob (Genesis 28:1; cf. Genesis 26:34–35; 27:46). Likewise, as Israel prepared to enter the promised land, Jehovah instructed them not to "make marriages with them; thy daughter thou shalt not give unto his son, nor his daughter shalt thou take unto thy son." The following reason is given for this command: "For they will turn away thy son from following me, that they may serve other gods" (Deuteronomy 7:3–4). Later, Ezra focused on this commandment as *the* hallmark of establishing a holy people (see Nehemiah 8:1–8).

At times, especially as Jehovah sought to establish them in their promised land, this required them to utterly destroy (Deuteronomy 7:2). Jehovah knew that the nations of Canaan would be a constant threat to the covenantal integrity of His chosen people (Deuteronomy 12:1–3, 29–32). When the Israelites failed to destroy all of the Canaanites, an angel declared for Jehovah, "[I commanded that] ye shall make no league with the inhabitants of this land; [that] ye

Wife/Sister Experience: Pharaoh's Introduction to Jehovah," in *Thy People Shall Be My People and Thy God My God: Sidney B. Sperry Symposium on the Old Testament* (Salt Lake City: Deseret Book, 1994), 150–65.

shall throw down their altars: but ye have not obeyed my voice: why have ye done this? Wherefore I also said, I will not drive them out from before you; but they shall be as thorns in your sides, and their gods shall be a snare unto you" (Judges 2:2–3).

The Old Testament records the recurring flirtations of Israel and Judah with the "other gods" of the local inhabitants (see Deuteronomy 7:4; Judges 2:17; 1 Kings 14:9; Jeremiah 1:16). Throughout Israelite and Judahite history, Jehovah sent prophets to call them to repentance, with mixed success. In addition to the prophetic work, the Southern Kingdom had three important periods of reformation that played significant roles in shaping the parameters of the Judaism we find in the New Testament and, by extension, the Jewish/Gentile boundaries.

Josiah became king of Judah when he was just eight years old. When he was sixteen and "yet young, he began to seek after the God of David his father" (2 Chronicles 34:3). The scriptures summarize his reign as follows: "He did that which was right in the sight of the Lord, and walked in all the way of David his father, and turned not aside to the right hand or to the left" (2 Kings 22:2). This reign is characterized by a religious reform that began with a zealous campaign to eradicate all forms of idolatry from his kingdom (2 Chronicles 34:3–7; see also Jeremiah 25:1–29). In addition, he commissioned the renovation of the temple. During this renovation, Hilkiah the priest found a copy of the law of Moses. This law was probably a copy of the book of Deuteronomy.[7] When Josiah had the contents read to him, he commanded his servant, "Go, enquire of the Lord for me, and for them that are left in Israel and in Judah, concerning the words of the book that is found: for great is the wrath of the Lord that is poured out upon us, because our fathers have not kept the word of the Lord, to do after all that is written in this book" (2 Chronicles 34:21). Accordingly, Hilkiah

[7] Margaret Barker, "What Did King Josiah Reform?" in *Glimpses of Lehi's Jerusalem*, ed. John W. Welch, David Rolph Seely, and Jo Ann H. Seely (Provo: Foundation for Ancient Research and Mormon Studies, Brigham Young University, 2004), 523.

went to "Huldah the prophetess," who declared, "Thus saith the Lord, Behold, I will bring evil upon this place, and upon the inhabitants thereof, even all the curses[8] that are written in the book which they have read before the king of Judah: because they have forsaken me, and have burned incense unto other gods, that they might provoke me to anger with all the works of their hands; therefore my wrath shall be poured out upon this place, and shall not be quenched" (2 Chronicles 34:22, 24–25).

Josiah then gathered his people together; covenanted to live by the commandments, testimonies, and statutes of the law; and caused his subjects to do likewise (2 Chronicles 34:31–32).[9] Ultimately, Josiah's reforms were short-lived. He was killed in battle with Pharaoh Necho at Megiddo in 605 B.C. His death opened the door for a number of puppet kings for the Babylonians under Nebuchadnezzar, eventually resulting in the deportation of many Judahites to Babylon. Josiah's effort was the first national covenant renewal since the days of Joshua. Perhaps the most significant contribution of Josiah's reform was the centralization of worship in Jerusalem.

The exile was a watershed event in the development of Judaism and Jewish/Gentile relations. Until this time, "the identity of the people had been shaped and supported by a number of complementary factors—common territory, political loyalty, ethnic continuity, common language, religious observance, and tradition."[10] During the exile, the people had to find ways to maintain their identity in a gentile environment. Their efforts were undoubtedly enhanced by

---

[8] The curses are probably a reference to the events recorded in Deuteronomy 27–28. Moses charged the Israelites that when they entered the Promised Land, they were to divide the tribes into two groups. One group would stand on Mount Gerizim and the other on Mount Ebal. Those on Mount Ebal were to shout the cursings that would come upon Israel if they broke the commandments. Those on Mount Gerizim were to shout the blessings associated with obedience.

[9] Not everyone agreed with Josiah's reforms. See Barker, "What Did King Josiah Reform?" 523–42.

[10] John J. Collins, *Between Athens and Jerusalem: Jewish Identity in the Hellenistic Diaspora,* 2d ed. (Grand Rapids, Mich.: Eerdmans, 2000), 1.

the prominent positions attained by Daniel, Shadrach, Meshach, and Abednego during the Babylonian captivity, and by Esther and Mordecai during the Persian rule. Nevertheless, "religious tradition and observance assumed an ever greater role in maintaining distinctive identity." They had to learn to "sing the Lord's song in a strange land" (Psalm 137:4).[11]

After the Babylonian exiles returned to Judea, Nehemiah and Ezra sought to reestablish their people by emphasizing their unique status—that they were a peculiar people who were not like the nations that surrounded them. Nehemiah banned foreign merchants from plying their trade in Jerusalem on the Sabbath and emphasized the use of Hebrew (Nehemiah 13:15–24). Ezra required that the returnees covenant to put away their "strange wives of the people of the land" (Ezra 10:1–5; see also Nehemiah 13:25–31).[12] Those who refused to do so were expelled from the community (Ezra 10:8). It is clear from the previous material in Ezra that the impetus for Ezra's actions was the report that "the people of Israel, and the priests, and the Levites, have not separated themselves from the people of the lands, doing according to their abominations, even of the Canaanites, the Hitttites, the Perizzites, the Jebusites, the Ammonites, the Moabites, the Egyptians, and the Amorites" (Ezra 9:1). In the scriptures, "abomination" refers to "that which God hates"—specifically idolatry and adultery.[13] The issue here cannot be adultery because the people were married. Therefore, the abominations must refer to the worship of the gods of the nations mentioned. In addition, Ezra gathered the people together to commit them to the study and observance of the law (Nehemiah 8:1–18). Apparently, the law they studied was from a book that Ezra had but that the people did not (Nehemiah 8:1). It

[11] Collins, *Between Athens and Jerusalem*, 1.

[12] Lee Levine, "Hasmonean Jerusalem: A Jewish City in a Hellenistic Orbit," *Judaism* 46/2 (1997): 141.

[13] Stephen E. Robinson, "Early Christianity and 1 Nephi 13–14," in *The Book of Mormon: First Nephi, The Doctrinal Foundation*, ed. Monte S. Nyman and Charles D. Tate Jr. (Provo, Utah: BYU Religious Studies Center, 1988), 178.

has been argued that the book Ezra brought with him out of captivity was the precursor to the Pentateuch in our current Old Testament.[14] We see under his leadership the seedbed from which New Testament Judaism would emerge. In particular, we see a focus on isolation from noncovenant people and a focus on the law, as interpreted by the intelligentsia (Nehemiah 8:7–8).[15]

The third major reform came during the period of the Maccabean Revolt. When Alexander the Great embarked on his campaign to unite East and West, he did not just conquer militarily; he also conquered culturally. There is good reason to believe that many Jews welcomed the cultural infusion. In 175 B.C., Jason transformed Jerusalem into a Greek city in exchange for receiving the office of high priest (2 Maccabees 4:1–10). The book of 1 Maccabees indicates that many Jews wanted to make a covenant with their Greek (Seleucid) rulers. They built a gymnasium in Jerusalem, "made themselves uncircumcised, and forsook the holy covenant" (1 Maccabees 1:14–15). The Seleucid king, Antiochus Epiphanes IV, entered Jerusalem and the temple, sacrificed a pig on the altar, and dedicated the temple to the worship of Zeus. In addition, in an effort to unify his empire under the religion of the Greeks, he outlawed the practice of Judaism (1 Maccabees 1:41–50).[16] The penalty for any infraction was death. The Maccabean Revolt was a response to this religious persecution. Under the leadership of Judas Hasmoneas and his brothers, Jews banded together to engage the

---

[14] K. Koch, "Ezra and the Origins of Judaism," *Journal of Semitic Studies* 19 (1974): 180–81.

[15] "The promulgation of Ezra's law as a rule for the people had consequences in the future which reached further than the promulgation of the Deuteronomy in the days of King Josiah. To this extent the achievement of Ezra became one of the presuppositions of later Judaism" (Koch, "Ezra and the Origins of Judaism," 197). We should note, however, that the ideal of isolation was rarely achieved. In the Hellenistic period, Jews voluntarily moved to other places of habitation and established Jewish colonies. Even though they maintained their identity, they also absorbed aspects of their host cultures. Philo of Alexandria worked to alleviate the negative Gentile assessments of Judaism by emphasizing the aspects "which were most acceptable to cultured Gentiles" (Collins, *Between Athens and Jerusalem*, 3–5, 15).

[16] See also Tacitus, *Histories* 5.8; Diodorus, *Fragments* 34/35.1.

Seleucid armies in a campaign of guerilla warfare. Their initial success swelled their numbers, and eventually they were able to recapture Jerusalem and rededicate the temple to the worship of Jehovah.

The Maccabean period is an interesting study in the historical relationship between Jews and Gentiles. It highlights the persistent tension between the desire to be a peculiar people and the yearning for acceptance among the other nations. On the one hand, the revolt forced the Jews to identify the core elements that made them a peculiar nation. Four elements were reenthroned as the religious and cultural markers of Judaism. As we saw with Ezra and Nehemiah, the temple was central, and "with the campaigns to ban idolatry and reemphasize the Temple's prominence came a greater emphasis on matters of ritual purity within Jewish society."[17] In addition to the temple, circumcision was reemphasized as the sign of the covenant, and Sabbath observance and dietary laws also rose in importance.[18] The rise of groups such as the Pharisees, Sadducees, and Essenes during this period is evidence "of a more concerted

[17] Levine, "Hasmonean Jerusalem," 142.

[18] See the account in 2 Maccabees 6 where Jews revolt against the edict of Antiochus outlawing the practice of Judaism by openly displaying their loyalty to these four aspects of Judaism. In the decree of Sardis, Jewish citizens are afforded the right to meet together to offer prayers and sacrifices to their God, and market officials are directed to "have suitable food for them brought in" (Josephus, *AJ* 14.259–261). Josephus also records Caesar Augustus' decree that Jewish monies sent to the temple are inviolable and that Jews are exempt from appearing in court on the Sabbath or Sabbath eve (*AJ* 16.6.1–8). Cicero says that each year Jews from Italy sent gold to the temple in Jerusalem (*Pro Flacco* 28.66–69; see also Tacitus, *Histories* 5.5). In addition, the New Testament shows that for Judaizers, the main areas for concern about letting Gentiles join the Church centered around circumcision (Acts 15:1; Galatians 5:1–13) and eating with Gentiles (Acts 11:3; Galatians 2:11–13). Worship on the Sabbath does not appear to be an issue because the early Christians continued to participate in the synagogue on the Sabbath and then added their service on the Sunday. In addition, the early Christians continued to worship at the temple (Acts 21:23–26). For a discussion on Pagan attacks on Jewish circumcision, Sabbath observance, and dietary laws, see Louis H. Feldman, *Jew and Gentile in the Ancient World: Attitudes and Interactions from Alexander to Justininian* (Princeton, N.J.: Princeton University Press, 1993), 153–70.

Jewish emphasis at this time."[19] But even though the Maccabean Revolt championed religious independence, it did *not* advocate cultural independence. The Maccabean rulers appropriated many Greek cultural traits. They adopted Greek names, their burial monuments and graves "reflect a significant appropriation of Hellenistic forms," their coins began to have both Greek and Hebrew inscriptions and symbols, and the literature of the time, even if the text berates Hellenism, often reflects strong Greek stylistic influence (e.g., 1 and 2 Maccabees).[20]

From Abraham down to the Hasmonean Period, the covenant people struggled to achieve the first blessing of the Abrahamic covenant: to be a great nation. The point of the reforms of Josiah and Ezra was that the covenant people had sought for greatness by trying to participate in the religions of their neighbors rather than giving their allegiance to the God of Abraham. Over time, the implementation and development of Ezra's reforms led outsiders to identify the covenant people as isolationists. Hecataeus, a Greek historian from the fourth century B.C., described the Jews of his time as "unsocial and intolerant" (quoted in Diodorus Siculus 40.3.4). Similarly, Apollonius of Molon, a Greek rhetorician from the first century B.C., declared that the Jews would not "have fellowship with those that choose to observe a way of living different from [them]selves" (as quoted in Josephus, *Against Apion* 2.258/2.37). Tacitus, in the second century A.D., describes Jews as extremely honest when dealing with their compatriots but notes that "they regard the rest of mankind with all the hatred of enemies" (*Histories* 5.5.1).[21] This tension between Jews and Gentiles is evident in the New Testament, particularly as the fledgling Church struggled to implement Jesus' command to teach all nations so that the second Abrahamic promise could be fulfilled.

---

[19] Levine, "Hasmonean Jerusalem," 142.

[20] Levine, "Hasmonean Jerusalem," 143–46.

[21] Feldman, *Jew and Gentile,* 45–47.

All the Families of the Earth Will Be Blessed

The second part of the Abrahamic covenant, that all the families of the earth will be blessed, is sometimes seen to be in tension with the first. Although God covenanted with Israel that they would be a peculiar people, the covenant was never intended to be an exclusive affair.[22] The command to destroy the inhabitants of Canaan must be understood within the context of the promise that "Abraham shall surely become a great and mighty nation, and all the nations of the earth shall be blessed in him" (Genesis 18:18).[23] It was always intended that the major focus of the covenant people was ultimately to bless, not destroy, the other nations of the world. But how was Israel to bless the nations of the earth? Abraham's commission indicates that it would be through the priesthood and the blessings of the gospel (Abraham 2:9, 11).

There is little biblical indication "that the Israelites were active missionaries,"[24] but there are some clues. Jehovah introduced the covenant by declaring, "I have purposed to take thee away out of Haran, and to *make of thee a minister to bear my name in a strange land* which I will give unto thy seed after thee for an everlasting possession, when they hearken to my voice" (Abraham 2:6; emphasis added). It appears that Abraham did not wait until he arrived in Canaan to respond to this injunction because when he left Haran, he took "Sarai his wife, and Lot his brother's son, and all their substance that they had gathered, *and the souls that they had gotten in Haran*" (Genesis 12:5; emphasis added). Apparently, Abraham

[22] For a discussion of early Jewish proselytism, see Feldman, *Jew and Gentile,* 288–341.

[23] It is this passage, rather than Genesis 12:3, that is at the heart of Paul's defense of his mission to the Gentiles (Galatians 3:8). Genesis 12:3 says that in Abraham "shall all the *families* of the earth be blessed" (emphasis added). The Hebrew word translated as "families" is *mishpehot,* which can also be translated as "tribes." Lest there be any room for ambiguity, Paul chooses Genesis 18:18 because it uses the term *goyim,* a word that means "nations" but will eventually come to be the technical term for "Gentiles."

[24] Feldman, *Jew and Gentile,* 288.

immediately began his missionary work.[25] Also, we learn that when the Israelites left Egypt, "a mixed multitude went up also with them" (Exodus 12:38), suggesting that others besides the Israelites were drawn to Moses and his God.[26] The later Rabbis interpreted the statement by Ruth to her mother-in-law, "Thy people shall be my people, and thy God my God" (Ruth 1:16), as proof of her conversion.[27] We also have Jonah's mission to call the inhabitants of Nineveh to repentance (Jonah 1–4). In addition, we have Isaiah's prophetic declarations that Israel would be "a light to the Gentiles" (49:6), that "the Gentiles shall come to thy light" (60:3), and that "the Gentiles shall see thy righteousness" (62:2).

In the Intertestamental Period, there appears to be a heightened awareness of, and attraction to, Judaism by Gentiles.[28] The antiquity of the religion and the ethical guidelines of the law of Moses were two characteristics that appealed to Gentiles.[29] Two Jewish writers, Josephus and Philo, make significant comments about Jewish proselytes. Josephus records that the Jews welcomed those who wished to adopt their laws (*Against Apion* 2.29), and that "the multitude of mankind itself have had a great inclination for a long time to follow our religious observances" (*Against Apion* 2.40). Philo says that those who have chosen to follow a single creator must be looked upon "as our friends and kinsmen" (*De Virtutibus* 33.179).

---

[25] This interpretation is consistent with that of the later Rabbis. Rabbi Hunia in the midrash on Genesis 12:5 comments, "Abraham converted the men and Sarah the women" (*Genesis Rabbah*, 39.14).

[26] Philo notes that the mixed multitude consisted, among others, of "all those who had admired the decent piety of the men, and therefore joined them; and some, also, who had come over to them, having learnt the right way, by reason of the magnitude and multitude of the incessant punishments which had been inflicted on their own countrymen" (*De Vita Mosis* 1.27.147). I have taken all Philo translations from C. D. Yonge, trans., *The Works of Philo: Complete and Unabridged* (Peabody, Mass.: Hendrickson Publishers, 1993).

[27] *Ruth Rabbah* 2.22–24.

[28] Tacitus says that proselytes "increase their [i.e., the Jews'] numbers" (*Histories* 5.5).

[29] Emile Schürer, *The History of the Jewish People in the Age of Jesus Christ*, 3 vols., rev. & ed. Geza Vermes, Fergus Millar and Martin Goodman (Edinburgh: T&T Clark, 1986), 3.1:150–76.

In part, this is because they "have left their country, and their friends, and their relations for the sake of virtue and holiness (*hosioteœs*)" (*De Specialibus Legibus* 1.9.52). What is the motivation for conversion? According to Philo, those who have their natural relations by blood, their native land and their national customs, and the sacred temples of their gods have "migrated with a holy migration, changing their abode of fabulous inventions for that of the certainty and clearness of truth, and of the worship of the one true and living God" (*De Virtutibus* 20.102).[30] In the New Testament, Jesus confirms that Jews actively proselyted converts. He declares that the scribes and Pharisees "compass sea and land to make one proselyte" (Matthew 23:15).[31] Josephus also records the conversion of the royal house of Adiabene in the first century A.D. (*AJ* 20.2.3–4).

In addition to proselytes to Judaism, we also find some evidence of people who were attracted to Judaism but did not convert to it. Philo mentions proselytes who had not undergone circumcision, and he insists that they were not true converts (*Quaestiones in Exodum* 2.2). Josephus, in describing those who sent contributions to the temple, makes a distinction between the "Jews throughout the habitable world" and "those that worshipped God" (*sebomenoœn ton theon;* Josephus, *AJ* 14.7.2). The same Greek phrase is also found in the New Testament as describing Lydia (Acts 16:14) and Justus (Acts 18:7). Another parallel New Testament phrase that seems to describe Gentiles who participate in Judaism to a limited degree are those who "fear God" (*phoboumenoi ton Theon;* Acts 10:2, 22, 35; 13:16, 26). Scholars sometimes identify

---

[30] We find the most detailed description of a conversion to Judaism in a late apocryphal work entitled *Joseph and Aseneth* (3rd–4th century A.D.). The impetus for Aseneth's conversion is meeting Joseph and the realization that he is not interested in marrying anyone who does not share his religious beliefs. The account, however, goes to great length to show that Aseneth's conversion is spiritual in nature.

[31] The only specific extracanonical evidence for "an organized Jewish proselytizing campaign is found in the policies of the Hasmoneans toward the Idumeans and Itureans in the late second century B.C.E." (Collins, *Between Athens and Jerusalem,* 262).

this group of Jewish sympathizers with the technical term of "God-fearers."[32] This group of people seems to be a fruitful source for early Christian missionary activity, and their existence may help us understand why two Gentiles, the centurion and the Canaanite woman (whom we will discuss below), could appeal to Jesus with such extraordinary faith.

In summary, the Abrahamic covenant was designed to accomplish two tasks: to create a peculiar and holy people who would become a great nation, and to bless all the nations of the earth. This brief sketch of Israelite and Jewish history highlights the fact that there was sometimes a pulsating tension between these two goals. At times, an emphasis on the first goal overshadowed the importance of the second, but in the intertestamental period, we see the planting of seeds that would mature to harvest in the New Testament. Although there is no evidence for an organized, large-scale Jewish program of proselyting, there is enough evidence to suggest that missionary work did exist on some level.[33] The evidence from Acts suggests that Paul's success during his gentile mission was often founded among both gentile proselytes to Judaism and God-fearers. Although Christ's responsibility to the covenant sent him Him first to the house of Israel (see 3 Nephi 20:26), it was always intended that the gospel would then be made available to the Gentiles (3 Nephi 15:22–23). It is in this context that we can now better understand Jesus' dealings with, and teachings about, Gentiles in the New Testament.

Gentiles in the Ministry of Jesus

Of the four Gospels, in many ways, Matthew provides the most detailed accounts of Jesus' interaction with, and teachings about,

---

[32] There is some debate whether *God-fearers* is a technical term for a well-defined class of Gentiles who were connected with the synagogue. The evidence suggests that there were many levels of attachment. For careful discussions on issues, see Feldman, *Jew and Gentile*, 342–82, and Collins, *Between Athens and Jerusalem*, 264–72.

[33] Contra Dieter Georgi, *The Opponents of Paul in Second Corinthians* (Philadelphia: Fortress Press, 1986), 84, 175n1.

Gentiles. This may be surprising to some because Matthew's Gospel was clearly written to a Jewish audience.[34] His account of Jesus' genealogy goes back to Abraham (Matthew 1:1–17) rather than Adam, as in Luke's Gospel (Luke 3:23–38). Matthew emphasizes that Jesus was the fulfillment of Old Testament prophecy. He prefers the phrase "kingdom of heaven" to the "kingdom of God" used in Mark. He also organizes his Gospel to emphasize that Jesus was the new Moses.[35] Even though Matthew's Gospel was directed to a Jewish audience, it was written at a time when some Jewish Christians were struggling to come to terms with the implications of the gentile mission. We know from Acts and Paul's letter to the Galatians that Paul's gentile mission was very unpopular with certain Jewish Christian circles. Matthew's Gospel, therefore, in some respects, reflects the same struggle that we have noted with ancient Israel: How do we acknowledge the concept of a chosen covenant people and, at the same time, embrace and promote a universal gospel? Here I will address four ways where the role of Gentiles is emphasized within the overall Jewish context of the gospel.[36]

Matthew's Introduction and Conclusion

Matthew has both introduced and concluded his Gospel with

---

[34] Papias, as quoted in Eusebius, *Ecclesiastical History*, 3.24.

[35] Like Pharaoh of Egypt, Herod issued an order to destroy infants (Matthew 2:16). Jesus came out of Egypt (2:12–15). He gave a new law on a mountain (5:1). Matthew organized his Gospel around five speeches that Jesus gave: the Sermon on the Mount (5:2–7:27), the Apostolic commission (10:5–42), the Parables (13:1–52), the Discourse on Community Regulations (18:1–35), and the Apocalyptic discourse (24:3–25:46). We know that Matthew intended to emphasize these five discourses because after each one he writes, "When Jesus had ended these sayings," or something close to it (7:28; 11:1; 13:53; 19:1). Then, after the final discourse, we read, "When Jesus had finished *all* these sayings" (26:1; emphasis added). Scholars have associated these five discourses as a link to the five books of Moses (this thesis was first proposed by B. W. Bacon, "The 'Five Books' of Moses against the Jews," *The Expositor* 15 [1918]: 56–66).

[36] For a more complete list, see Donald Senior, "Between Two Worlds: Gentile and Jewish Christians in Matthew's Gospel," *The Catholic Biblical Quarterly* 61 no. 1 (January 1999): 14–16.

passages in which Gentiles figure prominently. Matthew begins his Gospel with Jesus' genealogy (1:1–17). As we have already noted, this genealogy begins with Abraham. Within this list, however, we find mention of four women: Thamar, Rachab, Ruth, and "her *that had been the wife* of Urias." This is an unusual occurrence, especially because the most famous Jewish matriarchs, Sarah, Rebecca, and Rachel, are not included. Women are only rarely found in the Old Testament genealogical lists.[37] Even Luke, who often included women in his Gospel, does not do this in his genealogy. Why, then, would Matthew, who is reciting the patriarchal lineage of Joseph, include these women? The clue is in the way Matthew identifies the fourth woman. Unlike the rest of the women in his list, he does not identify her by name—only by her relationship to her husband, Urias. Why didn't Matthew choose this identification when her name, Bathsheba, is so prominent in the Old Testament record? What is it about her relationship with Urias that fits in better with Matthew's intent than using her own name? Her husband Urias (Urijah or Uriah in the Old Testament) was a Hittite, and thus a Gentile (2 Samuel 11:3), as were Thamar, Rachab, and Ruth. Matthew wants to show that even though Jesus' patriarchal lineage can be traced back to Abraham, He also has an important genealogical connection with Gentiles.[38]

In chapter 2, Matthew also includes the account of the coming of the Wise Men to pay homage to the Christ child. Elder Bruce R. McConkie suggests that the Wise Men were diaspora Jews.[39] This may be the case, but it is also clear that from Matthew's perspective, they represent the Gentiles. When they come to Herod, they inquire, "Where is he that is born King of the Jews?" (verse 2).

---

[37] Women are mentioned in the genealogical lists—Genesis 11:29; 22:20–24; 25:1, 12; 35:22–26; 1 Chronicles 2:18–21, 24, 34, 46–49; 7:24—but not in Genesis 5:3–32; 10:1–32; Ruth 4:18–22; 1 Chronicles 1:1–54; Ezra 7:1–5; 8:1–14; Nehemiah 12:10–21. On those occasions when women are mentioned, it is usually to distinguish between two family lines, which is not the case in Matthew 1.

[38] Ulrich Luz, *Matthew 1–7: A Continental Commentary*, trans. Wilhelm C. Linss (Minneapolis: Fortress Press, 1989), 109–10.

[39] McConkie, MM, 1:358.

They were apparently unaware of the Jewish scriptures containing the prophecy of the place of his His birth.[40] In the New Testament, only Gentiles refer to Jesus with this title (see Matthew 27:11, 29, 37; Mark 15:9, 12; Luke 23:37).[41] In addition, the role of the Wise Men in chapter 2 is to set up a scriptural foil for Herod (a nominal convert to Judaism) and the chief priests and scribes. In contrast to the Wise Men who followed a star, traveled great distances, and immediately paid homage when they encountered the Christ child, those who had the prophecies needed the help of outsiders to find himHim, even when He was at their door.

Matthew concludes his Gospel by rescinding the apostolic commission. When Jesus initially called his His Apostles, He specifically commanded them, "Go not into the way of the Gentiles [*ethnoi*], and into any city of the Samaritans enter ye not: but go rather to the lost sheep of the house of Israel" (Matthew 10:5–6). Matthew is the only Gospel author to include this injunction. It is an important issue for him because, later, he is also the only author to include Jesus' comment to His disciples that He was "not sent but unto the lost sheep of the house of Israel" (Matthew 15:24). These statements are centered on Christ's responsibility to His covenant people first (see Mark 7:27). The Book of Mormon makes clear that the Messiah would come first to the Jews and then, after they had rejected Him, He would "make himself manifest, by the Holy Ghost, unto the Gentiles" (1 Nephi 10:11; cf. 3 Nephi 15:22–23). Paul also taught that although the gospel of Christ is "to every one that believeth," the order is "to the Jew first, and [then] also to the Greek" (Romans 1:16).

Prior to His ascension, however, Jesus commanded His disciples, "Go ye . . . and teach [*matheœteusate*] all nations [*ethnoi*], baptizing them in the name of the Father, and of the Son, and of the Holy

[40] W. D. Davies and Dale C. Allison Jr., *A Critical and Exegetical Commentary on the Gospel According to Matthew*, 3 vols., The International Critical Commentary (Edinburgh: T&T Clark, 1988), 1:230.

[41] The only exception is John 19:21, but here the chief priests are reacting to the superscription that Pilate placed on the cross.

Ghost: teaching [*didaskontes*] them to observe all things whatsoever I have commanded you" (Matthew 28:19–20; see also Acts 1:8). This passage is pivotal for understanding the intent of Matthew's Gospel. It differs in significant ways from that found in Mark's Gospel. Mark records Jesus as saying, "Go ye into all the world [*kosmos*], and preach the gospel to every creature [*ktisis*]" (Mark 16:15). Although the meaning is the same in both renditions, by specifically using *ethnoi* instead of Mark's *kosmos,* Matthew has emphasized the importance of the Gentiles in this commission. In addition, Matthew uses "teach" in verse 19, where Mark uses "preach" (*krussoœ*). The Greek word that Matthew uses here is not the same Greek word as "teaching" in verse 20. In verse 19, it derives from *matheœteuoœ,* which has the basic meaning of "to make a disciple of." This has a stronger sense than preaching or teaching because it anticipates that the disciples will not just tell the Gentiles about Jesus but also make them His disciples. In Matthew's Gospel, this is the very last instruction that the resurrected Jesus gives to His disciples. Readers must appreciate the impact of the placement of that statement in a Gospel directed to a Jewish audience.

Matthew, therefore, has organized his testimony that Jesus is the promised Messiah by placing it between two "gentile" bookends. These bookends convey to the reader that the material the bookends hold together must be read within the context they provide. In other words, Jesus' ministry among the Jews must be understood within the context of the Gentiles. In the healing of the centurion's son and the Canaanite woman's daughter, we see two examples of Gentiles who, even though they were not part of the lost sheep of the house of Israel, still exhibited such tremendous faith that Jesus honored their requests for help.

Jesus' Healing of the Centurion's Son

The second aspect of Matthew's Gospel that brings focus to Jesus' interaction with Gentiles is His healing of the centurion's son. A centurion is a Roman officer in charge of one hundred foot soldiers. Although the KJV indicates that the miracle concerns the centurion's servant, the Greek word *pais* can also be translated as "son." The latter translation is to be preferred because in Matthew 8:9, the centurion uses a different Greek word (*doulos*) for servant.[42] Luke records that the elders of the Jews described him as someone who "loveth our nation, and he hath built us a synagogue" (Luke 7:5). This description suggests that he may have been a God-fearer. The healing story in Matthew is part of a two-chapter list of miracles that Jesus performed. Matthew has gathered these healings together to exemplify that Jesus is the Messiah in both word (Matthew 5–7) and deed (Matthew 8–9).[43]

The centurion approached Jesus seeking help for his son, who was grievously tormented with palsy. Jesus' response in Matthew 8:7 can be translated in two ways. The first, as it reads in the KJV, is "I will come and heal him." But it is also possible to render His response as "Should I come and heal him?"[44] The latter implies some hesitancy on the part of Jesus to respond to the request. This may be because, as we have seen, His primary responsibility was to the house of Israel. The centurion's response, however, exhibits a

---

[42] Compare Matthew 2:16; 17:14–21, where he uses *pais* for child/son (Ulrich Luz, *Matthew 8–20*, trans. James E. Crouch, *Hermeneia—A Critical and Historical Commentary on the Bible* [Minneapolis: Fortress Press, 2001], 10n17).

[43] We know that Matthew 5–9 is a distinct literary pericope because Matthew has marked it with the scriptural bookends of Matthew 4:23 and 9:35. Then, when John the Baptist's disciples come to him in chapter 11 and ask if He is the "coming one" (*ho erchomenos*), Jesus responds, "Go and shew John again those things which ye do *hear* and *see:* The blind receive their sight, and the lame walk, the lepers are cleansed, and the deaf hear, the dead are raised up, and the poor have the gospel preached to them" (Matthew 11:4–5; emphasis added). This "the poor have the gospel preached to them" hearkens back to the Sermon on the Mount, where the opening line is "Blessed are the poor" (Matthew 5:3). Then, in chapters 8–9, we have specific examples of each one of the miracles Jesus mentions in His response to John's disciples.

[44] Davies and Allison, *The Gospel According to Saint Matthew,* 2:21–22; Ralph P. Martin, "The Pericope of the Healing of the 'Centurion's' Servant/Son (Matthew 8:5–13 par. Luke 7:1–10): Some Exegetical Notes," *Unity and Diversity in New Testament Theology: Essays in Honor of George E. Ladd,* ed. Robert A. Guelich (Grand Rapids, Mich.: Eerdmans, 1978), 15.

depth of humility and faith that moves Jesus. He says, "Lord, I am not worthy that thou shouldest come under my roof: but speak the word only, and my servant shall be healed. For I am a man under authority, having soldiers under me: and I say to this man, Go, and he goeth; and to another, Come, and he cometh; and to my servant [*doulos*], Do this, and he doeth it" (verses 8–9).

In this declaration, the centurion "expresses on the one hand his submission to the 'Lord,' while on the other hand accepting the reality that Jesus is a Jew and is sent to Israel."[45] Then, Jesus turns to the crowd and declares, "Verily I say unto you, I have not found so great faith, no, not in Israel" (Matthew 8:10; cf. 3 Nephi 19:35). Such a statement would have caused some consternation among the members of the crowd. It was a ringing indictment against the covenant people. In Matthew's Gospel, this is the first statement by Jesus of this kind, but it is not the first time He has praised Gentiles above Israel. Luke records Jesus proclaiming in His inaugural speech, "I tell you of a truth, many widows were in Israel in the days of Elias, when the heaven was shut up three years and six months, when great famine was throughout all the land; but unto none of them was Elias sent, save unto Sarepta, a city of Sidon, unto a woman that was a widow. And many lepers were left in Israel in the time of Eliseus the prophet; and none of them was cleansed, saving Naaman the Syrian" (Luke 4:25–27).

Although Matthew's account of this miracle is very similar to the one we find in Luke's Gospel (Luke 7:1–10), Matthew includes an additional statement by Jesus: "Many shall come from the east and west, and shall sit down with Abraham, and Isaac, and Jacob, in the kingdom of heaven. But the children of the kingdom shall be cast out into outer darkness: there shall be weeping and gnashing of teeth" (Matthew 8:11–12). Elder Bruce R. McConkie wrote, "Many—not a few; Gentile hosts; members of the hated, alien nations—many would find glory in heaven with the ancient patriarchs, while the literal seed, . . . Jews who should have been the

[45] Luz, *Matthew 8–20*, 10.

children of the kingdom, would be cast out. How little His Jewish hearers understood the meaning of that which Jehovah had of old time said to Abraham: 'as many as receive this Gospel shall be called after thy name, and shall be accounted thy seed, and shall rise up and bless thee, as their father' (Abr. 2:10)."[46]

Jesus and the Canaanite Woman

Our third gentile passage deals with the healing of the Canaanite woman's daughter (Matthew 15:21–28).[47] In this story, not only the Canaanite woman but also her daughter represent the Gentiles and have important lessons to teach. Jesus had been teaching in the land of Gennesaret, responding to the taunts from scribes and Pharisees about the importance of washing hands before eating. His message was that what comes out of the mouth will defile a person, not whether people ritually wash their hands. Then, Jesus withdrew toward "the coasts of Tyre and Sidon" (Matthew 15:21).[48] As He does so, a Canaanite woman comes out to meet Him.[49] The desperation of the woman is highlighted by the fact that she does not wait

[46] McConkie, MM, 2:183.

[47] For the purposes of this chapter, I will address only the Jewish/Gentile boundary of this story. There are other boundaries, however, that also play important roles in the story, such as gender and socioeconomic ones. See Frances Taylor Gench, *Back to the Well: Women's Encounters with Jesus in the Gospels* (Louisville: Westminster John Knox Press, 2004), 11–20.

[48] Many scholars prefer "withdrew" rather than "departed," because Matthew uses the Greek verb *anachoœreoœ* when Jesus withdraws from a perceived danger (2:12–14, 22; 4:12; 12:15; 14:13). Gench prefers "towards" instead of "into" because the Greek phrase (eis + accusative) can be translated either way, and the Canaanite woman "came out of" the region the Jesus was traveling toward. This suggests that the two met at the borders of their respective countries. As Gench notes, "Matthew otherwise takes pains to emphasize that Jesus' ministry takes place exclusively within Israel, and this passage offers the only occasion in Matthew on which Jesus might be depicted as stepping outside its borders" (*Back to the Well*, 5).

[49] Mark identifies the woman as "a Greek, a Syrophenician by birth" (7:26). Matthew's use of "Canaanite" is significant: there were no Canaanites during Jesus' time. This is an anachronistic term to link the woman to people whom Joshua and the Israelites were supposed to destroy when they entered the promised land and who were a constant source of pagan worship for the Israelites (see Gench, *Back to the Well*, 5–6). The identification serves to highlight the significance of what this woman does.

for Jesus to come to her, but she comes out to meet Him and cries out, "Have mercy on me, O Lord, thou Son of David; my daughter is grievously vexed with a devil" (Matthew 15:22).

For some, Jesus' reaction to this woman's pain is difficult to understand. At first, He ignored her. This was a unique response for Jesus. The only other person Jesus had ignored was Herod, who had killed John the Baptist (Luke 23:9). Why did He ignore this woman? It can't be because she was a Gentile, because He responded to the plea of the centurion. With the benefit of hindsight, we can appreciate that Jesus was creating a situation where the woman could show her great faith. Even though Jesus initially ignored her, she was not put off. She persisted in her loud cries for Jesus' attention, so much so that the disciples interceded on her behalf. Then Jesus reminded the woman and His disciples, "I am not sent but unto the lost sheep of the house of Israel" (Matthew 15:24). Her use of the title *Son of David* in verse 22 indicates that she knew Jesus was sent to Israel.[50] So His response did not dissuade the woman; if anything, it intensified her actions, because she came and fell at His feet and worshiped Him, saying "Lord, help me" (verse 25). The Greek word for "worshiped" is *prosekunoœ,* the same word used by Matthew to describe the action of the Wise Men when they came into Jesus' presence (Matthew 2:2, 8, 11; see also 8:2; 9:18; 14:33; 15:25; 28:9, 17). It conveys a position of worship through prostration. The imperfect tense of the verb suggests that this worship is not confined to a single act but is a repeated one.

When Jesus did respond, His words sound harsh: "It is not meet to take the children's bread, and to cast it to dogs" (Matthew 15:26). The dogs, however, refer to household pets (*kunarion*). This reading is reinforced by the woman's response, "Truth, Lord: yet the dogs eat of the crumbs which fall from their masters' [*kurios*] table" (verse 27). In this response we see the amazing resiliency and humility of the woman, who acknowledges that, as a Gentile, she is

---

[50] Luz, *Matthew 8–20,* 339.

a beggar at Israel's table. We also must appreciate the play on words, which is more evident in Greek than in English. Whenever she addresses Jesus, she does so with the title *kurios* (Lord). This is the same word she uses to describe the master at the table from which the crumbs fall. The crumbs "must refer to the bread that Jesus, the Lord, gives. The 'children's bread' is his His to give."[51] The table itself represents the eschatological banquet, concerning which Jesus had already told another Gentile, the centurion, that "many shall come from the east and west, and shall sit down with Abraham, and Isaac, and Jacob" (Matthew 8:11). This woman wanted to be one of those many coming from the west.

Having proved her humility and commitment, Jesus responds, "O woman, great is thy faith: be it unto thee even as thou wilt." Then, the record states, "her daughter was made whole from that very hour" (Matthew 15:28). Matthew emphasizes that it is the woman's faith that brings forth the miracle.[52] It is noteworthy that in Matthew's Gospel, Jesus applauds two people for their faith, the centurion and the Canaanite woman, both of whom were Gentiles.[53] This detail stands in contrast to the theme of "little faith" among the Jews (Matthew 6:30; 8:26; 14:31; 16:8). It was the faith of these two Gentiles that enabled Jesus to bless their lives, even though His mission was to the covenant people of Israel. We recall the words of Elder Jeffrey R. Holland concerning the faith of the brother of Jared: "Is it possible to have faith so great that even God cannot resist it?" The faith of these two Gentiles may also be examples of cases of "mortal man's desire, will, and purity so closely approaching the heavenly standard that God could not but honor [their] devotion."[54] Elder John K. Carmack, referring to the great

---

[51] Judith Gundry-Volf, "Spirit, Mercy, and the Other," *Theology Today* 51 no. 4 (January 1995): 518.

[52] Mark does not record this statement about the woman's faith in his version of the story, where the woman's logic is the impetus for the miracle (see Mark 7:28–30).

[53] See also Jesus' comment about the Syrian army captain, Naaman: "And many lepers were in Israel in the time of Eliseus the prophet; and none of them was cleansed saving Naaman the Syrian" (Luke 4:27).

[54] Jeffrey R. Holland, "Rending the Veil of Unbelief," in *Christ and the New Cove-*

faith of these two Gentiles, has admonished us, "We can learn much about faith from such sisters as the woman of Canaan, from our friends of other faiths such as the Roman centurion, and especially from our children. No matter how we learn to use the power of faith, we need to have it to accomplish the awesome tasks assigned to us."[55]

The Canaanite woman, however, is not the only person in this story that teaches us about Jesus' ministry with the Gentiles. Her daughter, even though not present in the story, also represents the Gentiles. The fact that Jesus heals her from a distance, rather than personally attending to her, reminds us of the Book of Mormon's teachings that the Gentiles, as a whole, would not hear His voice; rather, He would manifest Himself to them through the ministering of the Holy Ghost (3 Nephi 15:22–23; 1 Nephi 10:11).[56]

The Parables of the Wicked Husbandmen and the Marriage of the King's Son

The third way that Matthew's Gospel highlights the Gentiles in Jesus' ministry is his record of parables such as the Wicked Husbandmen (Matthew 21:33–46)[57] and the Marriage of the King's Son (Matthew 22:1–14). Both of these parables have parallels in other Gospel accounts, but Matthew's account is most strongly grounded in the future place of the Gentiles in the kingdom.[58]

---

nant (Salt Lake City: Deseret Book, 1997), 23–24.

[55] John K. Carmack, "Faith Yields Priesthood Power," *Ensign*, May 1993, 43.

[56] The healing here is different from that of the Centurion's servant. Although Jesus accomplished both healings from a distance, He intended to come to the centurion's house. It was the centurion who stopped Him from coming.

[57] For a discussion of the differences between Matthew's and Mark's accounts of the parable, see Davies and Allison, *Matthew*, 3:177–78.

[58] For the parable of the Wicked Husbandmen, see Mark 12:1–12; Luke 20:9–19; *Gospel of Thomas* 65–66. For a discussion on the account found in the *Gospel of Thomas*, see William G. Morrice, "The Parable of the Tenants and the Gospel of Thomas," *Expository Times* 98, no. 4 (1987): 104–7. For the parable of the Marriage of the King's Son, see Luke 14:15–24; *Gospel of Thomas* 64. In this version, the contrast is between the rich and the poor rather than the Jewish leadership and the Gentiles. In the *Gospel of Thomas*, those who refuse the invitation are buyers and merchants.

Therein, the Parable of the Marriage of the King's Son immediately follows the Parable of the Wicked Husbandmen. Even though our modern Bibles have a chapter break between them, the two parables are part of the same speech. Matthew shows that they were specifically directed to the chief priests and elders who questioned Jesus' authority (Matthew 21:23–27). The purpose of the two parables is to contrast Jewish leadership's rejection of Christ and His kingdom with the future response of the Gentiles.

In the Parable of the Wicked Husbandmen, a householder planted a vineyard, put a hedge around it, and built a tower to protect it. He then hired husbandmen, or tenant farmers (*geoœrgos*), to tend to the vineyard while he was in a far country. The description of the vineyard is very close to a similar vineyard in Isaiah 5:2 (LXX), where the vineyard represents the house of Israel (LXX Isaiah 5:7). There is, however, evidence that by Jesus' time, the vineyard and the tower specifically represented Jerusalem and its temple.[59] Thus, this parable must also be understood in the context of Jesus' cleansing of the temple earlier in the chapter (Matthew 21:12–16).[60]

When the time of the harvest approaches, the householder sends a series of delegations to receive it. With each delegation, however, the husbandmen attacks them, beating, stoning, and killing them. These delegations symbolize the prophets that God has consistently sent to Israel. As a last resort, the householder decides to send his son, hoping that the husbandmen will respect his authority—a hope that is quickly dashed. The husbandmen, wanting to seize the vineyard, kill the owner's son. Then, Jesus poses a pointed question to the chief priests and elders: "When the

---

[59] Craig A. Evans, "God's Vineyard and Its Caretakers," in *Jesus and His Contemporaries: Comparative Studies* (Leiden: Brill, 1995), 397–401, and George J. Brooke, "4Q500 1 and the Use of Scripture in the Parable of the Vineyard," *Dead Sea Discoveries* 2 (1995): 283–85.

[60] Wesley G. Olmstead, *Matthew's Trilogy of Parables: The Nation, the Nations and the Reader in Matthew 21.28–22.14*, Society for New Testament Studies Monograph Series 127 (Cambridge: Cambridge University Press, 2003), 111.

lord therefore of the vineyard cometh, what will he do unto those husbandmen?" (Matthew 21:40). Their answer is a natural response: "He will miserably destroy those wicked men, and will let out his vineyard unto other husbandmen, which shall render him the fruits in their seasons" (verse 41).

Jesus then quotes Psalm 118:22: "The stone which the builders rejected, the same is become the head of the corner" (Matthew 15:21). He does so to reinforce in the minds of His audience that He is the Son who will be rejected (JST Matthew 21:52). It is Jesus' explanation of this passage that is unique to Matthew's Gospel: "Therefore say I unto you, The kingdom of God shall be taken from you, and given to a nation bringing forth the fruits thereof" (Matthew 21:43). The chief priests and Pharisees clearly understood thatJesus was comparing them with wicked husbandmen (v. 45). But who was the nation that would be given the kingdom? Some scholars interpret it as "the church and/or its leaders gaining the kingdom upon the death and resurrection of Jesus,"[61] but when Jesus later explained the parable to His disciples, the JST clarifies that He was specifically speaking of the Gentiles (JST Matthew 21:53). They would receive the kingdom because they would bring forth the fruits, such as the faith that the centurion and the Canaanite woman exhibited.

If the kingdom was to be given to the Gentiles, what did Jesus mean when He said, "Whosoever shall fall on this stone shall be broken: but on whomsoever it shall fall, it will grind him to powder" (verse 44)? This verse is often neglected in discussions of the parable.[62] Some even question whether it was part of the original text.[63] In the JST, however, Jesus interprets it for His disciples: "And when the Lord therefore of the vineyard cometh, he will destroy those miserable, wicked men, and will let again his vineyard

[61] Davies and Allison, *Matthew* 3:186.

[62] See Davies and Allison, *Matthew* 3:187; Anthony J. Saldarini, *Matthew's Christian-Jewish Community* (Chicago: University of Chicago Press, 1994), 58–63.

[63] For a discussion of the issues, see Olmstead, *Matthew's Trilogy of Parables*, 220–22 n. 102.

unto other husbandmen, even in the last days, who shall render him the fruits in their seasons. And then understood they the parable which he spake unto them, that the Gentiles should be destroyed also, when the Lord should descend out of heaven to reign in his vineyard, which is the earth and the inhabitants thereof" (JST Matthew 21:55–56). Thus, we are reminded that even the Gentiles will be held accountable, and if they do not bring forth fruit, they also will be destroyed.

The Parable of the Marriage of the King's Son consists of two parts: Matthew 22:1–10 and verses 11–14, which are unique to Matthew's Gospel. The first part describes the kingdom of heaven as a king's preparations to celebrate his son's marriage. He sends two sets of servants to call those who had already received invitations to the festivities. This was not the first time they had heard about the wedding; they had prior knowledge and responded to the invitations. Both sets of servants, however, met with rejection. The first group flatly refused to come. The second group at first minimized the importance of coming and returned to their businesses. Part of the second group, however, took the servants and "entreated them spitefully, and slew them" (verse 6). When the king heard, "he was wroth: and he sent forth his armies, and destroyed those murderers, and burned up their city" (verse 7). He then instructed his servants that, since the original guests were unworthy of the honor, they were to go out and extend invitations to anyone who was willing to come. "So those servants went out into the highways, and gathered together all as many as they found, both bad and good: and the wedding was furnished with guests" (verse 10).

The first part of the parable has numerous thematic and literary ties to the Parable of the Wicked Husbandmen. Both parables have three sets of ambassadors who are sent and rejected,[64] some of

[64] The language is the same in both parables although it is slightly different in the KJV: "he sent forth his servants" (*apesteilen tous doulous autou* in 21:34 and 22:3); and "again he sent forth other servants" (*palin apesteilen allous doulous* in 21:36 and 22:4).

whom are also killed. Because of that rejection, both parables show that the kingdom will be given to another group. Thus, the role of the second parable is to emphasize the message of the first. There are, however, significant differences between the two parables. In the Parable of the Wicked Husbandmen, the servants represent the Old Testament prophets. In the Parable of the Marriage of the King's Son, the servants represent Christian missionaries, sent to call God's covenant people to now respond to that covenant (cf. Matthew 23:34–39). Rather than the servants preceding the coming of the son, as in the first parable, the servants here are to bring people to the son. "The servants in this final parable no longer belong to a different era."[65] In other words, Jesus places these two parables together to show that the present rejection is a continuation of that which took place in the past. This present rejection brings the judgment of God upon them (Matthew 22:7) and probably refers to the destruction of Jerusalem and the temple.

Verse 10 provides a transition between the two parts of the parable. When the servants go out a third time to gather together whoever would come to the marriage, they brought "both bad and good" to the wedding. This group refers to the Gentiles.[66] The fact that the servants gathered this last group from the highways reminds the reader of Jesus' comment, after the centurion had shown his faith, that "many shall come from the east and west, and shall sit down with Abraham, and Isaac, and Jacob, in the kingdom of heaven. But the children of the kingdom shall be cast out into outer darkness: there shall be weeping and gnashing of teeth" (Matthew 8:11–12). Verse 10 also indicates that this gathering comprises both bad and good, and the second part of the parable gives an example of the bad.

When the king arrived at the wedding, he found someone who did not have on a wedding garment. When the king asked him why

[65] Olmstead, *Matthew's Trilogy of Parables*, 123.

[66] Graham N. Stanton, *A Gospel for a New People: Studies in Matthew* (Louisville: Westminster/ John Knox Press, 1992), 153; McConkie *DNTC*, 1:598.

he didn't have on the appropriate attire, "he was speechless" (Matthew 22:12). His silence suggests that he had no valid excuse. By failing to put on a wedding garment, the man showed disrespect for both the king and the banquet. What does the wedding garment symbolize? The Greek phrase translated as "having a wedding garment" is *endedumenon enduma,* where both the verb and the noun come from the same root. The same verb, in a different tense, is used at the end of Luke's Gospel where, just prior to Jesus' ascension, He tells His disciples to remain in Jerusalem until they are endowed with power from on high. The power they are to wait for is the reception of the Holy Ghost (Acts 1:5–8). Therefore, one way of understanding the garment is that it is the Holy Ghost. Another possibility is found in Revelation 19:7–8, where the "fine linen" of the wedding garment is the "righteousness of saints."

Thus, it is clear that not all Gentiles will participate in the kingdom of heaven; they must also show that they belong there. Membership in the Church is not a guarantee of salvation. Just as with the JST addition to the Parable of the Wicked Husbandmen, we learn again that Gentiles, as well as Jews, must take the obligations of the gospel seriously. Those unworthy to enter the kingdom are not just those who kill the servants; they are also those who accept the invitation but want to do things their own way rather than surrender their will to God. The result for Gentiles who do not measure up is the same as their Jewish counterparts: They will be "cast . . . into outer darkness; [and] there shall be weeping and gnashing of teeth" (Matthew 22:13; cf. Matthew 8:12). "For many are called, but few are chosen wherefore all do not have on the wedding garment" (JST Matthew 22:14).

Conclusion

God covenanted with Abraham that his seed would become a great nation and that his seed would bless all the families of the earth. Membership in the covenant, however, is not a privilege. John the Baptist taught the Pharisees and Sadducees, "Think not to say within yourselves, We have Abraham to our father: for I say unto you, that God is able of these stones to raise up children unto Abraham" (Matthew 3:9). His point was that participation in the covenant requires responsibility—to "bless all the nations of the earth," to take the gospel to all the world. Nephi taught, "As many of the Gentiles as will repent are the covenant people of the Lord" (2 Nephi 30:2). Matthew holds up the examples of the four women in Jesus' genealogy, the Wise Men, the centurion, and the Canaanite woman as Gentiles who belong to the kingdom, not because they were born into the chosen lineage but because they responded to the light and knowledge they possessed. Jesus knew that His primary responsibility was to covenant Israel, but He also recognized the faith of all people, and He responded to their needs. Ultimately, both Jew and Gentile will be judged by how they as individuals bring forth fruits commensurate with their commitment to Jesus the Christ, the Son of the Living God.

XII.

THE OLIVET DISCOURSE

KENT P. JACKSON

Then shall appear the sign of the Son of Man in heaven, and then shall all the tribes of the earth mourn; and they shall see the Son of Man coming in the clouds of heaven, with power and great glory.

JOSEPH SMITH—MATTHEW 1:36

Jesus had spent much of the Tuesday of His last mortal week in the temple in conversation with Pharisees, Sadducees, and others. His final recorded statement to the assembled group showed that He would soon be ending His earthly mission but that He would someday come again: "Ye shall not see me henceforth, till ye shall say, Blessed is he that cometh in the name of the Lord" (Matthew 23:39).[1] With those words, the disciples were reminded of their Lord's return—a subject that would play an important role in the discussion that would follow. As Jesus left the temple, the disciples asked Him about His earlier reference to the temple's destruction. That topic, too, would be important in the following discussion. Jesus responded, "Verily I say unto you, There shall not be left here one stone upon another, that shall not be thrown down" (Matthew

---

[1] For the Old Testament allusions in this statement and elsewhere in the sermon, see David R. Seely, "The Olivet Discourse," in Kent P. Jackson and Robert L. Millet, eds., *Studies in Scripture Volume 5: The Gospels* (Salt Lake City: Deseret Book, 1986), 391–92, 402n1.

24:2). With that, Jesus went up on the Mount of Olives, where the Twelve soon joined Him privately.

On the Mount of Olives

The Olivet Discourse is a sermon Jesus gave to the Twelve as they met on the Mount of Olives, the traditional name of the sermon coming from its location. Unlike most of the other sermons recorded in the Gospels, this one was not in front of a multitude but was a private meeting with the Twelve. They were His immediate audience, but readers in the latter days are also addressed, and much of the message is for us. The Olivet Discourse is Jesus' most prophetic discourse in that it deals entirely with future events, some not long after His day and some in the far-distant future.

The Mount of Olives, running north and south, lies directly east of Jerusalem, separated from the city by the Kidron Valley. It is more accurately a hill than a mountain, being only four hundred feet high from the middle of the valley and requiring about fifteen minutes to walk to the top. It is two hundred feet higher than the parallel hill to the west, where the temple stood. Herod's temple, known after the name of its builder, Herod the Great, was one of the architectural marvels of the Roman Empire. It was an extraordinarily large building, covering forty acres (four times the size of Temple Square in Salt Lake City) with a surrounding wall as much as 160 feet high, depending on the natural slope of the hill. Inside the vast paved courtyard stood the 150-foot-tall sanctuary, surrounded by other walls that formed concentric courtyards with increasing sanctity as they approached the middle.

From within the innermost walls, the smoke of the burnt offerings rose to the heavens, symbolizing the redemption of the children of Israel. In Jesus' day, the temple filled a person's view from any point on the west side of the Mount of Olives. Its nearest wall, more than fifteen hundred feet long, was balanced visually by the tall, imposing sanctuary within it, the roof of which was plated with gold. The stonework throughout the vast complex was superb, not only because of the extraordinary size of some of the stones and the quality of the architectural features but also because of the fine carved finishing on the surfaces. Herod's architects and engineers were among the best in the world, and his artisans were unsurpassed. Even so, Jesus said that not one stone of their work would be left standing upon another.

Our New Testament sources for the Olivet Discourse are Matthew 24–25, Mark 13, and Luke 17 and 21, each providing significant variations but each outlining Jesus' prophecies essentially in the same way.[2] But each of those accounts presents readers with the same fundamental difficulty: They intersperse Jesus' statements about the end of the world among His statements about the destruction of Jerusalem. As a result, for the past two thousand years, scholars and lay readers alike have been left with the impression that Jesus anticipated a speedy return and that His return would coincide with the tragedies that would come upon the Jewish nation, including the destruction of the temple.[3]

To the biblical accounts, modern revelation adds a wealth of clarifying information, the most important of which is found in two revelations to Joseph Smith early in 1831. On March 7, the Prophet received the revelation now known as section 45 of the Doctrine and Covenants. Part of it is a re-creation of the Olivet Discourse, in which the Lord made known to the latter-day Church what He had told His disciples anciently. Some time later, in May or June, the Lord revealed to Joseph Smith a revised text of Matthew 24 as part

[2] The discourse in Luke 21:5–36 is not identified as taking place on the Mount of Olives, but it is the same sermon as that recorded in Matthew 24 and Mark 13.

[3] Some standard commentaries include Craig A. Evans, *Mark 8:27–16:20*, Word Biblical Commentary 34B (Nashville: Thomas Nelson, 2001), 285–342; Joseph A. Fitzmyer, *The Gospel According to Luke (X–XXIV)*, Anchor Bible 28A (New York: Doubleday, 1985), 1323–56; Donald A. Hagner, *Matthew 14–28*, Word Biblical Commentary 33B (Dallas: Word, 1995), 682–747; William L. Lane, *The Gospel According to Mark*, New International Commentary on the New Testament (Grand Rapids, Mich.: Eerdmans, 1974), 444–84; and C. S. Mann, *Mark*, Anchor Bible 27 (Garden City, N.Y.: Doubleday, 1986), 498–542. For Latter-day Saints, the contributions of these studies are somewhat limited because most of the difficult exegetical questions of the Olivet Discourse are answered in modern revelation.

of the New Translation of the Bible. That text is one of the most significant contributions of the JST and, indeed, one of the great documents of the Restoration.[4] With small but stunning changes to the text that can be explained only as coming from a supernatural source, the Prophet—mostly through reorganization and repetition of Matthew's verses—dramatically changed the text of the discourse in such a way that both its overall meaning and most of its subtle details are now clear and easily understood.[5] Recognizing the importance of this revised text of Matthew 24, the Church printed it on a broadside in the 1830s.[6] In 1851 Elder Franklin D. Richards included it in his British Mission pamphlet, *The Pearl of Great Price,* and it is still in the Pearl of Great Price today, canonized as scripture since 1880 and now known as Joseph Smith—Matthew.

The key to the Olivet Discourse is verse 4 of Joseph Smith—Matthew, in which the disciples asked Jesus two questions: "When shall these things be which thou hast said concerning the destruction of the temple, and the Jews?" and "What is the sign of thy coming, and of the end of the world, or the destruction of the wicked, which is the end of the world?" Those two questions form the framework of the Olivet Discourse—the first question asking about trials that would come soon upon the Jews and Jerusalem, and the second about Jesus' return and the end of the world. The

---

[4] See Scott H. Faulring, Kent P. Jackson, and Robert J. Matthews, eds., *Joseph Smith's New Translation of the Bible: Original Manuscripts* (Provo: BYU Religious Studies Center, 2004), 217–21, 291–95.

[5] "To the basic text the Prophet added nearly four hundred fifty new words, representing about a fifty percent increase in the text size. Even so, there is only one verse (v. 55) to which there is no correlation in the King James Bible; but three verses are repeated [Matthew 24:6 = Joseph Smith—Matthew 1:23, 28; 24:12 = Joseph Smith—Matthew 1:10, 30; 24:15 = Joseph Smith—Matthew 1:12, 32]. This means that most of the additional material is an expansion of that already in Matthew. Yet it is not only in adding material that the revealed version gives understanding but more especially in the *reordering* of the material" (Richard D. Draper, "Joseph Smith—Matthew and the Signs of the Times," in Robert L. Millet and Kent P. Jackson, eds., *Studies in Scripture Volume 2: The Pearl of Great Price* [Salt Lake City: Randall Book, 1985], 290). See also Seely, "The Olivet Discourse," 395.

[6] See Peter Crawley, *A Descriptive Bibliography of the Mormon Church, Volume One, 1830–1847* (Provo: BYU Religious Studies Center, 1997), 60–61.

profound contribution of Joseph Smith—Matthew is that in it Jesus answers the questions separately and sequentially. The answer to the first question is found in verses 5–21a, and the answer to the second is found in verses 21b–55. This is the text, given by revelation to a modern prophet, that we will use for our discussion of the Olivet Discourse, supplemented with material from other sources.

Jerusalem and Josephus

As the Savior sat with His Apostles looking across the Kidron Valley toward Jerusalem, He already knew the fate of the temple, the city, and its inhabitants. Perhaps less than an hour earlier, He had lamented their future: "O Jerusalem, Jerusalem, thou that killest the prophets, and stonest them which are sent unto thee, how often would I have gathered thy children together, even as a hen gathereth her chickens under her wings, and ye would not! Behold, your house is left unto you desolate" (Matthew 23:37–38).

Indeed, their sacred house, their holy city, and their very lives would in time be desolated beyond their imagination. A generation after Jesus' day, war broke out in Palestine as Jewish groups hostile to the Roman occupation rose up in an effort to shake it off. The First Jewish Revolt, as historians now call it, was characterized by initial successes, much deadly fighting, and ultimate failure. But more than anything else, it was characterized by the unspeakable degradation and misery of ordinary people, who suffered beyond description at the hands of all parties in the conflict. Aside from some cleaning-up operations in outlying areas, the culminating event of the war was the destruction of Jerusalem and its temple in A.D. 70, four years after the revolt had begun.

Both archaeology and ancient history show that Jesus' prophecy of the destruction of Jerusalem was fulfilled; the archaeological record is unmistakable. A systematic dismantling and destruction of the temple accompanied a massive conflagration, doing away with the city of Jerusalem that Jesus knew.[7] Our best documentary

[7] See Ephraim Stern, ed., *The New Encyclopedia of Archaeological Excavations in the*

sources are the writings of Flavius Josephus, who witnessed many of the events of the war and portrays them and the circumstances that led up to them in vivid detail. His book *The Jewish War* provides thought-provoking analysis.[8] Josephus was a Pharisee from an upper-class Jewish family who was born about the time of Jesus' earthly ministry. He tells his readers that he opposed the war against Rome on moral grounds, believing that his people were wicked and that God would not be on their side. Even so, he was pressed into the service of his nation, and he became the commanding general of the revolutionary forces in Galilee.

When the Roman general Vespasian besieged a city Josephus was defending, Josephus, recognizing the futility of the defense and of the revolt in general, surrendered to the invaders. He announced that he had received a revelation from God that Vespasian would soon become the emperor of Rome—thus likely preserving his own life while the Roman general waited to see what would become of the prophecy. When Vespasian was, in fact, made emperor, Josephus' life and livelihood were secured. He was adopted into the new emperor's family, and he was permitted to accompany the Roman forces for the rest of the war to chronicle its events. When Vespasian left the war and went to Rome, his son Titus took command of the Roman forces and saw the suppression of the revolt to its conclusion, including the destruction of Jerusalem. After the war, the eyewitness Josephus joined Vespasian and Titus in Rome and wrote his books, now indispensable sources for the history of the ancient Jews. Although not without considerable self-interest, Josephus' record of the war is considered to be, for the most part, reliable, as much in the big picture as it is in many of its small details. Whatever anyone thinks of his integrity or of the quality of his loyalty to his own people, modern readers are indebted to him for recording the fulfillment of Jesus' prophecies.

Holy Land (New York: Israel Exploration Society and Carta, 1993), 2:720–57.

[8] See Josephus, *JW, Books I–III*, 203,; *JW, Books IV–VII*, 210; Flavius Josephus, *The Jewish War*, trans. G. A. Williamson, rev. ed. (Harmondsworth, U.K.: Penguin, 1970).

Tribulations of the Jews and the Church

As we learn from the Savior's words to the Twelve, the destruction of the temple and the holy city would not be the first of the trials that would come upon the Jews. Beginning in verse 5 of Joseph Smith—Matthew, Jesus outlined a series of developments that would precede the ultimate calamities.

Jesus warned His disciples to beware of, and not to be taken in by, the many false Christs who would come and who would then deceive many people (see Joseph Smith—Matthew 1:5–6). The English word *Christ* comes from the Greek *christós,* itself a translation of the Hebrew *māšîah,* "Messiah." Both in Greek and in Hebrew, the word means "Anointed One," and it was applied to Israel's kings and, more particularly in New Testament times, to the anticipated leader who would restore the kingdom of Israel and liberate Judea from its Roman captors. Jews in the generations of Jesus and Josephus were indeed expecting their Messiah—and with good reason. Some decades earlier, an angel had announced to Judean shepherds that the Messiah-Deliverer was born. They, in turn, "made known abroad the saying which was told them concerning this child." And "all they that heard it wondered at those things which were told them by the shepherds" (Luke 2:17–18; see 2:8–20). When the baby was taken to the temple to be circumcised, a prophetess who was in the temple daily recognized Him as the Messiah and "spake of him to all them that looked for redemption in Jerusalem" (Luke 2:38). Sometime later, magi arrived in Jerusalem seeking the new king, whose sign they had seen in the sky. King Herod was troubled, "and all Jerusalem with him," and "all the chief priests and scribes of the people" were involved in the quest to find where this messiah would be born, Herod's motivation being to destroy the young rival (Matthew 2:3–4, see also 2:5–6). Herod massacred all the children two years old and younger in Bethlehem and surrounding areas, accompanied by the lamentation, weeping, and mourning of the bereaved families (see Matthew 2:16–18).

Needless to say, those were all very public events, and although the Christ child and His family were able to slip back into general anonymity, for decades thereafter some Jews in Palestine certainly knew that somewhere their Messiah was among them, preparing to assume His anointed role. When Jesus of Nazareth came on the scene, He ultimately proved not to be the kind of messiah most were anticipating, neither reestablishing the kingdom nor delivering Judea from foreign oppressors. Thus, all but very few ruled Him out as their promised deliverer. Josephus tells us that others came forward as deliverers in subsequent years, each gaining followers. Each of those had his day of fame, yet each proved ultimately to be a disappointment.[9] The most famous early Jewish messiah figure came after Josephus' time. He was Simon bar Kosiba, called by his followers bar Kokhba, "Son of the Star." Bar Kokhba was the leader of another rebellion against Roman occupation, the Second Jewish Revolt (A.D. 132–35). That revolt, too, was put down by overwhelming Roman force.[10]

As with the false messiahs, Jesus foretold that many false prophets would come, and they would deceive many (Joseph Smith—Matthew 1:9). Josephus tells of men who came to the fore in Jewish society and identified themselves as prophets of God. Several of the would-be deliverers, in fact, claimed to be prophets.[11] During the First Jewish Revolt, as Josephus informs his readers, false prophets were responsible for the demise of thousands of people.[12]

---

[9] See Josephus, *AJ*, 20.97–99; *JW*, 2.258–65; and Keith H. Meservy, "Jesus and Josephus Told the Destruction of Jerusalem," in *The New Testament and the Latter-day Saints* (Orem, Utah: Randall Book, 1987), 202–6. See also Kent P. Jackson, "Revolutionaries in the First Century," in *Masada and the World of the New Testament*, ed. John W. Welch and John F. Hall (Provo: *BYU Studies*, Brigham Young University, 1997), 129–40; Craig A. Evans, *Jesus and His Contemporaries* (Boston: Brill, 2001), 53–81; and Richard A. Horsley, *Bandits, Prophets, and Messiahs: Popular Movements in the Time of Jesus* (Harrisburg, Penn.: Trinity, 1999), 88–189.

[10] See Benjamin I. A. Oppenheimer, "Bar Kokhba Revolt," and Michael O. Wise, "Bar Kokhba Letters," in Freedman, *ABD*, 1:598–606. Jerusalem was made a Roman colony, renamed Aelia Capitolina, and Jews were thereafter prohibited from living in it. The plan to make Jerusalem a colony was likely a major reason for the revolt.

[11] See Josephus, *JW*, 2.261–64.

[12] See Josephus, *JW*, 6.284–87.

Troubling times would also come to the early Christian Church. Jesus told His Apostles that the day would come in which they, the Twelve, would be persecuted, imprisoned, beaten, betrayed, afflicted, killed, and hated because of Him (see Joseph Smith—Matthew 1:7; Mark 13:9; Luke 21:12, 16). The New Testament tells of ample persecution against the Apostles (for example, Acts 4:1–21), but it records the murder of only one, James the brother of John, who was killed at the hands of Herod Agrippa I (see Acts 12:1–2). The Christian historian Eusebius, fourth-century bishop of Caesarea, records the deaths of four Apostles: James the brother of John, James the brother of Jesus, Peter, and Paul.[13] Aside from those accounts, which appear to be historical, the fate of the rest of the Twelve remains unknown to authentic history. But Jesus' words leave no doubt about what would happen to them eventually, and as He told them later, "The time cometh, that whosoever killeth you will think that he doeth God service" (John 16:2; see also Joseph Smith—Matthew 1:7).

As Jesus continued His somber warning concerning the future of the Church, He stated that many would "be offended" and betray and hate one another (see Joseph Smith—Matthew 1:8). The meaning of the word *offended* has changed since the publication of the King James translation. In religious contexts such as here, the passive voice of the Greek verb *skandalízō* conveys the meaning of giving up one's faith or apostatizing, and it is rendered with words of that sort in most modern translations.[14] The New International Version's "turn away from the faith" captures well the intended meaning. Jesus' words are an ominous statement about the future of the Church, clearly pointing to circumstances that would accompany the apostasy that would destroy it in just a few decades. Nephi wrote about the time of the early Apostles and prophesied of a "great and abominable church" whose founder would be the devil. It would bring the Saints "down into captivity," in part by removing

[13] See Eusebius, *History of the Church* 2.1, 9, 23, 25.

[14] See Arndt and Gingrich, *GEL*, s.v. "*skandalízō*."

things "which are plain and most precious" both from the scriptures and from the gospel itself (see 1 Nephi 13:4–6, 20–29). Both Jesus and His Apostles foretold the time when Church members would look beyond the simple doctrines and bring new ideas into the Christian faith.[15] It would be that, and not persecution by outsiders, that would be the fundamental cause of the apostasy, resulting in a spiritual transformation in the early Church and replacing the authority of Apostles with the pseudo-authority of intellectuals.[16] Nephi saw in vision that after Jesus' death, "the multitude of the earth," in a "large and spacious building," would oppose the Twelve. Indeed, "the house of Israel hath gathered together to fight against the twelve apostles of the Lamb" (1 Nephi 11:34–35).

The "great and abominable church," as described by Nephi, consisted of those forces and individuals within early Christianity who removed its leadership, changed its direction, and set it on a new course. The Greek word *apostasía,* "apostasy," does not mean "falling away," as unfortunately translated in 2 Thessalonians 2:3, but "mutiny," "revolt," and "revolution." The early Church died not only when wrong ideas replaced true doctrine but also when self-appointed teachers took power from the Lord's true messengers. And in time, Jesus' prophecy would come true: the Apostles themselves would be killed.

Jesus warned that the day would come among the Jews in which iniquity would abound and the love of many would grow cold (see Joseph Smith—Matthew 1:10). Of this calamity, Josephus bore the strongest witness. He tells the story of the growing wickedness of his people from the time of his youth, culminating in the atrocities that accompanied the war against Rome. Through the course of the

---

[15] See Kent P. Jackson, "Watch and Remember: The New Testament and the Great Apostasy," in *By Study and Also by Faith: Essays in Honor of Hugh W. Nibley on the Occasion of His Eightieth Birthday, Vol. 1*, ed. John M. Lundquist and Stephen D. Ricks (Salt Lake City: Deseret Book and Foundation for Ancient Research and Mormon Studies, 1990), 81–117.

[16] See Kent P. Jackson, *From Apostasy to Restoration* (Salt Lake City: Deseret Book, 1996), 1–30.

decades following the death of Jesus, lawlessness increased as both the Romans and the Jewish central government began to lose control. The resulting fragmentation of society invited opportunists to gather followers and sustain themselves by acts of banditry and terrorism.[17]

During the struggle with Rome, civil wars broke out as competing Jewish armies vied for power and unleashed unspeakable cruelty on each other and on the populace in general. The shifting alliances, intrigues, assassinations, and sheer butchery that Josephus described show well the abundant iniquity and diminished love for fellowmen that Christ foretold. As Josephus wrote, "Somehow those days had become so productive of every kind of wickedness among the Jews as to leave no deed of shame uncommitted; and even if someone had used all his powers of invention he could not have thought of any vice that remained untried."[18] He continued, "So corrupt was the public and private life of the whole nation" that they were "determined . . . to outdo each other in impiety towards God and injustice to their neighbours."[19] One group who was involved in "this lawlessness and this barbarity to [their] kinsmen . . . left no word unspoken, no deed untried, to insult and destroy the objects of their foul plots."[20] One of the usurpers "subjected his country to countless woes."[21] Concerning another, "What crime did he not commit?"[22] And concerning another group, "There was no crime in the records that they did not zealously reproduce."[23]

Civil war broke out within the walls of Jerusalem and continued even while the Romans were besieging the city from the outside. At the hands of their own countrymen, rival combatants and thousands

[17] See Horsley, *Bandits, Prophets, and Messiahs*, 48–87.

[18] Josephus, *JW*, 7.259. All Josephus quotations are from Williamson.

[19] Josephus, *JW*, 7.260.

[20] Josephus, *JW*, 7.262.

[21] Josephus, *JW*, 7.263.

[22] Josephus, *JW*, 7.265.

[23] Josephus, *JW*, 7.269.

of civilians alike were slaughtered, property was plundered, and many were tortured to death.[24] Large stockpiles of food, carefully prepared to feed the city during the anticipated Roman siege, were destroyed deliberately by the warring Jewish armies.[25] Both sides terrorized the civilian population.[26] Josephus reported, "The entire City was the battleground for these plotters and their disreputable followers, and between them the people were being torn to bits like a great carcase." And then, perhaps most indicative of the hardened hearts and abounding iniquity that the Savior said would overtake Jerusalem, "Old men and women, overwhelmed by the miseries within, prayed for the Romans to come, and looked forward to the war without, which would free them from the miseries within."[27]

Despite all these tragedies, Jesus said that those who would remain steadfast would be saved (see Joseph Smith—Matthew 1:11). Although horrible times would come upon Jerusalem and its people, His disciples could avoid being overcome. Both Matthew and Mark have "endure to the end" at this place in the sermon (see Matthew 24:13; Mark 13:13); the word *steadfast* is a JST change. Remaining firm and unmovable would provide a defense.

The Judahite prophet Daniel, in exile in Babylonia, twice spoke of what he called the "abomination that maketh desolate" (Daniel 11:31; 12:11). Both passages are in highly apocalyptic prophecies with meanings that have not been revealed beyond the context that Jesus provided in the Olivet Discourse.[28] Both speak of the cessation of the daily sacrifices. Jesus' words, "the abomination of desolation, spoken of by Daniel the prophet, concerning the destruction of Jerusalem," teach us that the reference is to the

[24] See Josephus, *JW*, 4.310–34.

[25] See Josephus, *JW*, 5.21–26.

[26] See Josephus, *JW*, 5.1–38, 251, 439–41.

[27] Josephus, *JW*, 5.27–28.

[28] For apocalyptic revelation, see Kent P. Jackson, *Lost Tribes and Last Days: What Modern Revelation Tells Us about the Old Testament* (Salt Lake City: Deseret Book, 2005), chapter 14.

cessation of the sacrifices brought about by the Roman destruction of the temple (see Joseph Smith—Matthew 1:12). Daniel's words suggest that the "abomination that maketh desolate" is an object that would be set up where the temple once stood. Eventually, a sanctuary for the Roman god Jupiter was constructed on the site, but the reference here could be to something as simple as a Roman standard planted in the rubble. But the JST change suggests that it may even be an event, rather than an object, that Jesus had in mind.[29] What is important, however, is that the "abomination of desolation, spoken of by Daniel the prophet, concerning the destruction of Jerusalem" represents God's great act of judgment against His people—the destruction of their temple and the cessation of the ordinances in His once-holy house.

Jesus told His disciples to stand in the holy place (see Joseph Smith—Matthew 1:12). He was not referring to the temple, for it would be destroyed. More likely, He was telling His disciples the same thing He told the Church in latter-day revelations regarding standing in holy places to find refuge from the world (see Doctrine and Covenants 45:32; 87:8; 101:22).[30] The phrase "whoso readeth let him understand" signals that metaphorical language is being employed here.

Jesus used explicit and practical words when He counseled His listeners to flee (see Joseph Smith—Matthew 1:13–17), speaking literally to address the real-life situation that early Christians would face. He said, "When ye shall see Jerusalem compassed with armies, then know that the desolation thereof is nigh" (Luke 21:20). Jesus warned the disciples that despite all spiritual preparation entailed in the idea of standing in holy places, the reality would be that before it would be too late, Christians would need to flee for their lives to

[29] That clearly is the case in the parallel passage in Joseph Smith—Matthew 1:32.

[30] President Ezra Taft Benson stated, "Holy men and holy women stand in holy places, and these holy places include our temples, our chapels, our homes, and the stakes of Zion" ("Prepare Yourselves for the Great Day of the Lord," *Brigham Young University 1981 Fireside and Devotional Speeches* (Provo, Utah: Brigham Young University Publications, 1981), 68.

find safety elsewhere. Josephus reported that Jews from all over Palestine were in Jerusalem when the Roman armies drew near, hoping for safety behind its enormous walls.[31] But those who heeded Jesus knew that walls would not protect them. Their flight would be in great haste and under difficult circumstances—hence the command not to return home to get one's possessions and the warning that it would be most difficult for pregnant women, for nursing mothers and their babies, and for anyone in the cold, wet, and muddy Palestinian winter. The historian Eusebius reported that Christians, under inspired direction, fled to Pella, a city to the east of the Jordan River.[32] There they remained safe from the horrors, torture, and death that overtook the population in Jerusalem.

"For then, in those days, shall be great tribulation on the Jews, and upon the inhabitants of Jerusalem, such as was not before sent upon Israel, of God, since the beginning of their kingdom until this time; no, nor ever shall be sent again upon Israel" (Joseph Smith—Matthew 1:18). Those who understand the atrocities that would befall the Jews nineteen centuries later can only imagine the meaning of the last clause in this lament of Jesus. The reprisals, massacres, and enslavement that followed the fall of Jerusalem must have been beyond comprehension. All the previous tragedies that Israelites had experienced were "only the beginning of the sorrows which shall come upon them" (Joseph Smith—Matthew 1:19).[33]

Signs of the Last Days

At this point in the sermon, the Savior made the transition from the tribulations of the first century to the dramatic events of our time and of the final days of the world's history. Beginning at verse 21 of Joseph Smith—Matthew, He presented a series of events and

---

[31] See Josephus, *JW*, 6.420–32.

[32] See Eusebius, *History of the Church* 3.5.

[33] The Greek word that underlies "sorrows" is more accurately rendered "birth-pain(s)." All previous trials had only been the beginning of labor; the hard labor and delivery would come with the destruction of Jerusalem. See Arndt and Gingrich, *GEL*, s.v. "*odín*."

circumstances that would serve as characteristics of the latter days and signs of His approaching Second Coming.[34] Some of these developments repeat those of the first century, showing that the circumstances of our time would be similar in many ways to conditions then. But others would be unique to the final generations of history. Although Jesus was speaking to His disciples, He was also speaking to His latter-day Saints, and thus we can treat His words regarding our time as addressed to us.

In the latter days, just as in the first century, there would be false Christs and false prophets (Joseph Smith—Matthew 1:21–22). Jesus warned that among the false Christs and false prophets would be those who would have such power that "if possible, they shall deceive the very elect, who are the elect according to the covenant" (Joseph Smith—Matthew 1:22). Concerning those words, Joseph Smith stated, "False prophets always arise to oppose the true prophets, and they will prophesy so very near the truth that they will deceive almost the very chosen ones."[35] He also told us that the true motive of false prophets and teachers would be power: "They strive to have power and by their pernicious ways lead off many."[36] Jesus did not say that it is inevitable that some of the "elect" will be deceived. In both Matthew and Mark, the Greek words *ei dunatón*, translated "if it were possible" (Matthew 24:24; Mark 13:22), govern a clause that is described grammatically as "assumed true for argument's sake."[37] The words indicate that the powers of the false Christs and false prophets would be so impressive that were it possible—which it is not—they could deceive even the "very elect."

[34] Alternatively, some scholars have suggested that the transition comes at verse 24. That transition point would not alter the message substantially.

[35] Andrew F. Ehat and Lyndon W. Cook, eds., *The Words of Joseph Smith: The Contemporary Accounts of the Nauvoo Discourses of the Prophet Joseph* (Provo: BYU Religious Studies Center, 1980), 367.

[36] Ehat and Cook, *Words of Joseph Smith*, 370; capitalization and spelling standardized.

[37] This kind of construction appears about three hundred times in the New Testament. See Daniel B. Wallace, *Greek Grammar Beyond the Basics* (Grand Rapids, Mich.: Zondervan, 1996), 689–94.

Elsewhere, we learn that the elect will not be deceived, and we are told why. Jesus said, "Whoso treasureth up my word, shall not be deceived" (Joseph Smith—Matthew 1:37). And "they that are wise and have received the truth, and have taken the Holy Spirit for their guide, and [therefore] have not been deceived . . . shall abide the day" (Doctrine and Covenants 45:57). And "so likewise, mine elect, when they shall see all these things, they shall know that he is near, even at the doors" (Joseph Smith—Matthew 1:39).[38]

Jesus taught that "wars, and rumors of wars" would be prevalent in the latter days (see Joseph Smith—Matthew 1:23). Yet He also pointed out that His Saints should not be troubled by the news of such matters because many events remain to be fulfilled and because "the end is not yet." This tells us that rather than being a sign of the imminent end of the world, warfare is to be seen more as a common reality of our time. Sadly, we have already witnessed the fulfillment of this in numerous parts of the world, especially in the past one hundred years. But more is to come.

Next, Jesus addressed the topic of His Second Coming (see Joseph Smith—Matthew 1:25–26). He had said before that if anyone should announce that He had returned already, the Saints should "believe him not" (Joseph Smith—Matthew 1:21, see also 24). No test would be necessary. The merism in verse 25 ("in the desert," "in the secret chambers") is meant to emphasize that if anyone has to inform us that Jesus has returned *anywhere,* we can know it to be false. The reason is made clear in the following verse: the Second Coming will be as obvious as the sun coming up in the east, moving slowly across the sky, and setting in the west. In other

---

[38] President Brigham Young said that if Latter-day Saints have their faith in the right things, their "lives pure and holy, [and] everyone fulfilling the duties of his or her calling," they will be "filled with the Holy Ghost," and it will be impossible for anyone to deceive them (*JD* 7:277). President Joseph F. Smith and his counselors stated that there are two types of Latter-day Saints who are most susceptible to being deceived: those who do not keep the commandments and those "who pride themselves on their strict observance of the rules and ordinances and ceremonies of the Church" (James R. Clark, comp., *Messages of the First Presidency of The Church of Jesus Christ of Latter-day Saints*, 5 vols. [Salt Lake City: Bookcraft, 1965–71], 4:285).

words, people living in that day will know it when it happens, and no one will need to be told about it.[39] As Joseph Smith taught, all who will be alive then will be witnesses of it.[40]

Another of the features of the latter days will be the gathering (see Joseph Smith—Matthew 1:27). Jesus' metaphor, however unsavory it may sound to modern readers, is more than effective. As vultures (generously translated "eagles" in the King James Version) are drawn to a target by some unseen force from many miles away, "so likewise shall [the Lord's] elect be gathered from the four quarters of the earth." And indeed, an unseen power today gathers good people from every land to find the Church and the gospel wherever they are.

Again Jesus warned of "wars, and rumors of wars" that would plague the earth, with nation rising against nation and kingdom against kingdom (see Joseph Smith—Matthew 1:28–29). Remarkably, verses 23 and 28 do not state that the Saints will *experience* warfare—only that they will "hear of" it. The implications of that are not clear, but elsewhere in scripture we are assured of the Lord's protective power over His people (see Doctrine and Covenants 45:66, 69; 63:33–34; 115:6; Moses 7:61).

Jesus foretold "famines, and pestilences, and earthquakes, in divers places" (Joseph Smith—Matthew 1:29). People living now have witnessed all three, sometimes in distant lands and sometimes closer to home. In this day of instant, worldwide communication, we are more aware of such natural disasters than any previous generation was, and thus their reality is much more immediate to us than ever before. In our own time—perhaps indicative of what we will see through the rest of history—famines are as much a product

---

[39] The JST makes an interesting change here that improves the text greatly. Matthew 24:27 has "the lightning" coming from the east and shining to the west. The JST replaces that with "the light of the morning" that comes from the east and shines to the west and then adds the phrase "and covereth the whole earth" (Joseph Smith—Matthew 1:26). The change from "lightning" to "the sun going across the sky during the course of a day" takes a weak metaphor and makes it crystal clear.

[40] See Ehat and Cook, *Words of Joseph Smith*, 181, quoted below.

of evil politics and government as they are of weather. And plagues are often preventable by adherence to basic laws of God and science. It is sometimes stated that earthquakes are increasing in frequency around the world, but scientists see a steady pattern through recent geologic history. Although we certainly live now in a time of fulfillment of all three of these tragedies, it is perhaps not unlikely that the pace of famines, pestilences, and earthquakes will quicken as the Second Coming draws nigh. Yet the Lord said that in spite of all these warnings, "men will harden their hearts" against Him (Doctrine and Covenants 45:33).

As in the generations following the mortal ministry of Jesus, the latter days would witness the flourishing of iniquity and the diminishing of love toward fellow humans (see Joseph Smith—Matthew 1:30). The symptoms of these signs are already so obvious today that they hardly need mentioning, and coming generations will likely witness an increase in iniquity and inhumanity hardly imaginable now. Jesus' prophecy and the examples of societies in secular history and in the Book of Mormon give us no cause to be optimistic about the moral future of our culture in general. But even so, just as He had done earlier when He foretold the decline of society among the Jews, Jesus promised that "he that shall not be overcome, the same shall be saved" (Joseph Smith—Matthew 1:30).

"And when the times of the Gentiles is come in, a light shall break forth among them that sit in darkness, and it shall be the fulness of my gospel" (Doctrine and Covenants 45:28). The Restoration would be the event that would initiate the work of God's kingdom in the latter days, ushering in the fulness of "the times of the Gentiles," in which God's work would reach its premillennial climax. Among the most important missions of the Saints of the latter days would be the preaching of the gospel throughout the earth: "And again, this Gospel of the Kingdom shall be preached in all the world, for a witness unto all nations" (Joseph Smith—Matthew 1:31). Elsewhere, the same message is repeated more emphatically: "And this gospel shall be preached unto every nation, and kindred, and tongue, and people" (Doctrine and Covenants 133:37). This is one of the greatest of the signs of the times, and every indication is that it is intended to be understood literally.[41] Its importance is highlighted by the fact that it is followed immediately by these words: "And then shall the end come" (Joseph Smith—Matthew 1:31). This is thus the first of only two prophecies in the Olivet Discourse that are accompanied by language stating that their fulfillment announces the end of the world (see also Joseph Smith—Matthew 1:34). And, perhaps uniquely among the events and circumstances foretold by Jesus in this sermon, this prophecy can be analyzed and quantified to determine the extent of its fulfillment. As earlier in verse 4, the end of the world is defined as "the destruction of the wicked," not the end of the planet (Joseph Smith—Matthew 1:31).

"And again shall the abomination of desolation, spoken of by Daniel the prophet, be fulfilled" (Joseph Smith—Matthew 1:32). Repeating the warning that was found in the context of the destruction of Jerusalem, Jesus again foretold the "abomination of desolation" of which Daniel spoke (see Joseph Smith—Matthew 1:12). This time, it seems clear that He was not speaking of an object, or even of a single event, but of God's collective acts of judgment against the wicked world—just as the destruction of the ancient temple was God's great act of judgment against Jerusalem. The Doctrine and Covenants provides two parallel scriptures that employ the wording "desolation of abomination" (Doctrine and Covenants 84:117; 88:85), each with reference to the desolation that God will bring upon the world in response to the abominations that will prevail in it. In one of those passages, we see the same sequence that Jesus foretold in the Olivet Discourse: the Lord's servants will preach the gospel for the last time throughout the world, following which the prophesied desolation will come (see Doctrine and Covenants 88:81–85).

[41] See Spencer W. Kimball, "When the World Will Be Converted," *Ensign*, October 1974, 5–7.

The Coming of Jesus

"Immediately after the tribulation of those days," great signs will be seen in the heavens that will show that the Lord's coming is near: the sun will be darkened, the moon will withdraw her light, stars will fall, and the heavens will shake (Joseph Smith—Matthew 1:33). This dramatic prophecy is found not only here but also in each one of the standard works of the Church—with remarkable consistency (see Joel 2:30–31; Mark 13:24–25; 2 Nephi 23:10; Doctrine and Covenants 29:14; 45:40–42; Joseph Smith—History 1:41).

Exactly what this prophecy means is not yet known, but two things about it seem certain. First, these events have not happened yet. The descriptions are vivid enough and the end-of-the-world context is clear enough that the prophecy does not represent an eclipse, polluted air, or anything else witnessed so far by humans on earth. Second, "this generation, in which these things shall be shown forth, shall not pass away until all I have told you shall be fulfilled" (Joseph Smith—Matthew 1:34). This prophecy includes a promise that those who witness it will be living in the generation in which all the other prophecies of the last days will reach their conclusion. If a passage in the Doctrine and Covenants refers to the same set of events, it places the fulfillment at the time of the Second Coming. When Jesus returns, "so great shall be the glory of his presence that the sun shall hide his face in shame, and the moon shall withhold its light, and the stars shall be hurled from their places" (Doctrine and Covenants 133:49).

Again, "after the tribulation of those days," people will witness a great sight in the sky. "Then shall appear the sign of the Son of Man in heaven, . . . and they shall see the Son of Man coming in the clouds of heaven, with power and great glory" (Joseph Smith—Matthew 1:36). Concerning those events, Joseph Smith taught, "How are we to see it? As the lighting up of the morning or the dawning of the morning cometh from the east and shineth unto the west, so also is the coming of the Son of Man. The dawning of the morning makes its appearance in the east and moves along gradually. So also will the coming of the Son of Man be. It will be small at its first appearance and gradually become larger until every eye shall see it. Shall the Saints understand it? Oh yes. Paul says so [see 1 Thessalonians 5:4–5]. Shall the wicked understand? Oh no. They [will] attribute it to a natural cause. They will probably suppose it is two great comets coming in contact with each other. It will be small at first and will grow larger and larger until it will be all in a blaze, so that every eye shall see it."[42] Twice in this quotation, the Prophet emphasized that "every eye shall see" the Second Coming of Jesus Christ, consistent with other revelations that teach that "all flesh" will see Him together (Isaiah 40:5; Doctrine and Covenants 88:93; 101:23), "all the ends of the earth" will hear His voice (Doctrine and Covenants 45:49), and He will stand "upon the mount of Olivet, and upon the mighty ocean, even the great deep, and upon the islands of the sea, and upon the land of Zion" (Doctrine and Covenants 133:20). The Prophet stated further, "The coming of the Son of Man never will be, never can be, till the judgments spoken of for this hour are poured out, which judgments are commenced. . . . All this must be done before [the] Son of Man will make his appearance: wars and rumors of wars, signs in heavens above [and] on the earth beneath, [the] sun turned into darkness [and the] moon to blood, earthquakes in diverse places, oceans heaving beyond their bounds, then one grand sign of the Son of Man in heaven. But what will the world do? They will say it is a planet, a comet, and so forth. Consequently, the Son of Man will come as the sign of [the] coming of the Son of Man."[43]

Jesus again gave counsel about how not to be deceived—by "treasuring up" His word (see Joseph Smith—Matthew 1:37).

When the Son of Man comes again, "he shall send his angels before him with the great sound of a trumpet, and they shall gather

---

[42] Ehat and Cook, *Words of Joseph Smith*, 181; capitalization, punctuation, and spelling standardized.

[43] Ehat and Cook, *Words of Joseph Smith*, 180; capitalization, punctuation, and spelling standardized.

together the remainder of his elect from the four winds, from one end of heaven to the other" (Joseph Smith—Matthew 1:37). A significant Joseph Smith Translation change at Matthew 13:30 reverses the order of the gathering in the Parable of the Wheat and the Tares, placing the gathering of the wheat before that of the weeds. In another revelation to Joseph Smith, the motif of the angels gathering is also used, with the same order of the gathering of wheat and weeds that is found in the Joseph Smith Translation: "Therefore, let the wheat and the tares grow together until the harvest is fully ripe; then ye shall first gather out the wheat from among the tares, and after the gathering of the wheat, behold and lo, the tares are bound in bundles, and the field remaineth to be burned" (Doctrine and Covenants 86:7).[44]

Recognizing the Signs

Jesus taught His disciples that the conditions and happenings He foretold in the Olivet Discourse would show them that His coming was "near, even at the doors." Like someone noticing the coming of spring by observing the budding of fresh leaves on a fig tree, the things Jesus foretold will be recognized by His elect as signs of approaching events. Even so, "of that day, and hour, no one knoweth; no, not the angels of God in heaven, but my Father only" (see Joseph Smith—Matthew 1:39–40). Concerning these words, Joseph Smith taught some especially remarkable doctrine: "Christ says, 'No man knoweth the day or the hour when the Son of Man cometh.' . . . Did Christ speak this as a general principle throughout all generations? Oh no; he spoke in the present tense. No man that was then living upon the footstool of God knew the day or the hour. But he did not say that there was no man throughout all

[44] It is not certain which of these came first. Doctrine and Covenants 86 was revealed on December 6, 1832. The JST change at Matthew 13:30 is not dated, but because all of the New Testament revisions were apparently in place by February 2, 1833, on balance, it seems most likely that the JST change in the order of the gathering (coming in Matthew, early in the New Testament) preceded the revelation of Doctrine and Covenants 86.

generations that should know the day or the hour. No, for this would be in flat contradiction with other scripture, for the prophet says that God will do nothing but what he will reveal unto his servants the prophets [Amos 3:7]. Consequently, if it is not made known to the prophets, it will not come to pass."[45]

The Prophet spoke of a man who claimed to have seen the sign of Christ's coming. He "has not seen the sign of the Son of Man as foretold by Jesus. Neither has any man, nor will any man, till after the sun shall have been darkened and the moon bathed in blood. For the Lord hath not shown *me* any such sign, and as the prophet saith, so it must be: 'Surely the Lord God will do nothing, but he revealeth his secret unto his servants the prophets'" (Amos 3:7).[46] Consistent with the message of all the scriptures, these words are reminders that the Lord's latter-day disciples will be prepared for the events that precede and accompany the Second Coming. In this, however, they will be unlike many others in the world. For most, it will be "as it was in the days of Noah," "in the days which were before the flood." Going on with the normal affairs of life, people will be oblivious to the signs all around them, signs that are intended to warn them to be worthy and prepared (Joseph Smith—Matthew 1:41–42; see also 1:43). But the elect will be saved. Treasuring up Christ's word, taking the Holy Spirit for their guide, observing the signs of the times, and following the prophets, they will "watch," and they will be "ready" (see Joseph Smith—Matthew 1:46, 48).

Six Parables of Preparation

To conclude the Olivet Discourse, Jesus related six parables. One is preserved only in Mark, and the others only in Matthew. After having discussed the end of the world and the Second Coming from the standpoint of doctrine, the Savior now shifted to

[45] Ehat and Cook, *Words of Joseph Smith*, 180–81; capitalization, punctuation, and spelling standardized.

[46] *Times and Seasons* 4, no. 8 (March 1, 1843): 113; emphasis added, capitalization and punctuation standardized.

application, teaching by these allegories the importance of being prepared for the future. Some of the parables can be applied to preparation for the events in Jerusalem not long after Jesus' day, but the main focus is on the last days. Thus, we who live at this time are the primary intended audience.

Mark's Parable of the Watching Porter (see Mark 13:33–37) is one of three brief stories with the same theme. The master of the house goes on a journey and places the doorman in charge of watching for his return. Readers are warned to be careful lest they be found sleeping when the master comes back. Punctuating Jesus' earlier warnings about His Second Coming, the story ends with the admonition, "Watch." The Parable of the Good Man of the House uses a different story line to convey the same message (see Joseph Smith—Matthew 1:47–48). Had the man known when the thief would invade his home, he would have been watching. Jesus' point is that we do not know when future events will take place, and thus we must always be prepared. This parable ends with the admonition to "be . . . ready." The Parable of the Ruler over the Household expands on the theme (see Matthew 24:45–51). Blessed is the servant if he is found doing his job when his master returns. But if he is not, the master will come when he is not expected, and the servant will be punished severely. This parable ends with the servant's intense sorrow, "weeping and gnashing of teeth."

Matthew 25 contains three long parables—the ten virgins, the talents, and the sheep and the goats. These allegories seem to form a progression, teaching different aspects of the readiness that Jesus encouraged of His listeners and readers. The Joseph Smith Translation of verse 1 places the story of the ten virgins clearly in the context of the Second Coming. In the parable (see Matthew 25:1–13), five of the young women were present when the wedding doors were opened, and five were not. The difference was that the five wise virgins had prepared themselves to endure to the end—whenever that might come—and the others had not. Such preparation is a necessary precaution because "ye know neither the day nor the hour wherein the Son of man cometh." This parable, like that of the porter, ends with the admonition, "Watch."

In the Parable of the Talents (see Matthew 25:14–30), the master, traveling to "a far country," leaves different quantities of his goods in the hands of three servants, to each one "according to his several ability." Two of the servants doubled their master's resources that had been entrusted to them. The third, however, hid his allotment for safekeeping. To the two who magnified their investment, the master said upon his return, "Well done, good and faithful servant; thou hast been faithful over a few things, I will make thee ruler over many things: enter thou into the joy of thy lord." The final servant returned the master's talent to him, yet he did not receive his lord's praise but rather his condemnation: "Thou wicked and slothful servant." The message for Jesus' audience seems clear. This is not a parable about the uncertain timing of Christ's return but about what we do with the gifts He has entrusted to us while we are waiting. As Joseph Smith taught, we should "improve upon all things committed to [our] charge."[47] This parable, like that of the ruler over the household, ends with the unprofitable servant's intense sorrow, "weeping and gnashing of teeth."

The final parable, that of the Sheep and the Goats (see Matthew 25:31–46), again addresses what people do with the blessings entrusted to them—but in a very different way. The setting in this story is not that of a returning master or an unexpected event. It is a judgment scene: "When the Son of man shall come in his glory, and all the holy angels with him, then shall he sit upon the throne of his glory: and before him shall be gathered all nations: and he shall separate them one from another, as a shepherd divideth his sheep from the goats." Those placed on the King's right hand will receive an inheritance in His kingdom, whereas those on His left hand will be sent off to "everlasting fire." Jesus explained in some detail the criteria for the King's just judgment. Those worthy of an

[47] *The Evening and the Morning Star* 2, no. 18 (March 1834): 142.

inheritance of glory will be those who fed Him when He was hungry, gave Him drink when He was thirsty, took Him in when He was a stranger, clothed Him when He was naked, visited Him when He was sick, and came to Him when He was in prison. Those who will be condemned will be the ones who had the same opportunities but did none of those worthy things. Both groups will protest having no knowledge of doing, or not doing, what Jesus ascribed to them—the first group out of wonderment and the second out of defensive self-justification. "And the King shall answer and say unto them, Verily I say unto you, Inasmuch as ye have done it unto one of the least of these my brethren, ye have done it unto me."

How we treat our fellow humans, particularly those who can be called "the least" among us, is thus the final test of whether we are prepared for the world-ending events of the future, including Christ's coming in glory. And as the rich young ruler learned earlier in Jesus' ministry, that is perhaps the final test of real discipleship as well (see Luke 18:18–23). Both the parable and the Olivet Discourse end with reference to the ultimate fate of those who are either prepared or unprepared when Jesus comes again: "everlasting punishment" for those on His left hand and "life eternal" for those on His right.

XIII.

THE FAMILY OF JESUS

RICHARD NEITZEL HOLZAPFEL

[Jesus] went down with them, and came to Nazareth, and was subject unto them: but his mother kept all these sayings in her heart.

LUKE 2:51

Few New Testament topics have captured the attention and imagination of ancient and modern commentators more than the scintillating issue of the family of Jesus.[1] There has naturally always been interest in the genealogies preserved in Matthew and Luke because of the unique insights they preserve regarding Jesus' progenitors.[2] However, others interested in Jesus' family have centered their inquiry on the individuals, named and unnamed, in the New Testament who may have been related to Him.[3] Scholars

[1] Two important studies provide a review of the debates surrounding Jesus' family, possible answers to the questions raised, and a remarkably complete bibliography on the topic; see Richard Bauckham, *Jude and the Relatives of Jesus in the Early Church* (Edinburgh: T&T Clark, 1990), and more recently, John Painter, *Just James: The Brother of Jesus in History and Tradition* (Minneapolis: Fortress, 1999).

[2] See Richard D. Draper, "Annunciation through Young Adulthood," *The Life and Teachings of Jesus Christ: From Bethlehem through the Sermon on the Mount,* ed. Richard Neitzel Holzapfel and Thomas A. Wayment (Salt Lake City: Deseret Book, 2005), 125–28. Additionally, see "The Lukan Genealogy of Jesus," in Bauckham, *Jude and the Relatives of Jesus,* 313–73.

[3] One scholar identifies some twenty-five individuals in the New Testament, not including those mentioned in Matthew's and Luke's genealogies, who he proposed were related to Jesus; see J. W. Wenham, "The Relatives of Jesus," *Evangelical*

have been equally eager to know how those identified as members of the family of Jesus were connected (as brothers, cousins, and so forth). This is particularly true of those identified as Jesus' "brothers" and "sisters" in various passages in the Gospels and Pauline letters. Some scholars and commentators argue that the Greek terms employed in the New Testament could reasonably be understood to mean cousins or other relatives and even nonblood relatives, depending on the context of the passage.[4]

Other avenues of inquiry have focused around Jesus' relatives in the decades following the close of the New Testament story, after the book of Acts stops reporting events in about A.D. 62. This investigation has centered around two related questions. First, what roles did Jesus' family play in the early Church? Second, what happened to Jesus' relatives in the centuries between the first Jewish revolt (A.D. 66–70) and the second Jewish revolt (A.D. 132–135)?

The primary sources for the study of the family of Jesus are the New Testament Gospels and the passing references in Acts and the epistles. Josephus, an early second-century historian, also reports some details about the family of Jesus.[5] A Christian historian, Eusebius, from the early fourth century, collected and published historical information about the family of Jesus that was available to him.[6] There also exist a few passing references to James in noncanonical sources, but they are, for the most part, legendary and incomplete.

Although each source noted above may provide additional clues, hints, and evidences beyond the New Testament itself, in the

---

Quarterly 47 (1975): 6–15.

[4] As the literal biological brother or sister or the figurative brother or sister in the faith; see Gingrich and Danker, *GEL*, 15–16.

[5] Steve Mason, "Josephus," *Eerdmans Dictionary of the Bible,* ed. David Noel Freeman (Grand Rapids, Mich.: Eerdmans, 2000), 736–37. See also, Eric D. Huntsman, "The Reliability of Josephus: Can He Be Trusted?" *Masada and the World of the New Testament,* ed. John F. Hall and John W. Welch (Provo, Utah: *BYU Studies*, Brigham Young University, 1997), 392–402.

[6] Charles Guth, "Eusebius," *Eerdmans Dictionary,* 434.

effort to draw conclusions from these texts, we must carefully sift and sort this information to retain only the "golden nuggets."

The current public interest in and scholarly debate about Jesus' family would certainly have surprised the authors of the New Testament. They could not have imagined a future generation asking these questions nor a hungry public appetite for legends and rumors regarding the family of Jesus. As a result, they did not tell us all the things a modern audience might want to know about Jesus' family.[7]

However, the absence of data that would allow thoughtful and careful historians to discuss some specific questions about Jesus' family has not stopped generations of commentators from filling in the gaps between the letters, words, and sentences in the New Testament text—providing an array of conflicting responses to human curiosity about Jesus' family. Despite the apparent lack of interest or focus on the part of the authors of the New Testament, it may be possible to reconstruct at least a basic picture of Jesus' family from the unintentionally embedded clues in the text. There can be no firm case built upon this fragmentary evidence, but an attempt to provide a coherent assessment of the data that do exist is possible. An effort to reconstruct, as best as is humanly possible, what we can know and what we cannot know about Jesus' family will at least reveal the limitations of such an investigation and establish a boundary for certitude.

Mary, the Mother of Jesus

Despite debate and controversy on virtually all aspects of the subject, there is universal agreement among all scripture texts, early

[7] It is certainly possible that even if they could have anticipated these questions they might not have wanted to address them, as their purpose in writing their stories and letters was motivated by the issues that mattered in their own day and not in the twenty-first century. Another possibility exists: Some of them might not have been aware of Jesus' family, did not especially care about those related to Him, or at least were not especially careful in telling the story, which may have revealed details about His family.

Christian Church Fathers, anti-Christian authors, and modern scholars on the identity of Jesus' mother as Mary (Greek *Maria*).[8] Her Hebrew name, *Miriam*, was a widely popular name in the first century among Jews living in Galilee and Judea, as is evidenced from the number of women with the same name appearing in the New Testament (see Luke 8:2–3; John 11:1–44; Matthew 27:56, 61; John 19:25; Acts 12:12; Romans 16:6). Although the Gospels all make reference to her, they also provide nuances about Mary's life that sometimes are difficult to harmonize.

Joseph, the Husband of Mary

If everyone agrees on Mary's relationship with Jesus, the opposite is true about Joseph's (*Iōsēph, Iosēs*).[9] Though Peter boldly proclaimed, "Thou art the Christ, the Son of the living God" (Matthew 16:16), many others questioned who Jesus' father was. Of course, who Jesus is was of utmost importance to the authors of the New Testament as they prepared their own witnesses. Jesus' poignant question, which elicited Peter's response in the first place, still resonates today as strikingly as it did two thousand years ago: "Whom say ye that I am?" (Matthew 16:15). Forever bound to this question is Jesus' relationship with Joseph the carpenter (Matthew 13:55). For some, Jesus was thought of as Joseph's biological son. For others, Jesus was Joseph's adopted son.[10]

James, Jose, Judas, Simon, and Sisters

In addition to Mary and Joseph, the Gospels identify at least six other individuals belonging to Jesus' immediate family—four named brothers and at least two unnamed sisters. The four males are

---

[8] Beverly Roberts Gaventa, "Mary," *Eerdmans Dictionary*, 863–864.

[9] Seung Ai Yang, "Joseph," *Eerdmans Dictionary*, 735.

[10] Anti-Christian authors, fueled by Jewish rumors and polemics, maintained that Jesus was the illegitimate son of Mary. In some cases, the father was identified as a Roman soldier named Pantera; see the critique of Jesus' supposedly illegitimate birth by the second-century Greek philosopher named Celsus and preserved by Christian apologist Origen of Alexandria; see *Contra Celsum* 1.28–32.

identified as James (*Iákōbos*), Jose (*Iosés*), Judas (*Ioúdas*), and Simon (*Símon*) (Mark 6:3; Matthew 13:55).[11] Because ancient sources tended to list individuals in order of their age or position, it is generally assumed that James was the oldest brother.

What may surprise anyone familiar with this information in the New Testament is that, like other issues related to Jesus' family, the exact relationship they had with Jesus is also contested, even though it appears to be a straightforward and plain announcement by Mark and Matthew that they are brothers and sisters of Jesus. When first-century authors referred to Jesus' brothers and sisters, they were faced with a limited vocabulary to describe a literal sibling relationship. The wording they chose to employ was the only natural way they could indicate that Jesus had siblings, either male or female. Therefore, the burden of proof remains for those who want to take the natural meaning of "brother" and apply it to a later context, one that derives from later Christian use of the term or from a supposed earlier meaning in another language that may have been used when New Testament authors recorded their testimonies and histories. The theological debate centers on the exact meaning of the terms used to describe relationships to Jesus; the KJV uses the term "brothers" (*adelfoi*) and "sisters" (*adelfes*). At least three separate and fundamentally different positions have been articulated over the centuries.

The first position, generally accepted by Orthodox churches, argues that the brothers and sisters are Joseph's children from a previous marriage; he was, according to this proposal, a widower when he married Mary.[12] This would make his children Jesus' older stepbrothers and stepsisters.

---

[11] Later tradition identified the two sisters as Mary and Salome; see discussion below.

[12] Artists have sometimes depicted Joseph as significantly older than Mary based on such an opinion—this is particularly true in the Orthodox tradition. Generally, Catholic, Protestant, and LDS commentators have rejected this suggestion outright based on theological grounds. Such proposals, they argue, would make Joseph's eldest son by the previous marriage the rightful heir to the throne of David, not Jesus.

The second position, generally accepted by Roman Catholics, argues that the brothers and sisters are the children of Joseph's brother, traditionally identified as Cleopas and his wife, traditionally identified as Mary (a different Mary from the mother of Jesus; see discussion below).[13] This would make them Jesus' cousins; their relative ages to Jesus are, therefore, unknown.

The third position, generally accepted by Protestants and many Latter-day Saints, argues that the brothers and sisters are the natural children of Joseph and Mary, born after Jesus' birth. This would make them Jesus' younger half-brothers and half-sisters.[14] Of course, others have suggested a variety of alternatives, some of which are variations of the above positions.[15]

Jesus' Family in Mark

Mark's story is the oldest Gospel, and it preserves "Peter's Memoirs," giving us an eyewitness account of some of the earliest stories in Jesus' ministry.[16] Mark does not provide a birth narrative or an account of Jesus' youth, so we should not be surprised that we learn very little about Mary and Joseph from Mark. In fact, Joseph is not mentioned once in this Gospel. Although the text is silent on this

---

[13] Catholics identify Mary as the "Blessed Virgin"; by this they mean she remained a virgin throughout her life.

[14] An exception to this generalization about LDS scholars and commentators is Jeffrey R. Chadwick, associate professor of Church History and Doctrine at Brigham Young University. Chadwick accepts proposal number two, generally held by Catholics, as representing the New Testament text; see "Was 'James' really the 'son of Joseph,'" an unpublished essay where he provides some thoughtful reconstructions of the data that might lead to different conclusions about the "brothers" and "sisters" of Jesus.

[15] Another proposal was offered on the Discovery Channel at Easter in 2005, "The Real Family of Jesus," which aired on 27 March 2005. The two-hour special argued that Joseph was previously married and that he had two sons (James and Jose) and a daughter (Salome) before the death of his first wife. Following Joseph's marriage to Mary, and after Jesus' birth, they had two sons (Simon and Judas) and one daughter, providing a complex picture of Jesus' family. Finally, some scholars believe that Jesus was Joseph and Mary's son, proposing a family consisting of five boys and two girls.

[16] See Richard Neitzel Holzapfel and Thomas A. Wayment, "Introduction: The World of the New Testament," *The Life and Teachings of Jesus Christ,* 1:xxv–xxvi.

subject, scholars and commentators have noted that Joseph's absence in Mark, which outlines only the period from Jesus' baptism until His resurrection, is easily explained by the fact that Joseph had died before Jesus began His public ministry.[17]

Though Mark does not provide us information about Joseph, he does about other family members: "The multitude cometh together again, so that they could not so much as eat bread. And when his *friends* heard of it, they went out to lay hold on him: for they said, He is beside himself" (Mark 3:20–21, emphasis added).

The word *friends* in this pericope is best understood as "those from the side of Him" (*hoi par' autou*), suggesting it was Jesus' family who came out to "lay hold on him" because they thought Jesus was "out of his senses."[18] This, of course, is an unflattering portrait of Jesus' family at the beginning of His ministry. Mark continues:

> There came then his brethren and his mother, and, standing without, sent unto him, calling him. And the multitude sat about him, and they said unto him, Behold, thy mother and thy brethren without seek for thee. And he answered them, saying, Who is my mother, or my brethren? And he looked round about on them which sat about him, and said, Behold my mother and my brethren! For whosoever shall do the will of God, the same is my brother, and my sister, and mother (Mark 3:31–35).

Some commentators have suggested that Jesus rejected his family connections as He established a new spiritual kinship based on faith and not biology. Certainly, this was a shocking new vision to Jesus' hearers, who, as first-century Jews, held strong feelings about the covenant people based on blood. However, Jesus indicates that water is thicker than blood. From Mark, it appears that Jesus' family had nothing to do with His ministry.

---

[17] When Joseph died cannot be ascertained, as eighteen years elapsed from the time that Joseph is last noted in the Gospel of Luke—from when Jesus was twelve years old (Luke 2:41–53) to when He was about thirty as He began His ministry (see Luke 3:23).

[18] See footnote in LDS Edition of the KJV Mark 3:21a.

It is not until Jesus returns to Nazareth that Mark provides additional information about Jesus' family. Mark, along with Matthew, records the names of "his brethren" but not the sisters, as noted above, when disbelieving members of the synagogue question Jesus' miracles and teachings (see Mark 6:1–6). Although it is impossible to demonstrate beyond a shadow of doubt that these brothers and sisters are Mary and Joseph's children, and thus half-brothers and half-sisters of Jesus, the preponderance of evidence allows a high degree of confidence in reading the pericope in the most simple and straightforward way.[19]

One argument against such a reading is that Hebrew or Aramaic did not have a specific word for "cousin"; therefore, authors often employed "brother," "sister," or a circumlocution, something like "the son of my uncle," to describe this particular relationship. According to this argument, the authors of the New Testament, while writing in Greek, continued the Hebrew practice of using the terms *brother* and *sister* to describe relationships such as cousin and kinsmen, making it impossible to determine with certainty what the exact relationship was. However, this argument falls apart with the inspection of another first-century author. Josephus, who spoke the same language as Jesus and was a younger first-century contemporary, maintained a difference between the words for brother and cousin when he wrote his histories in Greek. When wishing to designate a literal brother, Josephus employed *adelfos,* as do the Gospel authors when speaking of Jesus' siblings, whereas Josephus used a different word to designate a relative who was not an immediate sibling (*syngenēs*), as Luke does when referring to the relationship between Mary and Elizabeth (Luke 1:36; cf. Luke 21:16).

There seems to have been no significant first-century confusion between the terms, and authors had at their disposal a vocabulary that could sufficiently distinguish between a brother or cousin.[20]

---

[19] For a thorough and comprehensive treatment of the topic, see Bauckham, *Jude and the Relatives of Jesus,* 19–32.

[20] Josephus, *Life,* 177.

Another argument against this reading, given the infant mortality rate, suggests that it was impossible for Mary to have had six children who reached adulthood before Joseph died. The assumption is that the window for childbearing was from the birth of Jesus until shortly after the family returned from Jerusalem when Jesus was twelve years of age.

However, it is not difficult to imagine that Joseph and Mary could have had six children who all survived to adulthood if we expand the window of childbearing to near the time of the public ministry. The assumption that Joseph died shortly after the family returned from Jerusalem is without foundation. That Joseph had died before Jesus began the public ministry seems certain.

Additionally, the period of conception and gestation for six additional children could have been substantially shorter than noted above. It could have been possible for Mary to have conceived six children during the period after she and Joseph returned to Nazareth from Egypt and through a period that lasted a few years beyond their visit to the temple in Jerusalem when Jesus was twelve years of age. This is not as unlikely as it may first appear.

Another interesting issue revealed in the pericope deals with Jesus being known as the "son of Mary," not of Joseph. The convention of the day would have had a person known by his father, the "son of Joseph," not his mother. This wording most likely suggests that rumors were still circulating about Jesus' birth, which signifies that the designation was pejorative (see Judges 11:1–2). Even though Joseph had become Jesus' legal guardian through Joseph's marriage to Mary (see Matthew 1:24), the residents of the tiny town of Nazareth apparently had long memories reaching back some thirty years. Such clouds of suspicion apparently continued to plague Jesus for the rest of His mortal ministry and beyond.[21]

Mark indicates that members of Jesus' family were also among those who were offended, amazed, and startled by His claims:

[21] See Ben Witherington III, *The Gospel of Mark: A Social-Rhetorical Commentary* (Grand Rapids, Mich.: Eerdmans, 2001), 193.

"They were offended at him. But Jesus said unto them, A prophet is not without honor, but in his own country, and *among his own kin, and in his own house*" (Mark 6:3–4; emphasis added). Only Mark specifically mentions Jesus' "own kin [relatives]."

Jesus' Family in Matthew

Written sometime after Mark's Gospel, the book of Matthew provides both a birth and childhood narrative.[22] The genealogy preserves traces of Jesus' descent from Abraham and David. In the birth and childhood accounts, both Mary and Joseph play prominent roles.[23] Joseph, a "just man," acknowledges Jesus as his own child, despite misgivings that are resolved through a dream (Matthew 1:18–25).

Matthew indicates that Jesus spent the first one or two years in Bethlehem, most likely surrounded by a number of relatives (Matthew 2:1–23; note that Jesus is not identified as an infant but as a young child, and that the family lives in a *house* at the time of the visit of the wise men from the east; see Matthew 2:8–11, 13–14).

Of singular interest, however, in these narratives is a complete lack of any reference to other children in the family besides Jesus. Note Matthew's description regarding the family's journey to Egypt: "When he arose, he took the young child and his mother by night and departed into Egypt (Matthew 2:14; compare 21). Matthew's description seems to discount the proposal that Joseph had been previously married and that he had brought children into his marriage with Mary. It also raises a question about children born after the birth of Jesus, the existence of whom may be implied by these words: "And *knew her not till* she had brought forth her firstborn son: and he called his name Jesus" (Matthew 1:25; emphasis added).[24]

---

[22] See Holzapfel and Wayment, "Introduction: The World of the New Testament," *The Life and Teachings of Jesus Christ,* 1:xxv–xxvi.

[23] See S. Kent Brown, "Zacharias and Elisabeth, Joseph and Mary," *The Life and Teachings of Jesus Christ,* 1:101–20.

[24] This represents only one aspect of the argument and could not by itself provide

Like Mark, this Gospel records the story of Jesus' family waiting to talk with Him, which provided Jesus the opportunity to talk about how to become members of the family of God (see Matthew 12:46).

Matthew also records the story of Jesus' visit to Nazareth, but unlike Mark, he tells us that Jesus was the "carpenter's son" (Matthew 13:55). The list of the family members—Mary, James, Joseph, Simon, and Judas—is basically the same as in Mark, except that Matthew calls one brother Joseph instead of Jose (an acceptable abbreviation of Joseph), and he reverses the order of the last two brothers.[25]

Like, Mark, this account provides a hint about His family's general reaction to His ministry at this point: "They were offended in him. But Jesus said unto them, A prophet is not without honour, save in his own country, and *in his own house.* And he did not many mighty works there because of their unbelief" (Matthew 13:57–58; emphasis added).

Jesus' Family in John

Like the book of Mark, the Gospel of John does not provide a birth narrative or childhood narrative.[26] In John's Gospel, we are introduced to Jesus' mother as "the mother of Jesus" at a wedding in Cana (John 2:1–2). This is one of the unique features of John's account; he never refers to Mary by name (see John 2:3–5,12; 6:42; 19:25–27).

Following the marriage at Cana, John continues, "After this he went down to Capernaum, he, and his mother, and *his brethren,* and his disciples; and they continued there not many days" (John 2:12; emphasis added). It is difficult to ascertain the significance of this

---

any conclusive answer to the questions. However, it is part of the constellation of evidence that seems, taken together, to demonstrate some certainty on the issue.

[25] See discussion on the significance of this change in Bauckham, *Jude and the Relatives of Jesus,* 7.

[26] See Holzapfel and Wayment, "Introduction: The World of the New Testament," *The Life and Teachings of Jesus Christ,* 1:xxvi–xxviii.

pericope, especially in light of the synoptic tradition, which gives the impression that Jesus' family remained in Nazareth, or at least were not sympathetic to His mission.

In John 6, Jesus is recognized by Galilean Jews as the "son of Joseph, whose father and mother we know" (John 6:42). This statement suggests that although questions arose from time to time about Jesus' paternity, they were not the only things people believed or knew (see below).

Later in the Gospel, John provides an ominous setting for the story recorded in chapter 7: "After these things Jesus walked in Galilee: for he would not walk in Jewry, because the Jews sought to kill him" (John 7:1). Immediately, John informs his audience that Jesus' family attempted to pressure Him to go to Jerusalem, despite the threat awaiting Jesus there in the Holy City (John 7:3–4).

The passage remains obscure and meaningless, at least somewhat unintelligible, until the next verses are read carefully: "*For neither did his brethren believe in him.* Then Jesus said unto them, My time is not yet come: but your time is always ready. The world cannot hate you; but me it hateth, because I testify of it, that the works thereof are evil" (John 7:5–7; emphasis added). Here it seems that "his brethren" knew full well that danger awaited Him in Jerusalem but wanted Jesus to go anyway, because they did not "believe in Him"; a major theme in John's Gospel is "believing" in Jesus. Note John's introduction: "He was in the world, and the world was made by him, and the world knew him not. He came unto his own, and his own received him not" (John 1:10–11).

Only in John is the charge of illegitimacy explicitly portrayed: "They answered and said unto him, Abraham is our father. Jesus saith unto them, If ye were Abraham's children, ye would do the works of Abraham. But now ye seek to kill me, a man that hath told you the truth, which I have heard of God: this did not Abraham. Ye do the deeds of your father. Then said they to him, *We be not born of fornication;* we have one Father, even God" (John 8:39–41).

The question that has caught the attention of more than one commentator is found in John's crucifixion narrative. Jesus asked the "beloved disciple" to take care of His mother, suggesting that no male members of the immediate family were willing or able to do so (John 19: 26–27).

The crucifixion scene also provides an additional clue; Jesus' aunt is present: "Now there stood by the cross of Jesus his mother, *and his mother's sister,* Mary the wife of Cleophas, and Mary Magdalene" (John 19:25; emphasis added). Commentators have notoriously confused this passage when they have identified "Mary the wife of Cleopas" as Mary's sister, forcing the verse to talk about three women instead of four. The natural reading suggests that John had four women in mind. Because John rarely refers to living members of Jesus' family by name, we can assume that he does not name Jesus' aunt. Also, it would apparently have violated Jewish convention to give two daughters the same name while both were alive: Mary, the mother of Jesus, and Mary, his mother's sister.

This reconstruction is significant because it may reveal another possible family relation just under the surface of the Gospel narratives. Mark is the only Gospel to provide the name of one of Jesus' female disciples—Salome (*Salomē*): "There were also women looking on afar off: among whom was Mary Magdalene, and Mary the mother of James the less and of Joses, and *Salome*" (Mark 15:40, emphasis added).[27] Although Mark adds that other women were also present (see Mark 15:41), he chose to highlight these three women in particular.[28]

When we compare the four Gospels' accounts of Jesus' execution, several women dominate the story. Trying to line up the individuals in the group for comparison is difficult but not impossible. First, Mary Magdalene is noted specifically in each account (see Matthew 27:55–56; Mark 15:40; Luke 23:49, cf. 24:10; John

[27] See Jeni Broberg Holzapfel and Richard Neitzel Holzapfel, *Sisters at the Well: Women and the Life and Teachings of Jesus* (Salt Lake City: Bookcraft, 1993), 129–31.

[28] Salome was among the women who brought spices for Jesus' burial (Mark 16:1); Peter Richardson, "Salome," *Eerdmans Dictionary,* 1153.

19:40). Luke does not provide the specific names of any of the women at this point in his narrative (see Luke 23:49, 55) but will in the resurrection narrative: "It was Mary Magdalene, and Joanna, and Mary the mother of James, and other women that were with them" (Luke 24:10).

Second, Matthew's account notes, "Among which was Mary Magdalene, and Mary the mother of James and Joses, and *the mother of Zebedee's children*" (Matthew 27:56; emphasis added). This is the only Gospel to inform us that James and John's mother was present at the cross, "the mother of Zebedee's children." This wording has caused several commentators to suggest that the mother of Zebedee's children in Matthew should be identified with Salome in Mark, and with the mother of Jesus' sister in John—making James and John cousins of Jesus.

This relationship might explain why Jesus asked John (His cousin) to take care of His mother (John's aunt) at the cross (see John 19:25–27).[29] Additionally, if this reconstruction is possible, it may explain why John rarely refers to himself in the Gospel: his proclivity not to mention Jesus' living relatives by name. They modestly recede behind the message.[30]

Jesus' Family in Luke and Acts

Because Luke penned both the Gospel of Luke and the book of Acts, sometime in the later 60s or early 70s, he covers a longer time frame of the story than the other Gospel authors, beginning with the annunciation and going through Paul's arrival in Rome in about

---

[29] Why Jesus asked John to take Mary home has raised many questions, especially if she had several children who would naturally have taken care of their mother following the death of her eldest son (Jesus). One line of thought suggests that because Mary's children did not accept Jesus as the Messiah at this time, Jesus asked not only a relative, but a believing relative, to do so. At some point, some of the children accepted Jesus as Messiah and Lord and joined Mary when she met with the other disciples shortly before the Pentecost (see above and Acts 1:14).

[30] For a critique of this reconstruction, see Bauckham, *Jude and the Relatives of Jesus*, 12–13.

A.D. 62.[31] Because of this, Luke provides us an opportunity to learn more about Jesus' family than we could in the other Gospels.

We are introduced to Mary, Jesus' mother, in the very first chapter. According to Luke, Mary lived in the unwalled and insignificant village of Nazareth in Galilee (Luke 2:6). Like Matthew, Luke informs his audience that Joseph is Mary's husband (Luke 1:27; 2:4–5). She accepts the call to become the mother of the Messiah and soon makes the journey to visit her relative, Elisabeth (Luke 1:36). Therefore, Luke expands our view of Jesus' family to include Zacharias, Elisabeth, and John as extended family members.[32]

Luke preserves the story of Joseph with some remarkable additional insights beyond what Mark or Matthew recorded. According to Luke, Joseph was "espoused" to Mary and was a descendant of David (Luke 1:27). Luke informs his audience that Joseph took Mary to Bethlehem, his ancestral home, just before she delivered her firstborn son (Luke 2:4–5). According to Luke, Joseph was present at the birth, circumcision, and presentation at the temple (Luke 2:7, 21, 22).

The narrative continues when Joseph returns to Nazareth with Mary and Jesus (Luke 2:39–40). Luke informs his audience that Jesus accompanied Mary and Joseph to Jerusalem when He was twelve years old. While there for one of the feasts, Jesus remained behind while the extended family made their way back to Nazareth. When Joseph and Mary discovered that Jesus was not with the party, they returned to the Holy City and eventually found Him in the temple. There, Jesus reminded them that His father was God: "How is it that ye sought me? wist ye not that I must be about my Father's business?" (Luke 2:49). Luke added, "And [Jesus] went down with them, and came to Nazareth, and was subject unto them" (Luke 2:51).

---

[31] See Holzapfel and Wayment, "Introduction: The World of the New Testament," *The Life and Teachings of Jesus Christ,* 1:xxvi.

[32] For Elizabeth, see Jo Ann H. Seeley, "Elizabeth," *Eerdmans Dictionary,* 400. For Zacharias, see Stephen R. Miller, "Zechariah," *Eerdmans Dictionary,* 1412.

If Mary's or Joseph's families had moved to Galilee in the wake of the Hasmonean expansion during the century before, Jesus may have had a number of other relatives who migrated north themselves.[33] That Jesus grew up surrounded by family is suggested by the travel narrative when He was twelve: "And when they had fulfilled the days, as they returned, the child Jesus tarried behind in Jerusalem; and Joseph and his mother knew not of it. But they, supposing him to have been in the company, went a day's journey; and they sought him among *their kinsfolk* and acquaintance" (Luke 2:43–44).[34]

Like Matthew, the Gospel of Luke also provides a version of Jesus' genealogy—tracing the descent of Joseph from Adam (Luke 3:23–38).

Luke preserves a dramatic episode in Jesus' ministry when he reports the story about Jesus' visit to Nazareth: "He came to Nazareth, where he had been brought up: and, as his custom was, he went into the synagogue on the Sabbath day, and stood up for to read" (Luke 4:16). Nazareth at this time was a small hamlet with fewer than four hundred people.

It would not be unreasonable to suggest that Jesus' family, at least some of them, were present on the occasion. Luke informs his audience that Jesus read (from Isaiah) a messianic prophecy and immediately applied it to Himself (Luke 4:17–21; cf. Isaiah 61:1–4). Here, those in attendance rhetorically ask, "Is not this Joseph's son?" (Luke 4:22).[35]

The story continues as Jesus challenges them (Luke 4:23–27);

---

[33] See S. Kent Brown, *Mary and Elisabeth* (American Fork, Utah: Covenant Communications, 2002), 36–39.

[34] The oldest manuscripts say "his parents," but later orthodox scribes, concerned with issues discussed in their own day about Jesus' Sonship, altered the text to eliminate any confusion over who was Jesus' father; see the discussion about intentional scribal alterations of the New Testament in Thomas A. Wayment, "The Story of the New Testament," *The Life and Teachings of Jesus*, 1:35–40.

[35] If Luke's detailed information is correct, then Joseph was most likely dead only a short time because he is remembered, a conclusion that undermines the traditional view that he had died shortly after Jesus' twelfth birthday.

then it notes, "And all they in the synagogue, when they heard these things, were filled with wrath, and rose up, and thrust him out of the city, and led him unto the brow of the hill whereon their city was built, that they might cast him down headlong" (Luke 4:28–29). We can only wonder: Were members of Jesus' family in the synagogue that day? Were they offended also? Did they support the mob action to kill Jesus?

It is impossible to adequately reconstruct this story to answer those questions without additional evidence. However, it may be the result of this experience in Nazareth among some of His own family, along with others, that Luke intended as the historical setting for Jesus' teaching regarding the household (family) of faith: "And it came to pass, as he spake these things, a certain woman of the company lifted up her voice, and said unto him, Blessed is the womb that bare thee, and the paps which thou hast sucked. But he said, Yea rather, blessed are they that hear the word of God, and keep it" (Luke 11:27–28).

Jesus continued to emphasize the importance of accepting the "good news" and becoming part of God's family by responding to Jesus' call. Instead of rejecting all family ties and responsibility, the statement in Luke 14 is hyperbolic: "If any man come to me, and hate not his father, and mother, and wife, and children, and brethren, and sisters, yea, and his own life also, he cannot be my disciple" (Luke 14:26).

Although Luke does not mention any of Jesus' brothers or sisters by name, he most likely knows their names, as he will highlight James in the book of Acts—the second part of his two-part story. He notes, "These all continued with one accord in prayer and supplication, with the women, and Mary the mother of Jesus, and with *his brethren*" (Acts 1:14; emphasis added).

Sometimes lost on students of the New Testament is the fact that James, the Lord's brother, is immediately inserted in the narrative following the death of James, the son of Zebedee, by Herod Agrippa I in A.D. 44 (see Acts 12:1–2 and 17). Obviously, these are two different disciples. Luke then highlights the ministry of James (the brother of Jesus) when Paul and Barnabas arrive in Jerusalem in A.D. 49 for the famous and important Jerusalem Conference (see Acts 15). Here James plays a significant role as a mediator between the Pauline mission and those conservative Jewish-Christians who are still Torah-observant Jews. He appears to be one of the leaders of the Church, along with Peter.

Luke provides additional information about James. He appears to be solely in charge of the Church in Jerusalem. The other members of the Twelve were either dead or scattered throughout the Mediterranean Basin and most likely were unable to return frequently to the Holy City, as shown in this narrative when Paul made his last visit to Jerusalem in about A.D. 59 (see Acts 21).

Luke may have identified a special group, known as "the brothers of the Lord," as he rehearsed the story of Peter's escape from prison: "Peter continued knocking; and when they had opened the door, and saw him, they were astonished. But he, beckoning unto them with the hand to hold their peace, declared unto them how the Lord had brought him out of the prison. And he said, Go shew these things unto James, and to the brethren. And he departed, and went into another place" (Acts 12:16–17; cf. 1 Corinthians 9:5; Acts 1:14; Jude 1:1).[36] This special group may have included members of Jesus' family who were also witnesses of the Risen Lord.

Jesus' Family in Paul's Letters

Paul's letters provide another set of documents from the first century that help in reconstructing Jesus' familial relationships,

[36] This would not be the first time that Luke has provided the reader with the name of a special group. Throughout the book of Acts, he refers to "the way" (Acts 9:2). Today, many New Testament scholars recognize that this was actually one of the earliest nicknames for the Church, and, as a result, many recent translations have capitalized "way" in the printed editions of the New Testament. For example, the NIV states, "He went to the high priest and asked him for letters to the synagogues in Damascus, so that if he found any there who belonged to the Way, whether men or women, he might take them as prisoners to Jerusalem" (NIV Acts 9:1–2; compare 16:17; 18:25–26; 19:9, 23; 22:4, 24).

particularly to his brother James: "After three years I went up to Jerusalem to see Peter, and abode with him fifteen days. But other of the apostles saw I none, save *James the Lord's brother*" (Galatians 1:18–19; emphasis added).[37] Paul here indicates that James was an "apostle," one sent forth by Jesus to preach His message. A little later, Paul identifies James along with Cephas (Peter) and John as "pillars" who gave Paul and Barnabas "the right hand of fellowship" (Galatians 2:9), demonstrating that by this period, about A.D. 49–50, James was recognized as a figure of authority in Jerusalem.

In his first letter to the Corinthians, Paul sustains his authority and rights by citing examples of others who are known to have similar rights and privileges: "Have we not power to lead about a sister, a wife, as well as other apostles, and as *the brethren of the Lord,* and Cephas?" (1 Corinthians 9:5; emphasis added). This verse certainly suggests that Jesus' brothers, who traveled with their wives, were well known and that their authority was acknowledged, or such an appeal would not make sense.

In another section of the letter, his list of resurrection appearances, Paul unwittingly provides the modern audience, starving for information about Jesus' family, additional details about James: "I delivered unto you first of all that which I also received, how that Christ died . . . [and] was buried, and that he rose again the third day. . . . And that he was seen of Cephas, then of the twelve: after that, he was seen of above five hundred brethren at once. . . . After that, *he was seen of James;* then of all the apostles. And last of all he was seen of me also (1 Corinthians 15:3–8; emphasis added).

Paul emphasizes the appearance to male apostolic witnesses in this list and bypasses the women who saw Jesus. He confirms what the synoptic Gospels suggest, that Jesus appeared first to Peter (Cephas). Paul then informs the Corinthians that Jesus next appeared to the "Twelve"—not twelve men, because Judas was dead, but to the "Twelve," an organized group. Next, Paul informs the reader that the Risen Lord was seen by more than five hundred,

---

[37] Robert E. Van Voors, "James," *Eerdmans Dictionary*, 669.

most likely at the time of the ascension. The next appearance mentioned was to James (who was well known when Paul was dictating this letter), the brother of Jesus. The next group is all the "apostles," those called by Jesus and commissioned to preach His message, not a group ordained but simply a group "sent," the meaning of the term *apostle.*

What is surprising in this list is the fact that only Peter and James are highlighted as having had a personal experience instead of a group experience with the Risen Jesus. This may partially explain James' reputation.

Paul's account of the appearance to Jesus' brother James is confirmed in several early sources and helps make sense of Luke's comment in Acts 1, where he provides a list of those present at the early meeting of disciples following the death and resurrection of Jesus (see Acts 1:14). In other words, if Jesus' brothers, including James, were unsympathetic during Jesus' mortal ministry, a resurrection appearance would certainly have changed their minds about who Jesus was, helping us understand why they were in an early meeting with the other disciples.

Jesus' Family in the Remaining New Testament Documents

It has generally been assumed, if the books of James and Jude are dated earlier rather than later, that two of Jesus' brothers wrote letters that are now included in the New Testament.[38] The inclusion of two letters written by Jesus' brothers demonstrates the important roles and influence of Jesus' family in the early Church. Additionally, their influence could also be based on the fact that they, too, were of Davidic ancestry, which certainly would have been important to Jewish Christians. But of utmost interest is the fact that James, the best-known member of Jesus' family in the decades following the death and resurrection, did not claim special

[38] There are many positive arguments for dating both James and Jude quite early; see Luke Timothy Johnson, *Brother of Jesus, Friend of God: Studies in the Letter of James* (Grand Rapids, Mich.: Eerdmans, 2004), 37–38 and William F. Brosend II, *James & Jude* (New York: Cambridge University Press, 2004), 5–7.

privileges based on his relationship with Jesus; "James, a servant of God and of the Lord Jesus Christ," is the only introduction he provided his audience (James 1:1).

Although certainly known to the Church as the "brother of the Lord," James accepted Jesus' definition of family, a teaching he may have heard himself when it was first given: "Who is my mother, or my brethren? And he looked round about on them which sat about him, and said, Behold my mother and my brethren! For whosoever shall do the will of God, the same is my brother, and my sister, and mother" (Mark 3:33–35).[39]

The book of Jude begins, "Jude, the servant of Jesus Christ, and brother of James, to them that are sanctified by God the Father, and preserved in Jesus Chris, and called" (Jude 1:1).[40] Note that Jude (Judas), like James, does not claim authority based on blood relationship with Jesus. He is a "servant" of Jesus Christ; this is the emphasis in the opening line. He sees his relationship to Jesus not as familial but rather based on discipleship (see Philippians 2:6–7).[41] However, he does provide a link to James, demonstrating again the enormous stature James the Just, the brother of the Lord, held in the first-century Church.

References to Jesus' Family outside the New Testament

If reconstructing Jesus' family from the information preserved in the New Testament itself is challenging, doing so with other writings, including important postcanonical early Christian writings, is even more complicated. There are, however, some data worthy of consideration.

An important source for reconstructing the world of the New

---

[39] Typically for the period, a person would identify himself or herself by parentage, birthplace, or occupation. This is a stunning example of the radical redefinition of who one was, based on faith. For James, he was the servant (slave) of God and the Risen Jesus.

[40] A literal reading is "Jude [of] Jesus Christ a slave, a brother of James."

[41] Slave theology is rooted in the Old Testament, where Abraham, Moses, and David are described as "slaves" of God. The Septuagint used *doulos* in this context to translate the Hebrew word. This is the same Greek word used here.

Testament is the first-century Jewish historian Josephus. He was born and raised in Jewish Palestine, but he wrote from Rome in Greek to a gentile audience. In his history of the Jews, Josephus not only mentions James, the brother [*adelfos*] of Jesus, but he also provides an account of his death. The text, which is almost universally accepted as authentic, describes James as a respected member of the Jewish community in Jerusalem who was condemned to death by the Jewish high priest Ananus in A.D. 62. Josephus reports that Ananus "convened the judges of the Sanhedrin and brought before them a man named James, the brother of Jesus who was called the Christ, and certain others. He accused them of having transgressed the law and delivered them up to be stoned."[42]

Several Gentile-Christian sources, dating from the second century, provide the names of Jesus' sisters, unnamed in the Gospel accounts, as Mary and Salome (see Mark 6:3; Matthew 13:55).[43] A study dealing with the distribution of Jewish women's names reveals that, combined, these two names accounted for nearly 48 percent of the total number of women's names collected.[44] They are the two most popular names during this period, a fact that validates the claims of second-century sources about the names of Jesus' sisters, as it is unlikely that Gentile-Christian writers could have guessed that these two names were so common in the first century.

Another ancient source, the *Gospel of the Hebrews*, provides information about James.[45] In this text, which most likely dates from about A.D. 150, James is depicted as having perhaps been present at the Last Supper: "When the Lord had given the linen cloth to the servant of the priest, he went to James and appeared to him. For James had sworn that he would not eat bread from that

[42] Josephus, *AJ* 20.200.

[43] See Bauckham, *Jude and the Relatives of Jesus*, 37–44.

[44] See Tal Ilan, "Notes on the Distribution of Jewish Women's Names in Palestine in the Second Temple and Mishnaic Periods," *Journal of Jewish Studies* 40 (1989): 186–200.

[45] For a brief introduction to the *Gospel of Hebrews*, see George Howard, "Hebrews, Gospel According," *Eerdmans Dictionary*, 570.

hour in which he had drunk the cup of the Lord until he should see him risen from among them that sleep. And shortly thereafter the Lord said: Bring a table and bread! And immediately it is added: he took the bread, blessed it and brake it and gave it to James the Just and said to him: My brother, eat thy bread, for the Son of man is risen from among them that sleep."[46]

This second-century source may have direct bearing on Paul's reference to James as one of those who had seen the Risen Jesus (see 1 Corinthians 15:7), providing additional information about Jesus' family that was not recorded in the New Testament. However, if this account from the *Gospel of the Hebrews* contains information from the first century, it conflicts with the depiction of Jesus' strained relationship with His family presented in the Gospels. How do we reconcile James' presence with Jesus in Jerusalem if he and Jesus were at odds during the public ministry?

It would not have been unreasonable for Jesus' family to have gone to Jerusalem during the Passover, as the book of Luke suggests it was their custom to do so (see Luke 2:41). Would Mary have joined Jesus and His disciples for the Passover meal? Since she was present at the cross, we should assume that she had come to Jerusalem for the feast (John 19:25). Would some of Jesus' other family members have made the long journey with her? Would they have gathered with Jesus and His disciples to eat the Passover dinner? It is not beyond the realm of possibility.

Another source that likely preserves reliable ancient traditions going back to the first-century Church is the writings of Eusebius (died c. 342). Although it may be impossible to categorically prove that Eusebius' use of these earlier documents was accurate, it is, nevertheless, necessary to examine his writing and evaluate his use of sources to help in the reconstruction of what happened after the close of the New Testament era.

Eusebius preserves material from a second-century Christian,

[46] Wilhelm Schneemelcher, ed., *New Testament Apocrypha,* trans. R. McL. Wilson (Philadelphia: James Clarke and Westminster/John Knox Press, 1991), 178.

Hegesippus,[47] who claims that Cleopas (*Kleopás*), mentioned by Luke as traveling on the road to Emmaus (see Luke 24:13–32), was "the brother of Joseph" and that Simeon, a son of Cleopas, was Jesus' cousin.[48] As a result, some have identified Cleopas with the "Clopas" mentioned by John: "Now there stood by the cross of Jesus his mother, and his mother's sister, Mary the wife of Cleophas, and Mary Magdalene" (John 19:25). If this is true, then Jesus' aunt's name was Mary—again, one of the most common names among first-century Jews in Galilee and Judea. Because Cleopas was Joseph's brother, there is no problem having two sisters-in-law with the same name: Mary, Joseph's wife and Jesus' mother; and Mary, Cleopas' wife and Jesus' aunt. Additionally, Eusebius reported that Cleopas' son, Simeon, succeeded James, the brother of Jesus and Simeon's cousin, as the leader of the Church in Jerusalem.[49]

Another contribution from Eusebius deals with Jude's grandsons. According to Hegesippus, at the end of the first century, Domitian arrested and interrogated all the known descendants of David with plans to execute any who might be agitators.[50] Jude's grandsons were detained and questioned about their Davidic line and their relationship to Jesus Christ, the Messiah. According to this source, they were released when it was determined that they were not a threat to Rome, allowing them to return home and continue serving in the Church. Although it is highly unlikely that two Jewish peasants would appear before Domitian, the story most likely reflects the arrest of two extended family members of Jesus at the end of the first century. Even the names that the sources provide, Zoker and James, may, in fact, have some historical plausibility.[51]

---

[47] Eusebius, *Ecclesiastical History*, 3.11; see G. A. Williamson, trans. (New York: Penguin Books, 1989).

[48] Cleopas is the shortened form of *Cleopatros;* see Joe E. Lunceford, "Cleopas," *Eerdmans Dictionary*, 264.

[49] Eusebius, *Ecclesiastical History*, 3.11

[50] See Scott Nash, "Domitian," *Eerdmans Dictionary*, 353.

[51] Eusebius, *Ecclesiastical History*, 3:19–20 (the names are present only in the Bodleian Manuscript Barocc, 142).

Finally, Eusebius reports that other relatives continued to play significant roles in the Church until the end of the first century. Eusebius, reporting information from a letter by Julius Africanus dated about A.D. 200, said that the relatives of Jesus had settled in Kochaba and Nazareth. In addition, he reported that they preserved their Davidic genealogies.[52] By the end of the second century, Jesus' relatives disappear from the historical record, replaced by rumors, legends, and speculation about them and their posterity.

The Family of Jesus in the JST

Interestingly, the Joseph Smith Translation does not provide any additional insights about Jesus' family. Apparently, the original authors' data (preserved in the Greek manuscripts) about the family of Jesus have been passed down through the long history of transmission, leaving us with the same questions that began this study; Joseph Smith, who was called by the Lord to provide the Saints with the "fulness of [the] scriptures" (see Doctrine and Covenants 42:15), did not feel during this part of his ministry the need to add or restore information concerning the family of Jesus.

Conclusion

Any study regarding the family of Jesus must of necessity make modest claims because the information available is woefully fragmentary. The outline below is scarcely exhaustive and only suggestive of some of the conclusions that can reasonably be drawn from the evidence presented above. (At the end of the chapter, see Adam Hiatt's chart that provides a genealogical picture of Jesus' family members.)

Although each Gospel author provides distinctive views about Jesus' family, it seems that Mary should be considered Jesus' first disciple, a view highlighted by Luke. And although she did not always understand her son, she was one of His most devoted and

[52] Eusebuis, *Ecclesiastical History*, 3.11

constant followers. Her appearance in the first chapter of Luke and also in the first chapter in Acts made her a bridge—a witness of the birth of the Messiah and also a witness of the birth of the new Church.

Mary rarely dominates any Gospel story. The annunciation and birth narratives are the exception, but her presence is felt throughout the Gospels, and she appears at the end, at the critical part of the story. Following an important gathering after Jesus' death and resurrection, she disappears from the New Testament record. Joseph, on the other hand, played a similar role in Matthew's and Luke's Gospels in the beginning but disappears from the story before Jesus began His ministry.

The New Testament suggests that Jesus had brothers, four named, and at least two sisters, unnamed. However, they are absent from the birth and childhood narratives. But once the public ministry begins, they appear from time to time in various contexts and places. Apparently, some of Jesus' relatives thought He was "out of his senses" and did not accept His special status, at least during the early part of His mortal ministry.

However, several members of Jesus' family eventually became at least sympathetic to His mission and may have been with Him at the Last Supper. A few, including James, became witnesses of the Risen Christ. Most likely, one of Jesus' extended family, His uncle Cleopas, met Jesus on the road to Emmaus and also became a witness of the resurrection.

Some of Jesus' immediate family joined with Mary, their mother, at the earliest meeting noted in the book of Acts. Although Mary fades from view after Acts 1, James, the brother of Jesus, begins to rise in prominence as Luke continues to unfold his story about the Church in the decades following Jesus' ascension.

James, known as the "Just," eventually became an important leader in the Jerusalem Church and likely wielded authority beyond the Holy Land. His letter, the Epistle of James, was probably composed sometime in the 50s and was sent to the "twelve tribes which are scattered abroad." In addition, James' authority in Jerusalem was in line with that of the Twelve.

By the time Paul began his ministry, James was considered one of the "pillars of the church," along with Peter and John. Because James remained in Jerusalem, he may have become the leading figure in the Church there before his own martyrdom in A.D. 62.

Another brother, Jude (Judas), is the author of the book of Jude and claimed special authority based on his discipleship as "the servant of Jesus Christ"—but also partly on being the "brother of James." Written sometime before the destruction of Jerusalem in A.D. 70, Jude's letter was eventually included in the New Testament canon.

Some of Jesus' brothers were married and traveled with their wives as missionaries throughout the Mediterranean basin. Others remained in Jewish Palestine and continued to play significant roles in the Church there through the second century. We lose sight of Jesus' family by the end of the second century, but obviously they played a significant part in Jesus' own life, and their shadow continued to influence Christianity for generations.[53]

[53] It was James' letter that strengthened the Prophet Joseph Smith's resolve to enter into the woods near his home in the spring of 1820 to pray, opening a new gospel dispensation.

JESUS' FAMILY

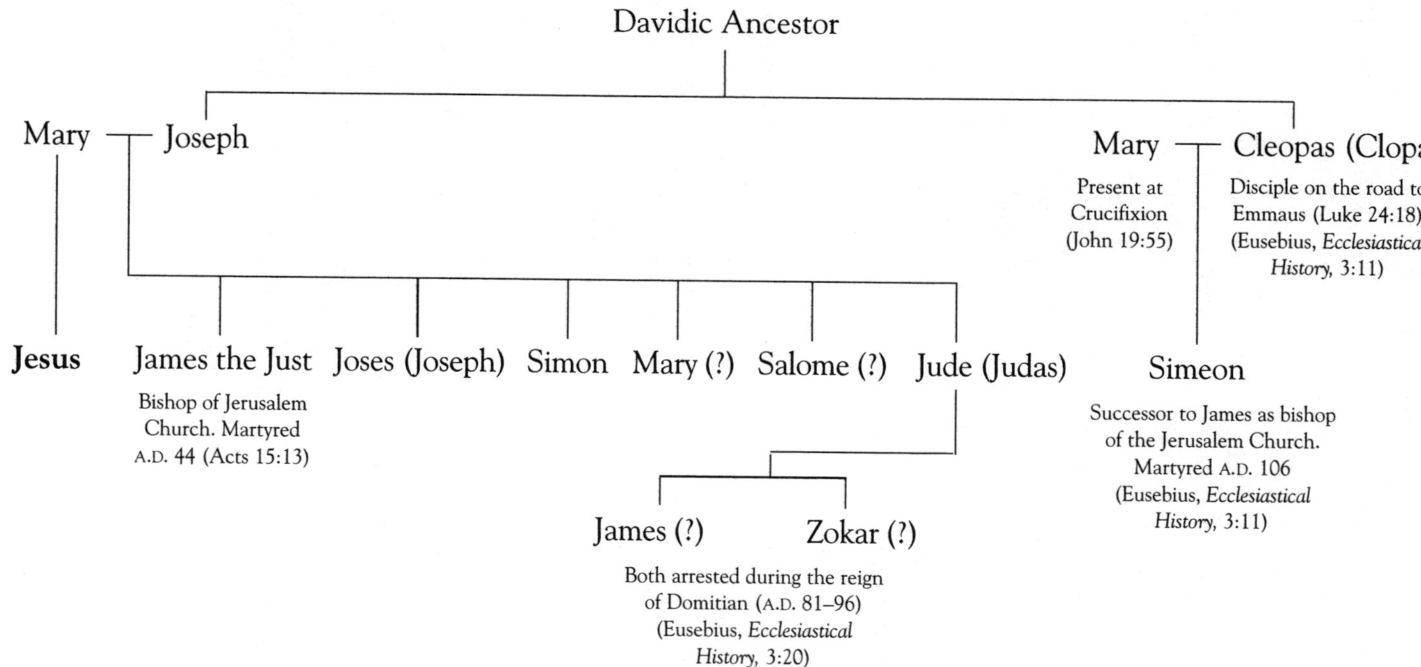

XIV.

THE WOMAN TAKEN IN ADULTERY AND THE HISTORY OF THE NEW TESTAMENT CANON

THOMAS A. WAYMENT

And early in the morning he came again into the temple, and all the people came unto him; and he sat down, and taught them.

JOHN 8:2

Describing and retelling the history of the development of the New Testament canon is a complex undertaking fraught with assumptions, innuendos, and presuppositions that often generate faulty conclusions. Popular reconstructions of the process of canonization, which occurred in the first four centuries of the post-New Testament era, place the majority of the decision-making process into the hands of Church leaders, who oftentimes, with conspiratorial intentions, limited and excluded certain books from the New Testament to substantiate their own doctrinal positions or undermine the beliefs of their opponents. This popular reconstruction also focuses on the purity of doctrine being protected by a few unsuspecting Christians whose true doctrines and practices were ultimately marginalized and excluded through the removal of precious truths by the corrupt ruling elite. This portrait, although entertaining and creative, lacks the depth and clarity of presentation accompanying the actual process of canonization.

A thorough treatment of the history of canonization would require several hundred pages, beginning with the perceptions of Jesus' first followers and their impressions of the immediate authority of Jesus' words and culminating in the development of principles used to include or exclude certain writings by third- and fourth-century authors such as Athanasius (A.D. 296–373), Origen (A.D. 185–254), and Cyril of Jerusalem (A.D. 315–86).[1] The principles developed by these and other early Christian leaders were meant to exclude pseudoapostolic writings of questionable authenticity and content.

In this effort, they should be congratulated, as the current New Testament canon contains a rich treasure trove of writings from the first century, written by faithful followers of Jesus and the Twelve, and does not include some of the fanciful apocryphal texts so popular among the next generations of Christians. Nevertheless, the principles they developed were formulated quite late in the history of the canon and were not the single definitive influence in creating and shaping the current form of the New Testament.

One of the major issues facing any modern reconstruction of the history of the New Testament canon is the lack of surviving sources and information during the decades after Jesus lived, particularly the decades during which the letters and Gospels of the New Testament were written (A.D. 49–90). Without doubt, the New Testament writings preserve the words of Jesus, but the reasons that induced the first writers to put ink to papyrus have been clouded by the passage of time. The Gospel authors may have written to preserve the story of Jesus, to correct erroneous presentations of His life, or to present an alternate interpretation of Jesus' life against those who were trying to pervert the historical accuracy

[1] The most authoritative treatment to date on the process of canonization remains Bruce M. Metzger, *The Canon of the New Testament: Its Origin, Development, and Significance* (Oxford: Clarendon, 1997).

of the eyewitness accounts of Jesus' life and ministry.[2] One of the most fascinating clues into the process of how the New Testament canon developed is the story of the woman caught in adultery (John 8:1–11), which preserves an event from Jesus' lifetime, even though the story was not originally part of the Gospel of John and was likely not written by the author of the Gospel of John.

The Textual History of John 8:1–11

The story of the woman caught in adultery is missing from almost all the earliest manuscripts of the New Testament, including all the earliest New Testament Greek papyri.[3] The story is also absent in the oldest Syriac versions (early second century), the Sahidic and sub-Achmimic Coptic (third century), and older Bohairic Coptic versions of John, as well as in some of the oldest Latin versions (end of the second century).[4] The story is found in some early Latin manuscripts as well as in the majority of manuscripts dating to the Middle Ages. The earliest manuscript to contain the

[2] Perhaps one of the most fanciful attempts in this regard is the pseudepigraphical writing known today as the Gospel of Peter, which claims to preserve a more correct portrait of Jesus. In the Gospel of Peter, Jesus cannot physically suffer, and many of those who were involved in the crucifixion of Jesus convert upon learning of their misguided actions. For a thorough, although controversial, study of the Gospel of Peter, see John Dominic Crossan, *The Cross That Spoke: The Origins of the Passion Narrative* (San Francisco: Harper & Row, 1988).

[3] The list of manuscripts that do not contain the reading is extensive and diverse—indicating additionally that the story of the woman caught in adultery was likely not a regional phenomenon either. The reading is absent from the important manuscripts p66 (c. A.D. 200), p75 (c. A.D. 200), Sinaiticus (fourth century), Vaticanus (fourth century), T (fifth century), Freer (fifth century), and probably also Alexandrinus (fifth century) and Ephraemi Rescriptus (fifth century), although the latter two manuscripts are defective at John 8 and cannot definitively indicate either its presence or absence.

[4] For a more complete discussion of the textual history of John 8:1–11, see Bruce M. Metzger, A *Textual Commentary on the Greek New Testament,* 2d ed. (Stuttgart: United Bible Societies, 2001), 187–89. See also Frederick Schilling, "The Story of Jesus and the Adulteress," *Anglican Theological Review* 37 (1955): 91–106; Gary M. Burge, "A Specific Problem in the New Testament Text and Canon: The Woman Caught in Adultery (John 7:53–8:11)," *Journal of the Evangelical Theological Society* 27 (1984): 141–48.

reading is Codex Bezae, dating from the fifth century A.D. The obvious conclusion, therefore, is that historically the story was inserted into the text of the New Testament at a surprisingly late date, perhaps as late as the fourth or fifth century. From a textual perspective, and based on the current collection of New Testament manuscripts, proving that the story of the woman caught in adultery was written by the author of the Gospel of John and that it was placed in its current location in the first edition of that Gospel would be nearly impossible.

In addition to the weak textual support for the story of the woman caught in adultery are the sparse quotations of that story in the first three centuries after the death of Jesus. If an early Christian author had quoted from the story in the first two hundred years after the books of the New Testament were composed, then we could logically surmise that the story was early and well known. Moreover, an exact quotation would confirm that the story was not only written early but also existed, at least in part, in that early stage in its present form. Unfortunately, in the instance of the account of the woman caught in adultery, no direct reference to the story is made until the fourth century A.D. In fact, prior to the recent discovery of the quotation by Didymus the Blind, the findings and ramifications of which were published in 1988, the first Greek-speaking commentator to make explicit reference to the story was in the twelfth century A.D.[5] Didymus the Blind (c. A.D. 310–95), the first author to quote from the story, quotes a version that is significantly different from that preserved in our New

[5] Eusebius also records a tradition that the story was contained in the lost Gospel to the Hebrews (Ecclesiastical History 3.39). The account in Eusebius relates that Papias used to tell another story about a woman who had been accused of sin, but no mention is made of the story belonging to one of the canonical Gospels, of which Papias and Eusebius were obviously aware. There is a debatable reference to the story in the third-century Apostolic Constitutions (8.2.24), but the reference there seems to be to another story because the woman is not guilty of adultery and because those who brought her to Jesus simply left, therefore losing the underlying theme of a setup as recorded in John 8:1–11. Bart Ehrman, "Jesus and the Adulteress," *New Testament Studies* 34 (1988): 24.

Testament and derives it from *tisin euangelliois*, "certain gospels."[6] Therefore, scholars have concluded that the story may have originally circulated in several different forms and that a scribe, working with the text in the fourth century or later, fixed the text in its current form and placed it in the Gospel of John in what he thought was the most appropriate position.

This theory raises several lively issues in the study of the development in the New Testament canon. First, immediately after the Gospels were written, they were circulated at least among the congregations nearest to the authors' residences—and likely among a much-wider Christian community. How long it took for a Gospel or epistle to circulate among all the branches of the Christian community is unknown, but perhaps it is not unreasonable to think that under the best circumstances, a document could circulate widely within five to ten years and, under poor conditions, up to several decades. For example, 2 Peter 3:15–16 is evidence that Paul's writings were already being gathered and circulated toward the latter half of the first century, possibly even within Paul's lifetime. In the majority of instances, regional awareness of a new document would have been almost immediate, whereas wider Church awareness could take some time in the first and second centuries when the vast majority of canonical and extracanonical texts were being composed.

Understanding this process is pivotal to appreciating the development of the New Testament canon because the original text, or autograph, became a control for all later copies of that same document. If a certain community, or group of conspiring leaders, wished to alter the text, then the autograph of that document, held by a specific community or individual, could be invoked as a control on corruption and change. As long as the autographs existed or the original authors were living, an immediate external control on textual corruption was present. This process does not mean that no alterations could be made to a document as long as

[6] Ehrman, "Jesus and the Adulteress," 25–27.

the autographs survived or the author was living, but those wishing to alter Christian documents had to face the additional task of discrediting the validity of the original or its author.

If the original community became marginalized or if their own views and beliefs were called into question, then the text of the original writing could be more freely altered because the control mechanism was now circumvented. Most likely, in the history of Christianity, the death of the disciples presented a major turning point in the preservation and accuracy of the New Testament documents, where corruption, alteration, and tampering could be more easily introduced into the original compositions. The ability to alter text, however, in the wake of the Apostles' deaths, could be greatly hindered by faithful communities who themselves held tenaciously to the truths that had been given to them. These believing communities became enclaves of textual preservation and were a major stumbling block for those who wished to alter the text.

A second major issue was the creation of different versions or recensions of the same text in close proximity.[7] If a conspiring group of Christians wished to alter the text dramatically, then the risk of revealing their fraud increased exponentially according to the number of texts in circulation. For example, if a text were altered regionally, then the local communities could perhaps be duped into following the altered text, but if that altered text came into contact with other copies of the same document that had circulated more broadly, then the alterations would be readily apparent. This process of textual alteration gave rise to numerous variants in the texts of the New Testament, yet, in the vast majority of instances, the process did not significantly alter the substance of the primary text.

---

[7] A recension differs from an edition of a text in that it is not carried out under the control of the original author. "Edition," in text-critical terminology, refers to a reworking of a text by the author, whereas a recension is a new version of the text that was created through inadvertent loss or corruption of the text—or even in some instances through intentional alteration.

To succeed in the conspiracy to alter texts, a responsible person would need to replace all, or at least the majority, of previously existing texts or to undermine the authority of existing copies by circulating rumors and falsehoods. In reality, altering existing texts was much more difficult than simply producing new alternative texts that were forged in the name of an Apostle or famous figure. However, finding "new" sayings of Jesus or new stories from His life was an ideal means of altering the primary traditions established in the texts of the New Testament.

The third obstacle was how a few contriving Christians could conceivably alter the beliefs and traditions of the majority when the majority of Christians had access to the same texts, ordinances, and traditions. Without a doubt, internal corruption was a major factor in the first centuries of the expanding Christian Church, yet within the Christian tradition, like-minded believers could form a social structure for the accurate preservation of tradition. A conspiring heretic could not simply alter the texts, pass them off to unsuspecting believers, and expect an immediate and radical alteration in their beliefs. Beliefs take time to shape, and variant texts are successful only to the extent that they are utilized and read by a community and to the extent that a single document can alter belief in the face of other established texts, which also need to be altered in the same way so the altered doctrine is more universally credible. Altering a doctrine in a single New Testament text ran the risk of being exposed as a forgery when the correct doctrine could be found in other books of the New Testament.

A related issue is the extent and influence of Church leadership on Christian practice and belief. A strong, localized Church leadership can easily alter texts to reflect changing Church practice and doctrine, but a weak central leadership may leave issues of practice and belief in the hands of local leaders. According to the portrait presented in the book of Acts, the overwhelming conclusion is that direct and well-organized Church leadership began to weaken in the fifties as the Church leaders and leading missionaries suffered martyrdom. In fact, after Acts 15, no significant gathering of the Twelve is mentioned again in the New Testament. James (the brother of Jesus) and Paul met around A.D. 58 (Acts 21), but their exact position is difficult to ascertain. James was most likely a member of the Twelve, but Paul's role in Church leadership is less certain. The gathering of three Apostles in the mid-fifties (Peter, James, and Paul) is noted in Galatians 2. Perhaps there were other significant gatherings of Church leaders that were not recorded, but Luke chose to present the latter half of his final work through the lens of a waning central leadership. Such sparse evidence does not lead to a convincing conclusion that the Church leadership remained centrally strong after the death of the Apostles or when only a few were still alive.

Regarding the canon of the New Testament, weak Church leadership creates a greater obstacle for textual alteration instead of becoming a vehicle for consistent and thorough textual corruption because textual corruption and alteration need to be made on a large scale to be convincing. However, if the central leadership becomes corrupted, then its ability to alter text in a negative way is dramatically increased. For example, if one denomination of Christians alters the texts of their Bible in any significant way (like the New World Translation or the JST), then the altered text will most likely have very little influence on other Christian denominations. The same holds true for early Christianity, where regional corruption of texts led to an ever-increasing number of recensions of the same text but not the complete wholesale alteration of a single text of the New Testament.

The greatest factor contributing to the alteration of text was loss and intentional removal. Removing text from a document cannot be so easily traced, and the mass removal of text can subsequently be used as an argument that the longer version of the text contains an expansion or forgery. Doctrinal alterations, on the other hand, are less likely to have a far-reaching influence because they reveal the perpetrator's doctrinal bias and run the risk of not being as convincing as the primary text. The ability to remove text is also directly linked to how widely disseminated the document has become; therefore, significant removal of text is likely to be a greater factor in the earlier periods of Christianity than in later periods, particularly in the period before Nicea (A.D. 325) when all the New Testament texts enjoyed wide circulation and a broad readership.

Oral Traditions and the Development of the Canon

The earliest traceable accounts of Jesus' life and ministry are the oral reports that have their origin in the region of Judea/Palestine and were passed along in Aramaic.[8] If there were written accounts that circulated contemporary with or prior to our earliest written sources (the epistles of Paul and the Gospel of Mark), then those sources have been entirely lost. Some passing references to other works have survived even in the New Testament, such as the lost epistle to the Laodiceans or the earlier sources known to Luke (Colossians 4:16; Luke 1:1–3), but no holy grail of documents, as it were, is mentioned by the earliest authors. If an unspoiled document on the life of Jesus existed or if a more complete history of the first thirty years of Christianity existed, then even the references to such works have been entirely lost.

On the other hand, the earliest Christians, particularly the eyewitness generation, knew and heard things that Jesus taught that were not included in the New Testament record. The author of the Gospel of John hints at such knowledge when he said, "And there are also many other things which Jesus did, the which, if they should be written every one, I suppose that even the world itself could not contain the books that should be written. Amen" (John 21:25).

Having eyewitnesses living while a historical account is being written would almost certainly lead to different versions and

[8] Matthew Black, *An Aramaic Approach to the Gospels and Acts*, 3rd ed. (Peabody, Mass.: Hendrickson, 1998), 272–77.

alternate ways of telling the same story. Nevertheless, the living eyewitnesses acted as a control to the main aspects or core of the story. The oral traditions, which derive their authority from those who had experienced the life of Jesus firsthand, shaped the way the written story of Jesus was told and presented, even though very few eyewitness reports survive to this day. Perhaps an even greater influence on shaping the canon was the collective memory of those who had heard the eyewitnesses teach.

Writing a Gospel as a second-generation Christian, such as Mark or Luke, must have been a tricky endeavor because eyewitnesses were certainly still alive in the sixties and seventies, if only John the Beloved; and even if they were not still alive, memory of what they had taught was still a major factor influencing the way any history of Jesus would be written. Therefore, if the author of the Gospel of Mark were writing in or around the region where John the Apostle was living, then his account would be shaped by what John remembered and by what the local community remembered John teaching them. If not, Mark's account would almost immediately fall into controversy. Fortunately, Mark was the earliest written of the four Gospels, with Matthew and Luke writing near the fall of Jerusalem (A.D. 71), and may not have had to contend with an earlier written Gospel account. However, even the oral traditions passed on by the Apostles acted as a type of external control on the transmission of the Gospels, particularly the Gospels most closely associated with eyewitnesses, John, Matthew, and Mark (which contains Peter's memoirs).[9] Those who wrote after the Gospel of Mark had been composed had to write in the shadow of another Gospel.[10] This may help to explain, at least in part, why Matthew and Luke relied so heavily on the Gospel of Mark for their wording, order, and accounts when they presented their own viewpoints on the life of Jesus.

---

[9] Eusebius, *Historia Ecclesiastica* 5.8.

[10] Martin Hengel, *The Four Gospels and the One Gospel of Jesus Christ* (Harrisburg, Penn.: Trinity, 2000).

Recent scholarship on the writing of the New Testament Gospels has increasingly turned away from the belief that the Gospel writers composed their accounts in isolation; and, in fact, the clear reliance of Matthew and Luke upon the Gospel of Mark when they wrote is certain evidence that at least the synoptic authors knew what the others were doing or had done.[11] Although direct collaboration can likely be ruled out, direct borrowing cannot. Therefore, the viewpoints in the earliest written sources must have shaped the later accounts in a positive way while, at the same time, limiting the variety and manner in which things could be presented. The greater the degree of divergence in the newer sources, the greater the likelihood that the new documents would either be rejected or lead to schism.

In the creative environment of pre-fall Jerusalem, when the oral accounts of Jesus' ministry were being passed on and when the accounts were also beginning to take on a more undeviating nature, several individuals began contemplating a more definitive form for transmitting the words and life story of Jesus. The dynamic interaction between oral traditions and written texts must have existed for quite some time in early Christianity as the eyewitnesses passed on and as those who had heard the eyewitnesses speak continued to tell and retell what they had heard.[12] In a living tradition, such as early Christianity, it is not unreasonable to expect that the reverence early Christians felt for their Savior would be passed on directly in some measure to those who had met Him or heard Him speak. The likelihood that eyewitness tradition would have a significant effect on the shaping of the texts of the New Testament and the canon for the first 150 years is considerable; and, in instances where the written texts differed from the eyewitness accounts, the influence could be significantly longer.

---

[11] Charles Horton, ed., *The Earliest Gospels: The Origins and Transmission of the Earliest Christian Gospels—The Contribution of the Chester Beatty Gospel Codex* P^{45} (London: T & T Clark, 2004), 13–26.

[12] Eusebius, *Historiae Ecclesiastica* 3.29, 36, 39.

The Woman Taken in Adultery

In the case of the story of the woman taken in adultery, which was almost certainly not included in the original text of the Gospel of John, the story was introduced into the canon because it had always been part of the oral traditions about Jesus' life but had never been recorded by any of the evangelists. In fact, after we look more closely at the story and how it was understood in early Christianity, it will become apparent why the story was placed in its current position after John 7:51. This evidence reveals that the canon continued to be an open book, inasmuch as additions could still occur for several centuries after the texts were written. By the early second century, many of the books now recognized as canonical had gained a strong foothold in early Christianity, a position they would never relinquish.[13] Over the course of the second century and into the early third century, the twenty-seven books of the New Testament gained wide circulation, and the foundation to their acceptance as canonical texts was laid. Slowly, over the course of the first three hundred years after Jesus' death, extracanonical books, many of them known today as the apocrypha, were pared away as their authorship, provenance, and doctrines came under suspicion.[14]

The Context of the Story

The story of the woman caught in adultery contains several internal features that may have contributed to the way it was passed on through the first centuries after the death of Jesus. First, and perhaps the most glaring issue, is whether Jesus forgave the adulterous woman too readily, particularly in a society where most of the members had been raised believing that those guilty of adultery should be stoned (Leviticus 20:10). How Christians of the first two

[13] See Bruce M. Metzger, *The Canon of the New Testament: Its Origin, Development, and Significance* (Oxford: Oxford, 1997); and Bruce M. Metzger and Bart D. Ehrman, *The Text of the New Testament: Its Transmission, Corruption, and Restoration*, 4th ed. (Oxford: Oxford, 2005).

[14] Metzger, *The Canon of the New Testament*, 39–108.

centuries dealt with adultery within their ranks is unclear, but it is not beyond the realm of possibility that they continued to believe that the principle of Leviticus 20 was applicable, even though they had no authority to carry it out in their respective societies. Jesus' statement to the adulterous woman, "Neither do I condemn thee: go, and sin no more," contains what many modern scholars have felt was an overly lenient stance on adultery (John 8:11).[15] Unfortunately, no commentary from the first centuries after Jesus' death survives to substantiate that such an interpretation was ever adopted by Christians.

The counter argument to this conjecture is that Jesus does not explicitly excuse or forgive the woman for her sins; in fact, His statement "Neither do I condemn thee: go, and sin no more" may be nothing more than a legal statement about Jesus' personal authority to carry out a punishment mandated in the law of Moses. In this particular instance, after the eyewitnesses to the act of adultery had departed, Jesus, as a sole testimony to the woman's adultery, could not legally convict her of her sins because at least two witnesses were required by the law of Moses; therefore, she was free to go. The Joseph Smith Translation adds an important detail to the story that supports this conclusion. When Jesus raised Himself from the ground, He "saw none of her accusers," a reading that supports the conclusion that Jesus' statement to the woman was based, in part, on the fact that He could not condemn her as a single witness.

Another option, which places the decision to exclude this story into the hands of those who heard it or knew directly of it, is that those who retold the stories of Jesus' life passed over this story in their accounts because of something they perceived in it. Stories and teachings are often withheld in particular settings because of their sacred nature, doctrine, or difficulty to be understood. The choice to withhold a story or teaching in a given setting is most

[15] See Harald Riesenfeld, "The Pericope *de adultera* in the Early Christian Tradition," in *The Gospel Tradition* (Philadelphia: Fortress Press, 1970), 95–110.

often made by the person speaking and is rarely mandated by an outside commandment or practice. In the story of the woman caught in adultery, where so often conspiring intentions or calculated decisions are presupposed, the eyewitnesses themselves may have chosen not to tell this story for their own personal reasons, possibly a result of what they felt to be a difficult teaching on adultery, particularly in light of Jesus' other teachings on adultery where its definition is sharpened rather than softened.[16] The eyewitnesses had the privilege of asking Jesus what He meant when He spoke to the woman caught in adultery if they did not initially understand what was meant, but such a privilege was not available to the masses of Christians who converted after the resurrection; therefore, this teaching may have been too controversial in communities where other greater issues of doctrine and practice existed (see 1 Corinthians 1:10–11). The fact that the story of the woman caught in adultery appears in none of the early manuscripts (nor is it quoted by any of the early Church leaders) favors the conclusion that the story was initially limited in its dissemination by those who heard or saw it take place instead of having it removed by conspiring individuals who wanted to alter the text of the New Testament.

A second internal issue of the story is the location where the event takes place. Regardless of the motives of those who brought the woman to Jesus, the fact that Jesus is in the temple when they approach Him raises a serious legal issue. At the time of Jesus, great teachers commonly taught within the walls of the temple; therefore, His presence in the temple would not have been viewed as disruptive or peculiar. However, the fact that a legal decision is being considered within the walls of the temple is surprising—

[16] In the Sermon on the Mount, Jesus expanded the common definition of adultery to include adultery of the heart (Matthew 5:28) and to include those who divorced (Matthew 5:32). In both of these instances, the traditional definition of adultery was expanded to include acts that were not proscribed in the law of Moses and, in the second instance, acts that were not looked upon with disfavor. Therefore, those who heard Jesus teach the Sermon on the Mount may have been surprised by His teachings to the woman caught in adultery.

particularly a legal decision by someone other than the members of the Sanhedrin.

During the first century A.D., while the temple was still standing, the Sanhedrin most likely met in the temple for official business. The members of the Sanhedrin were the only Jews who held the legal right to make decisions regarding the law; and, in many instances, their powers to make decisions and carry out sentences were limited because they were subject to Roman rule. In this instance, Jesus' opponents asked Him to make a decision that He could not legally make according to Jewish law. Moreover, the tension of the situation was compounded because it took place within the walls of the temple—where a directive to stone someone by one who has no authority to make such a decision could be viewed as treasonous.

The problem is often expressed in terms of the temple's proximity to the Antonia Fortress, which in the days of Jesus functioned as a garrison for Roman soldiers (see Acts 21:31–40), with the possibility that Roman procurators and governors stayed there while they were in Jerusalem. If the Antonia Fortress housed at least a small garrison of Roman soldiers, then an act creating a public disturbance in such close proximity to their domicile would immediately draw their attention, particularly a public riot, which would be dispersed without delay.

A third glaring issue of the story is the presence of only the woman caught in adultery. Regardless of anyone's definition of adultery, the act requires two individuals; and, in this instance, only the woman is brought forward for punishment. A host of possibilities exist that would explain why the man is not present or mentioned. The most fanciful possibility is that he bribed the arresting party, whereas the woman was unable to pay the price of the bribe.[17] The most common reasons given why the adulterous man is not present are that his sentence had already been carried out, the

[17] J. Duncan M. Derrett, "Law in the New Testament: The Story of the Woman Taken in Adultery," *New Testament Studies* 10 (1963): 7.

act of adultery was a setup by Jesus' opponents, or the man was able to escape. Another possibility would also explain why no man is present: Jesus had previously taught that remarried divorcees were guilty of adultery (Matthew 5:31–2), and therefore the Pharisees may have been presenting Jesus with the logical consequence of His teachings, which was that remarried divorcees who were considered by Jesus to be guilty of adultery should be stoned according to the law of Moses' punishment for adultery.[18] Given the current focus of the story, the reason for the man's absence is, in reality, a superfluous detail because the story in its present form is told in the context of a trap. However, almost all commentators have tended to point out the man's absence as a further detail in the conspiracy to trap Jesus. For the author of the story, as it is told in this instance, the man's whereabouts are not of interest; the fact that the woman has been caught in the very act of adultery is the central concern. Nevertheless, the absence of the man from the story may reveal the unconscious male prejudice of Jewish leaders at the time—providing readers with information that was probably not intended by the author but that is potentially revealing for those attempting to reconstruct the social reality of the first century.

These three central issues in the story of the woman caught in adultery likely had some influence on the way the story was told and retold in Christian congregations. To compound the problem, the off-color subject matter of the story—a woman caught in the very act of committing adultery—may have contributed to the limited circulation among Christian congregations. What is so important about the history of the transmission of this story is that generations of scholars have sought, with little success, a reason why Church leaders would expunge this story from the Christian canon when, in reality, a more convincing argument can be made that the eyewitness generation intentionally curtailed the dissemination of this story among early Christian congregations because of its inherent doctrinal complexity and subject matter. Placing the

[18] Alan Watson, "Jesus and the Adulteress," *Biblica* 80 (1999): 103.

burden of proof for the absence of the story of the woman caught in adultery on the simple matter that Jesus appears to have been too lenient on the adulterous woman raises the question of how obvious such an interpretation really is in this story.

This specific interpretation of Jesus' statement to the adulterous woman is not obvious from the current context, nor is it evident in the words "Neither do I condemn thee" (John 8:11). Modern Latter-day Saint commentators, many who may have not been aware of the textual problems associated with this pericope, have also insisted that such an interpretation of Jesus' words in this instance contradicts the doctrine of the kingdom as well as of His teachings elsewhere. For example, the following statement eloquently states the doctrinal problem with an immediate forgiveness of sins being granted in this instance: "This is not in any sense a pardon, nor is our Lord condoning an adulterous act. He does not say, 'Go in peace, thy sins are forgiven thee.' He merely declines to act as a magistrate, judge, witness, or participant of any kind in a case that legally and properly should come before an official tribunal of which he is not a member."[19] Instead of making this rather inconspicuous account fall victim to the conspiring intentions of Church leaders, who, in this instance, would have removed something with relatively little doctrinal impact, the history of this story reveals something of the way the canon came into existence.

How the Eyewitness Tradition Shaped the Development of the Canon

For the first century and a half after the death of Jesus, the history of the development of the New Testament lies in murky waters, clouded by the lack of surviving documents and made more difficult to understand because of the many opinions about how the canon came into existence. The story of the woman caught in adultery, however, is a vital piece of evidence for understanding

---

[19] Bruce R. McConkie, *Doctrinal New Testament Commentary: Volume 1, The Gospels* (Salt Lake City: Bookcraft, 1987), 451.

how the canon was shaped by the eyewitness tradition even after the written Gospels had been composed. Regarding the history of the story of the woman caught in adultery, the most likely scenario for its transmission is that those who experienced it firsthand chose to pass it on in limited fashion, perhaps being persuaded that its inherent difficulties made it problematic and that the subject matter of the story may have been inappropriate for some audiences. However, the story certainly originates from a historical encounter of Jesus, His opponents, and a woman who had been caught in sin. Moreover, the eyewitnesses, although they told the story sparingly, did indeed present this story on occasion.

Later, the evangelists, who either followed the lead of the eyewitness tradition in retelling this story or were unaware of it because of its limited circulation, chose not to include it in their Gospel accounts. This is particularly surprising because John, the author who is most closely associated personally with Jesus, did not tell the story. Instead, the Gospel of John lacked John 8:1–11, which, if read without this story in place, presents a continuous narrative. Read in this manner, the Gospel presents a division among the crowd regarding the Messiahship of Jesus, which goes unresolved—apparently because a substantial group among them had faith in Jesus. This story is then interrupted by a subplot of the Pharisees who had sent officers to arrest Jesus but who, upon hearing Him teach, were moved by the power of His words (John 7:45–53). This plot by the Pharisees falls apart because of internal dissension among them, initiated in part by Nicodemus; and, in the end, each man of the Pharisaic gathering went his own way, allowing for the possibility that at least some of them recognized the power and authority of Jesus.

Following the original outline of the Gospel of John, Jesus then seized on the opening in the conversation caused by the division among the people and taught them with power about His being the "light of the world" (John 8:12). The preceding focus of conversation had been on whether Jesus was the "Christ" (John 7:41), and

John 8:12 builds logically on that foundation, with Jesus teaching in power concerning His true identity. This outcome presents a logical conclusion to their dissensions, with Jesus offering personal testimony to those who were ready and willing to accept Him.

The absence of the story of the woman caught in adultery in the written Gospel accounts and its later incorporation into the canon based on oral traditions seem to be confirmed by a statement of Papias as recorded by Eusebius in the fourth century A.D.: "And he [Papias] recounted another story of a woman who was accused of a multitude of sins before the Lord, which the Gospel of the Hebrews contains" (Historia Ecclesiastica 3.39; author's translation). The identity of the enigmatic Gospel to the Hebrews has yet to be unraveled, but the way Eusebius tells the story clearly indicates that Papias recounted the story orally, even though it was supposedly written in the Gospel to the Hebrews. Papias' reference to another story of a woman accused of many sins appears similar to the story in John 8 as the woman caught in adultery, although Papias seems to know more about it than our present source provides. This piece of evidence suggests that individuals like Papias, who had actually heard the eyewitnesses teach, continued to pass on orally certain stories from the life of Jesus that were not found in the canonical Gospels. The remarkable feature of this story is that because of its obvious authenticity and reliability, it was introduced into the canon, even though it was not written by the author of the Gospel in which it was placed.[20]

[20] The conclusion that the story of the woman taken in adultery was not written by the author of the Gospel of John may seem to some to be overly hasty. Scholarly studies on the issues of similarity of grammar, syntax, and wording between the story of the woman taken in adultery and that of the Gospel of John has led to the conclusion that two different authors are at work. My own studies on the issue have led to a similar conclusion, and although it seems prudent to recognize that another author wrote the story of the woman taken in adultery, it also seems prudent to draw the conclusion that the author of the story of the adulteress was someone who was intimately familiar with the synoptic Gospels (Matthew, Mark, and Luke). For the most comprehensive study on the issue, see Daniel B. Wallace, "Reconsidering 'The Story of Jesus and the Adulteress Reconsidered,'" *New Testament Studies* 39 (1993): 290–96.

Ancient Interpretation of the Story of the Woman Caught in Adultery

In John 7, Jesus confronted His adversaries regarding a previous healing on the Sabbath for which He had been condemned because it violated the prohibition against work on the seventh day. Jesus then presented them with a logical corollary: If in the law a young boy is allowed to be circumcised on the eighth day, even when the eighth day falls on the Sabbath, therefore making him whole and pure, then would it not be more holy to heal someone on the Sabbath and thus make that person whole and pure? Jesus followed up with the directive, "Judge not according to the appearance, but judge righteous judgment" (John 7:23–4). The underlying argument is that hypocrisy, particularly in judging others, is a sin surpassing any supposed infraction of which they had accused Jesus. At issue is the narrow-mindedness of Jesus' accusers, whose sole point for judging Jesus so harshly is the definition of whether an act of healing constitutes work and therefore violates the commandment to keep the Sabbath day holy.

As a follow-up, Nicodemus reintroduces the same theme in his defense of Jesus to the Sanhedrin, where he states that Jesus cannot be condemned unless He is given an opportunity to defend Himself against His accusers. The theme of hypocrisy in judgment is again raised, this time in the Sanhedrin itself, where the Jews who have traditionally held the law of Moses to be absolute are on the verge of violating that law because of their united opposition to Jesus. As if to prove they are guilty of hypocrisy in judgment, the Jews cite the precedent that the requirement for a defense is superseded in this issue because there is no prophecy of a Galilean Messiah. Jesus, in their minds a Galilean, must therefore be a false Messiah (John 7:52).

John 8:12 continues clarifying the concept of righteous judgment, where Jesus teaches that His judgment is just because it follows what the Father has taught, whereas Jesus' opponents judge only according to the flesh. The issue is again hypocrisy and the point of reference because, in their haste to condemn Jesus, His opponents have considered only the minor issue of whether an act of healing constitutes work and not whether the will of the Father was carried out or whether mercy was extended. Therefore, Jesus' opponents had judged "after the flesh" (John 8:15).

The story line of John 7–8 is cohesive, presenting a continuous line of argumentation on hypocritical judgment that has led to the condemnation of Jesus and His message. As scribes were faced with placing the story of the woman caught in adultery into the canon, they must have sought to fit it into position within the story where they believed it took place. Perhaps they even had some tradition of where the story took place in the life of Jesus.[21] The most common location for placing the story was after John 7:53, which interrupts the flow of the larger story line but at the same time fits into the story line because of its similar theme about unrighteous judgment. In placing the story in this location, early Christian scribes have inadvertently revealed their understanding of the passage, which, interestingly, they placed in the context of a discourse on hypocritical judgment instead of placing it alongside another teaching on adultery to counteract what many modern scholars have felt was too lenient of a position on forgiving adultery.

The way the story works in its present context is to exemplify how a seemingly obvious case of judgment, a woman who has been caught in the very act of adultery and for whom there is no question of guilt, can demonstrate that judgment is not always as obvious as it initially appears to be. In fact, the adulterous woman should be a fairly straightforward case of judgment, and Jesus could have easily invoked the precedent that the Romans would not let the Jews carry out the proper sentence mandated in the law of Moses, even though that was the proper course of action. On the

[21] Scribes definitely had varying views on where the story of the woman caught in adultery should be placed because one family of manuscripts f^{13} placed the story after Luke 21:38, thus showing that although scribes had some disagreement over where the story belonged, only a limited number of possibilities existed. The story is also found in other locations in the Gospel of John in very late Greek manuscripts.

other hand, Jesus is shown throughout the Gospels to have been merciful and forgiving of sinners and therefore may have been merciful on this occasion. Behind the question of Jesus' opponents is an intentional trap that would turn the multitudes against Him in the event that He spoke against the mandate of the law of Moses or presented, at the same time, the possibility that Jesus would contradict Himself by ordering the woman to be stoned.[22]

In this heated and volatile environment, where Jesus' very answer could incite a riot of words and where the obvious conclusion to the question of the scribes and Pharisees is that the woman should be stoned, Jesus reveals a divine standard of judgment, a standard that sublimely undermined the obviousness of the supposed sentence and taught against hypocrisy in judgment. Standing in front of Jesus, with the woman in their midst, the scribes and Pharisees seemed to have adopted the foregone conclusion that they should stone the woman, an act that was very pro-Jewish but also very anti-Roman. Initially, Jesus ignored their challenging questions, likely providing Him an opportunity to formulate a response. After considering the matter at hand, Jesus stood up and presented the divine postulate, "He that is without sin among you, let him first cast a stone at her" (John 8:7). The brilliance of the response is that it answers their inquiry without answering it directly. The request for Jesus to make immediate judgment was avoided while the need for a judgment to be made was placed back on the shoulders of those who initiated the inquiry.

Profound logic has a way of undermining the perceptions of the five senses, and even though Jesus' interlocutors had clear evidence about the woman's guilt, the divine logic of Jesus placed in front of them a new precedent for their consideration. No one present on that day appears to have had a legal right to condemn the woman as the story is told in its current form, for neither Jesus nor apparently those who brought the woman forward were members of the

[22] Zane Clark Hodges, "The Woman Taken in Adultery (John 7:53–8:11): Exposition," *Bibliotheca Sacra* 137 (1980): 45.

Jewish council of elders. Therefore, the legal question of the woman's guilt could not be decided on that day. However, an astute observation by Jesus taught the powerful principle that even in situations of obvious judgment, other matters of divine importance should be considered. Whether Jesus intended it as a universal principle to be applied in all matters of judgment seems unlikely, but given the context of making judgments hypocritically, it seems that the underlying principle Jesus taught was that we may often make hypocritical judgments even when we think that we have all the facts necessary to decide the case. What could be more obvious than the case of a woman caught in the very act of adultery? Such a heinous crime deserved an immediate and harsh punishment. In the end, as Jesus taught, judgment should be made in consultation with the Father as He had done (John 8:16).

In placing the story of the woman caught in adultery after John 7:53, Christian scribes revealed their interpretation of this story as relating to hypocritical judgment and not the modern concern that Jesus was too lenient on adultery. In fact, such an interpretation may never have been a consideration for early Christians.

Conclusion

The history of the canon plays an important part in our relationship to the body of scripture known today as the Bible. Our understanding of the great apostasy and the restoration of the gospel in the latter days paints a picture of upheaval, conspiracy, wickedness, and corruption in the centuries after the death of Jesus and His Apostles. In this worldview, the New Testament was composed and passed on through generations of Christians, finally making its way into our hands. We believe that the Bible did not reach us unscathed; rather, "we believe the Bible to be the word of God as far as it is translated correctly" (Articles of Faith 1:8).

Believing that the Bible is both the word of God and also contains errors creates an interesting dilemma for our understanding of how the Bible came to be. The earlier the date of the beginning of the great apostasy, the earlier the Bible was subject to alteration; whereas the later the date of the beginning of the great apostasy, the greater likelihood that the Bible preserves the word of God as it was originally intended. Therefore, efforts to push the corruption of the Bible into the era around Nicea (A.D. 325) must contend with the possibility that the current New Testament existed largely unscathed for nearly 250 years after it was composed. On the other hand, those who date the beginning of the apostasy to the period immediately after the deaths of the first Twelve Apostles, circa A.D. 70, must contend with the possibility that the New Testament was subject to corrupting influences almost immediately after it was composed. The answers to these issues are complex; and, as more detail surfaces about the first and second centuries, the more nuanced the answers will be.

In a single instance, the story of the woman caught in adultery survives as clear evidence of textual alteration based on oral tradition. As the story unfolds, several likely conclusions can be drawn that shed some light on how the Bible was revered in the first centuries after Jesus' death and on how alterations were made. The eyewitnesses, in this case their identity unknown, passed on the stories of Jesus' life orally while at the same time inadvertently emphasizing certain stories through repetition and drawing attention away from other stories by infrequently retelling them. The desire to suppress some stories may have been intentional, in some instances, where audience or subject matter may have predetermined what could be taught. The story of the woman taken in adultery may have had limited circulation initially because of the aforementioned reasons. However, the story was certainly told and retold, as evidenced by Papias' later knowledge of a version of it around the year A.D. 100 attests.

Because the story of the woman taken in adultery had been told by those who witnessed it, it likely enjoyed canonical status, even though it was never placed in one of the written Gospels. As the Gospels took their final shape toward the end of the first century, many who had heard this story realized that no Gospel authors had included it in their narratives; therefore, over the next few centuries, it continued to be passed on orally alongside the written Gospel. For reasons now unknown, the story did not simply die out because of a decreasing lack of authority—a result of the passage of time between those who experienced it and those who were now retelling it. The story proved itself resilient to suppression, and at some time during the latter part of the fourth or fifth century, it was brought back into the canon and placed in the Gospel of John as well as the Gospel of Luke. Its position in the Gospel of John proved more convincing, and only a small percentage of manuscripts continued to place the story in the Gospel of Luke.

By placing the story in the Gospel of John, early Christian scribes also revealed their interpretation of the story. The story of the woman caught in adultery formed part of Jesus' teachings on hypocrisy in judgment and provided a physical example of how judgment based only on sense perception could be misguided, even when the sentence seems obvious. Who was responsible for composing the story in its present form is a detail hidden by the passage of time; but the authenticity of the story, as one that verifiably took place in the life of Jesus, seems unassailable.[23] Original context might help us learn more from the story as it currently stands; but, at the same time, the story teaches a powerful principle in its current context.

A corollary to this proposition is the fact that believing individuals continued to pass on orally the stories of Jesus that had not made it into the written Gospels. Their influence was so powerful in this instance that they were able to add to the text of the Gospel of John hundreds of years after it had been composed. This influence also bears record that at least some Christians in the late first and early second centuries A.D., and possibly even later, continued to offer an external check on alterations, and hopefully corruptions, of the text of the New Testament. Several other sayings of Jesus,

[23] Daniel Wallace, "Reconsidering," 290–96.

known today as the *agrapha* (not written or included), are also included in the New Testament, perhaps undergoing a similar process that the story of the woman caught in adultery experienced. For example, in Acts 20:35, Luke adds a saying that he failed to include in His Gospel: "Remember the words of the Lord Jesus, how he said, It is more blessed to give than to receive." Luke may have felt pressure to include this well-known saying elsewhere when he did not include it in his Gospel account. Likewise, Paul includes a statement from oral tradition when he says "that we which are alive and remain unto the coming of the Lord shall not prevent them which are asleep" (1 Thessalonians 4:15). In both instances, as in the woman taken in adultery, oral tradition shaped the written tradition in a positive way by introducing other teachings and sayings of Jesus that would otherwise have been lost.

XV.

THE TRIUMPHAL ENTRY

THOMAS A. WAYMENT

One of the few stories told in all four Gospel accounts is that of Jesus' triumphal entry into Jerusalem on the day that has come to be known as Palm Sunday, a day made famous because of the crowds who shouted "Hosanna" at Jesus' arrival and covered the road with palm branches and clothing (Matthew 21:6–11; Mark 11:7–11; Luke 19:35–38; John 12:12–18). The Triumphal Entry, which is historically placed on the Sunday prior to the Resurrection, marks the beginning of the last week of Jesus' life—or what many Christians refer to as the Passion Week.[1] In the context of the three-year ministry, the triumphal entry marks the official beginning of the events that led to the death of Jesus, including many of the most important acts that constituted the Atonement.

As with any historical event, the triumphal entry has been interpreted from a variety of different angles: as an act against the Roman government, as a statement of judgment against the Jerusalem temple, as an attempt to enthrone Jesus as king, and as a humble sign of Jesus' role as Messiah. Without doubt, the significance of the triumphal entry was interpreted differently by those who opposed Jesus and those who believed in Him, and perhaps

[1] The day of the week of the triumphal entry is ascertained from the Gospel of John, which records that "Jesus six days before the passover came to Bethany" (John 12:1). The Passover was celebrated on the eve of the Sabbath (modern Saturday); therefore, the triumphal entry must have taken place on the Sunday prior.

Jesus intended something different than even what His disciples and followers ascribed to it at first. No single interpretation of the event can comprehend the variety of possible explanations of the impact of Jesus' entry into the holy city at the time of Passover in the spring of A.D. 30.

The most important interpretation of the triumphal entry is that given the event by Jesus himself. Interpretations by others reveal something of their hearts and minds, providing another context for the study of the life and ministry of Jesus. However, only Jesus' intentions on that day can reveal what was supposed to happen and what He intended His followers to understand. From the surviving Gospel accounts, Jesus' intentions can best be described as an overt, deliberately public act, revealing His role as Messiah-King, an act that was made without equivocation and without any reticence to keep the Savior's identity secret as during the early part of His ministry.[2]

Social Context

It may seem strange to modern sensibilities to think that a prophet would walk for three years in the streets, "naked and barefoot," in an attempt to teach the Israelites that the Lord would bring another nation into captivity (Isaiah 20:2–4). Or it may seem strange that the prophet Ezekiel shaved his head and then divided the hair into three portions, burning a third, smiting a third with a knife, and scattering a third in the wind (Ezekiel 5:1–4). These dramatic signs, however, were not uncommon in ancient Israel—a people separated not only by time and space but also by a religious and cultural environment that often seems quite foreign to the modern world. In their dispensation, the Lord often chose to reinforce spiritual lessons using physical signs and demonstrations. These signs were intended to be dramatic, but in equal fashion, they were intended to be public demonstrations so that members from all levels of society could witness the message of the prophet.

[2] See, for example, Mark 7:36.

In this environment, prophets commonly asked equally physical demonstrations of believers. For example, the prophet Elisha told Naaman the Syrian to wash himself seven times in the river Jordan so he would be healed of leprosy (2 Kings 5:10). Such physical requirements, however unusual, were intended to reveal the inner faith of the believer, and certainly while they could be misinterpreted as the *reason* they were healed, these physical requirements were only outward manifestations demonstrating that the believer could muster enough faith to be healed. Although many of these events are quite distant historically from the first century, Josephus reports that such dramatic acts were commonplace among Jews in the first century, both in Galilee and Judea.[3]

Therefore, if generations of prophets had revealed the word of the Lord in both spoken and dramatic form, it should not be surprising that Jesus, living in that world, would do likewise during His mortal ministry. One important aspect of the triumphal entry is its dramatic character, which could not be overlooked by the crowds and which may have been witnessed by hundreds, if not thousands, of individuals at once. If a list were made of all the cities that Jesus was known to have visited during His mortal ministry, we would find that Jesus preferred to teach in very small towns and villages, usually with populations of less than two or three thousand people, and only on a few occasions did He visit larger cities such as Tyre, Sidon, and Jerusalem. The mortal ministry developed in the small hamlets of Galilee, where it would have been common for only a handful of individuals to witness what took place. What is surprising is that even among these small rural communities, large crowds of people began to gather in support of Jesus (see Matthew 14:13–21; Mark 6:33–44; Luke 9:11–17; John 6:5–14).

The social setting of the triumphal entry can best be interpreted in light of Old Testament prophetic signs. Jesus left the familiar environs of Galilee and traveled to the population center of Judaism, Jerusalem, to do something public, an act that had no

[3] See, for example, Josephus, *JW*, 2.17.6–9.

precedent in the mortal ministry. Such prophetic signs were always intended to reveal the mind and will of the Lord in a dramatic way. On this occasion, Jesus made known the will of the Father in a way that those who had followed Him up to this point could know His intentions, even though the potential to misunderstand was still certainly an issue for some, whereas those who opposed Him would have an equally clear picture of what He intended to do. Unfortunately, as the mortal ministry makes clear, the potential to misinterpret and misunderstand, both by Jesus' antagonists and believers, is still a significant obstacle in understanding the full import of His intentions.

Prophecies and Symbols of the Triumphal Entry

Two parallel prophecies from the Old Testament provide a prophetic backdrop for the triumphal entry, one from the sixth century B.C., Zechariah, and another that has been attributed to King David, Psalm 118. Zechariah taught the children of Israel in the days of her return from Babylonian exile, "Rejoice greatly, O daughter of Zion; shout, O daughter of Jerusalem: behold, thy King cometh unto thee: he is just, and having salvation; lowly, and riding upon an ass, and upon a colt the foal of an ass" (9:9). The second prophecy supplied some of the language of praise offered by the crowd, who shouted, "Blessed be he that cometh in the name of the Lord" (Psalm 118:26).[4] These prophecies helped lay the foundation upon which Jesus would build on the day of the triumphal entry, and for those who recalled the prophecy, these utterances would have created an environment of spiritual familiarity.

Looking more closely into the wording of these two prophecies reveals two features that are often unnoticed when we read the accounts of the triumphal entry. First, the prophecy of Zechariah relates that the "King" of Israel is he who would be riding on the donkey, and second that the same King would have "salvation,"

[4] See Edwin D. Freed, "Entry into Jerusalem in the Gospel of John," *Journal of Biblical Literature* 80 (1961): 329–38.

thus tying together the concepts of a royal Savior. Jesus, up to that point in the ministry, had never made any personal claims to the kingship of Israel, although in the Gospel of John, Nathanael calls Jesus "the Son of God . . . the King of Israel," and later some followers attempted to "take him by force, to make him a king" (John 1:49; 6:15). In either instance, Jesus did not rebuke those who called or attempted to make Him king; instead, He seems to have passed over the issue without significant comment. A specific public claim to the kingship of Israel waited until the day of the triumphal entry.

In ancient Israel, following the introduction of kingship in about 1000 B.C. and perhaps continuing until the Babylonian exile in 586 B.C., the Israelites celebrated an annual reenthronement ritual of their king. Among the many rituals that constituted this reenthronement ceremony, the king rode into the holy city on a donkey and was crowned again as the legal and just king of the land.[5] The king was also required to be abased or humiliated at the gates of the city previous to entering in triumphal fashion. The approach of the king was to take place from the eastern part of the city, the Mount of Olives in the New Testament, or from the direction of the Kidron Valley in Old Testament terminology.[6] The act of riding a donkey into the city of Jerusalem or into the temple became an act intricately intertwined with the enthronement of the king of Israel, and although certainly any individual could ride a donkey into the city without creating a stir, Jesus' entry made it clear that His was not an ordinary entrance.

In the Old Testament, Absalom, David's son, was riding a donkey when he became caught by the hair in the branches of an oak tree, thus allowing him to be slain by Joab. Absalom had tried to take the kingship away from his father, David, and he rode the donkey in defiance of his father's kingship (2 Samuel 18:9–18).

---

[5] James A. Sanders, "A New Testament Hermeneutic Fabric: Psalm 118 in the Entrance Narrative," *Early Jewish and Christian Exegesis* (1987): 177–79.

[6] Joseph Blenkinsopp, "The Oracle of Judah and the Messianic Entry," *Journal of Biblical Literature* 80 (1961): 55–64.

Later, Solomon rode a donkey to the Kidron Valley to circumvent Adonijah's claim to the throne of David (1 Kings 1:32–53). Riding a donkey was a common symbol of kingship, perhaps because of its association with abasement.

Perhaps the most vivid, and indeed recent, antecedent to the triumphal entry took place when Jewish troops under the direction of Simon recaptured the citadel in Jerusalem from Syrian domination. When the Jews reentered the city, they "entered it with praise and palm branches, and with harps and cymbals and stringed instruments, and with hymns and songs, because a great enemy had been crushed and removed from Israel" (1 Maccabees 13.51). Simon's triumphal entry was accompanied by the waving of palm branches, as well as public recognition of Simon's legitimacy to rule Israel, even if some did not agree with his methods or tactics. Simon's intentions were clear, and those who saw Jesus ride into Jerusalem in similar fashion would have known of this famous parallel as well as the ramifications of His actions.

As the synoptic Gospel authors are careful to point out, the donkey on which Jesus rode was provided miraculously, its owner having been prepared beforehand, probably through revelation, to allow the disciples to simply take it (Matthew 21:1–3; Mark 11:1–6; Luke 19:29–34). The Gospel authors are also careful to point out that Jesus did not ride the donkey all the way from where He had been staying previously but rather from Bethany and Bethphage, the eastern limits of the city of Jerusalem (Mark 11:1).[7] Therefore, when Jesus rode the donkey into the holy city, it was not an act born of fatigue or weariness but rather an intentional decision made on the outskirts of the holy city.

Following ancient tradition, particularly traditions associated

[7] On the importance of riding a donkey, see J. D. M. Derrett, "Law in the New Testament: The Palm Sunday Colt," *Novum Testamentum* 13 (1971): 255. Some scholars have seen in the statement from Mark 11:2 and Luke 19:30 that the donkey on which Jesus rode had never before been ridden, a further sign of royalty. A donkey on which others had ridden was not fit for the service of the king. See S. Lewis Johnson Jr., "The Triumphal Entry of Christ," *Bibliotheca Sacra* 124 (1967): 222.

with the enthronement of the king of Israel and the annual reenthronement ceremonies, Jesus made an intentionally bold move when He rode through the Kidron Valley and up to the walls of the Jerusalem temple. He seems to have made every preparation and to have gone "out of his way" to make a direct connection to the kings of Israel.[8] Jesus' ride into Jerusalem on a donkey was, in fact, much more deliberate and obvious than in the examples above. His claim was clear; the king of Israel had entered the holy city.

From the surviving evidence, Jesus' intent in riding triumphantly into the city of Jerusalem should be considered as a clarification of previously implied actions. Throughout the mortal ministry, believers and antagonists alike had questioned Jesus about whether He was the Messiah, a Davidic king, the son of David, the son of God, Elijah, or one of the prophets come back from the dead; but on each of these occasions, as represented in the Gospel accounts, Jesus avoided any direct response to their inquiries and, in fact, often permitted their misconceptions to remain intact. Unlike the earlier years of the public ministry, the triumphal entry was, in essence, a move to clarify intentions and identity, both for those who opposed Jesus and particularly for those who believed in Him.

Certainly some would have supported Jesus' actions on the day of the triumphal entry because He acted against the aristocracy and ruling high-priestly factions, but others would have felt their testimonies grow as they realized that the triumphal entry was also a clarification for those who could grasp its meaning. On the other hand, many would have seen the triumphal entry as overly judgmental or critical, and for those who missed the full impact of His statement, Jesus' true identity would remain hidden.

The Date of the Triumphal Entry and Its Implications

Scholarly attempts to associate the cleansing of the temple on the day of, or day after, Jesus' triumphal entry with the Feast of

[8] Sanders, "A New Testament Hermeneutic Fabric," 179.

Dedication or Tabernacles, which took place in autumn, have mistaken the cleansing as an act of rededication rather than an act of judgment and condemnation.[9] Moreover, the date of the triumphal entry cannot be directly adduced from the presence of palm branches because several varieties of palm trees were indigenous to the area and also have green foliage year round (see John 12:13).[10]

The most direct evidence for the Passover dating of the triumphal entry is the seemingly explicit statement in the Gospel of John, "Then Jesus six days before the passover," which explicitly states that Jesus came to Jerusalem before the Passover (ta pascha) (John 12:1).[11] One difficulty, however, with John's Passover dating is that it places Jesus' arrival in Bethany "six days" before the Passover and then proceeds to narrate that Jesus came into Jerusalem "the next day," which would be five days before the Passover and therefore on Monday rather than on the traditional Sunday dating. The Gospels are unanimous in their placement of the crucifixion on Friday and the Last Supper on Thursday.[12] If, however, the author of the Gospel of John counted the days between the Passover (sundown on Friday) and the day of the triumphal entry inclusively, then five days would be an accurate measurement, given the fact that the new day began at sundown rather than at midnight as in modern

[9] Matthew places the cleansing on the day of the triumphal entry (Matthew 21:12–13), whereas Mark and Luke place it on the day following (Mark 11:12, 15–19; Luke 19: 45–46), although Luke's account could allow the possibility that the cleansing took place on the day of the triumphal entry. F. C. Burkitt, "W and Θ: Studies in the Western Text of St. Mark (Hosanna)," *Journal of Theological Studies* 17 (1916): 139–52, ultimately opts for a Passover dating of the triumphal entry, even though the symbolism fits better in the context of the Feast of Tabernacles.

[10] John refers to *ta baia ton foinikon* (John 12:13), most accurately translated as palm branches, even though Mark is less specific about which type of branches were used (Mark 11:8). See N. C. Masterman, "The Date of the Triumphal Entry," *New Testament Studies* 16 (1969): 76–82.

[11] Compare with John 5:1, which refers to "a feast of the Jews." *The* feast, with the definite article, refers to the most celebrated Jewish feast, the Passover.

[12] See David Rolph Seely, "The Last Supper According to Matthew, Mark, and Luke," in Richard Neitzel Holzapfel and Thomas A. Wayment, *From the Last Supper through the Resurrection: The Savior's Final Hours* (Salt Lake City: Deseret Book, 2003), 64–74.

societies. The importance of this information is that the date of triumphal entry can be fixed with some degree of surety on the Sunday (Nisan 9 or 10) prior to the Friday (Nisan 14 or 15) crucifixion, which certainly took place at the beginning of the Jewish celebration of Passover.[13]

The importance of Nisan 9 or 10 can be surmised from Exodus 12:3, which states, "Speak ye unto all the congregation of Israel, saying, In the tenth day of this month they shall take to them every man a lamb, according to the house of their fathers, a lamb for an house." Nisan 10 had been designated by the Lord as the day on which the children of Israel should choose the paschal lamb, or the lamb that would be sacrificed as part of the Passover feast and celebration. If, therefore, Jesus rode triumphantly into Jerusalem on Nisan 10, He did so on the same day that the children of Israel were commanded to choose a sacrificial lamb, and therefore the triumphal entry presented Jesus as God's choice for the lamb of sacrifice. It is a powerful motif in the Gospels, and one that slips by with subtlety—but one that would have been readily apparent to all who were gathering as family units and busying themselves with making a proper selection for a paschal sacrifice.

The image of Jesus riding into Jerusalem triumphantly on the same day that the paschal lambs were being selected is filled with divine irony. Jesus in His most politically triumphant moment, in the very moment that His followers appear to outnumber the forces of opposition, is, in reality, the Son of God, proceeding innocently to His death as the divine lamb of sacrifice. Perhaps the authors of the Gospels wanted to underline the fact that Jesus' most triumphant moment was the act of atoning sacrifice.

Increasing Popularity and a Growing Threat

One point that the Gospel of John drives home more than the other Gospels is the growing undercurrent of opposition against

---

[13] For a discussion of the Jewish calendar and how it relates to the Roman and mondern calendar, see Appendix "Calendars" in this volume.

Jesus that resulted from the raising of Lazarus from death.[14] According to the Gospel of John, Jesus raised Lazarus shortly before the triumphal entry; in fact, the raising of Lazarus likely occurred in the winter months between the Feast of Dedication and Passover.[15] The miracle created a ripple effect in the Jewish community, for as some chief priests observed, "Because that by reason of him [Lazarus] many of the Jews went away, and believed on Jesus" (John 12:11). This ripple effect extended as far as the council of Pharisees and chief priests, likely a meeting of the Sanhedrin, which met to discuss the issue of Lazarus. As the group pondered the problem, they concluded, "It is expedient for us, that one man [Jesus] should die for the people, and that the whole nation perish not" (John 11:50). In other words, it would be better to take Jesus' life than to have the Romans come and take away their rights because of a possible insurrection initiated by the rabble-rouser Jesus and His ever-increasing following.

Jesus, in the months before the triumphal entry, had gained a sufficiently large following, one large enough that the Jewish leadership had taken notice. In Galilee, Jesus' followers had numbered into the thousands on several occasions, and on at least one occasion, they likely numbered more than ten thousand, perhaps as many as fifteen thousand (Matthew 14:21). Whether or not they believed in Jesus, the Jewish leaders were faced with a man who had pretensions of being the Messiah and who also was able to amass a crowd that numbered half as much as the entire population of Jerusalem.[16] The potential problem created by such a large following, led in this instance by one who taught that He was the Son of

[14] John A. T. Robinson, *The Priority of John* (London: SCM Press, 1984), 218–23.

[15] The Gospels, which consistently report Jesus traveling to Jerusalem to attend the various feasts, are silent during the period between the raising of Lazarus and Jesus' final trip to Jerusalem to attend Passover. Therefore, the logical conclusion is that no feasts took place between these two events, thereby placing the raising of Lazarus after the Feast of Dedication (early December) and the Feast of Passover (late March or early April).

[16] See Brent Kinman, "Parousia, Jesus' 'A-Triumphal Entry,' and the Fate of Jerusalem (Luke 19:28–44)," *Journal of Biblical Literature* 118 (1999): 289–93.

God—a term with definite messianic overtones—was that the Roman government in Judea was particularly suspicious of such groups and, in many instances, suppressed them with vigor.[17]

Jesus' growing popularity threatened to make inroads among the Jewish hierarchy, and in the minds of some Pharisees, their influence among the masses had been curtailed to a crucial point: "Perceive ye how ye prevail nothing? behold, the world is gone after him" (John 12:19). Whether Jesus posed a real or significant threat to the Jerusalem hierarchy, certain Jewish leaders perceived Him to be a threat, so much so that they decided to put Him to death as well as Lazarus (John 11:50–53; 12:10–11). Certainly, such actions represent the worst reactionary tendencies among the Jerusalem hierarchy, and some may question the Gospel author's knowledge of such subplots to kill Jesus and Lazarus. But the fact remains that all four primary accounts of the weeks before Jesus' arrest and crucifixion report that there was a palpable tension in Jerusalem and that several traps were set to turn the crowds against Jesus and His supposedly heretical teachings.

The social dynamics of Jesus' Jerusalem ministry had always been very different from those of His Galilean ministry. Unfortunately, many of the reasons for Jewish hostility toward Jesus in Jerusalem have been obscured by incomplete sources, but the difference in tenor is clear in the Gospels (see John 7:1–8).[18] Jesus' ministry in Galilee had been met with relative peace, and as the ministry progressed, an ever-increasing number of people were coming to see Jesus for themselves. What the triumphal entry was able to achieve was an infusion of Jesus' Galilean popularity into the hostile environment of Judaism. Jesus brought with Him a

---

[17] D. R. Schwartz, "Pontius Pilate," in Freedman, *ABD*, 5:395–401. For a balanced discussion, see Eric Huntsman, "Before the Romans," in Richard Neitzel Holzapfel and Thomas A. Wayment, *From the Last Supper through the Resurrection: The Savior's Final Hours* (Salt Lake City: Deseret Book, 2003), 272–80.

[18] An interesting discussion of the ramifications of Jesus' prophecies against Jerusalem can be found in Donald J. Verseput, "Jesus' Pilgrimage to Jerusalem and Encounter in the Temple: A Geographical Motif in Matthew's Gospel," *Novum Testamentum* 36 (1994): 105–20.

contingency of Galilean supporters into the capital of Judaism. His first action, on the very borders of the city, was to raise Lazarus from death, perhaps the most dramatic miracle of the three-year ministry. The raising of Lazarus had brought the popularity of the Galilean ministry close to the axis of the Jewish hierarchy. Their challenge was to surgically remove Jesus without causing a riot among His followers. The triumphal entry revealed to them the extent of Jesus' popularity, as well as the obstacle they faced in removing Him.

Increasing Popularity and Its Ramifications for Jesus' Followers

The Gospels reveal that Jesus taught His disciples about His true identity in small doses, couching the knowledge in terms they could more easily comprehend. For example, Nathanael called Jesus "Rabbi . . . the Son of God . . . the King of Israel," which is correct on one level but lacks complete comprehension of Jesus' identity (John 1:49). Later, after a dramatic miracle on the Sea of Galilee, the disciples proclaim, "What manner of man is this, that even the winds and the sea obey him!" (Matthew 8:27). The assumption that Jesus is a "man" with special powers is prevalent in this account. Later, Jesus tested the understanding of the disciples when He asked, "Whom do men say that I the Son of man am?" (Matthew 16:13). The question, intended to gauge both popular and apostolic opinion, drove home the point that the masses were still woefully ignorant of who He really was, whereas the disciples, personified by Peter, had come to a greater understanding of Jesus' true identity and mission (Matthew 16:14–16).

As the disciples' understanding continued to grow, so did that of the crowds, who with increasing fascination began to question whether "this is the Prophet [of Deuteronomy 18:18]" or whether "this is the Christ" (John 7:40–41). The crowds were continuing to grow in understanding, albeit comparatively at a slower pace than the disciples. As the mission of Jesus came into sharper focus for the crowds and for the disciples, even so Jesus began to make clearer, more precise statements regarding His mission and identity.

One way of doing this was to contextualize and interpret the prophecies of the Old Testament with regard to His own personal mission. For example, Isaiah 53, probably the clearest surviving prophecy of Jesus' first mission from the Old Testament, was not understood by Jews at the time of Christ to refer to the ministry of the Messiah. Once the connection is made between Isaiah 53 and the ministry of Christ, the interpretation of that passage seems to jump off the page, and a whole new depth of understanding comes into view. This can be said of Psalm 118 and Zechariah 9:9 also.[19]

In each of these two well-known prophecies, popular interpretation had taught the Israelites that they would be fulfilled in a moment of triumph, at a time when the monarchy in Israel would be restored. One of the prophecies, Psalm 118, envisions the return of Israel's king at a time when the temple was still standing. Therefore, the implications of someone fulfilling these two parallel prophecies would be that the person who did so would be both the legal king of Israel as well as God's anointed.[20] Whether the Jews believed that future king to also be the Messiah is now a matter of debate, and from our current sources, it appears that this future king was thought to be separate from the coming Messiah.

If, however, Jesus' disciples and followers had begun to look to Jesus as the literal fulfillment of the prophecy that Israel would once again have a king like David and that this future king would usher in a new dispensation of peace, then the triumphal entry would have been a positive sign to them that their king had arrived.[21] Pilate's inquiry of Jesus, "Art thou the King of the Jews?"

---

[19] On the Messianic nature of Psalm 118, see J. F. Coakley, "Jesus' Messianic Entry into Jerusalem," *Journal of Theological Studies* 46 (1995): 473–74.

[20] Coakley ("Jesus' Messianic Entry into Jerusalem," 463) has argued that the opponents of Jesus could not possibly have comprehended the connection between Jesus' actions and Zechariah 9:9.

[21] The belief that the future king of Israel, and in some cases the Messiah, would descend through the line of David is prevalent in Jewish thinking. Isaiah 16:5, for example, prophesies of the future king sitting "upon it [the throne] in truth in the

reveals that one of the popular beliefs about Jesus was that He thought Himself to be king of the Jews (Mark 15:2). This popular conception about Jesus continued throughout His life, likely until His crucifixion and death made it clear that He would not seize the throne of Israel.[22]

The antagonists of Jesus certainly did not believe that He was either the Messiah or the future Davidic king of Israel, and any such association would have been considered blasphemy by them (for example, Luke 4:16–32). Jesus was considered a commoner by them, one who had gathered a large following. If the Jewish hierarchy did not understand Psalm 118 or Zechariah—the Old Testament prophecies of the triumphal entry—to refer to the ministry of Jesus, then when Jesus approached the temple in literal fulfillment of those prophecies, those who believed in Him would be easily distinguished from those who did not.[23] The triumphal entry thus became a means of distinguishing those who were for and against Jesus, for those who shouted acceptance of Jesus' actions clearly believed in Him. The question that cannot be answered is whether Jesus intended the triumphal entry to be a demonstration of the strength of His followers, a revelation to the disciples of their future missionary field, or a test to see if the crowds would reject such a monarchical interpretation of Jesus' ministry and accept Him in His true identity as Suffering-Messiah—their Savior.

---

tabernacle of David, judging, and seeking judgment, and hasting righteousness." Jesus used this popular conception as the basis of a riddle when He asked, "What think ye of Christ? whose son is he? They say unto him, The Son of David" (Matthew 22:42).

[22] The theme of Jesus' becoming king, or being declared king, by some of His followers can be traced back to the feeding of the five thousand: "When Jesus therefore perceived that they would come and take him by force, to make him a king, he departed again into a mountain himself alone" (John 6:15).

[23] See Thomas A. Wayment, "Jesus' Use of the Psalms in Matthew," in *Covenants, Prophecies, and Hymns of the Old Testament*, ed. Victor Ludlow (Salt Lake City: Deseret Book, 2001), 281–85; Solomon Freehof, *The Book of Psalms* (Cincinnati: Union of American Hebrew Congregations, 1938), 338; Richard T. Mead, "A Dissenting Opinion about Respect for Context in Old Testament Quotations," *New Testament Studies* 10 (1963/64): 286–87.

The Ramifications of the Triumphal Entry

The triumphal entry revealed both the strengths and weaknesses of Jesus' followers. No one knew for certain until that point whether arresting Jesus would cause a serious backlash, inciting a riot that would encourage Roman intervention. According to the Gospel of Matthew, "a very great multitude" laid their garments in the streets and "strawed" the way with palm branches for Jesus' donkey to tread upon (Matthew 21:8). For the first time, it became abundantly clear that Jesus would have to be taken by stealth, away from the crowds, and hopefully away from His disciples. Apparently, according to the Gospel of Matthew, "All the city" had become aware of the triumphal entry (21:10).[24] As the Gospel accounts continue to narrate the final week of Jesus' life, the plot to capture Jesus unfolds to reveal that He was arrested quietly, in a grove of trees, away from the purview of "all the city" so that He might be taken with "subtlety" (Matthew 26:4).

A troubling feature of the triumphal entry, one for which there has been no satisfactory answer, is why there was not an immediate Roman response in answer to Jesus' actions.[25] A small Roman garrison was stationed in the Antonia Fortress, which was perhaps strengthened with additional troops with Pilate's arrival, within plain sight of the temple; and therefore the Roman occupying force would have been immediately aware of Jesus' actions.[26] Why they did not respond immediately remains unclear, but such a definitive act against the heart of Judaism warranted swift action. Perhaps

---

[24] This point has been made most forcefully by S. G. F. Brandon, *Jesus and the Zealots* (Manchester: University Press, 1967), 349–50.

[25] Some scholars have taken this as a sign that the triumphal entry is a fiction developed by the evangelists to perpetrate the idea of Jesus' popularity. See David R. Catchpole, "The 'Triumphal Entry,'" in E. Bammel and C. F. D. Moule, eds., *Jesus and the Politics of His Day* (Cambridge: Cambridge University Press, 1984), 319–34. Such studies have been received with great skepticism among scholars, yet they continue to represent the extremes of historical inquiry. For a more balanced inquiry, see B. C. McGing, "Pontius Pilate and the Sources," *Catholic Biblical Quarterly* 53 (1991): 416–38.

[26] Huntsman, "Before the Romans," 285.

historically the event went unnoticed by the soldiers in the Antonia Fortress. Certainly Jesus could, according to God's plan, ride a donkey into the temple amidst fanfare and then depart without reprisal. The reality of the matter, however, is that once news of this action came to the attention of the Roman soldiers, some type of correction to this unruly behavior would have to be offered.[27]

The triumphal entry warranted Roman intervention; it also made it impossible for Jesus to remain as a pacifist in the ensuing conflict. Jesus' triumphal entry into the Jerusalem temple, part of a continuing picture of denunciation of the Jerusalem hierarchy and of what the temple had become, was serious enough to warrant His death.[28] The triumphal entry spelled the end of Jesus' freedom; He could not continue to remain free after having acted so openly against the Jewish state.

For the disciples of Jesus, the triumphal entry had other serious ramifications, which are interestingly revealed by one evangelist and obscured by another. The immediate effect of the triumphal entry is that within a week, the twelve disciples would be without their Master. He had initiated the process that would result in His death, and the disciples had only a few days to spend with the Lord.

The second immediate effect is recorded only in the Gospel of John, which preserves a trace of the disciples' involvement on the day of the triumphal entry. The synoptic Gospels report that Jesus gave His disciples specific instructions regarding finding a suitable donkey for Him to ride into Jerusalem (Matthew 21:1–3; Mark 11:1–3; Luke 19:29–31). Only in the Gospel of John does the issue of finding an appropriate donkey escape mention, with the whole miracle associated with finding the donkey receiving no mention. John reports only, "And Jesus, when he had found a young ass, sat

[27] Josephus, *AJ*, 18:85–9 attests to Pilate's willingness to respond brutally to a supposed insurrection. Pilate misjudged the Samaritan problem and was subsequently called back to Rome, likely to answer for his actions in Samaria.

[28] Thomas A. Wayment, "Responsibility for the Death of Jesus," in Richard Neitzel Holzapfel and Thomas A. Wayment, eds., *From the Last Supper through the Resurrection: The Savior's Final Hours* (Salt Lake City: Deseret Book, 2003), 432–38.

thereon; as is written" (John 12:14). According to the synoptic Gospels, the disciples became complicit in Jesus' actions the moment they went for the donkey, whereas in the Gospel of John, the disciples remained on the sidelines when Jesus began His ascent into Jerusalem.

Later in the Gospel of John, however, John reports, "Then remembered they that these things were written of him, and that *they had done these things unto him*" (John 12:16; emphasis added). Whereas in the synoptic Gospels the disciples had been complicit in obtaining the donkey on which Jesus rode, in John, the disciples are responsible for the triumphal entry.[29] At the heart of this statement lies some important fact that has been omitted from the record. Did John intend to write that the disciples were literally responsible for the triumphal entry, that they had physically caused it to happen, or did he intend to say that their misunderstanding and inability to alter the course of events led to Jesus' death, which was precipitated by the triumphal entry? The synoptic authors all record that the disciples were involved; the Gospel of John reports that the disciples were *responsible.*

In either case, the disciples could not turn back from their devotion to Jesus in the wake of the triumphal entry. They became His disciples in the eyes of the multitudes and the Jewish leaders on that day. They became permanently associated with Jesus and His fate, for they had publicly declared and demonstrated that He was their king and Lord; and despite any misgivings by the Jewish hierarchy, they believed Jesus to be the fulfillment of Old Testament prophecy. The Gospels also report that great crowds gathered on that day to celebrate Jesus' entry (Matthew 21:8; Mark 11:8; Luke 19:37).[30] These followers also became permanently and intimately associated with Jesus the Savior-King and therefore were

[29] Coakley, "Jesus' Messianic Entry into Jerusalem," 478–80.

[30] The Gospels nowhere report that these believing crowds later turned against Jesus. In fact, the Gospels report that Jesus gained a large following in Jerusalem and that the Jewish hierarchy then began to consider taking Jesus by stealth, a clear result of His growing popularity and numbers.

equally complicit in His actions. The crowds of the triumphal entry are likely the leading reason the Jews had to arrest Jesus at night, by subtlety, and by using a guide who could report His whereabouts away from the crowds.[31]

Conclusion

The triumphal entry marks a turning point in the ministry of Jesus—a point when, like the ministry of John the Baptist, Jesus' ministry began to wane, while that of His disciples began to wax stronger. Even though the triumphal entry was viewed as an act of blasphemy or treason by many of Jesus' contemporaries, the act was one of the most provocatively clear statements that Jesus gave concerning His own identity. It was divinely planned and foreseen by prophets many generations beforehand. The simple fact that prophets had foreseen the triumphal entry but remained silent on many of the other significant events of Jesus' lifetime attests to its importance.

Carefully planned and executed, the Triumphal Entry demonstrated to Jesus' opponents that He had a significant following and that His disciples were not afraid to make themselves known. Jesus' popularity in Galilee had now been extended into Jerusalem, threatening to make inroads into the Jewish hierarchy. Ironically, what some have taken to be a humble act of submission was rather a bold act on the part of Jesus, who in this instance may have offered His greatest public testimony of His own mission.

After the triumphal entry, the growing problem of Jesus and His followers could no longer be dealt with in complacency. Jesus made it clear that lukewarm enthusiasm for Him and His ministry could not be tolerated; He was either the Christ who would come or He was a false Messiah, a pretender to the throne of King David. His disciples obviously believed the former and made their beliefs known openly on this occasion, whereas those who opposed Jesus now had a firm estimation of the number of Jesus' followers. They

---

[31] Wayment, "Responsibility for the Death of Jesus," 422–49.

acted decisively, likely in conjunction with Roman authority from the inception. Jesus' triumphal entry into the holy city revealed to them that they had to act quickly and secretly to isolate, arrest, and kill Him before anyone could muster a defense.

CONCLUSION

JESUS BEFORE EASTER

RICHARD NEITZEL HOLZAPFEL
AND THOMAS A. WAYMENT

In this series, *The Life and Teachings of Jesus Christ,* we have collected essays by some of the leading Latter-day Saint scholars currently working on the New Testament, dedicated disciples and faithful Saints who are using their academic training and skills to help us appreciate more fully the wonderful texts preserved for us on the life and ministry of the most important person ever to have lived on earth—Jesus Christ.

The purpose of our effort in preparing three rather dense and thick volumes focusing on Jesus has been to provide a fresh look at some of the most important issues raised in recent scholarly discussions and in the popular media about Jesus by utilizing the most recent archaeological discoveries and significant advances in other areas of New Testament studies that, through the lens of the Restoration, help provide a more complete and nuanced portrait of Jesus' world, allowing us to build upon the already significant collection of studies on the life and ministry of Jesus of Nazareth.

Because we live two thousand years beyond His life, it is sometimes difficult to adequately reconstruct that world, which has by and large disappeared, but the discovery of new evidence or old evidence reinterpreted keeps this effort amazingly alive and healthy. Additionally, we inevitably read the stories in the four Gospels through the lens of the Resurrection, making it difficult for any of us to travel *with* the disciples of Jesus as they did on the dusty paths across the Holy Land—discovering who Jesus was before the seemingly tragic events of fateful Friday and the glorious events of Easter Sunday.

As we conclude this volume, *From the Transfiguration through the Triumphal Entry,* we close for a season our discussions on the mortal ministry of Jesus Christ. Our final volume, number three in our series, *From the Last Supper through the Resurrection,* focuses on the last twenty-four hours of His life and the Resurrection, those events that properly provide a context for His birth, life, and ministry. However, we would like to consider, one more time, Jesus before Easter.

The circumstantial and cumulative evidence from the first century suggest that none of Jesus' profound words or amazing deeds recorded in the four Gospels were written down at the time they were first heard or witnessed. Even by the time Jesus had made His final, fateful journey to Jerusalem at Passover in about A.D. 30, it appears that no written record had been made of His singular life and ministry. This is not surprising, as Jesus and His disciples lived in a thoroughly oral culture—one significantly distant and foreign from our current literate culture.[1]

What was obvious then, and now largely forgotten, is that the written word was, in fact, secondary to the spoken word, given that the literacy rate in the first century most likely did not exceed 10 percent. Even when the Gospels were eventually recorded, they were written with the expectation that they would be read aloud in public and during worship services, before the time of mass literacy and the production of books, newspapers, and magazines (see Matthew 7:24, 26; 11:15; 13:9, 19).

Another significant difference between the first century and our

---

[1] A detailed study of this process is James D. G. Dunn, *Jesus Remembered: Christianity in the Making Volume 1* (Grand Rapids, Mich.: Eerdmans, 2003), 139–254. A more accessible overview is Ben Witherington III, *The New Testament Story* (Grand Rapids, Mich.: Eerdmans, 2004), 3–27. Both have established the theoretical framework for this discussion.

own is that even literate people in antiquity read aloud when alone (see Acts 8:27–30). The main reason for this practice was that ancient texts were written, without any breaks, in continuous script. The Greek letters were not separated into words, phrases, sentences and paragraphs. There were no punctuation, verses, or chapters in the original manuscripts, called "autographs" today. This writing convention forced readers to carefully sound out each word as they read to ensure that they got the story right. Ancient texts were meant to be heard, not just read.

It would not have immediately come to mind to those who both saw and heard Jesus to record the stories of His life because writing was almost unimaginably difficult and extremely expensive. For us living in the modern world, separated from the past by both time and technology, this may be hard to fathom, as our own experience is so fundamentally different: we have access to inexpensive pens and paper, and we have the almost effortless ability to write on computers, which record our thoughts, ideas, and experiences with an easy effort that appears quite pedestrian today.

Additionally, we live in a time when we can purchase relatively inexpensive scriptures. Many of us will own several sets in our lifetimes, and some will own more than one set at a time, which makes it difficult for us to imagine that Jesus, Mary, or Peter never owned a personal set of scriptures in their lifetime.[2]

Two thousand years ago, writing activities were well beyond the ability and the capability of most people. Even the wealthy and educated often employed scribes when they needed to communicate. We may not fully realize what a tremendous amount of labor and expense went into the production of a papyrus scroll. Even the process of recording something on expensive papyrus required

[2] There were exceptions, but these would have been rare indeed, as most people could not have afforded a personal copy of any of the scriptures, let alone a complete copy of the Hebrew Bible, the Old Testament (see Acts 8:27–28 where the Ethiopian treasurer apparently had a copy of the book of Isaiah). Later, Paul or Luke may have retained copies of the Pauline letters, but at that time they were not scriptures, though highly prized.

additional items beyond a simple reed pen and ink, such as a knife to keep the reed pen shaped, a stone to smooth the reed pen's point, an ink well, and a damp sponge or cloth to wipe up mistakes on the papyrus. Writing meant much more than merely translating thoughts into words and then transcribing them effortlessly onto paper.

Under these circumstances, there would have had to be some compelling reason to have taken what was seen and heard and to actually record it, when it was far easier to simply tell it to others.

Scholars have generally assumed that Jesus may have been forgotten, or at least would have become a mere footnote in the history of Judaism, if there had been no story of the empty tomb. This false line of thought argues that the reason the stories about Jesus were eventually written down was Easter—it was such a profound event that the disciples began recalling stories that helped them make sense of Jesus' life.

What is often missed by commentators is the fact that Jesus' words and deeds were not considered more important following the Passion and Resurrection. Certainly, these events intensified the need to remember and retell the earlier stories. But people were amazed and astonished by His teachings and deeds even before Easter (see Mark 1:22, 27, 45; 2:12; 5:42; 6:2, 51; 7:37; 9:15; 10:24, 26, 32; 11:18; 14:33; 16:8).

Certainly Jesus' life paralleled the lives of the Hebrew prophets; He sometimes quoted from them, and His teachings were rooted in the Jewish scriptures. Yet there was something new, even unprecedented and shocking, about Jesus' message and His life.

The impact Jesus had on people before Easter is adequately demonstrated by the fact that the disciples themselves left their fishing nets, boats, and simple lives; they left tollbooths and royal employers *before* that glorious Sunday, not after it (Mark 1:17–18; 2:14). They had been changed from common laborers, scribes, fishermen, and members of the royal bureaucracy into disciples of Jesus long before Gethsemane, Golgotha, and the Garden Tomb.

Before these places became permanently etched into the hearts and minds of Christians, there were other places and events that captured their minds and hearts that made these first fishermen and tax collectors disciples of Jesus, even though they did not always understand Him.

One story of many similar ones preserved in the New Testament illustrates this point if we take time to consider it carefully and read it anew, as though we had never read or heard the story before:

> And the same day, when the even was come, he saith unto them, Let us pass over unto the other side. And when they had sent away the multitude, they took him even as he was in the ship. And there were also with him other little ships. And there arose a great storm of wind, and the waves beat into the ship, so that it was now full. And he was in the hinder part of the ship, asleep on a pillow: and they awake him, and say unto him, Master, carest thou not that we perish? And he arose, and rebuked the wind, and said unto the sea, Peace, be still. And the wind ceased, and there was a great calm. . . . And they feared exceedingly, and said one to another, *What manner of man is this, that even the wind and the sea obey him?* (Mark 4:35–41; emphasis added).

We know who Jesus is, or at least we have an improved understanding that is informed by the light of the Resurrection and Restoration. Many of us grew up singing the hymn based on this story, "Master, the Tempest Is Raging"; therefore, we know how the story ends and sometimes wonder why the disciples did not![3] They were, of course, on a journey of discovery—learning who He was every step of the way. They were, as we would have been too, full of wonder, amazement, and even fear: "Who is this man?"

It is not difficult to imagine the disciples talking among themselves about this unforgettable experience again and again, recounting what they saw, heard, and experienced on the boat—that

[3] "Master, the Tempest Is Raging," *Hymns* (Salt Lake City: The Church of Jesus Christ of Latter-day Saints, 1985), no. 105.

which impressed them most, that which had the greatest impact on each of them. Obviously, the experience did have such an effect, as it was preserved. As the story was retold and repeated, its core remained the same, but the telling would be adapted to meet the needs of the particular occasion upon which it had been recalled and retold (compare the differences among Mark 4:35–41, Matthew 8: 23–27, and Luke 8:22–25).

Not only were the disciples impressed with what Jesus said and did, but they had also been commanded by Jesus to remember certain deeds (see Luke 22:19), even promising that the Holy Spirit would help them do so (John 14:26).[4] As the disciples treasured what Jesus said, they created a core tradition, maintained by living witnesses, that would be passed along during the next decades before any of the stories were eventually recorded.

In the meantime, before the Gospels became fixed texts, the disciples would have had ample time to think about what they had seen, heard, and experienced during Jesus' ministry. These stories would certainly have been refreshed from time to time because Jesus would have taken the time to repeat a parable again, heal once again, and teach one of the eternal truths again. Yes, there were those singular experiences like the Transfiguration and the Triumphal Entry, but the majority of the stories and sayings would have been repeated and experienced often by the disciples during the mortal ministry. Significantly, each time these stories were recalled and remembered, each time they were retold and passed along to others, there were reflection and pondering on their meaning and significance. This outcome ultimately led the disciples to conclusions about Jesus that are now reflected in the four Gospels.

These incidents would have not only revitalized the memories of the disciples but also given them another opportunity to recall the singular significance of Jesus.

---

[4] The disciples also commanded others to remember (see Acts 20:35; 2 Timothy 2:8, 14).

At some point, the telling of the stories went beyond the circle of those who walked with Jesus. Certainly, they would have recalled with fondness, with feelings, and with wonder those things that were of utmost importance to them as they shared their witness with others. Retelling the stories again and again was the first stage of recalling and remembering what Jesus said and did.

The second stage of recalling what Jesus said and did most likely followed that fateful Friday and glorious Sunday. At this point, some of the oral traditions associated with various events may have been recorded in a narrative framework for the first time. These early accounts, most likely written in Aramaic, would have focused on Jesus' life and death, early accounts of the stories that would eventually become the Passion and Resurrection narratives.

It was through this lens that the seemingly tragic events at Jerusalem during the final days became the "good news."

It naturally follows that there may have been attempts to record some of Jesus' teachings, His words and sayings—those that had been repeated over and over by the disciples who remembered them as they had heard them during Jesus' lifetime (see Luke 24:8; Acts 11:16).

During the next period of the early Church's story, before the Gospels were written, the first clues and hints that a written record was beginning to emerge appears. Paul and James began to prepare letters, the earliest documents from the New Testament period, about A.D. 49–50. Even then, these letters were considered a poor substitute for the oral presentation of the "good news." Paul would rather have visited the Saints himself if it had been possible (see for example, Romans 1:10), but he begrudgingly sent letters instead. Scholars have demonstrated that the Pauline correspondences were prepared to be read out loud; indeed, they contain the rhetorical aspects of oral discourse so prevalent in the first century.

It is important to remember that those who originally received these letters and heard them read aloud already knew the story of Jesus, especially the significant last twenty-four hours and the singular events of the first day of the week when Jesus rose from the dead (see 1 Corinthians 11:23; 15:3).

The principal way of learning about the "good news" was not by reading a missionary tract or a book—or even by hearing a well-prepared written talk; it came by participating in the living oral tradition—by hearing the stories of Jesus preached without a written text for reference (see Acts 2:14; 3:2; 4:8; 5:29; 7:2; 10:34; 13:16; 15:7, 13; 16:13; 17:22; 20:7; 21:40; 23:1; 24:10; 26:1–2; 28:30–31).[5] The spread of the gospel was primarily through the spoken word, not the written word.

The expansion of the gospel beyond Jewish Palestine presented another problem in recalling and remembering what Jesus said and did—one of translation. Someone, we do not know who, needed to translate Jesus' Aramaic into Greek. The authors of the four Gospels did not have the same command of the Greek language. Therefore, their translations of any Aramaic material were uneven. Nevertheless, the transfer had begun and now accelerated as the "good news" moved away from Judea and Galilee.

Eventually, the next stage of remembering what Jesus said and Jesus did arrived. By now, the early Church had entered into the second half of the first century. We cannot possibly provide a detailed and completely convincing interpretation of this remarkable and far-reaching moment in Christian history because the sources will not allow us to do so.

However, it does not seem unreasonable to assume that in the face of the death of an increasing number of eyewitnesses and ear-witnesses, some felt it important, necessary, and prudent to record the words and deeds of Jesus before those who had heard them in the first place were gone (Luke 1:1–4). Early Christians must have known by this stage that even important things could be lost.[6]

The primary motive for recording these stories is evident from at

[5] The Jewish scriptures, the Old Testament, were present in many of the synagogues (Luke 4:16–17; Acts 17:1–3).

[6] That Paul had written an early letter, now lost, to the Corinthians is well known (see 1 Corinthians 5:9–10).

least one account: "These are written, that ye might believe that Jesus is the Christ, the Son of God; and that believing ye might have life through his name" (John 20:31). Even then, the author knew that writers could not possibly preserve every detail of Jesus' life and every word spoken: "And there are also many other things which Jesus did, the which, if they should be written every one, I suppose that even the world itself could not contain the books that should be written" (John 21:25).

This significant and influential decision cannot be overestimated. There was not only a limitation on the size of a scroll, about thirty-five feet, but also a limitation on resources, including time. The work of recording was, we cannot forget, hard work.

These stories, which had been retold, recorded, and preserved, had, during the next stage of remembering Jesus, been accepted as the authoritative version of the stories—the gospel, the "good news." And although we have four Gospels, it is only one Jesus that we see and hear in their accounts—different facets of a beautiful, brilliant diamond. The early Church was right in rejecting efforts to make one Gospel from four; as a result, we are the beneficiaries of this decision fourfold. The newness of the New Testament comes partly because of this unique feature.

These four separate accounts contain the words and deeds of Jesus. They are a supernal gift of inestimable value and unprecedented consequence and significance. That Jesus was remembered is not at all surprising, when we consider what He said and did and how people responded to Him so long ago. That we have four separate Gospel accounts highlighting those profound sayings and amazing deeds is surprising. We are fortunate indeed.

CONTRIBUTORS

Richard Neitzel Holzapfel
Professor of Church History and Doctrine and Managing Director, Religious Studies Center—Publications, Brigham Young University
Ph.D. from University of California at Irvine in Ancient History
The Life and Teachings of Jesus Christ: From Bethlehem through the Sermon on the Mount, Volume 1 (Salt Lake City: Deseret Book, 2005).

Thomas A. Wayment
Assistant Professor of Ancient Scripture, Brigham Young University
Ph.D. from Claremont Graduate School in New Testament Studies
The Complete Joseph Smith Translation of the New Testament: A Side-by-Side Comparison with the King James Version (Salt Lake City: Deseret Book, 2005).

Richard D. Draper
Professor of Ancient Scripture and Associate Dean of Religious Education, Brigham Young University
Ph.D. from Brigham Young University in Ancient History
"From the Annunciation through the Young Adulthood of the Lord," in *The Life and Teachings of Jesus Christ: From Bethlehem through the Sermon on the Mount,* 121–59.

Frank F. Judd Jr.
Assistant Professor of Ancient Scripture, Brigham Young University
Ph.D. from University of North Carolina at Chapel Hill in New Testament and Early Christianity
"The Setting of the Sermon on the Mount," in *The Life and Teachings of Jesus Christ: From Bethlehem through the Sermon on the Mount,* 306–29.

S. Kent Brown
Professor of Ancient Scripture and Director of the Foundation for Ancient Research and Mormon Studies, Brigham Young University
Ph.D. from Brown University in Religious Studies with an emphasis in New Testament and Early Christian Studies
Richard D. Draper, S. Kent Brown, and Michael D. Rhodes, *The Pearl of Great Price: A Verse-by-Verse Commentary* (Salt Lake City: Deseret Book, 2005).

Jennifer C. Lane
Assistant Professor of Religious Education, Brigham Young University—Hawaii
Ph.D. from Claremont Graduate School in Religion with an emphasis in History of Christianity
" 'Come Follow Me': The Imitation of Christ in the Later Middle Ages," in *Prelude to the Restoration: From Apostasy to the Restored Church, The 33rd Annual Sidney B. Sperry Symposium* (Salt Lake City: Deseret Book, 2004).

Gaye Strathearn
Assistant Professor of Ancient Scripture, Brigham Young University
Ph.D. from Claremont Graduate School in New Testament Studies
"Jesus Teaches at Jacob's Well," in *The Life and Teachings of Jesus Christ: From Bethlehem through the Sermon on the Mount*, 247–68.

Jeffrey R. Chadwick
Associate Professor of Church History and Doctrine, Brigham Young University
Ph.D. from University of Utah, Middle East Center in Archaeology and Semitic Languages
"Discovering Hebron," *Biblical Archaeology Review* 31, no. 5 (September/October 2005): 24–33, 70–71.

Cecilia M. Peek
Assistant Professor of Classics and Comparative Literature, Brigham Young University
Ph.D. from University of California at Berkley in Ancient History and Mediterranean Archaeology
"Early Galilean Ministry and Miracles," in *The Life and Teachings of Jesus Christ: From Bethlehem through the Sermon on the Mount*, 269–305.

Brian M. Hauglid
Associate Professor of Ancient Scripture, Brigham Young University
Ph.D. from University of Utah in Middle East Studies, Arabic
Astronomy, Papyrus, and Covenant, ed. John Gee and Brian M. Hauglid (Provo, Utah: Foundation for Ancient Research and Mormon Studies, 2005).

Eric D. Huntsman
Associate Professor of Ancient Scripture, Brigham Young University
Ph.D. from University of Pennsylvania in Ancient History
"Galilee and the Call of the Twelve Apostles," in *The Life and Teachings of Jesus Christ: From Bethlehem through the Sermon on the Mount*, 213–46.

Kent P. Jackson
Professor of Ancient Scripture, Brigham Young University
Ph.D. from University of Michigan in Old Testament and Ancient Near Eastern Studies
Joseph Smith's New Translation of the Bible: Original Manuscripts, ed. Scott H. Faulring, Kent P. Jackson, and Robert J. Matthews (Provo, Utah: Religious Studies Center, Brigham Young University, 2004).

SCRIPTURE INDEX

SUBJECT INDEX